DUCKWORTH OVERLOOK

SICK IN THE HEAD

'Wonderful, expansive interviews – at times brutal, at times breathtaking – with artists whose wit, intelligence, gaze, and insights are all sharp enough to draw blood'   Michael Chabon

'Anyone even remotely interested in comedy or humanity should own this book. It is hilarious and informative and it contains insightful interviews with the greatest comics, comedians, and comediennes of our time. My representatives assure me I will appear in a future edition'   Will Ferrell

'I can't stop reading it… I don't want this book to end'   Jimmy Fallon

'A Bible for all aspiring comics and their fans… a lot of fun'   *Independent*

'The funniest man in Hollywood… spans more than a quarter of a century, with scores of interviewees, including Chris Rock, Harold Ramis, Mel Brooks, Jim Carrey and Jay Leno (to name a very few). There's some decent goss in it… [and] interesting points about the art'   *Sunday Times*

'Candid, unguarded discussions, including Mel Brooks on political correctness, Louis CK on drugs and Amy Schumer on sex'   *Esquire*

'Anyone interested in comedy should invest'   *Heat* (five-star review)

'Open this book anywhere, and you're bound to find some interesting nugget from someone who has had you in stitches many, many times' *New York Times*

'Fascinating'   *Washington Post*

'An amazing read, full of insights and connections both creative and interpersonal'   *New Yorker*

'It's funny (natch), gossipy, page-turningly readable and packed with hard-won observations about showbusiness and life'   *GQ*

'Fascinating and revelatory'   *Chicago Tribune*

'A must-read for just about any comedy fan'   *Irish News*

'The most intriguing part of *Sick in the Head* is … ching exploration of his own insecurit …bout career and family… vital for unc…

Judd Apatow is one of the most important comic minds of his generation. He wrote and directed the films *The 40-Year-Old Virgin* (co-written with Steve Carell), *Knocked Up*, *Funny People* and *This Is 40*, and his producing credits include *Superbad*, *Bridesmaids* and *Anchorman*. Apatow is the executive producer of HBO's *Girls* and the co-creator of Netflix's *Love* and was the executive producer of *Freaks and Geeks*. He created *Undeclared*, and co-created the Emmy Award-winning television programme *The Ben Stiller Show*. His latest film is *Trainwreck*, and he is the editor of the collection *I Found This Funny*. He lives in Los Angeles with his wife, Leslie Mann, and their two daughters, Maude and Iris.

All of Judd's proceeds from this book are being donated to 826 National, 826 LA, and 26 NY organizations that provide free tutoring and literacy programs.

@JuddApatow

SICK
IN THE
HEAD

First published in the United States in 2015 by Random House, an imprint and division of Penguin Random House LLC, New York

First published in the United Kingdom by Duckworth Overlook in 2016
This edition first published by Duckworth Overlook in 2017

LONDON
30 Calvin Street, London E1 6NW
T: 020 7490 7300
E: info@duckworth-publishers.co.uk
www.ducknet.co.uk
For bulk and special sales please contact sales@duckworth-publishers.co.uk

The interviews in *Sick in the Head* have been condensed and edited for readability.
Photographs not otherwise credited are used courtesy of the author.
Grateful acknowledgment is made to the following for permission to reprint the material specified below:

Condé Nast: Transcript from interview with David Denby, Judd Apatow, and Seth Rogan at *The New Yorke* ... ... Brooks interview by Jim ... ... *ks and Geeks* Oral Hist ... ... Nast. Reprinted by pe ... ... n the March 2013 iss ... ... han- dling" by Mike Sa ... ... nission. *Huck*: "Judd Apat ... ... ited by permission. WTI ... ... odcast. Reprinted by per ... ... Steve Allen. Used by pe ... ... Enter- tainment: Transc ... ... d Jim Ca ... rey. Courtesy of Sony Pictures Home Entertainment

The rights of Judd Apatow to be identified as the Author of the Work has been asserted by him in accordance with the Copyright, Designs and Patents Act 1988.
A catalogue record for this book is available fron the British Library

9780715651605

Book design by Elizabeth A. D. Eno
Printed and bound by CPI Group (UK) Ltd, Croydon, CR0 4YY

1 3 5 7 9 10 8 6 4 2

SICK
IN THE
HEAD

Conversations
About Life
and Comedy

JUDD
APATOW

DUCKWORTH OVERLOOK

For Leslie, Maude, and Iris.

And for Mom and Dad. Your support—and the mental health issues you gave me—made all of this possible.

CONTENTS

INTRODUCTION: WHY COMEDY?

How did I start interviewing comedians? That's a good question. I was always a fan of comedy and . . . okay, I have been *completely obsessed* with comedy for about as long as I can remember. I blame my dad. My dad was not a comedian, but he may have secretly longed to be one. When I was a kid, he would play us Bill Cosby records and even took me to see him perform at Hofstra University for my birthday when I was in fifth grade. (Note: In this introduction, I was going to talk at length about Bill Cosby, but I can't, in good conscience, because he has more sexual accusers than I have had partners.) From there I discovered Dickie Goodman, George Carlin, and Lenny Bruce, and then, when Steve Martin hit, I completely lost my mind. I bought every album he put out—and couldn't stop doing an impression of him for the next five years. The biggest fight I ever got into with my parents was when we were at an Italian restaurant for dinner and I was trying to rush them out so we could get home in time to see Steve Martin on *The Carol Burnett Show*. They refused to hurry through their chicken parmesan and, as a result, I never got to see it. I remain furious.

The mid- to late seventies was a golden age in comedy. You had Richard Pryor, *Saturday Night Live*, Monty Python, *SCTV*—all in their prime. The club scene was beginning to explode, too. In my room at night, I would circle the names of all the comedians in the *TV Guide* who were going to perform on talk shows that week so I wouldn't miss any. When I was in fifth grade, I produced a thirty-page report on the life and career of the Marx Brothers and paid my friend Brande Eigen thirty dollars to write it out for me, longhand, because he had better handwriting than I did. This, by the way, was not for school. I wrote it for my own personal use.

A comedy freak was born.

I'm not sure why I was so drawn to comedy. Part of it, I think, was frustration. Looking back, I was an angry kid who didn't feel like the world made sense. My parents were not particularly spiritual people in those days, so they couldn't help much in the existential angst department. The closest they came to religion was saying over and over again throughout my childhood, "Nobody said life was fair." It was the opposite of *The Secret*. It was *The Anti-Secret*. This left a bit of a void in my life, and I looked to comedy—and the insights of comedians—to fill it.

Plus, I was the youngest boy in my grade, so I was small. This size deficit led to me always being picked last in gym class—every day for thirteen years. When you're always picked last, you always get the worst position, like right field in baseball. Then, since you are always in the worst position, the ball never comes your way, so you never get a chance to show anyone that you are, in fact, good at this sport. But the truth is, you are *not* good at this sport because you are never involved in a play, because you are always in the worst position. When it is time to step up to bat, you feel so much pressure to do something incredible, like hit a home run, that you usually whiff. If you somehow manage to get a hit, your accomplishment is ignored by your peers, who chalk it up to luck. (No child in history has ever gone from last one picked to first one picked. That is a universal law that will never be broken.) Then the kid who is picked last never gets a girl to like him, because he has been labeled a loser.

Therefore, what else is there to do except decide that everyone else is the loser and you are the cool one?

That is how the cocky nerd comes to be.

So I had a lot of time to sit there, in right field, thinking about other things, like how unfair this whole setup was. If I wasn't handsome, how would I ever find a girl who would love me? Could someone who sucked at sports be popular? Was there a reason why nobody else was interested in the things I found interesting? Why did all the teachers think I was a pain in the ass and not someone special?

At that age, the comedians I liked most were the ones who called out the bullshit and gave voice to my anger—the Marx Brothers, Lenny Bruce, George Carlin, Jay Leno. I loved anyone who stood up onstage and said that the people in power were idiots, and not to be trusted. I was also drawn to people who deconstructed the smaller aspects of this bizarre and ridiculous life. I idolized the new generation of observational comedians like

Jerry Seinfeld, Paul Reiser, and Robert Klein. I related to them and imitated them, and even began to write really bad jokes of my own in a notebook I hid in a small metal locker in my room. "On *Gilligan's Island* they went on a three-hour cruise," I wrote, "so why did they bring so much luggage?"

During junior high, my parents got divorced and things got a little messy. It was the early eighties, and after my dad read the self-help book *Your Erroneous Zones*, by Wayne Dyer, I think he suddenly realized how unhappy he was—and that was that. He and my mom never figured out how to make it work. They were both warm, caring people, but neither handled the divorce well. For reasons I never quite understood, they fought in and out of court for years—until everyone was broke. I was lost and scared. At one point, I started shoplifting with the secret hope I would get caught so that I could finally have an excuse to yell at them: "This would never have happened if it wasn't for this divorce!" (Sadly, I only got caught once, and when Macy's couldn't reach my parents by phone, the store let me go.) It's hard to be a teenager witnessing your parents at their worst. This was way before the days of "conscious uncoupling." This was war. I remember thinking to myself at one point, *Well, I guess my parents' advice can't be any good—just look at how they are handling this situation. I need to figure out how to support myself financially and emotionally.*

Oddly, that pain and fear became the fuel in my tank. It inspired me to work hard and has led to every success and good thing in my life. It worked so well that today, a parent now myself, I am trying to figure out how to fuck up my daughters *just* enough that they, too, develop outsize dreams and the desire to get the hell out of the house.

When I was a kid, my parents owned a restaurant called Raisins. After the divorce, my mom, Tami Shad, moved out and got a job. A former bartender named Rick Messina (who went on to manage Tim Allen and many others) hired her as a hostess at a comedy club he ran in Southampton, New York, the East End Comedy Club. I was fourteen years old at the time and this was one of the great summers of my life. I was finally able to see comedians in person. My mom would get me a seat in the back of the house and I watched every comedian—people like J. J. Wall, Paul Provenza, Charles Fleischer, and Jay Leno.

My next move was to accept a job as a dishwasher at the East Side Comedy Club, located in Huntington, New York, near my hometown of Syosset. East Side was one of the first comedy clubs that existed outside New York City and Los Angeles, and I remember the day it opened. One day there was an old fish restaurant in the middle of a large parking lot, and the next day there was this place that had nothing but comedy, and lines out the door. Long Island legends like Bob Nelson, Rob Bartlett, Jim Myers, and Jackie Martling were regulars. I remember watching a young Rosie O'Donnell do her first weekend spot at the club, and how excited everyone was for her. Occasionally a twenty-one-year-old named Eddie Murphy would come in and work on new material. When he did, the staff would start a pool and take bets on how long his set would go; they were annoyed at—and probably a little jealous of—his marathon sets, which would bump all of the other comics for the night. Watching him one night, I remember some guy in the crowd started heckling him. "I don't care what you say," Eddie responded, "because I'm twenty-one, I'm black, and I have a bigger dick than you." In retrospect, it was not that great a line, but back then I thought it was the funniest thing I had ever heard. I didn't have a big dick (more medium-sized), but now I definitely wanted to be up there yelling at people and being funny.

By my fifteenth birthday, my obsession was full-blown. I needed to become one of them. The question was, how to do that? And the answer seemed clear:

Meet them. Talk to them. Get to know them. Learn their secrets.

But who was going to sit down with some junior high school kid and talk about comedy?

In the tenth grade, I started to work at my high school's radio station, WKWZ 88.5 FM, in Syosset! Headquarters was a nerd's paradise located in the basement of our high school. The station was supervised by Syosset High's film teacher, Jack DeMasi, a fiery, hilarious Italian guy who went to film school with Martin Scorsese. We all loved him because he talked to us and treated us, a sea of weirdos, like we were adults.

At WKWZ, the sports geeks produced sports shows, the news geeks produced news shows, and there was even room for jazz and classical. My friend Josh Rosenthal was a DJ at the station, and he loved music as much as I loved comedy. Occasionally he would take the train to the city and interview new bands like R.E.M. and Siouxsie and the Banshees. This blew my mind. Wait, so we could actually interview people we admired? They would talk to you if you asked nicely? It suddenly occurred to me that maybe I could do this with comedians. I asked Jack if I could start a show of my own, and he said yes.

In your life you come across people who encourage your voice and originality. For me, that person is Jack DeMasi. In fact, in an episode of *Freaks and Geeks* Paul Feig wrote many years later, there is a cool teacher who runs the AV squad, played by Steve Higgins (the announcer on *The Tonight Show* and the producer of *SNL*), who gives an inspiring speech about why the jocks won't get anywhere in life. "They are peaking now," he said, "but the geeks will rule the future." In my mind that was Jack, and this moment changed my life.

How did I get people to talk to me? Well, I would call their agents or PR people and say I was Judd Apatow from WKWZ radio on Long Island and I was interested in interviewing their client. I would neglect to mention that I was fifteen years old. Since most of those representatives were based in Los Angeles, they didn't realize that the signal to our station barely made it out of the parking lot. Then I would show up for the interview and they would realize they had been had. But they never turned me away, and every single one was gracious and generous with their time. (Except for one, who asked to see my dick. I won't mention his name but I said no. I didn't even realize this was probably just stage one of his plan. He told me he'd made "a bet with another comic" that he could get me to show it to him. I now realize the bet was probably a *little* more complicated than that.)

Over the next two years, I interviewed more than forty of my comedic heroes—club comics, TV stars, writers, directors, and a few movie stars. It was a magical time. I remember walking into Jerry Seinfeld's unfurnished apartment in West Hollywood, in 1983, and asking him directly, "How do you write a joke?" And meeting with Paul Reiser at the Improv and asking him what it was like shooting *Diner*. I took a three-hour train ride to Poughkeepsie, New York, to meet Weird Al Yankovic, and hung out with John Candy on the set of *The New Show*, Lorne Michaels's short-lived follow-up to *SNL*. Harold Ramis met me in his office as he prepared to shoot *National Lampoon's Vacation,* and I sat down with Jay Leno in the tiny office in the back of Rascals Comedy Club in West Orange, New Jersey. By the end of those two years I had interviewed Henny Youngman, Howard Stern, Steve Allen, Michael O'Donoghue, Father Guido Sarducci (Don Novello), Harry Anderson, Willie Tyler (not Lester), Al Franken, Sandra Bernhard, the Unknown Comic (Murray Langston), and so many others. Some went above and beyond the call of duty. The legendary comedy writer Alan Zweibel took out his phone book and hooked me up with a bunch of his famous friends. "Hey, here's Rodney Dangerfield's number. You should call him! Tell him I sent you!"

This was my college education. I grilled these people until they kicked me and my enormous green AV squad tape recorder out of their homes. I asked them how to get stage time, how long it takes to find yourself as an artist, and what childhood trauma led them to want to be in comedy. I asked them about their dreams for the future and made them my dreams, too. Did I mention I never even aired most of the interviews? I put a few out there, but even then I knew this information was mainly for me—and that the broadcast part was a bit of a ruse.

One thing I took from these interviews was that these people were part of a tribe—the tribe of comedians. My whole life I'd wanted friends who had similar interests and a similar worldview, people I could talk with about Monty Python and *SCTV.* People who could recite every line on the *Let's Get Small* album and who knew who George Carlin's original comedy team partner was (Jack Burns). It was lonely having this interest that no one shared. Even my best friends thought I was a little weird. In fact, just last year, my high school friend Ron Garner said to me, "I finally get what you were doing in your room watching TV all those years."

These interviews would inform the rest of my life. They contained the advice that would help me attain my dreams. Jerry Seinfeld talked about treating comedy like a job and writing every day. (I have never done that, but I certainly have written more than I would have since speaking to him.) More than one told me that it takes seven years to find yourself and become a great comedian. (Mystical-sounding, but kind of true.) From that piece of advice I learned patience. In my mind I thought, *If I start working hard now, in seven years I will be Eddie Murphy.* Well, that hasn't happened—yet. Harold Ramis talked about how when he started, he wrote jokes for comics like Rodney Dangerfield to pay his rent, so when I was green and behind on my rent, I wrote jokes for people like Tom Arnold, Roseanne, Garry Shandling, and Jim Carrey, and when they got TV specials or movies sometimes they would ask me to help. Harold's advice set me on the path.

When I moved to Los Angeles in 1985 to study screenwriting at the University of Southern California, a whole new world opened up to me. The comedy scene was booming back then. Suddenly I was able to go to clubs and make friends with fellow aspiring comedians. Many of those people, like Adam Sandler, Wayne Federman, Andy Kindler, David Spade, Jim Carrey, Doug Benson, and Todd Glass, are still my friends today. I felt like the bee girl in the Blind Melon video, running onto the field and looking around and . . . finding all the other bees I didn't know existed. I was so happy to no longer be alone. Later, when I pursued stand-up comedy for real, I would sit and talk all night with the future comedy legends who were performing at clubs like the Improv or the Laugh Factory, asking them questions while eating fettuccini Alfredo and hoping Budd Friedman would notice us and give us more stage time.

Even after my career took off, the interviews never stopped. Sometimes I would get interviewed while promoting a project, and other times I would be on panels, or doing commentary recordings for a movie, interviewing my funny friends just like the old days. I would always save the articles or ask for DVDs or audiotapes, knowing that one day I would need them for something (my wife calls it hoarding).

One day I was talking to the writer Dave Eggers about fund-raising ideas for his tutoring and literacy nonprofit, 826, and I mentioned that I had this huge cache of interviews I had done in high school, along with some I'd done later in life—and maybe that would make for an interesting book? I had always loved Cameron Crowe's book of interviews with Billy Wilder and those old *Rolling Stone* books filled with Q&As with my favorite rock stars. I thought maybe this could be like that but with all of my heroes and friends talking about why they became interested in comedy, and how they are doing as human beings on earth. It might be funny, too! Maybe this book could inspire some kid who is sitting in his room looking at weird Funny or Die videos, the way I used to sit in front of the TV and tape *SNL with an audio recorder* before the Betamax was invented. Maybe this book would make that kid feel a little less weird and alone.

Dave connected me with my editor, Andy Ward, who encouraged me to do some new interviews and bring the book up to date. I wasn't sure how many I had the energy to do, since I was in the middle of production on a movie and I was a little worried this project would turn into a giant pain in the ass. When I sold the book, I promised to give my proceeds to Eggers's 826 nonprofit. (Unfortunately it sold for more money than I thought it would and it was too late to change the deal to "5 percent of the money goes to 826 and 95 percent goes to the Apatow Vacation Trust.")

The first new one I did was Spike Jonze, two hours in my office on a hot Wednesday in Los Angeles—and, afterward, I found myself as inspired as I was when I first started doing this, thirty-one years ago. Spike talked about how artists who come from skateboarding are so inventive because it's a sport that is all about coming up with a new trick. That is why when he made music videos he was always trying to do them in a way they had never been done before. Incredible! Now I want to do that!

I followed that up by inviting one of my first bosses, Roseanne Barr, to talk about her journey with me. We sat for hours digging through the past, amazed and baffled by this bizarre and fantastic journey we are still on. And before I knew it, I was hooked all over again. Next came three hours at Louis C.K.'s house, talking while he made me dinner like I was one of his kids. I couldn't stop. I kept saying I was done, and then I would think, *Wait! I didn't get to do Stephen Colbert yet. And how have I not talked to Steve Martin? Let me get Lena Dunham!* Due to space and mental limitations, I had to stop, but I still have a long list of people I want to talk to. Sacha Baron Cohen, you are next! Will Ferrell—don't think you are not going to be in volume two!

I would like to thank all of the people who so generously agreed to speak with me. When I was a kid, I noticed that all of the comics I was speaking to shared a common humanity. Some were solid as a rock, some seemed on the edge of sanity, but all were filled with love and kindness. As an adult, I have tried to pay it forward by giving my time to young comics and mentoring the funny people I believe in. It has been the most rewarding part of my career. I hope you enjoy this book as much as I enjoyed meeting all of these remarkable people.

When can I start the next one?

SICK
IN THE
HEAD

THE BEGINNING: JERRY SEINFELD
(1983)

I became an official Jerry Seinfeld fan the first time he appeared on television on *The Merv Griffin Show* in 1980. This was before *Seinfeld*, of course. This was back when he was just some guy from Long Island, like me, who talked like me, and cared about the same kinds of things I cared about—and he was the best observational comedian I'd ever seen.

In 1983, I convinced someone in his manager's office to set up an interview, and not long after, I showed up at his completely unfurnished apartment in West Hollywood. Thirty years later, I can still see that slightly crestfallen look in his eyes when he opened the door and realized that I was not, in fact, a real journalist from a real radio station with a real audience. That I was just a fifteen-year-old kid with a tape recorder.

This was one of the most personally influential interviews I did, mainly because he said so many useful things that helped me later in life—it was like a blueprint for how one should go about pursuing a career in comedy, and how to write jokes. For the first time, it dawned on me that comedy is work, and precision and care.

Jerry Seinfeld: Is it water-driven, this camera?

Judd Apatow: I'd like to talk about your type of comedy that you do. How would you describe it? Some people just tell the joke, like an observation, and that's it. But you add a whole new dimension to it.

Jerry: Well, it's one thing to see something. And I think the next step is to do something with it. You know, I'm doing this routine now about this guy that was on *That's Incredible* last year, caught a bullet between his teeth. It's like, you see a thing like that and you go, *What the hell is that?* The guy caught a bullet between his teeth. I don't know what's funny about that—but I think to myself, *There is something funny about that.* And that's what I like to do. I think, *What job did he have before he got into doing that? What made him go, you know, "I'd rather be catching bullets between my teeth"?* I have a whole routine about it. To me, that's funny.

Judd: So how do you develop that?

Jerry: Trial and error. You know, just try out one joke. I had this other thing about how I don't remember this guy's name. I saw the guy do it, right? Caught the bullet. I don't even know his name. Now, if he knew that I didn't know his name after seeing that, wouldn't he feel like, *What the hell do I have to do? You know what I mean? Isn't that impressive enough for people to remember me? I mean, what do I have to do, catch a cannonball in the eye?* So it's like I just keep thinking on it until I—

Judd: You're there.

Jerry: You know, hit something.

Judd: So you work it out at the Improv?

Jerry: Anywhere. Wherever I'm working, I'm trying new material.

Judd: So what do you think of the other kind of comedy, just observation, or—

Jerry: Depends on who's doing it. Anything can be done either in a classy, interesting way or in a junky, easy way. It's not the form itself, it's the way someone approaches it. I mean, David Letterman has a hemorrhoid routine, Preparation H routine. It's classy and brilliant. No cheap jokes in it. It's something about how hemorrhoid experts agree and, like, who are these people? And you thought *you* hated your job, you know. It's clever. Know what I mean? Normally I hear someone bring Preparation H up, I just turn off. I think, *This is not gonna be a clever piece of comedy.* So it doesn't matter, you could be doing prop comedy. Rich Hall, who is brilliant, clever, interesting, doesn't rely on the props. Some comedians will hold up something funny and it gets a laugh. Rich uses the prop, you know. And so—there's no one type of comedy. It's who's doing it, and how they're handling it.

Judd: What do you think of this whole crop of comedians that just came out in the last five years?

Jerry: You mean like me?

Judd: Yeah.

Jerry: I think we're pretty good. Ah, well, it's interesting. I guess we don't seem too daring as a group, if you compared us to say, the sixties or the fifties.

Judd: But that ground had been broken already.

Jerry: Yeah, there's not too many people that are scary in terms of the type of things they talk about. Nobody seems to be treading on thin ice. That doesn't seem to interest people anymore. I mean, comedy hasn't changed really in thousands of years. It's the same. If it's funny, you're funny, and people like you.

Judd: Do you think that people have gotten into comedy who shouldn't have? Since there's so many jobs now with so many new clubs opening up.

Jerry: It's an interesting question. I've been thinking about that actually, and I think that there will always be only a very few great comedians because comedy itself is so difficult. No matter how many people do it, it's just a rare combination of skills and talents that go into making a great comedian. If everyone in the country decided to become a comedian, there would still only be six terrific ones like there are now.

Judd: Do you think that there's certain topics that shouldn't be spoken about, or certain things that shouldn't be done onstage? For instance, there's gonna be a guy on tonight, who I've seen, who does something about Linda Lovelace with a glass of milk. And it's—it's rather crude. I won't go farther.

Jerry: Right. Well, it depends on how you're asking me. Do you think I should do something? For me, I wouldn't do it. I think it's wrong.

Judd: What about the egg white? Do you think—

Jerry: I think anyone should do whatever they like. I don't think there should be any rules.

Judd: As long as it gets laughs?

Jerry: If it doesn't get laughs, you're not gonna get work, and you're not gonna be a comedian. So the audience ultimately decides. It's a very democratic system.

Judd: Are there certain topics that you stay away from in your act?

Jerry: A lot. A lot of topics I stay away from. Mainly the ones that have been covered or the ones that are easy. And I want—sex is easy, basically.

Judd: *Gilligan's Island.*

Jerry: *Gilligan's Island.* TV shows. Commercials. I won't go near it, because I'm trying to find new, fresh, original, interesting things. I want my comedy to be the things nobody else talks about. Not necessarily things people don't want to talk about, but just things that everybody else missed. That's what I like.

Judd: What is the difference between an audience at the Improv or a local club, and Atlantic City or Las Vegas?

Jerry: What they came to see. Basically, the audience at the Improv is interested in comedy, and if it's an easy joke or an obvious joke, it's less appealing to them than a really clever, original observation. The reverse applies in Atlantic City. They don't want to hear a comedian. They want to hear the main act. If you are a comedian, do something that we don't have to pay too much attention to. You see, at the Improv they're watching: We'll listen to you go with it. You know. We'll listen. Try that. Let me see how far you can go with that idea and if you can make it work. And at Atlantic City it's enough if you can just get them to listen to you. I do the same act, but it's a different type of performance. It's much more instructive because they don't know where the laughs are in my act because it's not "Two men walk into a bar—bum bum bum, punch line." And if the audience doesn't know where the punch line is, you can't get laughs. So I have to really slow it down and explicate exactly what I'm doing because to them, I'm like Andy Kaufman. They're not used to my kind of comedy.

They're used to an older style. Traditional jokes. Polish jokes. They don't understand. *Why is he talking about socks?*

Judd: Do you have to change your act in different parts of the country?

Jerry: Some people do; I don't. There's a central core of what I do that pretty much works everywhere, and the only variable is the way I perform it. I do the same jokes, but I do them differently. Little lines that some people come to hear. They love the little stray thoughts that you throw in. That makes the pieces interesting for people that know comedy and are beyond the very basic level of it. But in places where they don't want to hear you, you can only do the stuff that—the tips of the icebergs.

Judd: How do you handle improvisation and talking to the audience in your act?

Jerry: See, that's something I'm really getting into a lot now, having a lot of fun with it. When I do my act in comedy clubs, where I get to do like an hour, I'll take questions at a certain point and just, you know, ad lib. It depends on how much I can get the audience to accept me. If I can get them to accept me, a lot of times I'll take off on routines that I do normally and change them and take them a different way. Whenever I'm doing new material, I'm always ad libbing.

Judd: What is the strangest experience you've had doing comedy in a club?

Jerry: Strange? Um. I mean, I've played places where people didn't know I was on. I did a disco one time in Queens on New Year's Eve. And they're screaming, yelling, and screaming and yelling and they sent me out on the dance floor to do my act, and I stood there but the screaming and yelling never diminished by even a couple decibels and I just stood there for thirty minutes, and walked off and I don't think anybody even knew I was onstage.

Judd: Anything else like—

Jerry: Bombing is a riot. The looks on people's faces is just priceless. They look up to me going, "I don't know what you're talking about. I don't know what you're talking about. I came for a show, and you're the show and I don't understand you. You seem normal but you don't make any sense."

Judd: You did a show the other day that didn't go that good. That still happens to you?

Jerry: Oh, yeah, all the time. Every show varies and there are very, very few shows that go just right. Because every audience is completely different — a completely different group of people with a completely different personality. And you have to shape your act to their personality. Every set is an accomplishment.

Judd: Do you ever worry about, you know, say ten years in the future — a lot of comedians get bored after a while, they just cut stand-up out completely.

Jerry: Yeah, I know. I don't think I'll be one of those comedians. I have a lot of respect for it as a craft. I don't see it as just a stepping-stone. I mean, it's a hard life in some ways. But I have a fascination for it.

Judd: A lot of people do it and they just — they hate it.

Jerry: Well, they use it as a vehicle, which is fine. You know, you can get seen real easy. But it's a tough thing to do. It's a tough thing to put yourself through when it's not gonna be a career for you. It's a difficult thing to play at. It's kind of like catching bullets between your teeth: If you're gonna do it right, it would be something to learn it and then not make a career out of it.

Judd: When you're onstage and everything is going great, is that like the ultimate idea?

Jerry: I think so. Yeah, for me it is. Because that's what I like. I like jokes and laughing more than anything. Everybody has an appetite for a different thing. And comedy is something that I have an endless appetite for.

Judd: When did this all start, being funny?

Jerry: I wasn't a class clown per se. I mean, I wrote some funny things for the newspaper and I was always trying to be funny around my friends. And watching comedy was the thing I enjoyed more than anything else. I knew every comedian, I knew all their routines. That's how I got into it. I wanted to be around it, you know. I never thought I'd be any good at it. But that turned out to be an advantage because it made me work harder than most other people.

Judd: When did you first do it?

Jerry: I did Catch a Rising Star one night. I guess this would actually qualify as my strangest experience. This is definitely it. My first time on-stage, I write the whole act out, you know, and I put it there on my bed and rehearse it, over and over again. I'm standing there with a bar of soap, like it's a microphone. And I got the scene memorized, cold. I get up on there, and it's gone. I can't remember a word. I was—I stood there for about thirty seconds with—saying absolutely nothing, just standing there, freaking out. I just couldn't believe it, all these people were looking at me. And then, I was able to just remember the subjects I wanted to talk about. This is absolutely true, I'm not embellishing this at all, I stood there and I went, "The beach . . . ah, driving . . . your parents . . . ," and people started laughing because they thought this was my act. I couldn't even really hear them laughing; I was like absolutely panicked. I think I lasted about three minutes and I just got off. That was my first show.

Judd: How do you get steady work?

Jerry: Well, you audition; you start off at three in the morning and you fight your way through the order by doing better than the guy they put on ahead of you. Then the next night they put you on ahead of him. Then you try to do better than that guy. But if you're good, people notice you. That's the greatest thing about comedy. If you've got talent, it's unmistakable. No one misses it and you don't have to wait around for a break. It's very easy to get a break. It's very hard to be good enough.

Judd: When did you do your first TV appearance?

Jerry: *Merv Griffin* was my first talk show.

Judd: And how did you get that first booking?

Jerry: The same thing. I was out working at the Improv. If you're clean, and you're clever, and you're killin', they're not gonna miss you.

Judd: What's it like doing *Johnny Carson* or *Merv Griffin*?

Jerry: It's the ultimate. *The Tonight Show* is—to stand up there is a dream. It's like the Olympics of comedy, you know.

Judd: How do you prepare a certain ten minutes to go on?

Jerry: Well, you try to put it together like a small regular set. In other words, it's an hour set condensed into ten minutes. You can't have a mistake in it. Because it's—you can't recover. It goes by so fast so you try and put it together like an opening, and then you build, and you get the audience rolling and you have a big closing finish.

Judd: Is it like fifty percent of the fight is just going on and walking out there?

Jerry: Yeah, yeah. But you make one little mistake, or one stupid mistake and in five minutes it's very hard to get an audience back. People do it, but it's tough.

Judd: So where do you go from here? Like right now you're established as one of the top comedians and you get work, not only in the clubs but in Atlantic City. How much farther can you get?

Jerry: It's a tricky point that I'm at. But everyone that you'll be talking to is that. Because there's a lot you could do with TV series; you could do a sitcom, which a lot of people don't want to be associated with. You could do movies; they're hard to get and it's hard to have a hit. You could just do stand-up and hope that you catch on after a while—like Gallagher, you know. There's a lot of different ways. I'm gonna do some acting. Because it's easy for me and there's a lot of good vehicles for exposure as an actor. But stand-up is what I am. I'm a comedian, and the acting will just be to improve my visibility.

Judd: And what kind of vehicles are you looking for?

Jerry: Quality. That's my only real consideration. It could be anything, as long as the people are trying to do something good. I don't want to do a piece of junk. I'm not starving, you know.

PART ONE
A–J

ADAM SANDLER

(2009)

I met Adam Sandler when I was in my early twenties. He was known at that time as the stud man from the MTV game show *Remote Control*. He also happened to be an extremely original and gifted comedian. We all knew that Adam was going to rule comedy one day; we just didn't know yet how that would come to pass. What would the trigger be?

The first step was when he was asked to do stand-up on *David Letterman*, and killed; then he was flying off to audition for *Saturday Night Live*; and then, suddenly, I didn't have a roommate anymore. Those days living with Adam were, in some ways, the time of our lives; we still get on the phone every now and then, twenty years later, and reminisce about it. It was a time when all we did, all day long, was kill time and write jokes and then, at night, tell jokes at the Improv, then we ate fettuccini Alfredo with Budd Friedman and one of the many comedians we looked up to. It was a special, carefree time. We were all working so hard to succeed, but having fun being knucklehead kids, too.

In 2009, I got to make *Funny People* with Adam, which turned out to be one of the most rewarding experiences of my career. He was so successful at the time, I honestly wasn't sure I would be able to maintain control of the project; I worried about how far he'd be willing to go with so much on the line. But Adam was a true collaborator. He was incredibly brave. He never once said, "I don't want to do that," or, "That might make me look bad." And in the process, he revealed a side of himself that most people had never seen before. Even more fun than making the movie was the press tour. From the beginning, Adam declared he didn't want to do any interviews without me, which led to me and Adam being in rooms together, having to do interviews with a different person every eight minutes in countries all over the world, and trying to figure out ways to make each other laugh. One of the high points of that press tour, for me, was our appearance on the Charlie Rose show, because Adam is an extremely private person who rarely talks in public about his life and career. We did it together, like old roommates. I liked it so much that I put it on the DVD for *Funny People*. And I present it again here now.

Charlie Rose: I am pleased to have Adam Sandler and Judd Apatow back at this table. Welcome.

Adam Sandler: Great to see you.

Charlie: Now, where do we start? Tell me when you two first met.

Adam: After I moved out to L.A., I was twenty-two and went onstage at the Valley Improv. There used to be an improv at a hotel in the Valley. They had that for a few years. It's gone now but, uh, I did pretty well that night. That wasn't a normal thing. Usually I didn't do well and so I ran to a phone to call my dad—"It's going all right, Dad." And if I remember correctly, I think Apatow was lurking around the phones, kind of looking at me, and I'm, *All right, this guy's looking at me.* And then he came up to me and said, "Hey, I'm Judd, I saw you out in New York, you do that Baryshnikov bit." I used to have a bit I'd wear sweatpants onstage and say here's my impression of Baryshnikov and I'd pull them up and show the lack of bulge—

Charlie: The what?

Adam: The lack of bulge. Anyway, Judd mentioned he liked it and we started talking.

Judd Apatow: It sounds like a come-on. I love your bulge.

Charlie: So he started talking to you—and then?

Adam: And then we became friends—very good friends. I was out there with a few guys from NYU. We all made the move together and then they couldn't afford rent anymore so I was like, I need a roommate who's going to pay.

Judd: I don't remember that. I don't remember that.

Adam: Everybody was moving out of that house.

Charlie: Where were you in your life, at that point?

Judd: I went to USC cinema school for a year and a half and then I basically ran out of money and interest. How I knew that was, during college I went on *The Dating Game* and I won a trip to Acapulco, but it was happening during finals week—so I dropped out of college.

Charlie: Oh my God. How was Acapulco?

Judd: I got sunburned the first day and couldn't leave the room for the next two days. And so I was living with my grandma Molly and my mom and working the clubs at night and emceeing at the Improv. So I was happy to move out to L.A.

Charlie: You were doing stand-up and emceeing at the Improv?

Judd: For money, I worked for Comic Relief producing benefits during the day so I had enough to pay my four-hundred-and-twenty-five-dollars-a-month rent.

Adam: He was making five hundred bucks a week. He was the only one of us who was guaranteed to pull in five hundred a week. We'd always say, "How's he getting this Comic Relief job?" He would go in for a few hours and come back—he's getting five hundred for only a couple of hours a day. There was a lot of anger towards him.

Charlie: What was he like as a roommate? I mean you were, he was Felix and you were—

Adam: I guess I was Oscar, you know, yeah. Judd's a very, uh—

Charlie: Fastidious.

Adam: He is.

Charlie: And after being roommates, you remained friends? You stayed in touch?

Judd: When Adam got *Saturday Night Live,* he left and, you know, there was a question of whether or not he was going to keep the apartment in

L.A. I quickly realized that wasn't going to happen. And so I got another apartment.

Adam: That I had a room in.

Judd: That, yes, you had a room in.

Adam: He moved to another apartment, and just for my L.A. visits, which weren't that frequent, he had an extra room for me.

Judd: It was very exciting because Adam got the job on *Saturday Night Live* out of the blue, which shocked me because Adam's stand-up was kind of mumbling and bizarre and he didn't do characters. He didn't come from Second City, and then suddenly he's like, "I'm the new cast member on *Saturday Night Live*." How did that happen?

Adam: You know what is insane? How cocky I was back then. When I got offered *Saturday Night Live*, they offered me to be a writer and then eventually a performer and I was going, "I don't know if I want to do that. These guys don't understand." And all my friends were like, "Just do it, you idiot."

Charlie: Dummy.

Adam: Exactly.

Charlie: So why didn't you make a movie together until now?

Adam: We did. We've worked on a bunch of movies together.

Judd: I started doing *The Ben Stiller Show*, which was a show that Ben and I created and was on for a season on Fox. That was the first big TV gig I got after writing jokes for people for a long time. I was doing that while Adam was on *Saturday Night Live* and then we both started writing movies. Adam wrote *Billy Madison* and I co-wrote a movie called *Heavyweights* with Steve Brill, and our friend Jack Giarraputo that Adam went to college with was the associate producer.

Adam: He [Jack] was your assistant.

Judd: He was my assistant. And then he moved over to *Billy Madison*, and then we worked together a little bit when I did some rewrites on *Happy Gilmore*. So every few years, I would come in and help out. I always wanted to do this but I did feel like I needed to have learned enough to be able to take on something so ambitious.

Charlie: And what did you want to do?

Judd: To make a movie with Adam and to make it personal because, you know, we know each other so well. I always wanted to tap into that but I also didn't know how to direct so I needed ten or fifteen years to get that together.

Adam: I always knew Judd was—you know, we have similar tastes. He's doing movies differently than I did them but we always made each other laugh. We always felt comfortable with each other. We liked the same things. Judd liked a lot of stuff I never even heard about, a lot of music, a lot of movies. He brought me in to a different world. Then Judd gave me—he said, "Check out my movie, *Knocked Up*." I was shooting a movie at the time. I watched it in my trailer with a couple of my buddies and I was just like, *Apatow is unbelievable*. I called him up and said, "Judd, whatever is next, let's do it." And he said, "All right, I think I'm going to have something."

Charlie: See, that says something interesting about him, doesn't it? Looking out for himself by calling you up and saying, "You know I admire what you do, and think about me the next time you make something that might be right." And on the other hand, he's a huge star when he makes that call.

Judd: I was thrilled and then I instantly had to go in my notebook and be like, *What would be the idea for Adam? Oh, maybe this one?* I'd always wanted to make a movie about comedians. It's not a subject that's been handled great on film and if you do it badly, all comedians will hate you for the rest of your life. So you feel that pressure but in the back of my head I thought, *I think I'm one of the few people that know this world enough to get it across on-screen.* It just took a long time to work up the courage.

Charlie: Before we talk about *Funny People*, both of you know comedians, you understand comedians. You are comedians. What are the common denominators among the people you know who do what you do, whatever variation of it: write jokes, stand-up, comic films, whatever?

Judd: In personality, it's different. There are some guys who are kind of smart and witty and funny, and there are some guys who are just a little bit off, and there's some guys who clearly got a beat-down at some point during their young life and that made them feel the need to get attention.

Charlie: And so which one is he?

Adam: So many of those.

Charlie: All of the above.

Judd: There is a moment on Garry Shandling's DVD commentary for *The Larry Sanders Show* where he talks about this with Jerry Seinfeld and Jerry Seinfeld says to Garry, "Why can't you be a comedian just because you're talented and you're smart and that's why you're a comedian?"

Charlie: That's what I would ask, yes.

Judd: And Garry just goes, "Why so angry, Jerry?" I think that captures it.

Charlie: Okay, *Funny People*.

Judd: Yes.

Charlie: What's the passion you had for this?

Judd: I wanted to talk about when I first became a comedian and the moment I was allowed into the world of comics, which was very exciting for me. The people I worked with when I first started were incredibly nice to me and I was just in heaven being around them. You know, I wrote for Roseanne and Tom Arnold. That was one of my first jobs. They bought me a Rolex for Christmas. They paid me eight hundred dollars a week and suddenly I could afford valet parking. It was all positive so I knew I needed to fabricate something and then I had another idea, which is, I wanted to write a movie about someone who is sick who gets better—

Charlie: Who is sick with a terminal illness and thinks it's all over.

Judd: Yes, and it's about how he realizes that he's more comfortable being sick and the way that makes him feel, in terms of appreciating life, than he is when he gets better. Suddenly, there's time again and he starts becoming neurotic and has kind of a meltdown. That was the initial thought.

Charlie: In your mind, what's the push-pull between, I want to tell this interesting-but-serious story and at the same time, I make comedies?

Judd: I thought that if this story happened in the world of comedians it would inherently have a lot of humor in it. But what I thought in my head was, *I'm not going to let the joke count determine what the movie is.*

Charlie: I'm not going to go for easy jokes?

Judd: I'm not going to go for big set pieces. Usually when you make a comedy, you think, *Okay, every ten minutes something crazy has to happen. The energy has to kick in.* And here, I just said, *Well, there will be a lot of stand-up in the movie and the conversations will be funny and intense, but I'll let the emotional life of it rule the day in terms of how this works.* And that was tricky to do. It's tough to shake it off and just say, *Okay, no, this scene's intense and that's it.* When you're testing a movie, if it's a comedy, you hear the laughs and you go, *That scene works.* But if it's a sad scene and you've watched it two hundred times, it's a little trickier to go, *How did we do there? Did you feel something?* I wish there was a noise for feeling. Then I could go, *Okay, they made the weird noise.*

Charlie: Adam, tell me about George Simmons, your character. How is he different from anybody you played before?

Adam: He's a little more raw. He shows a darker, nastier side—you know, what I like about playing the guy is you're never sure what the response is going to be. Seth Rogen plays my assistant. He's a nice young kid and one second I'm warm to him and the next second I'm abusing him. Seth never knew which way we were going to go with it, and when I first read the script I was like, "Oh, man, I am such a bad person in this movie." And he would always say, "Really? You think so? I don't know. I think he's a nice guy," and I'd be like, "I don't know, I don't know." But the way Judd put the movie together was like, All right, you see why this guy became a certain way and you forgive him.

Judd: That was the thought I had. I had a little notebook and right before we shot I made little notes, things to remember. Like: *Don't forget these four things.* And one of them was the entire movie is just a journey to understand why the character is like this and when it ends you completely know him and you know what his struggle is. But it takes a while to connect the dots.

Charlie: All right. There's something called "Apatowian." Explain to me what that means.

Judd: I don't know, exactly—

Charlie: What do you think it means? In other words, what is it if you say it's an Apatow movie?

Adam: I guess it's used right now with saying it's, uh, there's buddies involved in the movie, and language that feels natural. And cursing.

Charlie: A lot of reference to sex and women.

Adam: Exactly. What I love about this movie, I—on occasion, Judd has heard some, you know, uh, what is it? What do they say? What's the negative on you right now?

Judd: That I'm a sexist?

Charlie: No, misanthropic.

Judd: How would you define that word?

Charlie: Someone who hates everything.

Judd: See, I think I'm a wussy. I'm a wimp.

Charlie: Tell me how you see this.

Judd: Okay. Well, what I thought about when I was making the movie was that there are traditional structures of comedies—and film in general—and when you go against it, it disturbs people. You know, it's the movies like John Cassavetes's movies and Robert Altman movies where they're meant to make you feel things you don't want to feel. Now that's not part of mainstream comedy but I thought it was important to think about. There's this quote from John Cassavetes. He said, "I don't care if you like me or hate me, I just want you to be thinking about me in ten years." I do want you to love the movie—I think that is the most important part—but I want to get under people's skin and provoke in addition to having a hopeful message.

Charlie: All right. *"Funny People* feels insular, as if Apatow's whole world consists of nerdy jokesters who were angry, lonely kids who got rich beyond their dreams and 'f' women who'd never have talked to them in high school but are deep down still angry." That's from *New York* magazine.

Adam: What is the problem there?

Charlie: Yeah, exactly. You've got to help me on this. We got to understand what's—

Judd: It's wrong in a couple of ways. One is, I had a fantastic girlfriend in high school who was very nice to me. Her parents were very nice to me. So I wasn't the guy who didn't have a girlfriend. In terms of it being an insular world of comedians, it's kind of a ridiculous criticism because it's a movie *about* comedians. And in terms of comedians who get successful or who are unhappy, you only have to look at Michael Jackson to see what fame does to people in terms of everyone giving them everything they want. How unhappy it makes them and how much difficulty they have connecting with individuals when they can only connect with the masses. I think it's all very real stuff I'm talking about. It may not be real to everyone, but—

Charlie: Who's it real to? Twenty-five-year-old males?

Judd: It's a way of talking about how we come up with our priorities for our lives through the eyes of a comedian, but we all deal with this. How much time do we want to spend at work versus how much time do we want to spend with the family?

Charlie: All right, here's another one: "[Apatow's] man-child universe, with its mixture of juvenile raunch and white-bread family values, has conquered American comedy." Is that you? Middle-class values and man-child universe?

Judd: Well, I don't think I've met a man who is not a man-child. If I meet a man who acts very proper I think he's covering up how goofy he really is. I'm forty-one years old, and when we lived together we were all immature, goofy guys. Now I have a lot of the same friends and I'm forty-one and we haven't made a lot of progress and I really don't think when me and Adam are sixty it's going to be much different.

Charlie: What is it that you think connects with the audience out there?

Adam: I get pitched ideas about movies. "Hey, such-and-such studio has a movie for you." They tell me the idea and three sentences in, I can either be like, *Whoa, that feels like something,* or, *I don't know about that.* It's a gut feeling. It comes from when I was young and what I knew excited me and my friends or what I'd want to see. I'm getting older, though. I don't know exactly what these young kids are talking about. I used to be kind of cocky walking down the street from my movies. When the young kids would see me I'd be like, *Yeah, that's right, here I am.* Now I'm like, *You still like me? Am I in the gang still?*

Charlie: But when you look at these things, what is the instinct you have? *Does this fit for me?* or *It doesn't fit for me?* Can you define it or do you just know it?

Adam: Most importantly, it's *Am I going to be proud of it and think it's funny?* The fact that I went in with Apatow blind and said, "Whatever you write, I'm in," it's because I trust him and I like his taste.

Charlie: How would you characterize his taste?

Judd: My pitch was not a funny pitch: "Adam, you're dying and you're a terrible person."

Adam: Stop there, just write it. You're going to get me out of this thing. Now his taste is very sexist and I identify with that.

Charlie: So if he was a misogynist that's okay with you?

Adam: Exactly. I love to hate.

Judd: Here's what I think it is. I'm trying to show warts and all, men and women. In most comedies, women are romanticized and they're pretty and they're not funny and the men try to attain them. And in my movies, starting with Catherine Keener in *The 40-Year-Old Virgin*, and Katherine and Leslie in *Knocked Up*, I was trying to show real conflict between men and women. And some of the scenes—which I think are kind of rough, where people really curse each other out and have big fights—are more like fights in real life. It's not like fights in the movies. For some people it's so different that it throws them, but I just look at my own sense of what's happening. In *The 40-Year-Old Virgin*, Steve Carell doesn't want to have sex because he thinks he's going to be bad at it, so he avoids it. Catherine Keener starts screaming at him because she thinks there's something wrong with her. In *Knocked Up*, the issue was that Seth cared more about his bong and his pot than his pregnant girlfriend, so she breaks up with and screams at him. And she *should* scream at him for that. I'm trying to show immaturity—and there is sexism in the immaturity. But it is a journey towards these guys realizing, *I've got to get my act together. This isn't the way to behave.*

Charlie: Are you making fun of their attitudes and what they talk about and how they view—

Judd: Yeah. I just think terrible behavior is funny. I'm not saying it's correct. I'm saying, Here's a starting point and most comedies—even if it's a Jerry Lewis movie—start with an incredibly immature person who needs to learn a lesson. I'm not like that in life. I'm a very timid person when it comes to women. I was not out and about too much. I was a shy guy. But I find that nerdy guys talking about women in a way that is over-the-top sexist makes me laugh because they do it out of insecurity. They make up for that by going, "Hey, check that girl out," because if the girl tried to kiss them they would cry because they would be so scared.

Charlie: What do you like and dislike about your character, George? What are his redeeming qualities?

Adam: You know, I couldn't find any. It's easier for me *not* to like him because I'm married with two kids and I certainly don't want my two kids to think that guy's me. I was nervous about that the whole movie.

Charlie: You were?

Adam: Absolutely. I have little daughters and I know they're going to watch my movies when they're older. Some of them I'm like, *Maybe that one presents me in a nice light for my kids,* and one like this, I'm like, *I hope they don't think I'm that guy and they become jerks because Daddy was a jerk so I'm going to be a jerk.* I don't know.

Charlie: You're thinking about that?

Adam: Oh my God. I let it go when Apatow would say what he wants in a scene, and I'd say, "Okay, let's go." But I would drive home that night and—I have this nice house. I have kids. I would look in their bedrooms and see them sleeping and I was just like, *What the hell am I doing? This is going to kill me one day. Can I pull out of this?*

Charlie: It might not be worth the millions.

Adam: Exactly.

Charlie: About him, tell me what you think. I mean, Adam has been the most successful comedic actor—

Judd: What is it about him? What is his appeal?

Charlie: What does he have?

Judd: When I lived with Adam, I wanted to be a comedian very badly and Adam had one of those things that you just can't define, which is charisma. People were drawn to him. I would enter a room before he was famous and you would just feel the room move towards Adam and I would be sitting in a corner going, *Why don't I have the magic fairy dust?* He's a great person and people can just tell. The camera's been up in his face for twenty years and they get a sense of where his heart is in addition to all his comedic chops. He was fearless because he signed onto this movie before I wrote it, just off of a short pitch and there was no time during the shoot where he said, "You know, let's not do that—that's cutting too close to the bone" or "That makes me look bad." I really thought at some point we were going to go to war—I mean, in my head.

Charlie: Over what?

Judd: Anything. You know, a lot of actors try to direct through their performance. They'll say, "I don't want to do that because you might use it." Adam produces his own movies. He knows exactly what he wants. And Adam kept saying, "I completely trust you. It's your vision. I'm not going to water it down. Just point me in the right direction." And even though we were satirizing comedy and satirizing the comedy career, he just said, "I'm going to go for it, one hundred percent."

Charlie: Tell me about the Cassavetes thing. Cassavetes was one of your idols.

Judd: Yes.

Charlie: Because Cassavetes was an extraordinarily incisive director, who would confront anything—

Judd: Yes. I mean, I'm certainly not as accomplished or brave as Cassavetes, but I do think that what he preaches when you read interviews with him is important. He says all his movies are about love, and obstacles to love. And that's something that Garry Shandling always said of *The Larry Sanders Show*. And that's how I try to approach the work. Some of the scenes do not *have* to be enjoyable. They just need to make you think or feel something.

Charlie: You know where the pleasure center is, though.

Judd: I do, and it takes work to avoid it.

Adam: It feels good there, though.

Judd: It does.

Charlie: Is it your comfort zone?

Adam: It's definitely what I came out to Hollywood to do. I mean, I was like: *I'm going to make people feel at ease.*

Charlie: Is there anything that would cause you to say, "I'll roll the dice on this"?

Adam: I don't have that right now.

Charlie: You don't have that creative urge?

Adam: I'm forty-two. I've been doing this since I was seventeen. I've always had an insane drive. I'm shooting a movie right now and everyone in the movie is saying, All right, what are you doing next? And in my head I'm going, *I just want to relax. I just want to sit down.*

Charlie: Do you love the *doing* of the thing?

Adam: I am nuts. I am dying to get in there. I want to destroy. And when we get on the set, I'm just, like, in that trailer going, *Why the hell am I here? I can't stand it. Why did I make all this money to end up in this stupid trailer again? I can't believe it.*

Judd: It is a lot of pressure when you're on that set. Every day is an experiment. Every scene might not work and so you're concentrating—*Is it working? Should I get an extra line for editing? What would I change if I had to, if I hated this in three months, why would I hate it?* And you're concentrating and you're exhausted but it's supposed to be light, funny work so you're also trying to stay loose and funny. It's pretty intense.

Adam: That's why, when you see a happy actor, you're mad at him because you're like, "You don't care enough, you jerk."

Charlie: It's like they say about CEOs—those guys who have low golf scores are not doing a good job at the office, you know. Might you two work together again?

Adam: Of course, absolutely.

Judd: Definitely.

Adam: You know what was great? The subject matter of being sick—we both saw each other go through it with people we love and it was just very deep to us, this movie. Also we both work hard and respect each other's work and, like, at the end of the day when I'd say good night to Apatow, I would tear up. I'd say, "All right, I love you, buddy."

Judd: Are you serious?

Adam: Absolutely. Because it was, I couldn't believe that we've known each other so long, that we're both getting to do what we wanted. We would talk late at night. He wasn't so sure on what he was going to do. I was like, "I'm going to be a movie star. That's a guarantee and no one's going to stop me." Judd wasn't sure what he was doing, but he was writing away all the time. I'd walk by his bedroom, see him typing away. I would go, "What are you doing in there, Apatow?" "Oh, I'm just writing some skit." And I was like, "For what?" He'd be like, "I don't know." *What the hell's the matter with this guy?* It's just neat that we've known each other this long and then got to make a movie together. Of course I want to do it again.

ALBERT BROOKS

(2012)

There are certain people I always figured I would never get the chance to work with in my career. Albert Brooks was one of those people. Comedy-wise, he was simply out of my league. He was on Mount Olympus. At a certain point, I resigned myself to never knowing him like I wanted to.

When I was writing for *The Larry Sanders Show*, I had the opportunity to have dinner a few times with him and Garry Shandling, and I sat there, terrified and practically mute, for the entire meal. Should I have said something? Should I have tried to be funny? When I got home, I would run to my computer and write down everything he'd said.

Then, when I was writing *This Is 40*, I decided to write a part for Albert, thinking I would maybe ask him, if it ever got to that point, if he'd be interested in playing it. I never thought he would actually accept it, and when he did, I was completely paralyzed by fear. *Oh, God. What if the movie is terrible? What if I pull him down into the muck with me?* But the truth is, he was as brilliant and creative as one could ever hope Albert Brooks would be. The night before we would shoot a scene, he'd send me this stream of emails, filled with jokes that topped my jokes, and ideas that topped my ideas, all offered in a generous and collaborative way. I was just in awe. In your dreams as a young guy, you imagine your heroes to be one thing, and then you get a chance to work with one of them and he's actually even better. Down deep, all comedy nerds hope that, at the end of our lives, we will have made one movie as good and true as Albert Brooks's best movies.

This interview was originally published in Vanity Fair *in January 2013 (Jim Windolf/*Vanity Fair; © *Condé Nast*).

Judd Apatow: Didn't you write jokes for Michael Dukakis?

Albert Brooks: Yeah. I was asked to go on the airplane and go to different events. And I actually spoke at a few. I was so disenchanted with him. I thought, *I pray he doesn't win.* I mean, there were arguments on the plane, and the guys hated him. "Can I ask him a question?" "Nobody can talk to him now!" So I'm thinking, *What if there's a war?*

Judd: Was that the first campaign you got involved in?

Albert: Yeah. I wrote a big joke for him at the Al Smith Dinner, in New York, which is a big political event. George Bush's slogan was "It's time to give the country back to the little guy," and all I was trying to do was to get Dukakis to try to be self-deprecating. I said, "They love that." So Dukakis is, like, four foot three, and he said, "George Bush says it's time to give the country back to the little guy. Well, here I am!" And it got written about: Dukakis makes fun of himself. But I think he took it too far, with the tank.

Judd: And the helmet.

Albert: I wasn't there for that. I would have disapproved of that.

Judd: I always think when someone's elected president they take them into a room and say, "Here's what really goes on on this planet."

Albert: Well, that was in my book. That's the two-week period where you go from thinking you can change the world to being scared out of your mind. You get the list of the nine people who run everything. I'm sure that's the way it is.

Judd: You've always been a bit of a futurist.

Albert: My friend Harry Nilsson used to say the definition of an artist was someone who rode way ahead of the herd and was sort of the lookout. Now you don't have to be that, to be an artist. You can be right smack-dab in the middle of the herd. If you are, you'll be the richest.

Judd: And so *Real Life* and even the *Saturday Night Live* sketches were—

Albert: Well, the first thing I ever did was *The Famous School for Comedians*, for PBS. I had written this fictitious article in *Esquire*, with a test, and they got like three thousand real responses, because mockumentary things weren't really there yet. "Oh, it's a joke? Why would it be a joke? There's pictures of the school!" So Bob Shanks, a lovely man, was a producer at *The Great American Dream Machine*, and he said, "Why don't you make this into a commercial?" That was the first time I ever picked up a camera and found out that, well, if I aim it here, and this person says that, and I think it's funny, hey, you think it's funny, too.

Judd: Then Lorne Michaels wanted you as permanent host for *SNL*, which was just starting.

Albert: Instead of hosting, which I didn't want to do, I was able to sort of dictate what I wanted to do, because they wanted my name. And so I made six films [for *SNL*] in five months. That was really a film school.

Judd: Before that, did you have any sense you would go into filmmaking?

Albert: No. But my comedy bits were like scenes. I would bring props and chairs and tape recorders. I was fleshing out fifteen characters, with different voices, and it would have been better if I had hired fourteen people.

Judd: Was it almost a combination of a modern style of stand-up comedy and the previous style? This idea of doing characters and creating situations, but in a new way?

Albert: Well, my roots were in acting. That's all I wanted to be. Even though my father was a radio comedian, it wasn't cool to say, at a young age, "I want to be a comedian."

Judd: Did your dad do stand-up?

Albert: My dad played a character on the radio called "Parkyakarkus." A Greek-dialect comedian. He did Friars' roasts and wrote material and made people laugh that way.

Judd: What was the character like?

Albert: The character was a Greek immigrant who couldn't speak very well, so there was a lot of dialect humor. He owned a restaurant. And the show was called *Meet Me at Parky's*. My dad died right after performing at the Friars' roast for Lucille Ball and Desi Arnaz. I have that tape somewhere. There's still a lot of good jokes in there. I mean, that was 1958.

Judd: How old were you when that happened?

Albert: Eleven and a half.

Judd: So that's just an earth-shattering . . .

Albert: Well, he was so sick before that that I—

Judd: Heart problems?

Albert: Yeah. And he couldn't walk. He had a spinal operation. Then he could walk slowly, like Frankenstein. And so he gained weight. Nothing about him was healthy. Every time we were alone and he called me, I thought he was dying. So when it happened, it wasn't like, hey, he was the second baseman and he woke up and died.

Judd: How did having a sick dad imprint you?

Albert: I think when you're very, very, very young and you get a sense of the end before the beginning, it imprints you. In all possible ways.

Judd: What did your mom do?

Albert: My dad and mom met each other in a movie called *New Faces of 1937*. My mom went under the name Thelma Leeds, and she did a few movies, and she was really a great singer, and when she married my dad and started to have a family, she sang at parties. She didn't continue, and my dad, he was working, saved his money, so we—

Judd: You were okay.

Albert: We were okay. And then my mom remarried, a lovely man in the shoe business.

Judd: You always hear this legend of Carl Reiner going on *The Tonight Show* saying, "The funniest person I know is my son's friend." Why did he think you were so funny?

Albert: This bit that I did, he said it was the hardest he's ever laughed in his whole life. I don't think it was the greatest bit. It was me pretending to be a terrible escape artist who gasped for air and begged for help.

Judd: Who were you developing it for?

Albert: Well, we all go to the area of strength in school, so we can be liked by girls. And if you're not going to be a quarterback and you're not going to be a biology honors student . . . so I was funny. At Beverly Hills High, there was a parent-student talent show. A big event once a year. Now, Beverly High, a lot of the parents were famous. So you had Tony Curtis, you had Carl Reiner. . . .

Judd: You had competition.

Albert: That's right. Rod Serling. So I was the host of the evening—and I was this kid. I wrote jokes and made comments. I still remember a joke that I told. One of the kids, for their talent portion, did those batons—you twirl them around and around—and I still remember, because it was an ad lib. I was like, "Wasn't she wonderful? Do you know, in practice, a 707 accidentally landed on the football field." People roared.

Judd: So you weren't like the class clown that couldn't get a girlfriend?

Albert: Humor-wise, I was confident. I mean, my two best friends were Larry Bishop, who's Joey Bishop's son, and Rob Reiner, who is Carl Reiner's son.

Judd: It was a world of comedy. Did you think at that point you would go into film?

Albert: I never wanted to be a director. When I started, when I wrote the script for *Real Life*, I didn't want to direct it. And I went to Carl Reiner. And, really, directing is just the dictation of the style. You wind up doing it because—"No, no, no, don't cast him." You know? "We'll put Elliott Gould in the thing." "Oh, no. He's wonderful, but don't put him in that. That's terrible."

Judd: That's exactly why I became a director.

Albert: I mean, Steven Spielberg seems to have wanted to be a director from thirteen. He put his dog in a certain position and made him eat at four o'clock. He liked to direct it. But, to me, directing is tedious. Especially if you're acting in it. And I'm inherently lazy. I would stay in the trailer until someone came to get me: "It's four o'clock. You're not going to be able to do the horse shot if you don't—" "Oh, okay." So when I act in people's films, I have this perverse thing of watching it rain, and I'm like, *I think I'll eat another scone.*

Judd: Do you ever wish you directed more?

Albert: Here's what I think. I think Woody Allen was the last person to get in under the radar of testing and promoting.

Judd: Because he doesn't have to do any of it?

Albert: Yes. And I admire that, because the hardest part of the movies I made was the release part. I mean, some of my movies tested well enough where they were confused, and others tested so terribly that it's like you killed their children. And that whole period where you have to dodge phone calls and figure out what to do. I came just at the time where I had to go on the plane with them. You just had to, or they wouldn't talk to you again.

Judd: Was it the *Real Life* screening where the studio executives flew home without you?

Albert: No, *Modern Romance.* Frank Price was the head of Columbia at the time, and they had seen all these dailies, and I had had screenings. I ran this film fifteen times, just for my own good, and the audience was great, and they laughed, and the executives, they'd laugh. So then, what they did is, they surprised an audience. They told them after they came to a movie that they had paid for, which was *Seems Like Old Times*, that Goldie Hawn–Chevy Chase movie. So we went up to San Francisco, and they surprised them with *Modern Romance.*

Judd: So they make it a double feature? And they are exhausted by the time your movie starts?

Albert: Yeah, yeah, yeah. And there was a big party planned at the Fairmont, with hors d'oeuvres and liquor, and everybody left and just flew back, and they didn't tell me or [my co-writer] Monica Johnson or [my co-star] Kathryn Harrold—and I think [my friend] Paul Slansky came up just for support, and the four of us just spent the night in that ballroom alone, and they tell me I was the funniest I've ever been in my life. And then, when I got back to L.A., it was as if I had secretly changed every minute of the movie in a dungeon. They had a box of cards and they said, "You need to read these cards." This was 1980, so I was still able to say, "I'm not going to read the cards." So they read them to me. Like Guantánamo.

Judd: I get the same cards.

Albert: So Frank Price said, "You need to add a psychiatrist scene to explain the problem, or you won't have a second week." And I didn't add a psychiatrist scene, and, of course, what he was saying was: If you don't fix this, we're doing nothing. And they did nothing. But the nice thing about that experience was that Stanley Kubrick befriended me.

Judd: Really?

Albert: He screened the movie, and I was really—I couldn't get out of bed. I was just feeling like: *This is impossible, this kind of work. How do you do this?* A very famous young director at the time said to me, "Why don't you just do what they want? What's the matter with you?" And I'm going, "I didn't make the movie to do what they want. I'm trying to say something." So Stanley Kubrick said it was the best movie on jealousy he ever saw, and he said, "This movie would make twenty-five million dollars with the right support." And I just thought, *Jesus Christ, this is great.*

Judd: You struck up a friendship with him?

Albert: We wrote back and forth. Then one day I said, "Maybe I should come and visit." And he went, "No, no, no, no, I don't really live anywhere."

Judd: And you never heard from him again. How were your reviews?

Albert: Remember, there were key outlets that could give you a career. *Real Life* got a rave in *Time.* By Frank Rich. So I got enough good reviews that I kept having a career.

Judd: You're always able to make the next movie.

Albert: I can make the next movie tomorrow. The thing that keeps me hesitant is the third act. What I mean is: The first act is writing, the second act is making, the third act is releasing. And if I can just get over that, nothing would stop me.

Judd: Do you ever just think, *I've done so much—I'm a highly respected person—who gives a fuck about all that?*

Albert: Yes, I do. Listen, I like acting. I liked acting in your movie. I liked *Drive*. I like taking these parts, and that's satisfying. I run into a lot of people who are really nice about "When's your next movie coming out?" And I think about it. I just have to make sure I'm at that place where the third act wouldn't bother me.

Judd: Does that get worse as you get older?

Albert: It probably gets better as you get closer to the end. It would be funny to think, *Oh, I have terminal cancer, but I'm worried about the cards.*

Judd: I've been done with *This Is 40* since the end of May, and it comes out at Christmas. It's a seven-month gap, which is like telling a joke and waiting seven months to see if people laugh. It's torture.

Albert: There's no real immediacy in movies. Even in comedy albums, the irony is, if I didn't bring a comedy album to a friend's and sit down and listen to it with them, I never heard my comedy albums played. I've never heard reactions to them.

Judd: That's what's interesting about Twitter. I get tweets every night where someone says, "I'm watching *Freaks and Geeks* right now." It's a great way to connect with people who are watching your work at that very moment. Do you have that experience?

Albert: Yeah, but Twitter is the devil's playground.

Judd: It sucked you in. You're addicted now.

Albert: I don't know if I'm addicted. It's a horrible waste of time for the writer of it, the reader of it. We will lose the war to China because of Twitter.

Judd: So why are you still doing it?

Albert: Well, because I always liked the ability to comment on a good story of the day. And it's the easiest thing when you read the morning newspapers and then you go: "Look at this—they're bombing Europe." And it's amazing, whenever you do anything political, I'm sure you know.

Judd: The vitriol.

Albert: "I hope you die!" It's just so funny to me.

Judd: If someone says, "I hope you die," and I tweet back at them—

Albert: They say, "No, I love you."

Judd: Yeah. Every time.

Albert: Every time. I know. I love that. And they are so shocked. I had a guy that said, "Go drive your car into the ocean and never come up, you vile piece of shit." And I said, "All of that from that comment?" And the guy said, "Oh, my God, I didn't know you'd answer back. I love *Modern Romance!*"

Judd: So you're not currently writing a movie? Do you have notebooks? Do you have ideas?

Albert: I have tons of ideas. One of the reasons I didn't go into it again was I am enjoying acting and there were so many movies I turned down as an actor because I was making my own movies. Every time I see *Boogie Nights*—you know, I got offered the part that Burt Reynolds got. And I remember going into a screening room and seeing Paul Thomas Anderson. No one knew him yet, and I watched *Hard Eight*, and I thought, *Oh, this is good—this is someone you would like to take a chance with*. But I was just getting the money to make *The Muse*, and if you're writing and directing and starring in a movie, you can't stop.

Judd: You said you were friends with Harry Nilsson?

Albert: I was. He was one of these comedy-freak guys. He would come and see my shows and he was very sweet and a massive drinker. I didn't drink and I wound up being the driver. And then he introduced me to John Lennon, because they were best friends. I spent a lot of time with Harry Nilsson and John Lennon during those May Pang years, when he was out here. Those guys would get rowdy, but John Lennon was certainly a fun person. And John Lennon, again, was a frustrated comedian. All these guys—comedy, to them, was the holy grail.

Judd: So three single guys running around.

Albert: Harry wasn't even single. He was married. His wife was very forgiving with him leaving and coming back the next month. Look, sometimes it was too much. He was friends with Keith Moon. The Who were staying in Century City, and Harry said, "Come over. Keith is here—we're having a thing." Now, listen to this. I had just done a *Mike Douglas* in the afternoon and flew back from Philadelphia. And I come walking down the hall, and the housekeeper says, "Oh, you were on *Mike Douglas*—you were wonderful." "Thank you so much." I go in the room, and in about twenty minutes Keith Moon threw the television out the window. It was sixteen stories up. And now the room is destroyed, and I'm going: *I was recognized—I got to get out of here! How can I get out of the Century Plaza without being seen?* Because I know in court she's going to go, "The guy on *The Mike Douglas Show!*" You know? And I'm sitting there with Keith trying to be a Jewish mother: "Don't throw the TV. If you want to get your frustration out, go run around the block, because the TVs, they don't want them thrown out the window."

Judd: So how old are you when you're hanging out with John Lennon? Are you, like, twenty-three?

Albert: Twenty-five.

Judd: And did you grow up so much around show business that it didn't blow your mind?

Albert: It's a great question, because nothing blew my mind in show business, and he was the only person—the first time I met him, Harry said, "Get in that car there," and I got in the backseat, and there was John Lennon, and the one thing I prided myself on in my comedy, you know, I'm not a person that was ever on. I was funny. I knew when to stop. I wasn't that manic on, and I was on with him, and I didn't know how to get out of it. I didn't know what to do. And he said—that still remains the greatest thing to me—he leaned over and said, "I've known you for a thousand years." And I just never felt bad again.

Judd: That's right in the post-Beatles moment.

Albert: He was going through a lot. He was separated from Yoko, but I remember my album, *Comedy Minus One*, had just come out and was in

Tower Records. So he and Harry and I went in. He bought them all. He bought three boxes of them. Then he drove down Sunset and hurled them out like Frisbees. And again I'm going, "Don't do that. You'll get a littering fine." Boom. He's just throwing them out on the street. So it's good and bad. I mean, it helped my *Billboard* number, but now they are all over Sunset.

Judd: Was that inspiring creatively?

Albert: It was interesting to know what they think of comedy. They love comedy so much. It's a language they don't speak as eloquently. As much as you listen to the Beatles and say, "How do you write that song?" they're going, "How did you say that? Where did that come from?"

Judd: Were you doing stand-up in those years?

Albert: I started on television. I had five years of network television before I ever got up on a stage. The first thing I ever did was in 1967. This guy Bill Keene had a little talk show at noon, and Gary Owens took over for a week. He knew about this dummy bit I used to do, this ventriloquist thing, and I was on *Keene at Noon*. From that I got an agent and three Steve Allen shows in 1968. I only had one bit. I did that and then I made up two other bits.

Judd: Did you have to show them before?

Albert: No. No. It was a time when people trusted you. They said, "What are you going to do?" "I'm going to do this—it will be four minutes." Almost nobody laughed, but Steve Allen laughed so hard. And that was the laugh you needed. From that, in '69, I was offered a spot as a regular on a Dean Martin show. Then, from '70 to '73, I must have done eighty variety shows. There were so many. Glen Campbell. Helen Reddy. The Everly Brothers. Johnny Cash. *Hollywood Palace*. After all of these shows, I did Merv—I did Merv Griffin's CBS show fourteen times. And then, after all these years, I got a call from Neil Diamond. His manager said, "Would Albert want to open for Neil?" And I had never done that.

Judd: You'd never done it live, on the road.

Albert: My first couple of months was taking television bits and trying to make them fit into a live act. Eventually I felt comfortable onstage, but I went back to doing primarily television. In the early 1970s, *Dick Cavett* was very hot. And I hadn't done *Johnny Carson*. I'd done everything but, and I said to my agent, "I'd like to do *Dick Cavett*. I think that's a cool show." And they didn't want me, and I went to *The Tonight Show*. By default. And that was one of the lucky breaks I had. I did, like, forty of those shows. Half of them don't exist, because it was during those years in the seventies where they erased over the tape. It breaks my heart. I would do a new bit every time for Johnny, and that was a hell of an experience. Just once every five, six weeks. Make something up in the bathroom and go do it on *The Tonight Show*.

Judd: That's a lot of bits.

Albert: A lot of bits, but you had Johnny's confidence, and it didn't matter if the audience laughed. Johnny laughed, and that's all that ever mattered. But eventually they laugh. When Johnny laughs, they laugh.

Judd: Did you develop a friendship with him?

Albert: I would pay my respects and go to Las Vegas and see his stand-up, and he wasn't an easy guy to be a friend with. He came into my dressing room one night before the show out of the blue and he sat me down and said, "You need to be married." And this is a guy that's been married three times.

Judd: How old were you when he said that?

Albert: I was twenty-eight. And I said, "How come?" And he said, "This is too hard to do alone." Now, by the way, he's right on that account. But I didn't want to go through four wives just to accomplish that.

Judd: How old were you when you got married?

Albert: My forties. And I was very fortunate when I met Kimberly—things gelled. There weren't all these problems, everybody who has these relationships. I was an expert at it. I made *Modern Romance*. People used to stop me on the street. I get this a lot, where they honk their horn and roll down the window and a couple says, "We got married because of *Modern Romance*." I don't know what to do. I feel so bad.

Judd: What does that mean?

Albert: I don't know.

Judd: That means, "We both like it."

Albert: That means they're both screwed up. I had a very wise person tell me that he thinks marriage, when you're younger, you keep thinking you can fix things. That's what people do. And you can't really fix anything. It shouldn't be a massive difficult thing every day. Life's difficult enough. You can fix little teeny things. If a person likes to eat their peas off a plate, and you like to eat them in a bowl, you might win at that. But that's about it.

Judd: Were you a difficult person to date?

Albert: I wasn't a bad boyfriend. I had relationships with some of the women who were in the movies. And I wasn't a cheater. I was a pretty loyal guy.

Judd: You weren't like the guy in *Modern Romance*.

Albert: Very early on I was. I had a relationship that was immensely physical without the other components. And when you're young, that's confusing, because you're being told, Well, what do you think relationships are? They are physical. But you need a little bit of everything. I tried my hand at the most funny women, but I'm not a person who believes you want a person like yourself. You want key things in common, but you don't want the nutsiness to be the same, because that's too much.

Judd: What kind of dad are you? What are the TV rules?

Albert: TV isn't an issue. It's more the screens. It's the games, and there's rules about that, and there's nothing before homework. They are not big TV watchers during the day. They are at night. When I was a kid, that's all we had, and I watched a lot of it. We could trick our parents and say it was good for us.

Judd: What are your kids into?

Albert: My daughter, Claire, is an amazing singer and writes songs. And is a good writer. And very creative, and can draw. Jake is the funniest kid I know. He's got a real sense of humor. He's become a reasonable magician.

I take him to these places on the weekend where they have what's called Magic: The Gathering. And there's like forty people who look like they work for Microsoft and my son. And he wins most nights. But the most important thing is that they've got good souls. They've got good hearts. They know what kid to befriend when that kid needs it. . . . I don't see the kind of cynicism that you see in other people.

Judd: In us.

Albert: Yeah, well, I don't think I was a person who made fun of other kids. That wasn't my style of comedy. . . . I've never talked this much about myself.

Judd: Do you like the idea of your kids going into show business?

Albert: If I can't talk them out of it, yes. My mother kept trying to talk me out of everything. "Honey, fall back on business." I never knew what it meant, and that's the way it should be. I sum up all of show business in three words: Frank Sinatra Junior. People think there's nepotism in show business. There's no nepotism on the performing side, especially in comedy. I don't know of any famous person that can tell an audience to laugh at their son.

Judd: You once said you got such a kick out of making people laugh on the phone that it slowed down how much you would write for yourself.

Albert: That was a big problem for me and still is. I have to be careful. I'm going to go do *Letterman* for *This Is 40*, and I told my wife and a couple of friends of mine what I'm going to do, and it makes them laugh. We were having dinner, and my wife goes, "Tell them what you're going to do on *Letterman*." I said, "No, no, no." Because my problem was always that when I thought of something funny, if I called up a buddy, and I did it, the ship had sailed. I didn't need seven thousand people. One person worked. The chromosome had clicked and I had an orgasm. I was done.

Judd: And so you didn't need to write a movie.

Albert: It's terrible. It's not a commercial gene.

Judd: At some point it's like: How much need is there to—how much is too much?

Albert: Let's ask you that. You work a lot. I mean, if you enjoy it, it's good. If you wake up and it feels like it's destroying you, then you need to think about it.

Judd: True.

Albert: There are many aspects of work that are amazingly rewarding. The actual doing of it. The writing, when it goes well, there's no better creative high. A day on the set where you assemble a bunch of great actors and you brought this to life. That's a wonderful thing. There are other aspects where I've fought for things in movies. The movies that I've directed, for the most part, I've been able to win at the cost of alienating people.

Judd: Such as?

Albert: I wrote this movie with Monica Johnson called *The Scout*, that Michael Ritchie directed. I can't stand the way it ends, and it was a fight that I lost. I yelled so loud at Peter Chernin, I never worked at Fox again. I lost my temper. I went crazy, and I said, "Look, you're not the one in the paper getting . . ." And, sure enough, *The New York Times*, it was like the reviewer was listening. She said, "I'm so surprised that Albert Brooks would end a movie this way." And I'm going, "Albert Brooks didn't end a movie this way!"

Judd: The work can really bring out the worst side of you when you feel like someone else is ruining it. I can completely lose my mind.

Albert: But you're supposed to. If you're in a position where an argument can win, you're supposed to argue. I mean, I've lost only a few arguments. That was the good thing about writing and directing my own movies. For *Lost in America*, they were telling me, "He doesn't have enough stupid jobs before he decides to go back to New York. Put in more jobs." And I said, "When you have a man in a crossing guard outfit, there's no other stupid job." They said, "Just try some." So that was easy, because I was able to say, "Here's one: Find someone who looks like me and you film it. If it works, we'll put it in." That argument I can win.

Judd: How does it feel for you that these movies that were painful at the time and didn't make that much money are now classics?

Albert: It's cool, but it's not an active feeling. You don't get up in the morning going, "My movie's still here—fuck you." That's not a joyous daily feeling. I mean, as I told you, there's no line at the bank for being ahead of your time.

Judd: How did you find the process working on *This Is 40*?

Albert: I liked it with you, because of the rehearsal. I like the idea of what the father was going to be. People ask me all the time about improv, and I tell them improv is just the final icing. You need a structure. It's like, if you're going to commit suicide, you need the building to jump out of.

Judd: Which comedians made the biggest impression on you when you were starting out?

Albert: The biggest influence was Jack Benny. Because of his minimalism. And the way he got laughs. He was at the center of a storm, he let his players do the work, and just by being there made it funny. That was mind-boggling to me.

Judd: Were you around him at all?

Albert: I knew him a little. He was very sweet to me once. I did a bit on *The Tonight Show*, early on, this bit Alberto and His Elephant Bimbo. I was a European elephant trainer. I came out and I was dressed up with a whip, and I was distraught because the elephant never arrived, and I said, "Look, the show must go on. *The Tonight Show*, all they could get me was this frog, so I will do my best." So I took a live frog and put it through all these elephant tricks. Every time he did a trick I threw peanuts at him. And the last trick, I said, "I call this trick 'Find the nut, boy!'" I gave the peanut to somebody on the stage. I walked over and gave it to Doc Severinsen. "The elephant will find the peanut!" I took this frog. I threw this black huge cloth over him, the one I said I used to blindfold the elephant, and this black rag started hopping all over the place till it eventually hopped over to Doc Severinsen. It actually found him. I didn't know what the hell the frog was going to do. So after the bit I sit down at the panel, and Jack Benny was on. There was always that last two minutes where Johnny was asking people, "Thank you for coming—what do you have coming up?" And during the last commercial Jack Benny leaned over to

Johnny Carson and said, "When we get back, ask me where I'm going to be, will you?" So they came back. Johnny said, "I want to thank Albert. Jack, where are you going to be performing?" And Jack Benny said, "Never mind about me—this is the funniest kid I've ever seen!" And it was this profound thing. Like, *Oh, that's how you lead your life. Be generous and you can be the best person who ever lived.*

Judd: When I used to do stand-up in the late eighties at the Improv, you'd always hear, "Albert might be coming in, Albert might be coming in." I don't think you ever came in. Ever. Why did people think you were coming in?

Albert: Because I'd ask the guy to say that. Paid him forty bucks a week.

Judd: So you thought about jumping onstage but—

Albert: I did once. I even got a heckler. It was like I picked the wrong night. "Who are you?" I talk to a lot of friends now who tell me I would enjoy doing this again, because it's different, and people would appreciate it. It's a nice thing, because it's so in the moment. That's the lure.

Judd: Do you miss that part of your career?

Albert: I get it from the occasional talk show. The other thing would be to go do a stand-up special, something in front of a large audience. That's what you're really talking about. If I do *Letterman*, and it goes well, it's a fun feeling, when I'm leaving. And I get back to the hotel—and I'm the same person. There was nothing more exciting in the early years than when Johnny Carson was still in New York. You'd go there and do a Johnny Carson show. You travel alone. And the show would be great. And then you go out by yourself and you have a meal and you go back to the hotel and you watch it. And then you'd go to bed and then you wake up at three-thirty and picture all your friends watching it in Los Angeles. That doesn't work anymore, because people don't watch shows like that. You can do a *Letterman* and somebody will catch it months later. "Hey, I saw that thing." "It was two years ago."

Judd: What do you feel there's left to write about?

Albert: The subject of dying and getting old never gets old.

Judd: It's shocking as you realize: *Are we all going to have these horrible things happen to us?*

Albert: Well, aren't we? I mean, this getting-old stuff is something. I sound like Bob Hope. I think I envy my dog, because my dog is sixteen and she's limping and she's still living, but she doesn't look at me like she knows. She's not thinking what I'm thinking. It's a cruel trick, that we all know the ending.

Judd: Are you religious at all?

Albert: It's funny, I don't believe in the images of what God is, a thing or a person. I do wonder often the reason the sea horse is here, or a tree, or why I'm here, and so I don't know if I'm religious. But it's interesting when you're part of a group—the Jews, to be exact—that the world has had such problems with. It has really nothing to do with religion. That's why, if my kids didn't want to go to temple, I used to say, "Let me explain something to you: If Hitler came back, he's not going to ask if you went to temple. You're already on the train. So you might as well know who you are and why they're going to take you."

Judd: What do you get out of temple?

Albert: I went to a memorial service and brought my kids and we thought about my dad and my mom, and the rabbi gave kind of a cool sermon, and you're sitting in a room with everyone who would have to go on the same train. So there's a bit of community there.

Judd: That's dark.

Albert: But it's true. Here's what we know. We know meditation is healthy. Everybody says it slows your heart rate and everything, and the basis of religion seems to be that when you pray . . . I don't know what people who are religious think when they pray, but it's very close to what meditation is. It's sort of ritualistic, it's habit, it's like exercising, so you might be able to get something out of that. I'm sure some people enjoy thinking it's out of their hands. There's all these people who think it's "meant to be." But I don't buy that.

Judd: I'd love to buy it, though. I wish I could.

Albert: I don't buy it, but I love it.

Judd: It would make the day so much easier.

Albert: Look, only a few people get to die peacefully in their sleep after a wonderful life. So that's like not making the football team. There's lots of things you don't get to have. That's probably one of them. Thank God, I consider myself lucky that I live after anesthetic. Can you imagine those days? "Sit down. Tuesday, we're taking off your arm."

Judd: The whole setup sucks. And comedy is a constant exploration of it. I still can't figure it out, because it's so absurd and so awful that I can't do anything but laugh in its face.

Albert: But it's really not awful. If I've learned anything—anything—getting older, it's the value of moment-to-moment enjoyment. When I was young, all my career was "If I do well tonight, that means that Wednesday will be better. That means I can give this tape to my agent and . . ." It was this ongoing chess game. And that is a really disappointing game, because when you get to checkmate, it never feels like it should. And there's another board that they never told you about. So if I come here and talk to you, if I have an enjoyable three hours, god damn it, that counts.

Judd: Do you ever have a spiritual feeling when you're creative?

Albert: I used to hate when people say, "I feel it come through me," but there are moments where two hours go by and you don't know what happened, and you got all these words, and it's the highlight of my life.

AMY SCHUMER
(2014)

I was sitting in my car one day, listening to *The Howard Stern Show,* when Amy Schumer came on. I think I had seen her do a little stand-up on television once or twice before, or maybe just some jokes at a roast, but that's about it. But sitting there in my car, listening to her talk to Howard, I was blown away by how funny and intimate and fresh she was. You could sense that she had stories to tell and was a lot more than just a comedian. I instantly thought: *I need to make a movie with her.*

So we did.

Amy and I spent the next few years working on *Trainwreck,* and I found that she was, indeed, so much more than just a comedian. She is someone who is willing to go emotionally deep, as well as work obsessively hard, and there's a frankness to her work that I find inspiring. The stories tumble out of her. She is able to make important points about our culture and feminism and relationships and what it's like to be a woman in America right now, and to do it in a way that is consistently insightful and hysterical. Here is someone at the beginning of a very exciting career.

Amy Schumer: I did an interview with Jerry Seinfeld the other day.

Judd Apatow: You did? Did you know him at all?

Amy: We met a bunch of times at the Cellar, but I didn't know him well. He picked me up in a Ferrari, and then it broke down on [the] West Side Highway. It was a real piece of shit. It was smoking, it was real scary.

Judd: That's awesome.

Amy: Yeah, that was awesome. It was the best time.

Judd: And how was the interview?

Amy: He completely changed my philosophy about stand-up. He was like, "This idea that your generation has about 'you have to burn your material and start fresh every time'—it's just so self-important. Not everybody's watching everything you do, you know." He said, "Focus on coming up with your best act for a live show. Remember: Seventy-five percent of the crowd has never seen you, and they'll never see you again, so you should be working on the best possible show."

Judd: He's the main voice railing against the modern comic constantly turning over her act.

Amy: He changed my thinking. For TV, you always have to do new stuff, obviously. But for a live show, rather than trying to work out a whole new act, just do the stuff that's pretty well worked out.

Judd: But he goes beyond that. He's also saying that, at any time, half your act can be greatest hits. Like, who decided you couldn't do that?

Amy: I don't know why that became the thing. I don't know why the idea of doing an older joke is supposed to make you feel embarrassed. It's not about impressing the five comics in the back of the room. As Jerry said, if he sees someone, he wants to see their best jokes. Jokes are like works of art and they take years to figure out. He said you only get six closers in your whole life. Like six big jokes—

Judd: In your whole life.

Amy: Yeah.

Judd: I think the first person who turned over his material like that was George Carlin. He did a special every three years or so. Robert Klein put out a lot of specials, and I assume he was writing new material, too. But Seinfeld put out one special in his entire career. Leno has never put out a special. It's a generational shift. The modern comic says, "Hey, this is what I'm going through right now."

Amy: Yeah. "Check in with me, here's where I am now."

Judd: So maybe the secret is doing more specials than Seinfeld and less than Louis C.K.

Amy: I'm going to do one every couple of years, but I want it to be really great. Because the thing about specials is, they're going to be there forever.

Judd: Do you think Seinfeld will ever do another special?

Amy: I don't think so, no. He's been doing Caesars for ten years, maybe fifteen, and the crowds are great. He gives them a great show and they leave happy. He asked me, "Do you want people to come and say, 'Oh, she was good,' or do you want them to come and say, 'You *have* to go see that show'?"

Judd: But modern comedy fans *will* go see you again. That is something Jerry doesn't understand. Young people will go see Marc Maron every year.

Amy: That's a good point. I guess the question is, is it better to please the twenty percent of the crowd who comes to see you every time, or is it better to give a killer show, like an epic performance, for the rest?

Judd: This may not apply to anything, but I was watching a movie about women in comedy recently—I think it was called *Women Aren't Funny*? And I noticed that you weren't in it. Was that by choice?

Amy: I got cut out. Actually, I am in one scene. But I don't talk.

Judd: Oh, I thought maybe it was a political choice, a way of saying, we shouldn't even be debating this anymore.

Amy: No, that debate is insane to me. It doesn't even make me mad. It's like asking, "Do Jewish people smell like orange juice?" It's just such a weird question. It's not even a question. The thing that gets to me is the question "Isn't this a great time to be a woman in comedy?" I mean, all the TV I watched growing up featured funny women.

Judd: People said the same thing when *Bridesmaids* came out. We never thought about that when we were making it. I just thought, *Kristen Wiig is funny. It would be fun to make a movie with Kristen Wiig*. And then she had this idea to make a movie about bridesmaids. We never thought of it as a female movie. At some point, in the middle of it, it occurred to us: *Oh, it's kind of cool to have so many funny women in one movie*. But it wasn't conscious or anything. At the end of the process, we realized that it meant something to people. But what is shocking to me was that, even after the movie did well, there was almost zero follow-up in the culture.

Amy: In terms of what?

Judd: In terms of funny movies that are dominated by women. The studio system didn't embrace them. They don't know how to do it.

Amy: In my experience, there will be a script and you'll be like, *This is funny, I think I'll audition.* And you'll know other women, who are hilarious, are auditioning, too. And then they give it to, like, Jessica Biel. They're great actresses and they're really pretty, but they're not funny. Nobody's like, "Oh my God, you guys have to hear Jessica Biel tell this story."

Judd: When we did *Undeclared*, the note from Fox was: You need more eye candy.

Amy: Do you think that's true? Do people really need more eye candy?

Judd: I have thought about that a lot. I don't know. But what if people do want it?

Amy: I'm not above that. I want to look at Jennifer Lawrence eating cereal.

Judd: I mean, it depends. People are pretty happy looking at James Gandolfini, or Bryan Cranston. They're happy looking at Nurse Jackie and everyone on *Parks and Rec.* So I don't know. There's escapist television and soap opera–type television, but for the most part, you just want a hilarious person or an interesting person. Are you someone who believes that life is easier if you're attractive?

Amy: I think that beautiful people are not any happier than people who are not as beautiful. Even with models—there's always someone who is more beautiful or younger. So no matter what realm you're operating in, it's all relative. I didn't develop my personality, or my sense of humor, because I felt unattractive. I thought I was attractive until I got older. It was probably a defense mechanism for whatever pain was going on around me. But I don't think that people who feel beautiful feel like, *I don't need to do this other thing.*

Judd: You're in a weird area. I would describe it as: Everyone thinks you are beautiful, but maybe you don't agree with their opinion.

Amy: Um.

Judd: I'll talk about me for a second. I always thought I was right in the middle, looks-wise, and that if I had a good personality, it could put me over the top. But it wasn't like, behind my back, everyone thought I was handsome. I get the sense that you feel like some days you're looking great, some days you're not, but the audience sees you in a certain way that maybe you don't agree with. Does that make sense?

Amy: I think that's probably true. I think that's probably dead-on. I feel, like you just said, that some days I am like a real monster, completely unlovable and unfuckable, and then there's a moment, every now and then, when I'm more like Elaine on *Seinfeld*: "Is it possible that I'm not as attractive as I had thought?" Or maybe it's the opposite of that. Anytime I start feeling better about myself, physically, someone will say something that pushes me right back down. I think every woman feels this way.

Judd: I ask about it because it is about who you think you're speaking to.

Amy: That's a really good point.

Judd: I was a year younger than everybody in school. I was the youngest kid in class, always. But I only realized, later in life, that I was much *smaller* than everybody.

Amy: Physically?

Judd: Yeah. And by the time I caught up a little bit, in sixth or seventh grade, I had been defined. On some level, I guess it made me feel less masculine. And as a result, I always feel like a nerd. I have a beautiful wife, I'm successful. But I still feel like the kid who's picked last in gym class. And that shaped my idea of comedy being about outsiders. It was a way for me to attack all of these systems that I thought were unfair to me.

Amy: I would say the same for me.

Judd: What was your version of that? What happened to you as a kid that made you think and defined your sense of humor? Just the darkness of your house, primarily?

Amy: Yeah, and one thing that's too dark and private to even talk about. But I would say, with the physical stuff, that I was always pretty but not beautiful. And that was something that you were punished for. I was very aware of this stuff early on.

Judd: With girls, it's weird because it changes dramatically. In high school, girls don't look anything like they looked in third grade. Whereas guys, the handsome third-grade dude is still handsome in high school. Girls blossom and change. That was the kind of girl I always tried to date: the girl who, near the end of high school, got pretty but still acted insecure.

Amy: Well, that's the jackpot. That's my favorite kind of guy, too. The guy that blossoms but still sees himself as the fat kid.

Judd: Al Roker.

Amy: Al Roker is the *perfect* example.

Judd: He lost the weight but he's still nice to you.

Amy: Because he remembers. But I had no perspective on myself physically. All I knew was that I was pretty enough to get by. I remember in fifth grade, a guy who I was friends with said something to me about being pretty. I got my period in fifth grade. I had, like, boobs. I had an ass.

Judd: Well, that changes everything. That's just pollution on Long Island.

Amy: Only recently have I got any sort of ownership over my body as a woman.

Judd: What does it feel like, going through puberty so early? Are you getting hormones, like a teenager?

Amy: I was totally boy crazy, running around trying to kiss them. My parents were getting calls. But I wasn't very sexual or anything. I remember growing pains, and my boobs hurt and I was just getting a body that no one else had yet. I remember being sexualized by gardeners—gardeners are the construction workers of Long Island, you know. I'd walk past a gardening truck and I remember feeling like, *Wow, I'm way too young to be getting this kind of sexual energy from these guys.* I only wanted that attention when I wanted it. I guess that's what every woman wants. No one wants unwanted sexual attention. But I felt confused by it, and it's why I talk about it onstage so much. It's the confusion of trying to figure out how attractive I am and laughing at myself—I can be easily convinced that I'm gorgeous. Someone will be like, "You really are a beautiful girl." And I'll be like, "I know." But then, an hour later, you're in an environment where you feel like a troll.

Judd: How does that relate to wanting to be funny?

Amy: That was so interesting, when you asked me before about who I was talking to when I'm onstage. I just thought of that two nights ago. I was in Rochester and I was onstage and this is probably bad to admit, but I was like, I really am speaking to the women in the audience. I'm appreciative of the guys that can come along for the ride and not feel alienated because this isn't some "pro-women, down with men" thing, but the reality is, I'm speaking to the women and trying to keep the guys interested enough that they still want to come to the shows.

Judd: And what are you saying to them?

Amy: "You're doing the best you can and you're good enough." And that came from just sitting around with my girlfriends in high school and not having to pretend. You could just be like, "Well, I haven't washed my hair in almost a full week, and do you want to hear what I ate last night?" You would feel so human—and, as a result, less apologetic.

Judd: Your act is like that now.

Amy: Well, I think it's really comforting to people. It makes everyone feel better to acknowledge that no one has it together. I mean, I don't know anyone that doesn't have this big, dark cloud hovering over them. Just knowing that makes me feel better.

Judd: At what age did you become aware of comedians?

Amy: Really young, when we would watch the Muppets. And then I discovered stand-ups. I loved Gilda. I was so drawn to funny chicks. I remember watching Rita Rudner and George Carlin and Richard Pryor. My dad must've had it on. And Letterman.

Judd: How old were you?

Amy: Ten or younger. Stand-up trickled in over the years but it wasn't until I was in college, early college, where I discovered Margaret Cho, and got really into it.

Judd: At what point did you think, *Stand-up is something I can do?*

Amy: After college. I was twenty-three.

Judd: What did it take for you to think, *Okay, I'm going to try this?* Because it's a crazy leap. The need to show up at an open mic — to even write your first joke. I was a lunatic about it. I was trying to write those jokes at twelve.

Amy: How old were you when you got up for the first time?

Judd: Seventeen. I had wanted to do it really badly since age fourteen, but I was afraid to admit it to anybody.

Amy: My experience was like this: I was in an abusive improv troupe after college. This guy set it up to get fifty bucks a month from each of us, but it was not really improv — it was a crazy, schizophrenic, delusional situation. I went one night to see one of the girls do stand-up at Gotham. It was like at six P.M. and she was bombing. Everyone was bombing. I thought, *I want to try this because I'm not digging the improv but I like it when I say something and I get a laugh.*

Judd: That's interesting. Because it's not about being inspired by watching someone murder, it's like, *Oh, this is as bad as it gets. And I can do better.*

Amy: I still think that all the time. It's not that I feel like what I'm doing is so amazing, but it's pretty good compared to what other people are doing. So that same week, I was walking past the club and it was my birthday and I was like, *I'm from New York, so I can get people in the seats.* I had three hours to prepare.

Judd: You wrote it in one day?

Amy: I wrote it in two hours.

Judd: How did you do?

Amy: Pretty good.

Judd: Do you remember any of it?

Amy: I have a tape of it. I remember it. I talked about how skywriting annoys me. Don't you find that when you talk about your early jokes, even though you *know* they were bad, you're still trying to sell them? Like, I still want you to think this is funny shit but I know it's not. Anyway, I talked about skywriting, how it's annoying and it fades and you can never read it. I was like, "If somebody proposed to me that way, I'd be like, 'Fuck you.' And so, like, this summer, do me a favor: Keep it at eye level," or whatever. So horrible. But it went okay, I think. People came up to me and asked how long I'd been doing it, which suggested that maybe I could do this if I wanted.

Judd: What were you doing for a living back then?

Amy: Waiting tables at Michael Jordan's Steakhouse.

Judd: Trying to get acting work?

Amy: Yeah, auditioning. But one day, this woman came into the restaurant and she really liked me. She was like, "I'm going to hook you up with my agent." So I went in and I did a one-act play to audition for the agent and he was like, "You're pretty mediocre and I have too many girls like you that are better than you."

Judd: That happened to me and I never acted again.

Amy: Are you serious?

Judd: Yes.

Amy: Well, it made me furious. At some point, I started doing open mics. They were the worst shows in the world.

Judd: So how long until you were okay at it?

Amy: Four years. It wasn't until the end of the *Last Comic Standing* tour that I was okay. I could do five minutes, but to do a twenty-minute set and have it be okay? That took three or four years.

Judd: What was it like for you on *Last Comic Standing*?

Amy: It was a reality show, so people were basically pulling for you. I was young, and I was excited, and I hadn't been at all hardened by the business or anything. I was just so happy about it all: "This is great, guys, we're telling jokes!"

Judd: How far did you make it?

Amy: Fourth place. And the other guys had all been doing it for twenty years, but I had an advantage in that way because I was funny off the cuff and on my feet. The competitions were good for the people with fresh minds rather than the hardened road dogs.

Judd: And then you guys all toured the country and you hated everyone, right?

Amy: Five of us toured and I died onstage every night. I would cry on the tour bus, and then go out and do it again the next night—sometimes two shows a night. We had this mandatory meet and greet after each show, so I'd have to stand out there and talk to everyone who had just not laughed at me.

Judd: Did you get better over the course of the tour?

Amy: My material was good, but I got better at selling it. By the end, I was pretty desensitized. I'd just been in so much pain every night that I stopped caring—and once that happened, it became more about my experience onstage. I was worried that I was going to offend someone because I'd be in Fayetteville, North Carolina, making a joke about how I think all gay people have AIDS, and then I'd look out and wonder, *Is that okay?* And the crowd was like, Well, we weren't even going to question it, but now we see that you are. And then I would say something way, way worse right after that, so if they thought they were uncomfortable then . . . That became my thing, tricking people into laughing. Like, the real joke would be a subliminal thing that came after what you thought was the punchline. It was comedy boot camp, and I feel like it gave me years of experience.

Judd: Do you think you have a much different experience, as a woman on the road, than guys are having?

Amy: Not in terms of the audience or anything, but in terms of fun? Yeah. Like, I've never hooked up with somebody after a show.

Judd: I did.

Amy: You did?

Judd: Once.

Amy: What happened?

Judd: It lasted eight seconds and I looked in her eyes as she realized what a horrible mistake she had made. And then we had sex again and this time, it lasted six seconds and she really looked disappointed in herself for choosing to do this. If she became a nun after that, it wouldn't have shocked me.

Amy: Oh my God.

Judd: And I thought, *I'm never going to do this again. This is terrible.*

Amy: That's why I've only dated two comics.

Judd: It's so boring on the road. If you're on the road and you're a guy and you're bored, it's almost like there's nothing else to do.

Amy: I'm just so lazy about what you do *after*. It just doesn't seem worth it to me. The thought of leaving or having the guy leave afterwards, I'm just like, argh.

Judd: Once I was playing the Dallas Improv and I hooked up with this woman after. This is how bad I was: She slept over and we didn't have sex. I told a friend about it afterwards, who was a comedian, and he told me that every time he was with a girl, they would have sex. And I was like, "They go all the way with you every time?" I was like a thirteen-year-old.

Amy: That's amazing.

Judd: She drove me to the airport in the morning.

Amy: Oh my God.

Judd: And her makeup was all smeared down her face. She looked crazy. And we had this weird goodbye, one of those things where you know you're not going to ever call each other.

Amy: Are we supposed to kiss goodbye like we're a couple?

Judd: And I thought, *This is just heinous.* I always tried to avoid all of that but every once in a while you would get so bored, you would think, *I guess I should see what this is.*

Amy: And then you're reminded that it's vile.

Judd: It's never delightful.

Amy: I've had one one-night stand in my life.

Judd: And yet people see your act as very sexual.

Amy: Right.

Judd: So is that a character you're playing?

Amy: Well, it's a part of me, too. Because the stuff you're copping to and the saddest, worst moments of your life—that's the stuff people connect to and appreciate. In reality, I've almost always had a boyfriend. But in those phases in between, I've never held out on sex at all. Like, I'll sleep with a guy right away. That's just what's in my nature. If I want to, I'll do it. I haven't ever used that like as a trading or a bargaining chip but I am also thirty-three and single, so . . .

Judd: You're allowed to.

Amy: Every year, if I have like one or two sexual experiences, they might both be hilarious.

Judd: And then they add up, and people think, *She must be doing this all the time.* I have maybe six experiences from my whole life. But if I go onstage and tell three of them, it sounds like I have hundreds of them.

Amy: Right. But you can get up there and do that, and you're not the Sex Guy. But if I do it, I am. So I just embraced it.

Judd: But those experiences are funny. That's the thing. Your worst sexual experience can be so humiliating and hilarious, both in movies and in stand-up. They're always the best stories. A guy who has got a lot of terrible sex stories is the best dinner companion of all time.

Amy: It's the best. I did one last season on my show, about the biggest penis I've ever encountered. It was like, that year I was single and I hadn't been single for four years. I dated a wrestler and there was so much preposterous sex stuff from that relationship, and then I happened to go out with a guy and realized that his penis was way more than I bargained for. I probably already told you who the guy was, but he was an athlete. He was this guy my sister loved, a hockey player. I don't watch sports but we winded up going out, mostly because my sister was like, "Oh my God, you have to go out with him! I've had a dream about you two falling in love!" So I go out with him mostly so she would think I was cool, but he was really hot and it was fun. I was like, *There's no way he's going to be attracted to me. He could have sex with supermodels.* So at the end of the night, I said, "I'm going to get out of here because I feel like a little insane with you." And he was like, "No, I'll go with you." We went to another bar and then back to his place and—what happened with his penis, it was just so horrible and embarrassing.

Judd: I haven't heard that bit.

Amy: You're supposed to be really excited about a big penis, but when you're faced with one, it's like a unicorn—in theory, you've always wanted to see one up close but if it were ever standing in front of you, you'd be like, *Fuck that,* and you would run. You'd be like, *Oh, it's actually a horse with a weapon on its head.* But in the moment, I was like, *No, you have to do this. Everybody talks about how great it is.* And I was like, okay, and I have a bunch of jokes in there about him going down on me because he was raised well but then I just realized that the guy has to do that, I mean he's like lighting candles. This guy needs to get the girl relaxed. And then he kind of pulled it out and acted like it wasn't a big deal. He was almost whistling like I wasn't going to notice. And then I tried to get myself psyched: *You can do this! You played volleyball in high school!*

Judd: You have to slow your heart rate down. Like a Buddhist monk.

Amy: And then I say, "Do you have a condom?" He says no. And I was like, *Way to call my bluff.*

Judd: They don't make condoms that big.

Amy: So then we tried and it didn't work at all. It was not a possibility. I would have had to alter my body.

Judd: He must be used to this, right? He must know it's going to happen.

Amy: At one point, I say to him: "Are you serious?" He's like, "No, it's usually—" And I'm like, whatever. In my twenties, I would have given it the old college try, but I'm in my thirties now and I was just like, I have Olive Garden leftovers in the fridge, see you later. It's not happening. I'm not going to walk around New York with a gaping vagina because I had sex with you once.

Judd: You tell that story and then you become known as a sex comic.

Amy: It makes me feel like a little bit of a fraud, actually, and a little misunderstood. Onstage, I'll talk about how I've never done anal, or no one's ever cum in my face. I haven't done anything out of the ordinary. I've been so boring. But people don't hear that. All they hear is that you're talking about sex.

Judd: How does that affect what you decide to do on your show? There's a certain amount of gender politics at play here, for sure, in what you decide to write about and talk about. Every sketch, in a way, ends up being about your position on certain things.

Amy: Right.

Judd: And your point of view is strong. That's what people like about it.

Amy: I'm only choosing and pitching what I'm interested in. If there is a great idea—something that I think that is kind of vulnerable and untouched, uncharted territory—I say, let's do it. I try to think of the ideas that are the most awkward.

Judd: What has been the most talked-about political sketch on your show so far?

Amy: We did one about rape in the military.

Judd: And does taking on a subject like that change the way you approach your work going forward? Does that inspire courage to write about different things?

Amy: I'm going to pitch things that I think are funny, but I will also pitch things about subjects that I think are unfair. I do feel a responsibility to be exploring some issues and so I try to always stay up on that stuff, reading every article I can get my hands on, trying to stay up on what's going on. I want to do something about the Equal Pay Act this season. I read every article on feminism.

Judd: Not too long ago, you gave a speech at Gloria Steinem's birthday party. Did people have a strong reaction to that?

Amy: Yeah. I got asked to do a monologue the year before, for some event, I can't remember what it was called. It was me and all these tiny actresses and I just felt like I needed to joke about it because we looked like an evolution chart or something. I felt like a big, blond monster, standing with a bunch of girls who had never seen semen before. But my speech really came off strong because I was actually talking about some real things, bad things that had happened to me—and the other speeches weren't as hard. And so Gloria asked me to come talk the following year at her birthday party. So I wrote this speech about losing all my self-esteem in college, and a kind of painful night that I tried my best to make funny.

Judd: What about it do you think connected with people?

Amy: Just the feeling of losing all your confidence and feeling like you're worthless because of how other people are treating you. And then having to realize that the real issue is actually how you're treating yourself. I think that's something most people have experienced, feeling like they don't deserve love.

Judd: Do you ever go back and read your own speech, to cheer yourself up?

Amy: Yeah, and my friends will quote it to me.

Judd: That must be a big change, to go from doing stand-up, just trying to get laughs, to realizing that people are paying attention to what you're saying. And that they're moved and inspired by certain things you say. It's not just about being funny.

Amy: I'm taking this responsibility seriously. I'm looking at it as an opportunity. What do I want to say? What have I really learned? Where am I, really? I'm not interested in just saying something for shock value anymore. I do feel more of a weight about the message that I'm sending because I know what it's like to be on the other end of that and I don't want to be in denial about what success means—and like how many people I'm reaching now. I want to make people feel better.

CHRIS ROCK
(2014)

I remember watching Chris Rock's act in the late eighties and thinking, *Not all of this guy's jokes are perfect, but his best jokes are better than everybody else's jokes by far.* And slowly, over the next decade or so, we all watched as his entire act became as great as his best jokes, and he ruled the comedy world.

When I started doing stand-up again in 2014, I spent the better part of four months at the Comedy Cellar in New York, waiting for my turn on-stage, watching other comedians. I saw so many incredible performances, so many inspiring new voices and original acts. But I also came away from it thinking, *Chris Rock is not only the best comedian in the world, he is WAY better than everyone else. Period.*

Judd Apatow: It's funny. We've been in the business for twenty or thirty years now, long enough to where, you know, we've seen the winds blow in both directions.

Chris Rock: Oh, it's unbelievable. If you put it in a movie, no one would believe it.

Judd: Right.

Chris: No one would be like, "Really?" You're in a big movie, and suddenly, people call you up who haven't talked to you in years. "Yeah, we've got to hang out! Come on the boat." Whatever.

Judd: "Come on the boat."

Chris: Get hot, you're on the boat. Cool off, and you don't get that boat invite like you used to.

Judd: It's almost impossible to keep success going because you have to stop at some point, to rest and learn something new. It's essential. People's interest in you goes away so quickly, but you have no choice but to step off the boat sometimes.

Chris: Yeah, if you're going to try to stay interesting.

Judd: People don't get that. In Hollywood, they think you going onstage to do a play means: Whatever happened to Chris Rock?

Chris: Exactly. I mean, doing a play is literally the equivalent of: Oh, he's doing open mics again.

Judd: When was your last HBO special—2008?

Chris: Yeah, about then.

Judd: How do you decide when you're in the mood to pursue stand-up again, and do a new special?

Chris: To me, the key is, you got to ask yourself, what kind of comedian do you want to be? You can be a guy who plays every night or every week, the guy who has the same act, or maybe the same act with a tiny bit of turn-over. Seinfeld and I always have this debate: the guy versus the act. You can keep the same act and work all the time, like Jerry does. But I don't want to be that guy. I have nothing against that guy. Most guys I love are that guy.

Judd: Like Leno. He never did a special.

Chris: Leno, yeah. And Rickles. Most guys have the same act, they really do. But then you've got this other crew of guys—the Carlin/Pryor school—who never wanted people to know what they were going to say. And in order to make that work, you have to live life. You've got to live like a musician, basically. You go on the road and drop an album and then you go off and live life for a couple of years. You come back and, hey, the world's changed a little bit. And so *you've* got to change a little bit.

Judd: Who are the comedians that have had the most impact on you?

Chris: Eddie Murphy. Even though the guy hasn't been onstage in twenty-five years or whatever, he was really into the idea of: It's got to be an *event*.

He's the main influence. I got spoiled hanging around him at a young age. And from him, I came to realize that my words have to be an event. It has to be a big deal. It can be big. You know, I saw Chappelle at Radio City not too long ago. It's like, you're seeing me in the same place you see Prince; why can't it be as good? Some guys look at it that way. When I was young, though, most guys didn't think that way.

Judd: Today, I feel like people put the special out, and then think they have to have the next act written, too, so they can tour off the special with a completely new act. That's a crazy amount of work.

Chris: I've never done that. I do a special. I tour for—until it's literally like, "Okay, I've been everywhere." But you want to leave some money on the table. The best advertisement you can have is for there to be a person out there that *didn't* get to see your show. That motherfucker's like, "Oh my God. You've got to leave a few of those in every city." Once you get to that point, it's like, "Okay, let's do the special now. Let's film it. Let's put it on HBO." And that's it. And hopefully it's good enough that you don't have to work for the next three years or whatever. Hopefully it's good enough that it plays. If you get people's attention as a stand-up, you don't really have to do anything for a while. That special will last.

Judd: Do you get the urge to do stand-up again because you feel like the culture has changed and you have something new to say? Or is it just, like, "Okay, I guess it's time to start thinking about a special again"?

Chris: It comes from having something to say. It comes from being a new person. Have you lived enough life? Are you seeing the world differently? It can be something as simple as getting up onstage and talking about your kids, you know. I didn't really talk about my kids in my last special, but the special before that one, I was talking about Lola being born and keeping her off the pole. You know what I mean? So if I decide to talk about her tomorrow, twelve *years* will have passed. I'll be talking about a thirteen-year-old kid. You're talking about a different person.

Judd: Suddenly the stripper joke's not as silly.

Chris: I have two daughters. That joke is never silly.

Judd: And then, the older your kids get, you have to think about their awareness of your act. My wife is going to see me do stand-up tonight. We've been together for nineteen years, and she has never seen me perform live. She's only seen a video of me doing stand-up once, and that was like the first week when I was hitting on her. And my older daughter, too. She has never seen me do stand-up. She's about to turn seventeen. And half of my act is about her.

Chris: Wow. That's my dream, that I can stay big long enough for my kids to come see me, with their friends, and it's a cool thing. It's not charity.

Judd: How aware are they of what you do? Do they go on YouTube when you're not looking and watch?

Chris: They must. I mean, the oldest one must. I'm sure when she's at her friend's house or whatever. When I pick them up from school, I can tell every boy has seen everything I've done. They're way too nice to me. They talk to me like I'm Mingus or something. Like I'm Monk. They're freaking.

Judd: Do you ever think about changing your act as your kids get older, to help them digest it?

Chris: Nah. I'm not going that far. I always say I've got kids like Eminem's got kids. Having kids hasn't seemed to affect his act.

Judd: It's funny, I've been going through your career, just looking at all the stuff you've done—and it struck me, how you seem to have done everything. I mean, I didn't realize that you wrote a memoir—in 1997!

Chris: I wouldn't call it a memoir, but yeah.

Judd: Okay, but you've been around a long time.

Chris: I try never to brag but I'm probably the only person who has been on *60 Minutes* twice and isn't dead.

Judd: That's hilarious. But you've done everything from *Beverly Hills Cop* to *Lethal Weapon* to some records. Wasn't your first album a rap album?

Chris: No, my first album was a comedy album. I put out a comedy album eight years before I got on *SNL*. At one point, I did have a record deal,

though. I had a deal for a rap record before I had a deal for a comedy record. I used to rap. I used to be a DJ. I sucked at it. I sucked at rapping. I
sucked at DJing.

Judd: What's your connection to hip-hop? Are there rappers you've been
close with?

Chris: All the old-school guys, yeah. We're like the same age. Me and Run
are literally the same age and we've lived near each other. Jay, Doug E.
Fresh, Flash is an old friend. MC Lyte, Kid 'n Play, Latifah, Busta. We're
all the same age, hung out at the same clubs. It's like we went to high
school together, in a way. I've known Queen Latifah for twenty-five
years—as long as I've known Sandler or any of those guys. Now we see
each other at funerals.

Judd: It's freaky.

Chris: Yeah. When I was on *SNL*, and even when I started doing stand-up,
there were no young black stand-ups around. George Wallace was it.
George Wallace, Mike Ivy. No one was hanging out with me. Everyone
was like, "Get away from me, kid." So I would do sets and then I would go
to the Latin Quarter or wherever the younger black people were at—and
they were mostly these rap clubs. There was nothing else. Stand-up
was—me and Sandler were younger than everybody for a long time. It was
not a thing a twenty-year-old would do.

Judd: How does it feel hanging out in the clubs now?

Chris: I'm the oldest guy at the club every night now. Sometimes the guys
are into me and sometimes they're just humoring me. Sometimes I can
tell they think I suck or I'm a hack or it's like, "Fuck you and your Mase-
rati out front." I can feel it sometimes. You know.

Judd: It is weird to be this elder statesman. You feel this need to really
show them why you're in this position.

Chris: Oh, I totally feel that. I love going to the Cellar and spanking the
shit out of everybody. I love going there, at my age, and having an act
that's better than the guys who are fifteen or twenty years younger than
me. I'm like, "This is my seventh special. What's your fucking excuse? I
got rid of six hours of shit. Why aren't you funny yet?"

Judd: Do you feel like comedians have gotten better? Are people funnier now?

Chris: I don't know. In some ways, they are better. There's more comedy to choose from, I would say. Hannibal Buress is kind of weird and Demetri Martin is kind of weird and, you know, Sarah Silverman has a totally different act than Kathy Griffin. So in that aspect, yes, I think there's more variety in comedy today. People are talking about different things. On the other hand, I don't know if comedians know how to work an audience anymore.

Judd: Yeah.

Chris: You know, that thing where it's just like, it literally doesn't matter who's in front of you. I find more and more comedians complain about the crowd these days. Or they're always asking, "How's the crowd?" And I'm like, "Why do you give a fuck about the crowd? I mean, if you kill tonight, is the crowd going to get the credit? And so don't give it to them if you bomb. It's not them, it's you." But I don't know. We have a lot *more* comedy, I would say that. There's a lot of risk taking.

Judd: Are you still engaged, creatively? Do you still feel as enthusiastic about your work as you always have? Are you on fire right now, or do you have a sense of fatigue, of just, *Wow, I've done this for a long time. It's hard*?

Chris: The only time I ever feel fatigue is the fact that it's really hard being up with kids early in the morning and being at a club late at night.

Judd: It's brutal.

Chris: I've got to make myself take a nap during the day if I'm going to properly do stand-up. So I do feel that fatigue. But as far as creativity? I honestly feel the energy even more now, I think. It's like that Tiger thing. Tiger is chasing Jack Nicklaus. He just is. And what is it, how many Masters does he need? I'm chasing Richard Pryor, man. I have not done — I still haven't done my version of his Long Beach concert. I've done some good stuff, but Richard Pryor in Long Beach? It's the greatest piece of stand-up ever done. It just is. I haven't got there, in my act. I got some stuff—you know, some of it is good and some of it is good in comparison to other people of my era. Pryor's special was kind of late in his career. He's not a kid doing it. That's what I'm going for.

Judd: What was your relationship like with Pryor?

Chris: I met him on the set of *Harlem Nights*. It was quick and funny. I was just hanging out and we were talking about Eddie and he was like, "Yeah, he'll get married as soon as he find a pussy that fits." It's like *exactly* what you want to hear from Richard Pryor. But I had no career then. I might as well been the water boy. I met him again, years later, when I was getting ready to do the *Bring the Pain* special. At that point, he was in a wheelchair, full-on MS—helped onstage, helped offstage. We were both performing at the Comedy Store every night for a month, and I would follow him.

Judd: Wow.

Chris: And a lot of nights he would actually watch my set and he would say nice things afterwards. One of the last times I saw him was—oh, I wish I could find this picture. The last time I saw him, he came and saw me at the Universal Amphitheatre. I was coming offstage and there's Richard Pryor, in a wheelchair, telling me I did a great job. It's one of the highlights of my life. One of the greatest stand-ups—you know, the Willie Mays of comedy. You know, Pryor's Willie Mays, and Cosby's Hank Aaron. Because Hank Aaron has more hits, more home runs, more RBIs than anybody. He's number one or two in every freaking category.

Judd: I was listening to the Richard Pryor box set that they put out last year. It has one disk, which has all sorts of odds and ends on it, and there's a lot of stand-up that he did about being sick. It's remarkable.

Chris: He was funny, even then. That's the crazy thing.

Judd: He was doing a bit about a girl walking up to him in his car—he's flirting with some pretty girl and he's pissing himself because he's sick and he can't control himself. He's trying to act cool as he pisses his pants.

Chris: Wow.

Judd: It was amazing. But even the great stuff he was doing around 1976 — about, you know, the Bicentennial and Patty Hearst — it all sounds like he's playing for a hundred people, in tiny clubs.

Chris: That was the genius of the guy. The guy believed in working it out. He was like, "Okay, so I'm going to have a bad set tonight, big deal. But when you pay to see me, it's going to be right." Most comedians just don't have the guts — especially famous comedians — to get up there and not be funny, to just feel your way around this thing.

Judd: How tragic is it that Eddie Murphy won't do stand-up anymore?

Chris: Tragic. Because he can do it, you know what I mean? It's like, what if Mike Tyson could still knock people out and didn't fight? That would be sad, right? Eddie Murphy, right now, would be top three in the world. Probably number one if he worked at it. But he doesn't want to. Only financial ruin will get that guy back onstage.

Judd: I do understand how it happens, though. You feel like, *I've made a lot of stuff and I don't feel the need to get up there and go through that again.* But as somebody who hadn't done stand-up in twenty-two years and then just started doing it again, I see instantly why it's necessary for people like him, if they want to do interesting work in whatever medium they're doing. You have to force yourself to experience it again, and to connect with the crowd.

Chris: You should go to Eddie Murphy's house on the next fight night. You'll be entertained by the funniest man on earth. He has amazing fight parties. There's lots of people there, every black comedian imaginable — and he's funnier than everybody there. But I've given up asking him. I don't even bring it up anymore.

Judd: As you're preparing your new act, do you begin by thinking about what's important, what really needs to be said right now?

Chris: A little bit, yeah. Some of it's for the crowd, and some of it's for you. There's definitely a part of you that goes like, *Okay, there's a lot of this police brutality going on. I got to look over this and figure out what my take is because people want to hear about it. I'm going to have to find a real, original take on it — not just, you know, "Hey, stay away from football play-*

ers!" I'm going to have to dig deep, regardless of what else I want to talk about. You have no choice. You've got an obligation because people are paying to hear that. But again, it also depends on what kind of comedian you are. If you're Demetri Martin, you probably don't have to do that. Jerry Seinfeld doesn't have that pressure, either.

Judd: Jerry doesn't have any pressure, apparently.

Chris: Jerry's got no fucking pressure. God bless him. Jerry Seinfeld, one of the greatest comedians of all time and one of the cockiest bastards to ever live.

Judd: How did he get that cocky? If you're neurotic in any way—like, in a normal way—he looks at you like you're insane for not getting it.

Chris: To his credit, he writes some of the best jokes ever. He really does. I mean, they're like Billy Joel songs, you know what I mean?

Judd: Yeah.

Chris: There's a lot of hip guys in the world, but who can follow Billy Joel in America, you know what I mean? I don't give a fuck who you are, I don't give a fuck if you're Sting or Bono—if you're onstage in America, there's a part of you that just hopes Billy Joel doesn't walk in. I remember going to see Billy and Elton John in concert. I kind of wanted to see Elton a little more, and I came out of it thinking, Billy Joel is actually more American than Bruce Springsteen, you know what I mean? Bruce Springsteen's a fucking Russian soldier compared to fucking Billy Joel, man. That shit's American. Everybody likes those records. And Jerry Seinfeld writes jokes like that. *Everybody* gets those fucking jokes. I've seen that guy work fucking Mexican crowds, black crowds, it doesn't matter. It doesn't matter. He's fucking cocky and kills every night.

Judd: I sometimes think it seems everyone in our circle had their kids at the same time. You, me, Seinfeld, Sandler—it's a real shared experience.

Chris: It's weird. Our kids are all the same age. And we're all kind of married to the same woman.

Judd: We all have the same issues in our lives. Several decades in, everybody's kind of in the same place, trying to figure out the next phase. When people have had success and they've made money and they have families —and they're not dying to be accepted anymore, with a long career ahead of them—they're *still* trying to figure it out.

Chris: We're going to be old for a long fucking time, dude.

Judd: Then you see certain people, like Martin Scorsese, who just go on a tear, a late game tear. And that makes you wonder, *Who am I going to be when I'm not a young punk?*

Chris: You've got to make yourself scared. When I did that play not too long ago, it was like, *Oh, this shit is scary. I'm out of my comfort zone. I'm the low man on the totem pole. I could really suck at this.* But it's in moments like that that you are going to learn the most. Directing, too: *What the fuck was I ever doing directing anything,* you know what I mean? It scared me and I did some things that sucked. But you learn more from fucking up than you do from success, unfortunately. And failure, if you don't let it defeat you, is what fuels your future success.

Judd: What made you realize it was time to make *Top Five*, which is such a personal film?

Chris: Doing that play, a few years ago, inspired me. It showed me what work is again. The thing about the play was, it wasn't a revival. It was an original play. If you're doing a revival, you can rehearse it at your house— the lines aren't going to change or whatever. But when you do an original play, when you're in previews, you get new pages, new lines, every day. "I'm going to get rid of that scene and we're going to do this scene instead." What? But being around actors really helped me. Being around creative people that had talents I didn't helped me. It opened my eyes. I don't know, I mean, I had directed two other movies in my life, but I haven't had a hit in a long time. There was a part of me that was like, *Okay, if this one doesn't work, I'm kind of done.* There was a part of me that was pushed against the wall, but there was also a part of me—there's a part of *Top Five* that's really personal, and it works. It plays like my stand-up. I did stand-up for fifteen years before I broke, you know.

Judd: So then you make this more personal movie. You show it in Toronto and the place goes crazy and you sell it to a big studio. That's the weird thing about creativity, right? When you get real, you have your biggest success.

Chris: It's the smallest movie I've ever written. Actually, it's the first time I wrote a movie. It's the first time I've written by myself.

Judd: I just finished a movie with Amy Schumer. At first, she wanted to write it with someone else, but I said to her, "I think, in ways that are hard to describe, your point of view will shift because you're going to make all sorts of concessions that are destructive to—"

Chris: You're going to have a consensus. You're not going to have a vision. That's what happens. So I wrote this movie by myself. Every other movie I've done—*Head of State* or whatever—was like, I wasn't even writing a movie. I was writing a poster. I was thinking about the pitch meeting before I was done with the movie.

Judd: I feel like, for a lot of people, there's that moment when you go personal with your work and everything changes. Look at Louis C.K. When he revealed himself, the whole world connected with him. I felt that way with *The 40-Year-Old Virgin* and *Knocked Up* and *Freaks and Geeks*—that's when I realized that if I just come clean, people connect in a completely different way.

Chris: I mean, there was an episode of *Louis*—the one where Melissa Leo gives him a blowjob in the car. And then she says, you know, "Now you're going to eat my pussy." And that blew my mind. I watched that episode, and it was like the first time I heard NWA. It was like, *Oh shit, you can do this?*

Judd: Yeah.

Chris: And I thought, *So why am I so scared? Why do I give a fuck about testing?* All the nonsense I spent so long giving a shit about. And then there was the fact Louis C.K. is a guy who literally used to—you know, I hired him on my writing staff and here he is, doing *this*. It was like, *Oh shit. Okay, whatever I do next has to be this honest.*

EDDIE VEDDER
(2013)

I am aware that Eddie Vedder is not a comedian or a comic actor. Yes, he was hilarious in *Walk Hard*, but I think most people still see him as a musician, not a funny person. I was thrilled to be asked to interview Eddie Vedder—and all of the members of Pearl Jam—to help them promote their last record, *Lightning Bolt*. Even though Eddie is way nicer and cooler than I am, and has the kind of artistic accomplishments I can only dream about, I have always felt like we are on a similar journey. We are about the same age. We have used our lives and experiences, our joy and pain, to create personal work that we can stand behind. We have tried, above all, to keep our careers going with our integrity and humanity intact. Plus, I am fanatical about his music.

Judd Apatow: Did you ever see the *Quadrophenia* documentary?

Eddie Vedder: I saw, like, an hour version. There's got to be a version that's longer and more detailed, but—

Judd: Yeah, you want the early cut, from before they tightened it up. For me, that was the big record. I've heard that was a mind blower for you, too.

Eddie: Yeah. And a lifesaver. A life ring to hang on to because, for some reason, I just didn't feel like there was anybody I could relate to on the whole planet. Nobody at school and certainly no one in the household. And then, all of a sudden, it was like here's some guy from London named Pete, and he knew everything that was going on.

Judd: How old were you?

This interview took place at the Pearl Jam offices and rehearsal space.

Eddie: Probably about thirteen, fourteen. And all kinds of stuff was happening in my life. It was really like, just, you know, it was like a bridge with the planks covering a big, deep chasm—and the planks were just falling. That whole period, I was just hanging on.

Judd: I feel like I had the same exact experience. My parents broke up in between eighth and ninth grade and had a crazy divorce. They didn't actually even get fully divorced until I was in college. They fought. For some reason, *Quadrophenia*—even now I try to think, what was it about *Quadrophenia* that made me feel a little better, and part of it was that song "I'm One." Which we later used in *Freaks and Geeks* because it captured exactly how I felt. Like, *How am I gonna get noticed? Why am I getting treated so badly? Why am I invisible at school?* But I was unconscious to it for decades, what it meant to me. Was that your experience?

Eddie: Absolutely. I mean, it was a number of things—I was finding messages in, like, Split Enz and Talking Heads. But as a whole, *Quadrophenia* was the one that . . . thank God the record store prescribed that drug, because that's what got me through. Even though it didn't offer any answers, in the end it was just knowing that you weren't the only one going through these things.

Judd: When I was a kid, no one was into comedy. I felt so alone with this weird interest and it was only when I moved to Los Angeles and went to college and met the comedians at the Comedy Store and the Improv that I thought, *Ohh, so there's hundreds of people who like everything that I like and who want to talk about it all night long.* Did you have that experience getting into the music scene?

Eddie: I remember—I still remember distinctly that somebody ended up obtaining a small bag of mushrooms and we were all gonna have a surf, and it ended up being a great experience. But while we were waiting for things to happen, we were playing a Kinks record and I said to my friend, "Yeah, see the guitar tone, the distortion, the space in between," and he was like, "You know, some people don't listen to music like you. Some people just listen to it to enjoy it." He was basically telling me to shut the fuck up.

Judd: (*Laughs*)

Eddie: He was just trying to listen to the song. And he had a valid point. But it was just always that way. With me—and I think eventually you— you find that. And then certainly with the group of guys in the band, you know, after a show, if we have a night and we have to travel or we're still up and awake and sitting in a confined space talking, we can talk all night about music. We'll talk until we get to the next place, laughing hysterically, remembering this thing, or "Oh yeah, so-and-so produced this one." You realize how fortunate you are and how involved everybody is to this day. The passion for music is as strong as it was when we were naïve little kids and it seemed like the most exciting thing in the world.

Judd: With a lot of comedy people, I feel like there's like a moment where you realize that certain friends have figured out their mental state, calmed down and evolved, and others kinda spin out. In the beginning, you do it because you're crazy. You're angry, you're trying to show somebody, you have low self-esteem—as a comedian, you go onstage because you so desperately want approval, you're willing to risk rejection by hundreds of people at a comedy club to get it. But at some point that kind of goes away and then you start creating for a different reason.

Eddie: I just try to always remember where that initial spark came from. It's like a pilot light, and you try to make sure it doesn't go out.

Judd: Sometimes I forget my pain. I try to remember what I was so neurotic about. It's still there, almost as a vibration, but I forget the specifics.

Eddie: An interesting moment for me was the movie *Into the Wild*, when Sean Penn asked me to contribute a song. I thought, *Yeah, I can relate to this kid, this character*—and I was a little surprised at how quickly it all just came back. I thought I'd processed all that. But it was crazy. It was just like a rash that had been slightly just under the skin the whole time. It was upsetting, you know. But you're just kind of putting it out and turning it into something hopefully worthwhile that other people can kind of experience, too. They can share in that and not feel like they were the only ones.

Judd: Who's been most helpful to you in your career? I've always had mentors who have shown me the way, who showed me, This is how you can do this work and not go crazy. Garry Shandling talked a lot about honesty and the importance of telling the truth in your work and honesty, and as a kid, I'd never heard about any of that. At each stage of my career, I find myself thinking, *Wow, I can have lunch with Mike Nichols or Marshall Brickman*—people who have done this work so well, for so many decades. Like, how do you stay engaged for that long? Who have you learned from?

Eddie: Oh, I feel like I've been learning from everybody. The other night, I got to sit with Tom Petty for a little bit and then, you know, there's Bruce and Neil and Pete and Kim and John Doe and Ian MacKaye and Thurston and it's all—in a way, you're so fortunate because you're working in something where it's a bit of a craft or whatever. It's an endless learning cycle.

Judd: I can never believe that I can sit and talk to any of these people. Does that ever go away for you?

Eddie: I think, at some point, you have to get out of that state. And I think it's more comfortable to them, too, to know that you feel like you've earned the right. That's only happened recently. That I feel like I've at least earned their respect enough to be sitting across the table from them. It probably makes them less nervous.

Judd: Exactly. (*Laughs*) What is your spirituality? Are you religious? Or are you still trying to figure that out?

Eddie: It's a curiosity, for sure, and an unanswered question. I think we can all agree that there's no evidence to say that it's just this one thing. But I think about the people who have stopped asking the questions, who have stopped searching and stopped looking for answers. I think that when you're committed to one religion—let alone into the level of being fundamentalist—you close yourself off to things that might be out there. There becomes a closed-mindedness where you don't allow anything more in, and I think you're missing out on half the plot, or half the experience of life on this planet.

Judd: You have two daughters, right?

Eddie: Yeah.

Judd: What's your theory, going forward, regarding the war with kids to be a part of the digital generation? What will your boundaries be?

Eddie: Well, raising them Amish is maybe the answer. We've been doing a lot of calligraphy.

Judd: Farming?

Eddie: Yeah, farming.

Judd: But it's a war with kids, isn't it? They want to be a part of it so badly. My daughter always says, "That's how we communicate, Dad, you can't stop it." But you can tell it's hurting them. They are not comfortable in silence and you hate to be that groovy person who's like, "It's hurting their imaginations!" But you can tell that they don't allow anything to come forward because they're just constantly filling all the mental space.

Eddie: When we were kids, back in the day, it was like, "Don't sit too close to the TV." That was our only electronic boundary.

Judd: (*Laughs*)

Eddie: Ten feet back, at all times! But now I'm worried about myself and certainly worried for them. I'm not really sure how it's gonna—I think it's just giving them enough they can at least balance it out. Our freedoms are going up in smoke, but if you still like take a walk, or take a hike or have a surf—if you're lucky enough to be in a situation where you do these things or go to the park or whatever, at least that can still feel free for a while.

Judd: Do you ever think about what, emotionally, you're giving away in your music? When I make a movie I think, *Oh, that person knows that I'm talking about them.* Like if I made a record and there were three songs about being married and two of them were like, this is really hard or a drag, I'd get in trouble immediately for it—

Eddie: Well, no. If the emotion is real and the idea—I guess one thing you do is try to mask it slightly.

Judd: (*Laughs*)

Eddie: But if it's the real thing, then you just do it and deal with the circumstances.

Judd: Are you happy, family-wise?

Eddie: My type of personality is that even when things are going really good, then I feel like something bad could happen at any minute. I think a lot about the fragility of life. From knowing people like Tomas Young, who's a soldier who lost the use of most of his body due to a couple of gunshot wounds in Iraq, and the challenges he faces, or just having friends who are dealing with diseases—knowing these people has given me a great appreciation for life and the moment. I just see that fragility at all times.

Judd: When you start a record, do you have an idea of what it's going to be, or is it something that evolves once you guys start working?

Eddie: Whatever the music is dictates what the record is, especially if I'm writing lyrics to someone else's piece. What you're listening for is, like, *What does this mean? What is this? What are these sounds or what is this rhythm or momentum of it?* I think the faster songs are easier, because it seems like there's plenty of aggressive stuff to write about these days. But maybe the more atmospheric stuff comes, you know—those become a little more of a puzzle, trying to line everything up and then have it create a meaning for you, or a story or something that relates to the sound of the song.

Judd: Are you writing actively or is the music the beginning of your process in writing lyrics?

Eddie: It's pretty much the beginning. I should do that more, you know, but usually it's just something that connects all at once. Something lands on my shoulder and then it's just a matter of waiting and getting it down. And then there's this great writing tool—I don't know if you've heard about it. It's called a vaporizer.

Judd: (*Laughs*)

Eddie: And so, you put your tools out on your desk and then you just start, you know, bricklaying and then you see what happens the next morning.

Judd: I think my whole process is wrong. I'm just stressed all day long trying to think of things. I'm sitting there thinking, *Why aren't you thinking of anything? You're behind. You need to get going.* I'm going to try this "vaporizer" you're talking about.

Eddie: I think we have a signature model coming out soon.

Judd: You should just be a sponsor of that. You could have your own brand, like the George Foreman Grill.

Eddie: Well, certainly in a few states, we could air those commercials.

Judd: But what will you tell your kids about the rock star life, and what your journey has been like? They can start googling you pretty soon. My daughter said to me recently, "You took mushrooms at a Frank Sinatra concert."

Eddie: I think I need to get home and check on the kids.

Judd: (*Laughs*) No, no, but I never thought, *Oh yeah, I did an interview five years ago where I told this story.* I wasn't prepared for my reaction and explanation—which was that someone force-fed them to me. It was a terrible, terrible incident. I was dosed. I guess it happens at some point that they have to understand everything you've been through.

Eddie: Right. Well, umm . . .

Judd: I just blew your mind. (*Laughs*)

Eddie: I'm a little paranoid about the computer. . . .

Judd: Yeah.

Eddie: A crazy thing happened the other night. My daughter likes to listen to this ukulele record that I did—she goes to bed to it, and especially if I'm not around, at least I'm there playing her to sleep. There's a sad song about sleeping by myself or something and it was pretty intense. She started by asking me, you know, "What's that song *about*? Why are you singing that?" And I said, "Oh, that was before I met Mom," and the whole thing. And then she started bawling. She said, "It's so sad, it's so sad." I had to comfort her, but she really kind of lost it, it was pretty intense, so we skip that song now. It was interesting to see the empathy that she had for her dad. I don't know if I ever had that, or an opening to have that. I was raised differently.

Judd: How much Disney Channel are your kids making you watch?

Eddie: I don't want to say anything, you know, because there are certain good things about Disney.

Judd: Yes.

Eddie: But that channel is not one of them. I challenge you to find a single character, if not just even a single line in a half-hour show, that has anything of value and that isn't said with an attitude other than, you know, being snarky.

Judd: Yeah.

Eddie: And it rubs off, you know. It's a bad influence. I probably sound like my parents. I mean, I was listening to Country Joe and the Fish and George Carlin and, you know, Jimi Hendrix and all of that. We were pretty excited about this stuff.

Judd: You never went with the Shaun Cassidy records?

Eddie: Mmm, no.

Judd: No Partridge Family period?

Eddie: No. But Michael Jackson? Yeah.

Judd: I read somewhere that you could sing like Michael Jackson for a short period, a short prepubescent period.

Eddie: He's an amazing singer.

Judd: Oh, absolutely.

Eddie: I had this period in Chicago where we lived with some foster brothers — it was like a home for boys kind of thing — and there was a basement and we had a lot of Motown records, Sly and the Family Stone and

James Brown, and we had kids of all races and all—it was a really good upbringing in that way. It made you grow up and toughen up a little bit, even though I was only like seven or eight. But man, Michael Jackson was an anomaly. The stuff coming off of that record player. That wasn't kitsch. He could really sing.

Judd: I used to watch the Jacksons' variety show.

Eddie: That was after the cartoon and all that, right?

Judd: Yeah, the cartoon. What was the animal he had in the cartoon? Did he have a mouse or—

Eddie: They had a snake and two mice. I show my kids that thing.

Judd: You have those shows on video?

Eddie: No, sixteen-millimeter film. We like to watch films on the wall.

Judd: Oh, wow.

Eddie: It's a part of their Amish upbringing.

FREAKS AND GEEKS
ORAL HISTORY
(2013)

I was given the chance to guest-edit the comedy issue of *Vanity Fair* a few years ago, and one of the first articles I assigned was an oral history of *Freaks and Geeks*. Why? Well, beyond blatant self-promotion, I figured: I've been so fortunate to work with a lot of talented people and we've done a lot of things I am proud of, but at the end of the day, *Freaks and Geeks* was our *Revolver*. That show was the moment where I think we got it right, and I don't say that in a cocky way, because really, it wasn't me. It was the success of a hundred people simultaneously. It was our magical moment, and this is the story of how it went down. If it never happens again, I'm okay with that. At least it happened once.

Judd Apatow: I first met Paul [Feig] in the mid-eighties, hanging around "the Ranch," this incredibly cheap house a bunch of comedians rented really deep in the boonies in the San Fernando Valley. It was all these guys who had come out to L.A. from the Midwest, and all they did was smoke cigarettes and watch infomercials. I also used to see Paul in comedy clubs and thought he was really funny.

Paul Feig: We would go out and do our stand-up shows and reconvene at the Ranch and play poker and drink coffee until the sun came up. That

This interview was originally published in Vanity Fair *in January 2013 (Robert Lloyd/*Vanity Fair; © *Condé Nast).*

was our routine every night for years. Judd was younger than everyone else—he was really considered to be just a kid. At the same time, he was booking his own stand-up night at some club, working for Comic Relief. I would say, "This guy is really smart. Everybody should be nice to him because he could be running the town someday." He was the most mature seventeen-year-old I'd ever met in my life.

Judd: By the late nineties, Paul's acting career wasn't going anywhere, so he started trying to write. One day I bumped into him and said, "If you have any ideas for TV, let me know." I didn't think he would hand me a finished script a few months later, and I certainly didn't expect it to be the best thing I have ever worked on. That just *never* happens.

Paul Feig: I had just come off of a year of trying to promote this movie I'd written, directed, produced, and paid for, and I had lost a good-paying acting job before that on *Sabrina, the Teenage Witch.* Everything had kind of hit the rocks; I was really at my lowest point. But I'd always wanted to write a high school show. I'd seen so many where it was like, *Who are these people?* I felt like they weren't honest at all. I kicked the thing out really fast—I think it had just been gestating for so long in my brain—cleaned it up and gave it to my wife, and she told me to send it to Judd. He called about twelve hours after I sent him the script. He was like, "I love this. I'm going to have DreamWorks buy it." It was that moment when you go, *Wow, my life's just changed.*

Dan McDermott (*then head of DreamWorks Television*): Within twenty-four hours, I'd say, we got a pass from Fox, from CBS, from ABC. A day or two later, we heard from Shelley McCrory, a development exec at NBC. She said, "If we don't make this show, I'm quitting the television business." Scott Sassa had come in as president of NBC West Coast, and Scott wasn't a content guy [he was previously in charge of NBC's owned-and-operated stations], so he was deferring to his people more than other network heads do.

Scott Sassa: Networks then programmed towards something called "least objectionable programming," which meant the show that would suck the least so people wouldn't change the channel. *Freaks and Geeks* wasn't one of those least objectionable shows.

Paul Feig: We went over to NBC, and I remember feeling that "new person in the industry" kind of indignation, like, "If they want to change this at all, I'm not going to do the show." So I start to make that speech and Shelley goes, "Don't change a thing." It was like, *This is not at all what I've always heard network development is like.*

Dan McDermott: Judd and Paul said, "We want to try to cast real kids—we don't want to cast TV kids." And, again, Scott basically said, "Sounds good to me!"

Paul Feig: My friends and I weren't popular in high school, we weren't dating all the time, and we were just trying to get through our lives. It was important to me to show that side. I wanted to leave a chronicle—to make people who had gone through it laugh, but also as a primer for kids going in, to say, "Here's what you can expect. It's horrifying but all you should really care about is getting through it. Get your friends, have your support group. And learn to be able to laugh at it."

Judd: The pilot had a very daring existential idea, which was that a young, really smart girl sits with her dying grandmother and asks her if she sees "the light," and her grandma says no. And all the rules go out the window. The girl decides to have a more experimental high school experience, because she doesn't know if she believes anymore. I was always surprised that the network didn't notice that that's what our pilot was about.

Paul Feig: I also really wanted the show to be about the fear of sex. I got tired of every teenager being portrayed as horny and completely cool with sex, because that was not my experience.

Judd: Paul felt like most kids are not trying to get sex, but trying to avoid that moment. You could split them into kids who are constantly trying to get older and kids that are desperately trying to hold on to their immaturity.

Paul Feig: First day of prep, we get into the office, and Judd's like, "Let's tear the script apart." And I said, "What do you mean? They don't want us to." And he said, "Yeah, I know, but let's see if we can make it better." And it was this stripping away of the old Paul Feig, who was a complete control freak, who wouldn't let people change a word of anything he wrote.

Judd: Paul showed up when we started production with this bible he'd written about the show, hundreds of pages long, with every character in detail—what they wore, their favorite songs. I asked him to write another few episodes to explore the world, and he banged out two more. We took a lot of moments from them and put them into the pilot.

(Jake Kasdan, twenty-four, is hired to direct the pilot; he will stick around for the run of the series, directing nearly a third of the episodes and helping edit the rest.)

Judd: Jake and I had the same agent, so I was always hearing a lot about this amazing young director. He had made a detective movie called *Zero Effect*, which, for some reason, I didn't bother to watch until the day after I hired him. Thank God it turned out to be good.

(Casting begins.)

Judd: In Paul's pilot, he really understood the geeks, but you could tell he didn't hang out with the freaks because it wasn't as specific. So I said we should just try to cast unique characters and rewrite the pilot to their personalities.

Allison Jones (*casting director and winner of the show's one Emmy*): I had never had any experience like that before—inventing while casting. It had always been about trying to fit the person to read the lines correctly.

Justin Falvey (*DreamWorks development executive*): From the moment the actor walks into what is usually the sterile, anxiety-ridden room of casting, Judd's applauding and everybody's got great energy. Judd and Paul created a carnival atmosphere.

(Linda Cardellini, then twenty-three, is cast in the lead as sixteen-year-old Lindsay Weir.)

Linda Cardellini: Here's this girl [Lindsay] who desperately wants to be away from her parents and what they know her as, but at the same time truly does not want to disappoint or rebel against them and really loves them. It was a more interesting approach than all the other teenagers I was reading, who just hated their parents.

Paul Feig: Lindsay was the only character not based on somebody I knew. But Linda was the exact person I had in my head. When she walked in, it was just, like, "She's alive!"

Jake Kasdan: We used to say in editing that you could always cut to Linda and she's doing the right thing.

(After a long search, John Francis Daley, thirteen, gets the role of Lindsay's younger brother, Sam.)

John Francis Daley: I was really sick when I auditioned. And I think that helped me ultimately, because it let me put my guard down. I was just focused on not throwing up.

Linda Cardellini: John was so natural. One day on the set I was sitting thinking about my part, and John was shoving his spaghetti in his mouth that we were supposed to eat in the dinner scene, going, "It's so great! All we have to do is act! It's, like, the easiest job in the world." I thought, *My God, he totally has it right.*

(James Franco, twenty, is cast as freak Daniel Desario, a slightly goofy bad boy.)

Jake Kasdan: The first impression was "This guy's going to be an enormous movie star. We should grab him immediately."

Judd: We didn't think of him as handsome. We thought his mouth was too big for his face and he seemed perfect to be a small-town cool guy who wasn't as cool as he thought he was. When all the women in our office started talking about how gorgeous he was, me and Feig started laughing because we just didn't see it.

John Francis Daley: Franco went to Michigan for two weeks to get into character, and we were joking that he lived under an overpass for a few nights. He was always the one that had a Camus novel, heavily dog-eared, and his car was so full of junk that it looked like he lived out of it.

James Franco: I knew that Paul had grown up just outside of Detroit, and I found his high school. I ran into his audio/video teacher, who showed me where Paul used to sit in the AV room. I saw all the kids at summer school, and there was this guy the teacher pointed out to me, this kind of rough-around-the-edges-looking kid. He had a kind face, but he looked like he'd been in a little bit of trouble. And I remember thinking, *Ah, there's Daniel.*

(Jason Segel, nineteen, is cast as pothead drummer Nick Andopolis.)

Jake Kasdan: The actors would walk in and we'd be like, "Hey, how's it going?" A little casual kibitzing to get some sense of who this person is. Jason walked in, and he said, "I'd like to just get into this, if I could." And we were like, "Let's do it!" and he was just hilarious and endlessly charismatic. Judd connected to him immediately and deeply.

Judd: I loved writing for Jason. That's what *I* felt like in high school. I felt goofy and ambitious and not sure if I had any talent, and I would be in love with these women and didn't actually know if they liked me that much. I'd never know if I was being charming or a stalker. Jason really captured that desperation.

(Seth Rogen, sixteen, who will play acerbic freak Ken Miller, is found on a casting trip to Vancouver.)

Judd: Everything he said made us laugh. The smart, sweet, grounded person we now know him to be seemed impossible back then. He seemed like a mad, troublemaking Canadian lunatic who was quiet and angry and might kill you.

Seth Rogen: At the time, I kind of had a chip on my shoulder, you know, because I hadn't gotten any girls to sleep with me yet. I was incredibly angry and repressed, and I think they saw me as this kind of weird, sarcastic guy and started writing towards that. But then they got to know me and saw me as a nice guy, and that revealed itself as the show progressed.

J. Elvis Weinstein (*writer, "Noshing and Moshing"; co-writer, "Beers and Weirs"*): It was clear that Judd had a mission to make this kid a star. There were some kids that Judd thought were immensely special and was going to beat that into them until they believed it.

(Busy Philipps, nineteen, is cast as Daniel's tough blond girlfriend, Kim Kelly—initially Lindsay's antagonist, but eventually a friend.)

Seth Rogen: Busy scared me at first. She's just kind of intimidating. She's a little loud and she's kind of physical. She'll punch you and smack you if she doesn't like what you did, as an exclamation.

Busy Philipps: I ran into Linda, who I knew peripherally. And she said, "Hey, are you going to do that thing? You have to do it—it'd be so fun to do together." So I decided, against my agent's better judgment, to do what essentially at the beginning was a guest-starring role.

(Martin Starr, sixteen, is cast as Sam's friend Bill Haverchuck. Gangly, shuffling, bespectacled, he is the most outwardly strange and inwardly deep of the central geeks.)

Paul Feig: You're seeing hundreds of kids, so every person you see you're like, *Yeah, he could do it.* But then you have these moments when somebody walks in and it's like, *Okay, everyone else is out of my head now.*

Martin Starr: I probably more than anything was focused on what came after that audition in my life. Like going to get food or going to a friend's house. My life wasn't focused entirely on whatever this audition was.

Jake Kasdan: The blank stare and the way Martin's doing those affects, mouth hanging open—it's just this incredibly subtle, inspired comic character. We figured out how to write to it and play to it, but it was not on the page initially and it wasn't him playing himself, either. He could make you cry laughing by doing almost nothing. Then it turned out he could do anything.

Thomas F. Wilson (*actor, "Coach Fredricks"*): The slightly sad seriousness with which Martin approached his role, to me, is the fulcrum of the whole show. It was really acting of a very high order.

Debra McGuire (*costume designer*): That first fitting, Martin went into the dressing room and every change was like twenty minutes. I'd knock on the door: "You okay in there?" And to this day I don't know if he was busting my chops or if it was for real.

(Samm Levine, sixteen, who will play Sam's other best friend, Neal Schweiber, a self-styled sophisticate and wit, is discovered on a tape from New York.)

Samm Levine: My audition wasn't terribly good, but I had asked beforehand if I could do my William Shatner as part of it.

Paul Feig: He looks past the camera to the casting director and goes, "Now? Can I?" and then he goes into a William Shatner impression that was so corny and silly. And Judd's like, "That's all of us when we were in school just trying to be funny, doing stupid shit."

John Francis Daley: Flying from New York to shoot the pilot, Samm Levine came up to me and said, "Hey, are you on the show as well? Come up to my row at some point and we'll chat." Who talks like that at that age? We told each other jokes for a couple hours and became friends. Martin was the exact opposite, very mischievous, liked to get a rise out of people. Samm was more the Vegas comedian with the puns and the quips. They got on each other's nerves immediately, but were friends at the same time. It was a very odd, bickering-family kind of friendship. That I got a lot of enjoyment out of.

(The pilot is completed by early spring of 1999. In May, NBC picks up *Freaks and Geeks* for thirteen episodes.)

Paul Feig: I remember I had looked at Judd right before we showed the kids to the network and said to him, "Are we about to ruin these kids' lives? What do we do to not let that happen?"

Joe Flaherty (*actor, "Harold Weir," Lindsay and Sam's dad*): Early on, Judd held a cast meeting. It was something like "This is your chance right now as actors, but you have to concentrate on the show, and don't get caught up in any of this Hollywood stuff. Don't start using drugs, because we still have a show to do here. I don't want to see you guys on *E! True Hollywood Story*."

(The producers assemble a writing staff.)

Mike White (*writer, "Kim Kelly Is My Friend," "We've Got Spirit"*): I had done two years on *Dawson's Creek* and was trying to never do TV again. But I took a meeting with Shelley McCrory at NBC, and she pops in the pilot of *Freaks and Geeks*, and I was like, "Oh my gosh, this is exactly what I told them you could do on *Dawson's Creek*, but everyone had said you can't"—the unmannered way that the characters spoke, the idiosyncratic way they all looked.

Paul Feig: We did our infamous two weeks with the writers locking ourselves in a room and telling personal stories. I wrote a list of questions for everybody to answer: "What was the best thing that happened to you in high school? What was the worst thing that happened to you in high school? Who were you in love with and why?"

Judd: "What was your worst drug experience? Who was your first girlfriend? What's the first sexual thing you ever did? What's the most humiliating thing that ever happened to you during high school?"

Paul Feig: That's where most of our stories came from. Weirder stuff happens to people in real life than it does on TV. It was a personal show for me and I wanted it to be personal for everybody else.

Gabe Sachs (*writer, "I'm with the Band," "The Garage Door"*): We thought the questionnaires were a private thing between us and Judd and Paul, so we wrote really honest. And the next day at work we get them all bound together. We're laughing with everyone but going, "Oh, man!"

Jeff Judah (*writer, "I'm with the Band," "The Garage Door"*): A lot of people kept going, "Hey, I read your questionnaire—sorry about that."

Patty Lin (*writer, "Girlfriends and Boyfriends," "The Garage Door"*): You could bring up the most embarrassing thing and it was accepted as "You're a great person."

J. Elvis Weinstein: Paul was the heart of the show, I always felt. I think everyone wanted Paul to be the heart of the show.

Steve Bannos (*actor, "Mr. Kowchevski"; also writer, "Smooching and Mooching"*): So many of the characters, so many of their voices, are Paul at some point. The freaks *and* the geeks.

Judd: Paul remembered every detail of everything that had happened to him in high school: every happy moment, every humiliation. The running gag in the writers' room was that Paul would tell a horrible story and I would say, "How old were you when that happened?" Implying probably twelve, and it was always seventeen. I had seen him as this cool comedian. I hadn't realized he had all these incredibly funny, dark stories. He *was* the guy who wore the "Parisian night suit" to school [as Sam does in the episode "Looks and Books"].

Paul Feig: There was a store I used to shop in during high school, a disco-flavored men's clothing store. One day one of the salesmen drags me over. He goes, "This is the hottest thing, man," and shows me this big denim jumpsuit with the flare pants and the big collar. To this day if I get a new piece of clothing I can't wait to wear it. So I could not be stopped from wearing it to school, and the minute I walked in the front door I knew I had made a huge mistake. It was fun, on the show, re-creating the most horrific moments of my past.

Jake Kasdan: From the beginning, we thought that everything about the show should be painfully, painstakingly real. We were going to separate it from all of the other high school shows by being radically unglamorous.

Miguel Arteta (*director, "Chokin' and Tokin'"***):** It felt a little more organic and handmade than the television I had seen.

Russ Alsobrook (*director of photography***):** Paul and Judd had a very specific aesthetic they wanted. No crazy gratuitous camera moves. No elaborate, precious lighting. They said, "This is Michigan in the fall and winter—pretend it's overcast all the time. Strip away all the turbocharged cinematography and get back to the basics of good storytelling."

Busy Philipps: Paul and Judd awkwardly tried to talk to Linda and me about how, now that we're on a TV show, we shouldn't think about losing weight, which had never even occurred to me. They were like, "Don't get crazy now—don't think you have to be an actress that's really skinny." And I was reading things in the press about how we were the anti–*Dawson's Creek.* There was one quote I remember very clearly, like, "You won't find any pretty people on *Freaks and Geeks.*" That was interesting as a nineteen-year-old girl to read.

Linda Cardellini: They didn't want us to look like people in other shows—which you don't really know how to take. It was comforting on one hand, and not so much on the other.

John Francis Daley: Paul talked to me about the fact that I was basically playing him, but he didn't try to steer me in any direction. They encouraged your true personality to shine through and shape your character. The way Sam is so amused by his dad was totally because I thought Joe Flaherty was the funniest guy in the world.

Bryan Gordon (*director, "Tricks and Treats," "The Garage Door"*): When we first began, Joe Flaherty was the star in everybody's mind. He was the *SCTV* hero. He was the comedy rock star.

Jason Segel: I just watched and learned, doing scenes with him. He's so fast. There's a lot of improv on all the stuff we do with Judd. When you're young, you kind of think, *I don't know if the old man can keep up.* And then you're like, *Oh, shit—this is the guy who created this style.*

(Between NBC's making the pilot and picking up the show, Garth Ancier arrives from the WB network—home of *Dawson's Creek*—to become president of NBC Entertainment.)

Dan McDermott: I remember getting the call that said, "Garth doesn't get the show. He went to boarding school and Princeton—he doesn't understand public school." And that was the first flag that went up.

Paul Feig: We flew to New York for the up-fronts [annual presentations of new shows to potential advertisers]. I go to this NBC party at "21" and Garth's there. And I go, "Hey, Garth, thank you so much for picking up the show." And he's talking to some guy and looks at me and goes, "Deliver the goods, man. Just deliver the goods." And he points to the guy with his thumb and goes, "Don't end up like this guy." I don't know who that guy was, but he gave this sort of sad laugh. And I walked away going, "We're dead."

(The show gets a time slot, Saturdays at 8 P.M., and a premiere date, September 25, 1999.)

Justin Falvey: You hear "Saturdays at eight" and you think, *Who's home Saturday watching television?* But we also thought it was an opportunity—the bar's really low. It was like coming in second or third place—it was qualifying for the next round.

Judd: We were up against the tenth season of *Cops*. I thought, *If we can't beat the tenth season of* Cops, *we don't deserve to be on the air*. And, of course, *Cops* kicked our ass.

Seth Rogen: You just have to conclude that people would rather watch shirtless dudes get tackled than a TV show about emotional shit that's funny.

Paul Feig: The reviews were great, and the premiere had a really high rating. The first Monday back I stood on a table and read the ratings and everybody cheered. And the next week we just dropped huge. And Joe Flaherty was quoted as saying, "Yeah, Paul never came back in and read the ratings to us again after that first week."

Joe Flaherty: I never got my hopes up. I'd gone through something similar with *SCTV*. My daughter had a poster of the front page of the *Soho Weekly News* with a sketch of me that said, "Is *SCTV* too good for TV?" and once again I thought, *I'm living on shows that are too good for TV*.

Paul Feig: We were the lowest-rated show on NBC several weeks in a row.

(Despite the ratings, the cast and crew continue to refine and improve their show.)

James Franco: I remember Judd saying, "You guys are acting too cool. You're acting like young guys who just got cast in a TV show. We need dudes that are a little insecure." He said, "We're going to show you your audition, because this is what we liked." So I watched it and I'm like, *Oh, man, I'm horrible*. It was so goofy. But I think what I didn't like is one of the better aspects of Daniel. I maybe took myself too seriously when I was a young actor.

Busy Philipps: Judd and Paul early on said they liked the weird physicality between James and me. Presumably both of our characters come from abusive households, and you parrot what your family does. In the pilot, James did all of that stuff. Kicking me and all sorts of rough behavior. But I would always go back at him. We had a real intense thing when we worked together.

Sarah Hagan (*actress, "Millie Kentner," Lindsay's old mathlete friend*): James is kind of a flirty guy. He gets really close and smiles that James smile. So that made me a bit nervous. I remember drawing him on one of my scripts, wearing a beanie on his head. I still have it.

James Franco: I always wanted to wear the beanie, and the network didn't like it. They were all about "We need to see his hair. He needs to look handsome."

Seth Rogen: James would do stuff at times just to push people's buttons. I think he threw milk in someone's face as an improv, and I remember thinking, *That's not the best improv.*

Judd: We used to say, "Two out of ten of Franco's improvs are good, but those two are just historic."

Natasha Melnick (*actress, "Cindy Sanders"*): There's a certain responsibility you feel when you're shooting on film. Every second you're goofing off is just, like, money.

Russ Alsobrook: It wasn't wasted: We were trying to find these comedic nuggets of gold that might be scattered throughout a ten-minute take. At one point Eastman Kodak gave me a lot of swag because we'd shot a million feet of film.

Judd: There were moments when I would say to the actors, "We're going to do the long version of this. I don't care about the words—I just want it to be truthful." In "The Little Things," the episode where Seth finds out his girlfriend has "ambiguous genitalia," it was important to us that it was legitimate and thoughtful. I took him into my office with Jessica Campbell [who played the girlfriend] and asked, "How would this go down if she was telling you this information?"

Seth Rogen: He had us improvise and rewrote them to what we improvised. That was the first time I saw you can make weird moments work if you treat them totally honestly.

Judd: That story came about because I was listening to Howard Stern and there was a doctor on, talking about ambiguous genitalia. I thought,

There's a way to do that that's real and sweet and compassionate. A lot of the writing staff thought it was going to be sentimental or in bad taste.

Jon Kasdan (*writer, "The Little Things"*): I remember Judd and Mike White and I sitting in Judd's office discussing it. It was *not* my idea. At first I thought they were just kidding. But it became clear that they weren't.

Judd: It became one of our favorite episodes. In a way, it was a fuck-you to NBC, like, "Now we're going to get really ambitious and aggressive with story lines that you would never approve if the show had a chance of surviving."

Jake Kasdan: There was this sense that it wasn't going to last, so the network wasn't really going to try to fix it. I'm not sure you could get away with those things on a show that isn't about to be canceled.

(As with the improvised scene between Rogen and Campbell, the series's depth and nuance owes much to the chemistry of the cast.)

Paul Feig: John and Linda would do this thing where they would talk to each other like brother and sister, just on the set when they were waiting around. They kind of got on each other's nerves, but it was their game. That's when I was like, *God, this cast is so good.*

Miguel Arteta: Judd knew how to get into the heads of these kids. He really knew their psychology. He made them bring what was happening in their real life into the performances.

John Francis Daley: Over the course of the show, Martin and I would hang out, and Samm would be the odd one out, and then Martin and Samm would hang out, and I'd be the odd man out. There were scenes when we had to act all lovey-dovey with each other and felt exactly the opposite.

Jeff Judah: Seth was stuck studying for his GED and wasn't happy about that, because he wanted to hang out with Franco and Jason and Martin.

Seth Rogen: I dropped out of high school when I started doing the show. I told them I was doing correspondence school from Canada and just wrote *Superbad* all day.

James Franco: I was interested in the writing, so after hounding Judd and Paul they said, "You want to see how it's written?" They took me into Judd's office, and they wrote a scene right in front of me, just improvising as the characters out loud. That was really important for me.

Judd: There's that moment early in your career when you will work harder than any other point afterward. And you can see that in *Freaks and Geeks*. Just total commitment in every frame of the entire series.

Linda Cardellini: Everybody was so talented and nobody knew it yet. People would hang out with each other and practice and play and think of things.

Jason Segel: We would get the script on a Friday, and Seth and James and I would get together at my house every Sunday, without fail, and do the scenes over and over and improve them and really think about them. We loved the show. And we took the opportunity really, really seriously.

Seth Rogen: We felt if we made the scenes better on the weekend, if we came in with better jokes, they would film it. And they would! And we didn't know it at the time, but that was completely unindicative of probably every other show that was on television.

(Ratings remain low as the series becomes hard even for fans to find.)

Paul Feig: We were on for two weeks, off for four weeks because of the World Series, on for another six and then off for two months, moved, put up against *Who Wants to Be a Millionaire*. And then the nail in our coffin was definitely the *Mary and Rhoda* reunion show [an ABC TV-movie sequel to *The Mary Tyler Moore Show* that ran opposite the tenth aired episode of *Freaks and Geeks*].

Judd: We started a website, but NBC refused to let us put the address on any of our ads because they didn't want people to know the Internet existed. They were worried about losing viewers to it.

Becky Ann Baker (*actress, "Jean Weir," Lindsay and Sam's mom*): They sent four of us to do the Thanksgiving Day Parade. It was a really cold, windy, icy day, and at one point we were on a street corner and the float was stopped and someone yelled up to us, "Who are you?!"

Scott Sassa: We had this constant battle with Judd about making things more upbeat. He thought we were going to put ponies and unicorns in, and we just wanted some wins for the characters—without losing the essence of the show.

Judd: There were tough episodes. The toughest was probably when Jason Segel tried to be a drummer, and he went out and auditioned, and he was horrible. And we really played that moment out there, when he realizes he's not good enough to do the thing he dreams of doing.

Linda Cardellini: Life is filled with moments where you have to sit alone with yourself, and I think this show let our characters do that in a way that wasn't normal at the time. You don't really know what to say or do, so you just have to sit there in the uncomfortableness.

Bryan Gordon: The show played silences, and television is afraid of silences. But silences just speak to so much about teenagers.

(A series finale is shot as the last episode of the initial thirteen-episode order, in case of cancellation.)

Paul Feig: Judd came to me and was like, "This thing could be dead, so you should write the series finale now." And then it was going to be the one I got to direct. It was terrifying, but it came out really well. Then the network ordered five more.

Judd: Paul was supposed to direct one of the first episodes, and at the last second I pulled him off it because we weren't in a groove with the staff writing the show yet, and it was so much Paul's vision that he couldn't disappear. Then when I realized the show was probably going to get canceled, I said to Paul, "You should write and direct this finale." And it's clearly the best episode of the entire series.

Linda Cardellini: To do the last episode in the middle felt rebellious, like we were part of dictating our own fate.

Becky Ann Baker: In the finale I'm putting Lindsay on the bus, where she was supposedly going off to a summer college experience. "I miss you already" was the last thing I said to her. And that was all so unfortunately true.

Samm Levine: We'd be out on location. Judd's phone would ring, and he would walk twenty feet away, and he'd be pacing on the phone for forty minutes. And I remember thinking, *That can't be a good phone call.*

Judd: We were saying to the network, We need a full season [twenty-two episodes] to attract an audience. And the order wouldn't come, and I would just rant and rave. It was like begging your parents not to get divorced, trying to save the show. And then they did order one episode.

Samm Levine: Judd said, "Scott Sassa said, 'If you get a ratings share higher than my shoe size, we'll order more episodes.'" And mercifully he was not a tall man.

Jake Kasdan: The thing they always used to say was "We want these kids to have a victory." I think what they were trying to say was "Is there any way it could be a little less depressing?" And it's a fair question when no one's really watching. We were telling really unconventional stories where the victories were so small they could be confused with not actual victories.

Judd: Garth took me out to lunch once and asked for more victories. And so we did an episode where Bill plays softball. We have this triumphant moment where he catches the ball, but he doesn't realize everyone's tagging up. He's celebrating catching the ball, but he's actually losing the game by not throwing it to home plate. That's as far as we could get.

Paul Feig: The irony was that the network was very, very supportive. The interference we had was the interference of people that wanted to make it as good as they could. But Judd was a screamer back then. He would take them on, hard-core.

Judd: We were willing to go down for the show. It would have been awful if one of us said, "Let's do all these changes—I really want to keep this job."

Jason Segel: We didn't really have to be told we were being canceled. We watched the craft service table: It started out with, like, cold cuts and delicious snacks, and it was reduced to half a thing of creamer and some Corn Pops by the end.

Judd: What happens is they shorten your order. Not that they officially shorten the order—they just *don't order any more.* Then you're in purgatory, wondering if someone's going to say, "Next year we're going to give you a better time slot because it deserves to be on the air." That's your prayer.

(One week after the wrap party, March 19, 2000)

Paul Feig: My mother died suddenly, and a couple of days later we got canceled. I was sitting with attorneys when Judd called. And I was just so bombed out from my mom and from the season, and the episode that aired the night before hadn't done well at all. And so part of me is going, *Of course we got canceled.*

Judd: An underling calls and tells you the show is canceled and then they say, "Garth is going to call in a little bit." They give you an hour to digest, so by the time he calls you don't really have the energy to argue. I always wondered if Garth had me on speakerphone, with his underlings laughing as I cried and begged.

Leslie Mann (*actress, "Mrs. Foote"*): Dealing with all the ratings bullshit was hard, but then when it was finally canceled it was like Judd lost a family member. It was just horrible, horrible.

Paul Feig: I remember everyone at the network coming to my mom's funeral. And Judd getting some secret joy of "Good, I'm glad they're all here." It made me laugh: He's enjoying the fact that they had to come and see me in a diminished state.

Linda Cardellini: I was asked to go on *David Letterman*—a lifelong dream. So I fly to New York and I'm in the limousine on my way to the show and I got a call from my publicist, and she said, "I'm so sorry, honey, the show's been canceled." And I said, *"David Letterman* has been canceled?" And she said, "No, *Freaks and Geeks."*

Judd: I felt like a father to everybody, and I felt like everyone's world was about to collapse. I felt responsible, like I had to fight to have it survive so that their lives would be okay, so that their careers could get launched. And so to completely fail was devastating to me. And especially for Paul, because this was Paul's story.

Paul Feig: We were still in postproduction on the last three episodes. The network was like, "Finish them up," but we didn't have anywhere to show them.

Judd: We stayed in editing for months, obsessing over every detail, in both rage and depression, for a show that had been canceled. I was so upset, I herniated a disk and had to have surgery.

Paul Feig: And that's when we did that day at the Museum of Television and Radio in L.A., where we showed the four episodes that hadn't aired. That was the coolest thing ever, in a theater packed with fans, with every episode just rocking the house.

Samm Levine: Scott Sassa called me himself and said, "I loved the show. But at the end of the day, it's a business." I've been on a lot of canceled shows since then and I've never heard from the network president.

(Sassa had decided to cancel the show when he saw a rough cut for Paul's final episode, in which Lindsay, apparently headed for a summer school program, instead runs off with Kim to follow the Grateful Dead.)

Scott Sassa: They show Lindsay traveling in the bus—I almost popped the tape out, because I thought I knew where they were going—and all of a sudden the bus goes by and the freaks are there in that van going to the Grateful Dead concert. And I thought, *That's not how this thing should end.*

Judd: I only found out later that when Scott Sassa saw the cut of the finale and he saw them get in the van he realized we would never do the things that would make the show commercial. That doesn't take away from the fact that Scott was the biggest supporter of the show; it's only good because he gave us all this creative leeway. But that's the funny thing about this work: You can do something you really like and someone else just looks at it and says, "I need to end this today."

Paul Feig: There was a moment when we got canceled where I was like, *Thank God—I can't do this anymore,* then immediately filled with regret: *Oh, fuck! I love these characters!* And I had so many things I wanted to do in the next season. It really is like losing your family. It's very bizarre.

Judd: Whenever I see an opportunity to use any of the people from *Freaks and Geeks*, I do it. It's a way of refusing to accept that the show was canceled. In my head, I can look at *Knocked Up* as just an episode of Seth's character getting a girl pregnant. All of the movies relate in my mind in that way, as the continuous adventures of those characters. The show was the kids' entire life. It was their high school: They're literally going to school on the set. They're falling in love on the set. It's actually happening. And those relationships are still happening; they're still close.

Paul Feig: I'm still very friendly with them all. Judd was the one who really kept on working with everybody; he brought them along to their next level. I'm like the mom who sits at home and watches the kids become successful and takes great joy in their accomplishments.

Judd: Part of the problem of the show was it should have been on HBO. Everything that's popular now you might call "independent television." *Mad Men* is a little like indie TV. But there was no home for us in 1999. It wasn't niche television—you were competing against Regis Philbin hosting a game show.

Martin Starr: I can't express how fortunate I feel to have been a part of something so appreciated and so loved. I'd feel so sorry for myself if I had done a teen movie and people were quoting the dumbest lines in the world everywhere I went. I feel so fortunate that it's something I care so much about and that I can connect with the people that connect with it. I got really, really lucky.

GARRY SHANDLING

(1984)

From the beginning, Garry Shandling was one of my favorite comedians. I used to watch him religiously when he was the guest host on *The Tonight Show*, in the seventies, and he was basically an unknown comedian filling in for the legendary Johnny Carson. He slaughtered every time. Unlike most of my high school interviews, this one was conducted over the phone. Garry was in a hotel room at Lake Tahoe, preparing for a show that night, but he took the time to talk to me and, in the process, to lay out every single thing he intended to do in the rest of his career. All these years later, I look at it and think: *Everything the guy said he would do, he did.* The lesson here, for me, was that you have to have a dream before you can execute it. That the people who succeed are the ones who think through what the next stages of their careers might be, and then work incredibly hard, day after day, to attain their goals. They don't just flop around like fish. They have a vision, and they work their asses off to make it a reality.

Judd Apatow: So you guest-hosted *The Tonight Show* recently. That's a pretty big step up. It was the talk of the town. How did that come about?

Garry Shandling: I think I had done the show eleven times. And I had done well, fortunately, just about every time. What happened was that Albert Brooks was supposed to guest-host, but he got sick the day before and so they called me, twenty-four hours ahead of when the show was being taped, and said we'd like you to guest-host tomorrow night. I had twenty-four hours to prepare.

Judd: Really?

Garry: Yeah. I mean, it was very weird. But *The Tonight Show* has always been supportive of me. And they said, if the opportunity ever arose, I could be used as a guest host. But you really don't believe it until it happens. So I knew the opportunity existed, but I didn't think it was gonna happen that fast.

Judd: What kind of preparation would you do for the show? I mean, you're interviewing people, which is new to you. Plus, you have to have a ten-minute monologue okayed. How did you go about preparing all that?

Garry: It was interesting because I hadn't worked in about twelve days—which is a long time for a comic to go without working. Because you don't keep your chops up on the stage otherwise. So I assembled a monologue of material I had done before—there was nothing else to do. And I went out to two clubs that night, tried to figure out what I wanted to do for my monologue. And just try to get my feet back on the stage, because I hadn't worked in two weeks.

Judd: And when you watched it, were you happy?

Garry: Pretty much. I mean, it's hard for me to look at it and be objective. I can't see it. But it seemed like it went well, for my first time. I don't think it was, like, amazing or anything. Did you see it?

Judd: No, I didn't. I was doing interviews that night at the Improv. But you must have been scared to death, right?

Garry: Well, I wasn't real scared because I had mentally prepared for doing that all along. I mean, *The Tonight Show* has been so supportive of me. They made me feel comfortable, rather than putting me under pressure. They simply said, "We think you're the guy for this and we don't have any question that you can do a good job." That kind of support made me feel comfortable instead of frightened. There were certainly nerves.

Judd: What kind of feedback did you get? Did you get offers afterwards?

Garry: My manager doesn't tell me about all the offers. But I did get requests to do what we call personal appearance work, which is in clubs and stuff. And I guess there were some sitcom offers, but I'm just not that interested in that.

Judd: Acting is something you're *not* interested in doing?

Garry: I'm interested in acting, I just don't know in what vehicle yet. My immediate goal is to sell a show and get it on the air. A talk variety show. Something like *The Tonight Show*, I guess. Or *David Letterman*. I would like to do something more than a situation comedy. And I have a show in my mind that we're actually going to pitch to the networks when I get back off the road, which will be the end of October.

Judd: *The Tonight Show* was taking a major chance with you, because you're not really in the public eye. It's a big chance to put someone like you on there, as far as ratings go. Someone turns the TV on and sees you behind the desk—

Garry: They were smart. Ratings-wise, they know I'm not going to get any ratings. But they were smart because they slipped me in when Albert Brooks had dropped out. The night before, they didn't even mention that I was going to be guest-hosting, so everybody who tuned in assumed it was Albert Brooks. And then I'm sure, out of curiosity, they watched for a while. I think, in their minds, they were taking a risk putting me in there. But I had pretty much proven that I was strong and in control of what I do. I think they felt that I could do it, and I think they were more than satisfied with how I did. It was exciting. It was very emotional.

Judd: So you're working bigger rooms these days. You're in Tahoe right now, right?

Garry: I'm in Tahoe, opening for Tony Orlando. But I've been doing big rooms for about two years.

Judd: And how does that compare to, you know, playing clubs in Los Angeles?

Garry: It's very different. For one thing, it depends who you're opening for and what kind of crowd they draw. Sometimes in these big rooms—like Reno, or Tahoe, or Vegas—they draw an older audience that's totally unlike what you find in a comedy club, which is generally younger, and a little hipper. So you work it differently. You have to work it in a broader, more commercial way. I have to take out most of my hip material. And some of my singles material has to go because it's been so long since some of these people have been single, they just don't relate to it.

Judd: How would you describe your type of humor?

Garry: Oh man, I can't see it objectively.

Judd: It's not that conventional. It's ideas and thoughts with observation. Some comedians now, they're just doing straight observational humor. But your act has a whole new dimension to it.

Garry: You should tell *me* what you think it is, because I'm always curious how people see it from the outside.

Judd: That's how I see it from the outside—you know, it's like your ideas on things, and I think it's great, just—

Garry: The most important thing a comic can do is write from his insides. As cliché as that sounds, a lot of comics start out thinking that they just should write something funny. Which is not the answer. You have to write from personal experience. What you see on the stage is really how I am when I'm funny.

Judd: Like with your friends?

Garry: I can't see how it's different. All I know is when I watch, I go, *Yeah, that's Garry*. I write about my life, and then I exaggerate it because I do like to write jokes. You know, I was a comedy writer before I was a comedian.

Judd: Who did you write for?

Garry: I wrote for *Sanford and Son*; *Welcome Back, Kotter*; and *The Harvey Korman Show*. I wrote for about six sitcoms before I decided to do stand-up. So I have an ability to write jokes, which I like to do. Every now and then, I'll be writing about my life and I'll just think about a joke, and it's really just purely a joke.

Judd: What would be an example of how a piece of material developed?

Garry: I'll tell you an interesting story—I mean, this is unlike other material of mine. I do this joke in my act: I say, "I've heard every excuse for a woman not going to bed with me. I think I've heard them all. I remember this one girl actually said to me, 'Look, not with this Falkland Islands thing.'"

Judd: (*Laughs*)

Garry: "And I said, 'That was over a year ago!' And she said, 'I still haven't gotten over it yet.' And I said, 'Well, I can understand that, Mrs. Thatcher.'"

Judd: (*Laughs*)

Garry: I could tell you about the derivation of so many jokes. Because some of them take a year—literally—from the time I get an idea to the time I get the line exactly right. With the Falkland Islands joke, I originally wrote a joke where I would come out and say, "Boy, I'm just not meeting any women. I don't know if it's this Falkland Islands thing or what."

Judd: (*Laughs*)

Garry: And then, as time went by, I changed it to "I've heard every excuse for a woman not going to bed with me. I remember this one girl said, 'Not with this Falkland Islands thing.'" Which is a little more hip, and gets a laugh. And I was telling David Brenner that joke, and he said, "At that point, you oughta say, 'That was over a year ago,' because that's funnier." And then I added, "Well, she still hasn't gotten over it yet." The Thatcher line came later. So it just kind of kept going, you know.

Judd: Can you tell me about another one?

Garry: Okay, there's one I'm working on now. I actually did this joke on *The Tonight Show*, but in a different way. It's just a stupid joke, really. But I said, "I went to a health food store recently and I've been taking bee pollen. Bumble bee pollen. It's supposed to increase your lovemaking stamina. So I've been taking about two thousand milligrams of bee pollen a day and, ah, the other night I woke up in the middle of the night and started to fling myself against the screen door."

Judd: (*Laughs*)

Garry: "And I started to shout: 'Someone turn off the porch light!'" And it's interesting, because I don't know yet how this joke is ultimately going to evolve. I actually did this joke on *The Tonight Show* where I just said, "I took two thousand milligrams of bee pollen, and now I'm afraid that when I make love, I'm going to die right afterward."

Judd: Yeah.

Garry: Because that's what bees do. And then I said, "Or I'll wake up the next morning, and I'll be flinging myself against the screen door." And then I added the part about "turn off the porch light," which I think paints the picture of what bees do—which is go for the light, you know.

Judd: That is really great. When did this all begin, this interest in comedy?

Garry: When I was a kid. I had a total interest in comedians when I was ten years old.

Judd: Who were the comedians that you idolized?

Garry: Woody Allen is my idol, period. I mean, I think he's as funny as you can get. Others? I like a lot of people. Mort Sahl. He is hip and funny. Dick Shawn, Johnny Carson. I think he's underrated in a way. I think he's a really funny man.

Judd: Did you ever see Woody Allen work live in a club?

Garry: No. I grew up in Tucson, Arizona, where there's just nothing. I'd only seen comedians on TV. But my folks started going to Vegas when I was like thirteen, fourteen, fifteen, and I saw Joey Bishop and people like that there. And I actually remember knowing some of his jokes before he delivered them, and thinking, *Oh man, he's doing old jokes.* So it was always an instinct for me. But to answer your question there, I didn't see a real comedian in a club until I was like twenty. I went to see George Carlin, who I'm just a major fan of.

Judd: Who isn't?

Garry: And it's really a wonderful story. The first time I ever wrote any comedy material, I was nineteen. George Carlin was working in a club in Phoenix. This is when he had just let his hair grow long and he was starting to do honest material about his life and stuff. And I met him and I asked him to read my material, and to tell me what he thought. And he read my material. He was so supportive. He said, "I don't buy material, I write all my own material." But he gave me a lot of feedback and encouragement. Then, ten years later, I met George again and was able to thank him for that moment. He's a wonderful guy.

Judd: What kind of background did you have that you could just write this stuff?

Garry: I was an electrical engineering major, if you can believe that. And then I switched to marketing, and then I switched to creative writing. I finally got a degree in business and I went to graduate school for one year. And just took writing classes. I'd always been a pretty good writer. It's just one of those things. I can sit down and fill a page pretty easily. And so I moved to L.A. and I didn't know exactly what direction I was going to take, and I met a guy who said, "Well, try writing a script and see what happens." I wrote a script for *All in the Family* that they didn't buy. But someone else saw it and said, "Wow, you have a lot of potential," and they helped me along. Then I wrote a script for *Sanford and Son* and they loved it, and started giving me work. It all went pretty fast. And I got pretty hot as a writer. People start to say, What would you like to write? What kind of show would you like to create?

Judd: Yeah.

Garry: But then I was sitting at the typewriter one day and I realized that this was not what I wanted to do the rest of my life. And so when I was twenty-eight, I sort of had a midlife crisis—you know, twenty-eight is midlife for a Jewish guy. I said, *If I don't stop now and start doing stand-up* . . . So I went to some real dive clubs, but it's real hard getting onstage when no one knew who I was.

Judd: Were there audition nights?

Garry: Yeah, I went to audition nights. I was working in discos and health food restaurants. It was bizarre.

Judd: Jerry Seinfeld, when I interviewed him, said that he did a disco and no one even knew he was performing.

Garry: I'm sure we've all had the same experiences. I worked a health food restaurant for about four months where people would just come in—there would be six people, eating rice and vegetables, and I would do forty minutes.

Judd: Only in Hollywood, I guess.

Garry: When you're first starting, it's just important to be on the stage. It doesn't matter if people respond, because you just have to get over your stage fright.

Judd: Was *The Tonight Show* the big break, as far as stand-up goes?

Garry: Yeah. They like me and they're supportive of me and they know that I work hard at what I do. I try to get better all the time. And I still don't think I'm near my potential.

Judd: You feel you have a ways to go?

Garry: Yeah, I don't think the things I'm doing on the stage now are what I'll be doing five years from now.

Judd: What will you be doing?

Garry: I hope it'll be even more honest than it is now, more personal. Because it takes time for people to get to know you. I mean, Richard Pryor is the perfect example. If you look at what he was doing ten or fifteen years ago, it's different than what he does now, because we *know* him. He can just get up and start talking about his life—and that's the funniest stuff.

Judd: What are your long-range goals?

Garry: Well, first of all, my long-range goal is to be funnier. It really is. And to get better, and to keep digging inside myself. Number two, I guess, is to find the right vehicle, either on television or film, that'll allow me to be funny in the way that I'm funny, you know.

Judd: Well, thank you very much.

Garry: I'm sorry I wasn't funny this morning.

Judd: This show is pretty serious.

Garry: Okay.

Judd: This is the comedy interview program that talks serious about comedy.

GARRY SHANDLING
(2014)

Most of the important breaks and rewarding experiences in my career can be directly traced to Garry Shandling. Let me run through it quickly here for you: One of the first jobs I got as a writer was writing jokes for the Grammys for Garry Shandling in 1990. After that, he agreed to do a cameo on the pilot of *The Ben Stiller Show*, and I've always believed that those celebrity cameos, in that first episode, were one of the main reasons the show eventually got picked up. Then, when the show was canceled, Garry hired me to be a writer at *The Larry Sanders Show*. Then, one day at *The Larry Sanders Show*, Garry walked into the writers' room and, without even asking me, said, "Judd, you're going to direct the next episode." And I did.

There is no one who has taught me more or been kinder to me in this comedy world than Garry Shandling. As a kid, my only dream was to be a comedian. I never thought about being a writer. Garry was the first person who ever sat me down and said, "Look, this is what a story is about. This is how you write in this format." He talked a lot about how the key was to try to get to the emotional core or the truth of each character, which I had never heard before. He taught me that comedy is about truth and revealing yourself, and these are all lessons I apply every day in my work. In fact, when we started *Freaks and Geeks*, I always thought of it like this: *Freaks and Geeks* is *The Larry Sanders Show* if *The Larry Sanders Show* was about a bunch of kids in high school.

Judd Apatow: Who made you the man you are today?

This interview was conducted by Mike Sager and originally appeared in Esquire *in October 2014.*

Garry Shandling: I can't discuss that without having a shitload of coffee first.

Judd: To get it all out? Oh, he's spilling it. He spilled it already.

Garry: See, this is why I don't eat in therapy. Do you ever eat?

Judd: The second you said, "That's why I don't eat in therapy," I thought, *Wait. Can you? Because I would* definitely *do that.*

Garry: I know I've had sessions where I've said, "You should think about having at least a salad bar," to the therapist. Seriously, though, I don't know who made me the man I am except to say what I feel in my heart relative to Roy London.

Judd: Yeah.

Garry: Roy influenced me gigantically when I was about twenty-seven years old and I stumbled into his acting class. Instead of talking about act- ing, we ended up talking about the world and people. Those conversa- tions are what gave me the confidence to move on. Up until then, I was a confused young man who was writing for *Sanford and Son*.

Judd: Who were you best at writing for? Which character?

Garry: That's a good question. Lamont. (*Laughs*) And Aunt Esther. The first script I ever wrote was Ah Chew opens up a Chinese restaurant with Fred. And then the health department closes it down.

Judd: The Asian character's name was Ah Chew?

Garry: Well, this was when political correctness was required nowhere in the script.

Judd: Do you think the world was better when you could name a charac- ter Ah Chew?

Garry: I cannot judge that right now. Even just alone with you, I cannot judge that. But I will say, the two producers on that show, Saul Turteltaub and Bernie Orenstein, taught me a lot. When I used to turn in my script, they'd go, "You don't have an ending," and I realized, "Oh, the writer ac- tually is supposed to do the *whole* script." I was assigned to write one in which Fred and Lamont went camping for the whole half hour, and then had to—

Judd: There's nothing *not* racist in that premise.

Garry: Well, I didn't know how to make it funny unless someone caught fire, and that certainly wasn't an option. Nor was I equipped, as a younger man, to write the father-son emotionality that they were looking for at the end—so they had to help me. I remember I wrote three of those scripts in one season and then I went to the story editor Ted Bergman, who really helped me, and said, "How do you write fifteen more? Or *seasons* more?" And he looked at me and said, "Burnt out at twenty-six, huh?" When I told my therapist about this, he said, "No, you might be bored." And it shocked me, because I never knew that that could be my own opinion. That's when I turned to doing stand-up and looking at other types of television and what I could do that was different.

Judd: So your shrink made you the man you are today.

Garry: She really did help me. Because I didn't think I had the right to be bored. You're just so grateful to have this job. Who am I to be bored by writing for *Welcome Back, Kotter* and all these great shows?

Judd: That's what we do: We instantly go to guilt and shame. *I'm not allowed to have a feeling about this. I should just appreciate it and shut the fuck up.* Right?

Garry: That's totally right.

Judd: In all situations, I go straight to that feeling. *Just shut up.*

Garry: Who were your early mentors?

Judd: Well, my grandfather Bobby Shad was this guy who produced Sarah Vaughan and Lightnin' Hopkins and Charlie Parker and Janis Joplin. He raised money when he was a kid—he was a poor kid—and would pay jazz musicians to let him record them and then he would make records and sell them in stores. Eventually, he started his own label, in the forties, and then—

Garry: You kind of saw the whole creative process right there.

Judd: Yeah, that's what I thought. I remember feeling like, *Oh, you can just do it. You can just start.* But I had no musical abilities. I like music, but I just—I tried to play guitar as a kid and I couldn't. What I liked was comedy. When I was a kid I said, "I want to know how they do it." So I started this show for my high school radio station, interviewing comedians. I interviewed you, Garry, on the phone from Las Vegas and you had just hosted *The Tonight Show* for the first time—

Garry: It was the only interview I could get.

Judd: (*Laughs*) Here was this fifteen-year-old calling you on the phone, and you were very nice and funny. I asked you what your plans were for your career, and you basically laid out everything you would go on to do. You said, "I'd like to do a show, probably a sitcom, probably something personal, I'd like to play myself, I might play myself," and this was in 1984.

Garry: That's right. You remind me of two or three things. One, for some reason, is that so many of the comedians and comedy writers I know all pretended like they had radio shows, talking into their tape recorders or whatever when they were kids—it seems to be a common theme. I used to do that, too, but I never actually called anyone and interviewed them. You've always had bigger balls than most kids in comedy. The second thing is, I was a late bloomer. I was confused until I was twenty-seven and, as I said, started to get into that Roy London mentality. That's when I realized I wanted to take the self-discovery path. I figured that would fit naturally into whatever project I felt was right, where I could continue to search this human condition thing we always talk about—because the human condition is hilariously awful.

Judd: I never thought about any of those things until I worked for you. I didn't think in terms of the human story. You started thinking about it from Roy, and then I worked for you, and then you started talking to me about it, and—

Garry: Yeah, this is the big bang of it. By the way, my own belief is that I know how the big bang started—everyone's confused—which is simply that shit happens.

Judd: Just random?

Garry: It may not be random, but "shit happens" is what we end up writing.

Judd: We're getting into chaos theory right now.

Garry: When we were doing *Larry Sanders*, it was all about life and the question of self and what you were bringing to it.

Judd: You always used to say that *Sanders* was about people who love each other, but show business gets in the way.

Garry: And what people are always covering up—the tension between what they're covering emotionally in life and what's really going on inside them. What you really want to write is what they're covering; otherwise you end up writing the exposition—which is just words. That's what the struggle was in the writers' room, in a nutshell: getting people not to write just words.

Judd: I remember you said once that it's very rare that anyone says what they actually feel, that we're always trying to project on to other people, hiding our true motivations and feelings, and when you finally tell someone how you feel about something, it's a big deal. As a kid, watching TV, I think I was learning all those things without even realizing it. I watched *M*A*S*H*, *All in the Family*, *Taxi*—you know, all the James L. Brooks shows—and those are all human comedies. I didn't understand that what I liked about them was seeing normal people with their daily struggles, trying to be good people in spite of all of the obstacles that are in their way, trying to find connection. That's what I enjoyed the most, but I didn't understand how it was made and I didn't understand how I would get there, until I worked with you at *The Larry Sanders Show*.

Garry: There's a way I mentor that's a bit on the Zen side, which is a little hard to understand because it happens in the writers' room. Let's just talk about you, Judd, okay? You, clearly, had youth and a point of view and energy and were really funny, and so what I wanted from you was whatever was pure that was coming out of you. The same pure thing will work for *The Larry Sanders Show,* or it will work for *This Is 40* — it's just got to be pure. What I'm doing in the writers' room is trying to sense whether that's organic or not, trying to help people find themselves. That's the lab we were in. And it turned out that we were filming it. Is that fair?

Judd: Yeah. I would notice things that were happening in your life, or things that you were thinking about, would make their way on the show. After *The Larry Sanders Show,* when I did *Freaks and Geeks* with Paul Feig, it was so personal to Paul. When we were making that show, I was always nervous about — what's the tone of this show? And how can you do it really funny? And in my head I always thought, *You know what this is? It's a spinoff of* The Larry Sanders Show. *If we did* Larry Sanders *in high school, it would be this.* That was always my secret thought.

Garry: Whenever you turn to what the organic state of any given character is, the fears and the anger and the struggle, you're going to get conflict and a lot of hilarious stuff.

Judd: It also led me to realize that certain stories can be very small, but if you're incredibly honest about them, there's so much to do there. Take *Knocked Up,* for example. This is how we came up with that idea: Seth Rogen was pitching me a big science fiction movie, and I said, "Seth, you know, you could stand there and it would be interesting. In *40-Year-Old Virgin,* you're just in a stockroom and you're interesting. You can do a whole movie where you get a girl pregnant and I would watch to see how that works."

Garry: That's right.

Judd: We were all going, "Oh, maybe we should do that," but we were just joking around and then we realized, "Wait, maybe that actually *is* enough."

Garry: You allow the actor to be, as opposed to do. People are fascinating. They don't really need to do much.

Judd: I've always thought that mentoring comes from being in a place where you want to learn. When you hired me at *The Larry Sanders Show,* you said, "Oh my God, you're going to learn so much." You didn't say,

"You're going to be so helpful to me." You said, "You're going to learn so much." And I took that seriously. I'm here to make as much of a contribution as I can, but it's just as important for me to take as much from it as I can. Some writers struggled with this because it was all ego, like, *What can I get on the show? Does Garry like me? Does Garry like my scripts?* They didn't approach it like, *I'm going to get my own show by observing this process and learning from what Garry's doing.* I had fun because I didn't feel that pressure. It wasn't ego-driven. It was, *Hopefully I can get some jokes in, but I just got to watch Garry re-outline that script.* I knew that watching was helping me.

Garry: That's the way I was when I was just starting out. I was really open to being taught. When I see talent, I want them to be all they can be. I really want to help—and by doing so, I am helped as well. Whenever I mentor, I notice I'm learning something myself. You are right that there were writers who were not willing to look deeper inside themselves to get the material we were talking about. It's like being at a therapist and saying, "No. No more sessions." Whereas you would keep going back in the room and rewriting until you just, I could see how successful you would be because that's what it takes. It's just, keep reworking and reworking—and man, you listened and you went back in and you ended up, of course, contributing enormously. I don't know, I'm just interested in life and teaching. I care.

Judd: The bar was so high on that show, it was fun just to try to meet it. But I think for some people—when you struggle to get there, your self-esteem collapses. If you write a bad script and someone calls you out on it, you either go, "How can I make it better?" or you get mad about it.

Garry: You get defensive.

Judd: You get defensive. But I always thought, *Oh, this is fun.* The quest to make you happy, I enjoyed. It's fascinating because I've had the same experience with Lena Dunham on *Girls*—here is a writer who is running a show, who stars in the show, and we know, based on how much work we get done each week, how much sleep Lena gets, and how sane she can be based on how much she's sleeping or how stressed she is about upcoming episodes. It's a very similar type of experience. And I think Lena benefits from my experience on *The Larry Sanders Show* in some ways because, for six years, I got to watch how the show was made—what helped you, and what didn't. So when we built her show and figured out how to staff it and how to write it and how to pace ourselves, I was able to tell her about what happened at *The Larry Sanders Show* and maybe help her do it correctly.

Garry: It sounds like you are saying that it's everything in the moment. On any given day, you can see everything that Lena brings to the stage, to the writers' room, that day. So you start there and try to take her somewhere.

Judd: Yeah. It's Lena's show, and we're all there to help her. Some weeks she may love our ideas, she may love our whole script. Other weeks, we're just trying to feed her so she gets excited and goes off and writes a script without us.

Garry: So it's not a discussion of ego, it's actually a discussion of someone's emotional life and where they are in the moment, which is incredibly usable for the writing and the shooting of the episode itself. That's what we were teaching in the room at *Larry Sanders*: The answer isn't on this piece of paper. It's in this space right here.

Judd: Her insecurity about being a writer is what her show's about, really—a lot like Larry's insecurity about being a talk show host. The battle in the writers' room, on some level, has all the same issues of the battle of trying to be a writer in New York.

Garry: So, as an example, if a writer came in and got defensive about a script he was going to rewrite for *Larry Sanders*, we might in fact find a scene where Larry's saying, "You know, Phil's just—he doesn't want to rewrite these jokes, he's just fighting with me." Instead of getting caught up in this real-life theater that's going on in the room, observe it. Because that may be what goes on the paper in the end.

Judd: It all becomes fodder for the show.

Garry: Translating experience to paper. That's so hard to teach, isn't it?

HAROLD RAMIS
(2005)

Harold Ramis was the original cocky nerd. He was the guy, more than anyone else in this book, whom I secretly thought I could be like. He was tall and lanky and goofy, the guy standing next to Bill Murray who was, in his own quiet way, every bit as funny as Bill Murray. Harold Ramis had a hand in almost everything of note that happened in comedy over the last few decades. He wrote for *Playboy* and the *National Lampoon*; he was the first head writer for *SCTV*, as well as one of its stars; he co-wrote *Animal House*, *Stripes*, *Meatballs*, and *Ghostbusters* (which he also starred in); he directed *National Lampoon's Vacation*, *Analyze This*, and God, the man co-wrote and directed *Groundhog Day*, which is in the running for greatest comedy of all time. *Groundhog Day* is hilarious and spiritually deep, a perfect encapsulation of the Ramis Worldview, and definitely one of those movies that people will be watching in a thousand years—if people are still here in a thousand years.

I first interviewed Harold when I was in high school, and he was thirty-nine years old, about to make *Ghostbusters*. "Why do you think so many people from Second City and *National Lampoon* have become famous in the field of comedy?" I asked, as if there was an easy way to answer this. And he very patiently said, "The same reason that all the doctors who graduated college when I graduated college are now taking over the medical profession. It's our time, you know. Second City is great training. I won't deny that it's a great way to learn how to do comedy, but as far as us all coming into prominence, you know—it's gonna happen to our generation soon. We'll be the old guys."

I was lucky enough to work with Harold on the film *Year One*, in 2009.

Everyone who was involved in that movie was thrilled to have a reason to be associated with him and to have a chance to download his thoughts about life and his legendary career. Harold was very interested in Buddhism, and he had taken everything he liked about the religion and condensed it onto one folded piece of paper. He gave me a copy of it on the set of *Year One*, and I still have it at home. He once said to me, "Life is ridiculous, so why not be a good guy?" That may be the only religion I have to this day.

Judd Apatow: When you look back, not in terms of quality but in terms of a good time, what movie do you look back on and say, "*That's* the one we had a great time making"?

Harold Ramis: The good-time movie for me has been every single one of them, without exception. I don't say that as a Pollyanna, because there have been nightmare situations. I thrive on disaster. I'm very excited when things go wrong. I'm really attracted to outlandish and excessive human behavior. Any experience with Bill Murray is better than any other experience because he does things no one you know would ever do. Every ride with Bill is a potential adventure. I say this with love and considerable distance, because I don't talk to him and I don't see him, but the memories of doing those films with him or even doing a film like *Vacation* — it's kind of the best of all possible worlds for a social person, which I am, because you assemble everyone you like, and if you're lucky you pick a beautiful place to make a movie or a real interesting place, and then you're with them for months with nothing else to do but focus on the work. It's like an excuse: "Can't drive the kids to school. Can't help you with your homework. I'm working." I know a director, Marty Brest — even when he was shooting in L.A., he'd move out of his house. He'd just say to his wife, "I'm not going to be any use to you anyway while I'm making this movie."

Judd: My wife is so onto that. She considers all work play. If I'm not working and I say, "I'd like to go to the movies with my friends," she's like, "You goof off with your friends all day long."

This interview originally took place as a panel at the Austin Film Festival in 2005.

Harold: I had the same thing with my first wife. I said to her, "I'm working so hard for you. . . . Blah, blah, blah . . . You don't appreciate . . ." She said, "You love your work. Don't ever claim this is hard for you."

Judd: What was the first movie you directed?

Harold: *Caddyshack.*

Judd: So you started at a very low level.

Harold: It *was* a low level. We were already kind of corrupted by the initial success of *Animal House,* which I'd written. I had been professionalized for ten years before *Animal House.* I'd been paid for writing and performing starting in 1968. So 1978 was when *Animal House* came out, and I felt I could always support myself. I was through the job-struggle period, and things were happening just as I thought they should. I went from improv comedy on the stage to doing television stuff, and then the treatment for *Animal House* gets bought, the movie gets made, and it's a huge hit. Producers literally waited outside screenings to meet me, Doug Kenney, and Chris Miller, and they asked, "What do you guys want to do next?" It was like a dream. So I said, "I want to direct the next thing I write." Jon Peters, best known as the hairdresser who married Barbra Streisand and a fine producer in his own right, looked at me and said, "You look like a director." I was wearing a safari jacket and aviator glasses at the time.

Judd: Did you guys all get money from *Animal House,* or did you all get screwed?

Harold: Well, we didn't get rich. I got $2,500 for the treatments, and Chris, Doug, and I split $30,000 for the final product, $10,000 apiece. They slipped me another two grand because I did the final polish. We shared five net points of the movie, 1.6 each. There were no gross players in the film, and it was relatively low budget. When the movie came out, we did a quick calculation and thought, "We're going to make some money." I think we made in the under-$500,000 range, but in 1978 that seemed like a lot of money. I literally went to the bank in Santa Monica with the review and bought a house.

Judd: Tell me a little about Doug Kenney, who is a *National Lampoon* legend, and also a little bit about your thoughts on having a group of people that's doing a lot of work together but separates as the years pass. What was that social world like for those people?

Harold: Having Second City as my first professional experience was great. Second City is so different from stand-up. In the world of stand-up you really talk about killing, not just killing the audience but killing the other comedian. It's a competition every night. You want to be better than anyone else. But the whole thrust of Second City is to focus on making everyone else look good because in that process we all look good. It's more than collaborative. Your life onstage depends on other people and on developing techniques for creating cooperative work. We have rules, guidelines, games, and techniques that teach that. It fosters a spirit that exists to this day. Anyone who's ever worked at Second City can run into any other generation of Second City players, and they instantly share a language and an approach to their work. John Belushi got hired from Second City. We were in a show together, and he got hired to do *National Lampoon*. They did a big Woodstock music festival parody called *Lemmings*—it was a big breakout show for John. Chevy Chase and Christopher Guest were discovered in that show. John was able to write his own ticket at the *Lampoon*, and when the *Lampoon* wanted to do a nationally distributed radio show, they let John be the producer. John brought me, Gilda Radner, Bill Murray, Brian Murray, and Joe Flaherty from Second City. We all moved to New York and had this great, cohesive Second City spirit. Doug Kenney was a really sweet guy, a hippie dropout from Harvard that started the *National Lampoon* and then took a year off to live in a teepee in Martha's Vineyard. He'd written a book called *Teenage Commies from Outer Space*, and he was their resident adolescence and puberty expert. He did the *High School Yearbook*. He did "First Lay Comics" and "First High Comics." So we did a stage show from *Lampoon*, John, Gilda, me, Bill, Brian, Joe. We took it on the road, then we did the *Radio Hour* for a while, and then Ivan Reitman saw us perform in Toronto. He wanted to do a movie with the *Lampoon*, so I said, "What about a college movie?" He said, "Who do you want to work with at the *Lampoon*?" I thought Doug was the smartest, funniest, nicest guy, so Doug and I teamed up, and then later we brought in Chris Miller. Doug was always really elegant. He wanted to be Cary Grant. He wanted to be Chevy Chase, basically, but he didn't have the performing chops. He was as smart as could be. Doug used to do a thing where he would stand at my bookcase in my house, close his eyes, pick a book, randomly flip to a page, start reading from that page, and at some point start improvising. You wouldn't know where the book ended and Doug's improv began. He could do it with any book on the shelf, just his little parlor trick.

Judd: So those were the salad days, socially, for that group? It wasn't like, "Oh, no, the group broke up because . . ."?

Harold: Not then. After *Animal House* was successful, Doug and I joined with Brian Murray and wrote *Caddyshack*. Doug produced it, I directed it, and Brian acted in it. We were so arrogant and deluded that we thought *Caddyshack* would be as big as *Animal House*, but to have your first movie be, what was then, the biggest comedy ever sets the bar a little high. Doug was already troubled, already wrestling with self-esteem issues because of family problems and substance abuse issues. We had a horrific press conference for *Caddyshack*. It was one of the worst public events I've ever attended, and it was kind of my fault. I said, "Wouldn't it be great to get Chevy, Bill Murray, Rodney Dangerfield, and Ted Knight on the stage to talk to the press?" Well, they scheduled it at nine-thirty in the morning. None of those four had ever been up at nine-thirty in the morning. Doug showed up at the press conference drunk, stoned, coked up, and sleepless. He hadn't gone to bed the night before. Chevy was rude to the press. Rodney was totally out of it. Bill was crude and off-putting, and the press was hostile. At one point, Doug stands up and tells them all to fuck themselves, and then passes out at the table. Chevy concludes his last TV interview of the day with Brian Linehan from Toronto, and Brian says, "Chevy, what would you say about so-and-so?" Chevy says, "What would I say? Can I say, 'Fuck you, Brian'? Could I just say, 'Fuck you'?" This is a televised interview. The next day someone sends me a clipping that says, "If this is the new Hollywood, let's have the old Hollywood back." So Doug was depressed, and I get a call — I don't know why I'm being so self-revealing. Doug says, "I'm going to Hawaii with Chevy for two weeks to clean up." You do not go anywhere with Chevy to clean up. I thought, *This is a potential disaster. I cannot go on this trip.* Chevy came back. Doug did not. Doug fell from a high place on the island of Kauai, and his body was found a couple of days later. It was beyond tragic. I'd been in a room with this guy eight hours a day for two movies. He's like my brother and best friend. And he's much loved by a great number of people. It was sobering, but in a way it became like a Rorschach test for each member of our group. Some thought suicide: Doug was a victim of his own substance abuse, his own depression, whatever. Some thought accident: He was careless. It was just fate, an existential accident. Others thought he was murdered by drug dealers on Kauai. There was no evidence for any of it. It just depends on how you see the world. We eventually concluded that Doug slipped while looking for a place to jump. Same with John Belushi. John died two years later of an administered overdose, but it's not suicide when you let a stranger shoot you up and you don't know what's in the needle. If you've even gotten to the point of putting a needle in your body, it's a form of suicide. John Belushi—as a nice segue from Doug Kenney, just to really perk up your morning—was pulled twice from a burning bed. If it happens once, it's kind of a wake-up call. If it happens twice, you start thinking, *Maybe I have a problem.*

Judd: You always hear that when *Caddyshack* was being made everybody was on drugs and partying during the shooting.

Harold: Everyone in the world of that age was on drugs and partying. It was the eighties in Florida. There were hotels literally built of pressed cocaine. They had so much cocaine, they just used it as construction material.

Judd: I'm always fascinated when you hear about people being on something when they're making *Saturday Night Live.* I think we got drunk once in the *Larry Sanders* writers' room, and then just went home and wrote nothing. So I'm just fascinated.

Harold: Well, one of the miracles of substance abuse—when you use something enough, it eventually loses its effect, whatever it is. That's why addicts have to take more and more of it to get high. You're not even high anymore. Eventually, John Belushi—people would come up to him at parties and just hand him drugs because they thought that was the way to John's heart. They'd give him a little gram bottle of cocaine and go, "John, you want some coke?" He'd go, "Yeah, the whole bottle." You become a glutton. It's a form of gluttony. If you're high all the time, that becomes your sober state. Eventually, all your judgments become relative to that state. That was the miracle of getting sober for me. It's not different. It's the same. I have the same problems, urges, desires, ideas, and thoughts. I don't need to be high. Eventually getting high, I realized, just made me sick. I was sick.

Judd: How does it feel—I would assume you would become numb to it at some point—to have a body of work that . . . in a way, I guess it's kind of like being the Beatles. Does it get boring dealing with the impact of your body of work on people, how much it means to people? Can you feel that anymore?

Harold: Grandiosity is the curse of what we do. There's a great rabbinical motto that says you start each day with a note in each pocket. One note says, "The world was created for you today," and the other note says, "I'm a speck of dust in a meaningless universe," and you have to balance both things. I once did a public talk and told them that story, and I said, "I literally have a note in each pocket." I took one out and said, "This one says, 'You're great,' and this one says, 'You're great.'" The culture is what it is. I'm as much a product of our culture as I am a participant in it. It's very gratifying on a personal level to know that people responded so much and cherish those films. Any of us who make films or work in any of the arts aspire to have a dialogue with the culture and with our audience. Our audience could be an audience of one, like when you grab your best friend and say, "Read this. What do you think?" Our little hearts pound as our friends read our poem, look at our painting, or read our script. If they like it, our spirits soar. It's great. We can get grandiose from the approval of very few people.

Judd: If you look at the entire generation of people you began with, it seems that very few of them have continued to work at a high level. There are a lot of people that crashed, or their work crashed. Then you look at other people. . . . Larry Gelbart is still a great writer after fifty years. Do you attribute that to anything?

Harold: What eventually happens in all our lives is that we're faced with developmental challenges. It's always, "Now what?" We all start to work for certain reasons, and I think most guys in the room would recognize that we work to meet girls. The last line of *Caddyshack* is, "Hey! We're all going to get laid!" It was an improvised line I can't even believe I edited into the movie. Getting laid is just a metaphor for getting all the things we're supposed to want when we're adolescent. We want to be rich, we want power, we want to be attractive to people, and we want all the perks of success. We'll leave out of the discussion what happens when you don't get it. But let's say you're Chevy Chase and you do get it. You're getting all the perks, people offer you money, women are throwing themselves at you, and you're famous. Now what? Now it becomes a measure of character, growth, and development. Who do you want to be from that point on? You're rich and famous, so what do you have to say? You've got the stage. You're on it. You're there. Now what? Once you've got people's attention, what do you want to do with it? Growth is hard. I've said this to Chevy. I see him. We bump into each other every couple of years. A few years ago, twenty years after *Vacation*, and after he's already done *Vegas Vacation*, he says, "We've got to do something together." I said, "Well, what are you thinking?" and he says, "'Swiss Family Griswold.'" My first thought is, *Do I need to do another* Vacation *movie? Does he need to do another* Vacation *movie?* So I said, "Maybe it would be better to do something you're actually interested in, like an issue in your life." When you're almost sixty years old there's got to be something more going on. What are the challenges of being a grown-up in the world? Start with something that's important or interesting to you, and that's what you make movies out of. It's like the rat in the experiment that just keeps going back and hitting the lever to get the same reward each time. It's all about growth and development. I've tried to find meaning or create meaning in each of the films, a meaning that's specific to me at that time in my life. All I can address is the sincerity and the meaningfulness for me. If I do a movie like *Bedazzled*, as broad as that is, or *Multiplicity*, or any of those films, I'm really examining those aspects of life that are portrayed in the film. If I had to do a Vegas film, I would be looking for what Vegas says about society. What does it mean to me? What does it say about the addiction to gambling? What does it represent? Everything means something, intended or not. Every story tells a big subtextual story. It's all rich. It's all subject to interpretation. That's the fun, isn't it? When we see generic work that has only one interpretation, so what? You might as well stay at home and watch another rerun of *Friends* than see another romantic comedy. And I don't mean to be down on romantic comedy.

Judd: Unless the guy's never had sex for forty years.

Harold: That was a good one, though. That transcended romantic comedy.

Judd: You talk about how you enjoy the disasters and the difficult moments. I'm not like that. I usually end up on my back in surgery when something like that happens. I don't get that, the enjoying-the-pain part. But maybe that's because I'm in pain the whole time, and you're not. When it gets even worse, it's like, *Can't I just have my low-level hum of stress and suffering as we do this?* When you think of the worst fights, or the worst kind of conflict making a film with Bill Murray, what's the one that comes to mind, like, *Wow, that was really ugly?*

Harold: As my first job out of college, I worked in a mental institution for seven months. I learned how to deflect insanity, or how to deal with it, and how to speak to schizophrenics, catatonics, paranoids, and suicidal people. It sounds funny, but it really expanded my tolerance for the extremes of human behavior, which turns out to be great training for working with actors. They have an incredibly hard job, and most of them are already a little bent. That's why they're actors in the first place. They have a desperate need to get out there and reveal something about themselves. Even as a teenager, you're in a room full of people and someone is acting out. God, that's interesting, isn't it? It's always the person who's in big trouble. The rest of the class sits there and goes, "Wow! Did you hear what he said to the teacher? That was great!" We all wish we'd said it, and we're fascinated by the result: "He's going to get in trouble!" Then you meet someone like Bill, who says things to people you can't believe. Like a sociologist or a psychologist, you watch for the impact: "God, you can say that and get away with it?" I've seen a total stranger come up to Bill on the street in New York: "Bill, love you on *Saturday Night!*" He says, "You motherfucker, I'm going to bite your nose!" He wrestles him to the ground—total stranger—and bites his nose. I guess you *can* do that.

Judd: What is that? Is he having fun, or is he mad? Does it make it impossible to maintain a relationship with somebody like that?

Harold: It keeps you constantly alive to possibility. Anything can happen here. It's great. It kind of frees your imagination. Actors are nothing if not self-revealing or at least self-presenting. It's kind of remarkable. It almost seems like a cliché to say comedy comes from pain, but real comedy is connected to the deep pain and anguish we all feel. I worked with Robin Williams on an obscure film called *Club Paradise*. Peter O'Toole, Jimmy Cliff, and Twiggy are in it. It's a wonderful mess, but it's a wonderful movie in a lot of ways. Robin is one of the most deeply melancholy people you'll ever meet. You can just see it all over him. It's what makes him so human, and I love and respect him. Deep down, Bill is as serious as a person could be. He's raging, angry, and full of grief and unresolved emotions. He's volcanic. Comedy gives them a place to work out ideas and entertain—and these guys love to entertain—but they want you to know that they feel. I think that's part of it. You go see Robin Williams do stand-up, and you can't get more laughs than that. I've been onstage. I know what it feels like to have those waves of laughter. It's like being bathed in love. Once you've had it, it's like a drug. It wears off, and then you need something more. I want the audience to feel something more than that. I want them to feel my pain.

Judd: You always hear stories of conflict during *Groundhog Day*, but was there any conflict trying to rein Bill in and focus his energy?

Harold: Never a creative problem. Bill kind of passive-aggressively takes his anger out on the production itself, but never me. I'm too calm. I don't offer him anything to go after. He would go after the producers, or the costumes. . . . Whoever was around had to take it from him. Or he'd go back and trash his motor home. I'd say, "Well, now you've trashed your motor home. Good idea." No one fights with me. I'm just a detached observer of this extreme behavior. One time, we were shooting *Vacation*, and it was 110 degrees in Arcadia. We're shooting a scene where Chevy and his family have arrived at the amusement park, Wally World. They park a mile away so they can be the first ones out at the end of the day. They run across the parking lot to the tune of *Chariots of Fire* in a slow-motion shot. It's 110, and the pavement's about 130 because it's been sunny all day in Arcadia. Everyone's really angry. Anthony Michael Hall gets heatstroke and has to go to the hospital. We continue to shoot with

Chevy, and he's really irritated because it's so hot, and he kind of blows a take. He's loading luggage on top of the station wagon, and he's holding this duffle bag. He screwed up, and he's really mad. I'm sitting in my chair, and I think, *He's going to throw that bag at something.* I see him look to his left. There's a light stand. I know he's processing, *I can't throw it at the light. There's the sound cart. I can't throw it at the Nagra* [a professional audio recorder]. *I can't throw it at the camera.* Then he looks at me, and I go, *He's going to throw that bag at me.* All this takes place in a split second, and of course, he throws the bag. I was so ready that I just put my foot up and knocked it to the ground. Then I say, "Come here," and I take him away from the set, but not so far that everyone won't hear us. This is my opportunity. The whole crew can hear. I say, "You fucking asshole, everyone's been out here all day. The crew's been out here longer than you have. They've been here since six in the morning. We're all tired, and we're all hot, so if you can't control yourself, why don't you . . ." Blah, blah, blah. So the crew is ready to applaud me. I've both cooled Chevy and made allies with the crew. So I try to turn adversity into something positive.

Judd: At what time in your life did you get acquainted with or interested in Buddhism? It seems like it influences your approach.

Harold: My best friend in college, we went to San Francisco together and graduated college in '66. The word *hippie* had not been coined yet. We called ourselves freaks and beatniks. We went to San Francisco. The Haight-Ashbury was flowering. Jimi Hendrix was playing, the Grateful Dead, Janis Joplin, Big Brother and the Holding Company, Jefferson Airplane, the whole thing. My roommate, David Cohen, was really stunned by it. We were both really powerfully affected by this radical energy that was going on. It was political, cultural, consciousness, religious . . . it was everything. David went back to San Francisco. He'd been in four years of psychoanalysis—all through college—formal, Freudian psychoanalysis. So when he got to San Francisco he made a methodical investigation of all the new religious and spiritual movements, from bioenergetics to yoga. He moved systematically through all these movements and finally came to the San Francisco Zen Center. Zen Buddhism is the cleanest, sparest, most rigorous religious practice there is. You sit for forty minutes in an extremely painful cross-legged position trying to keep your mind centered and focused. He became a full-fledged Zen monk and finally a Zen priest. He worked his way up through the Zen Center and stayed there more than twenty years. I so admired his practice and this amazing calm it brought to him. I started reading Buddhism and thinking about it. I don't claim to be Buddhist. I'm too lazy. Then I met my wife. She'd spent her college years in a Buddhist meditation center in L.A., and her mother lived for thirty years in a Buddhist meditation center. Everything I'd heard and read about it so impressed me. I grew up Jewish, and then I found out that American Buddhists are less than five percent of the population, but thirty percent of them are Jews. It's kind of an amazing statistic. It fit nicely with the Talmudic approach to life, which I'd been evolving. I'm so lazy that I just did a very superficial investigation of Buddhism and distilled it down to something the size of a Chinese takeout menu. It's literally that size. It's threefold, and I call it the "Five-Minute Buddhist." It reminds me how to think—not what to think, but how to think. It's a good response to existentialism, which is a psychology I embrace. There's an actual school of existential psychology—a discipline—and that's the one that makes the most sense to me. I wear Buddhist meditation beads. As Tony Hendra says in *Spinal Tap*, "It's an affectation."

Judd: As someone who is an existentialist with a dash of Buddhism, if that's your philosophy, you seem like a serene, happy person. How have you taken the darkest philosophy there is and found peace for yourself?

Harold: Serenity is an illusion, but if anything is possible and I can do anything, then there's a limitless capacity to do good. That's what *Groundhog Day* is about. In *Groundhog Day*, Bill destroys all meaning for himself. Buddhism says our self doesn't even exist. The self is a convenient illusion that gives us ego. In conventional terms, of course, it exists. There's a name and picture on your driver's license, you have to get dressed in the morning, and your paycheck is addressed to somebody, so you have a self. But it's really an illusion. I did a group exercise, and we were asked to face another person and describe ourselves in two minutes. I started describing myself, and from the very first statement started thinking, *That's not really true. That's what I like to think about myself, but I'm not as good as I'm saying.* It's all a projection. So then we switched partners, and they said, "Now tell this person who you are." So I did a corrective on the first, wrong view of myself, and as I'm talking I'm thinking, *That's not me, either.* The whole point of the exercise is that we're not who we think we are. We're only occasionally who we want to be. We're not what other people think we are. The self kind of evaporates as a concept. If you can take yourself out of these existential issues, life gets a little simpler. If life is full of possibility, and I stop thinking about myself, I end up where Bill ends up at the end of the movie: in the service of others. I called it the "Superman Syndrome." By the end of the movie he has every moment scheduled so he can do some good. He's always there to catch the kid. He's always there when the old ladies get a flat tire. We even cut some things out where he's always there to put his finger on a package someone is wrapping so they can tie the string. How the hell does Superman find the time to talk to Lois Lane when he could be stopping a dam from breaking? There's always some good you can be doing, which can make you crazy, too. There's a condition I call "altruistic panic," where you feel like you have to do something for someone somewhere. If life only has the meaning you bring to it, we have the opportunity to bring rich meaning to our lives by the service we do for others. It's a positive thing.

HARRY ANDERSON
(1983)

Yes, I was a Harry Anderson fan, too.

When I sat down with him, he was a magician and stand-up comedian whom I'd seen on *Saturday Night Live* a few times, doing his bit, and on *Cheers*, where he had done some memorable guest spots as an actor. I interviewed him just before *Night Court* started airing, so to me he was just this demented, semi-famous magician whom I happened to find hilarious. We talked for a long time—much longer than a teenager with a high school radio show should ever have hoped for—and he went pretty deep. He talked about some very personal things with me. I remember being a little taken aback by how open he was about his life—his successes, his struggles, and his pain. I remember having this vague sense of being moved by it all, but in ways I didn't fully understand yet, and am only coming to understand now. What I took away is a lesson that has proved absolutely vital in my career: Do not be afraid to share your story, or to be vulnerable and open when telling it.

Judd Apatow: On *Cheers* you play a con man—and it seems to be true, right?

Harry Anderson: If I were, I guess I would lie and say no.

Judd: No, but I saw you on *Letterman* the other day and you said you got in trouble in New Orleans for—

Harry: A shell game. I ran a shell game for about three years on the street.

Judd: Taking people's money?

Harry: Yeah.

Judd: And living off that? Were you doing stand-up at the same time?

Harry: No, I didn't do stand-up. I got into magic when I got my jaw broken doing the shell game, and I gave up gambling and then turned it around and did a comedic exposé of the shell game, which really wasn't an exposé but it was more of—there was no gambling, I just passed my hat at the end of it. This is back before street performers were so common. I was on the street from the time I was fifteen until I was twenty-five.

Judd: When did you get into magic?

Harry: I've always done magic as a hobby. I've done it professionally, too. I played at amusement parks in Southern California when I was a kid, did birthday parties and things.

Judd: At fifteen you started hustling?

Harry: When I first went out at fifteen, I did a street act with linking rings, but I wasn't very serious about it. I didn't make much money at it. When I was twenty-one, I went to San Francisco and started hustling full-time with the shell game because the money was better that way.

Judd: You just had people bet and they thought they could beat you out? Just like the guys on Eighth Ave.—

Harry: And Seventh Ave. and Sixth Ave. and Fifth Ave. . . .

Judd: And you made a lot of money doing that?

Harry: Well, no. I made better money but I didn't—too dangerous. I wasn't really cut out for it. I wasn't tough enough and, if it comes right down to it, I wasn't black enough to be doing that kind of work. Because the mobs that were running were black mobs, and I never had a mob. I never had shills. I did rough hustling, what they call playing against the wall. I just played myself with the players so I would pay, I would make them shill. I would pay certain players and then take from others. But it's a real rough way to do it. Sometimes it's called dumb hustling.

Judd: You were able to support yourself?

Harry: Well, yeah, I made a living, but then I got my jaw broken so—

Judd: How did that happen?

Harry: A guy didn't like where he found the pea. And that was—

Judd: So was it a—

Harry: It was a fix. There's no way to play the game fair. Because the pea won't stay under the shell.

Judd: What kind of fix? How did you work that?

Harry: The pea was not under the same shell where it started. Obviously, I was cheating the man. It should have been under that shell.

Judd: So you just lift up the shells without him knowing?

Harry: I can't explain the technique, you know. But it's a cheat and the fellow didn't like it. It was just one punch. I didn't even see him coming. He just was there and I was down on the ground. Somebody else took my money and left. So after I had my mouth wired shut for six weeks, I had a lot of time to think about what I should be doing. I'd always been a reasonably funny guy, so I decided to take a less serious, more comic approach to things. I went back out and did the shell game but it became more of a lampoon—a parody of the shell game. I created this character that I still have of a guy who is a little bit of a nincompoop—I'm poking fun at street hustlers. I didn't make quite as much money as one would gambling, but it was a lot safer.

Judd: You did this on the street?

Harry: Yeah.

Judd: So instead of people betting, you just passed around a hat?

Harry: I would demonstrate how the game is played and I'd fool them, and uh, I'd do the shell game and then a couple of card things and then just pass the hat.

Judd: And then how did the magic get into it?

Harry: If you do sleight of hand without trying to cheat someone, that's what magic is. A card trick is what a gambler does, only you're not cheating someone, you're entertaining them. It's the same technique, applied differently.

Judd: Did you have training from anybody?

Harry: Oh, from all sorts of people. I hung around these kinds of guys when I was a kid. But no formal training. I picked it up the same way most guys do. A lot of guys when they're seven or eight, and they're going through the variety of hobbies, will do magic for a while. Pretty much everybody starts around that age and then they stick with it or they don't.

Judd: What kind of childhood did you have if you were out on the street at fifteen?

Harry: Fine. Fine. I was just anxious to make some money. We weren't particularly rich.

Judd: Where was this?

Harry: I lived all over the country. We traveled. We never stayed anywhere much.

Judd: What did your parents do?

Harry: Well my mom and dad split when I was young and my mom hooked. She was a hooker, and that's how I ended up meeting the people I did and learning what I learned.

Judd: When did your act move into a club atmosphere?

Harry: Oh, about four years ago. Ken Kragen asked me to open for Kenny Rogers in Las Vegas.

Judd: Just off the street?

Harry: Not off the street, I was playing the Magic Castle in L.A. He saw me there and asked me. I had not done much nightclub work. I was playing colleges in Texas, Arizona, and California. It was a lawn show— I would put up a tent and do a noon show and pass the hat. And then I would go to L.A. and play the Magic Castle. I haven't played the streets since then.

Judd: Not at all?

Harry: Not at all.

Judd: And after you got signed, what kind of work did you do after that?

Harry: I started doing talk shows. Merv Griffin and John Davidson, Dinah Shore, Mike Douglas. And then last year I was signed to do *Cheers*. I did three episodes.

Judd: Do you have an ongoing contract with *Cheers* to do it next year?

Harry: I'm going to do at least one episode of *Cheers*, yeah. But we don't start taping *Night Court* until October thirty-first, so I'll have time to do at least one teaser. Not a major episode. I did one major episode for *Cheers*.

Judd: The poker game?

Harry: Yeah. And I did several episodes where I just popped in for a teaser and I'll do at least one of those next year.

Judd: And wasn't that, I guess that episode must have been, like, handwritten for you?

Harry: Well, I wrote it. I didn't write the script but I wrote the sting. I designed the game and the swindle for them. I told them who should cheat who at what time and that's part of the work I do. I have a consultation company called the Left-Handed League and we advise scriptwriters on plots like that. So the League would, if you look at the credits, the technical consultation for that episode is by the Left-Handed League.

Judd: Wait, you work for it or it's yours?

Harry: It's my company. I am co-founder of it with a fellow named Martin Lewis, who is a British cheat, and a sleight of hand expert.

Judd: So you're doing many things. All grounds are covered, really.

Harry: Oh yeah, I don't know how long anything is going to last so I have to make sure I have something to do tomorrow.

Judd: Are there any films that you are going to be starring in?

Harry: I did a film called the *Escape Artist* for Francis Coppola. I had the title role.

Judd: You were the escape artist?

Harry: Yeah, a very small part because I'm dead during the film but I'm seen in flashbacks.

Judd: I saw part of that. I saw a trailer—it got a good review with the two guys on Channel 11.

Harry: Siskel and Ebert?

Judd: Siskel and Ebert.

Harry: They gave it a good review?

Judd: They gave it a mediocre review.

Harry: Well, it was never released nationwide. So it wasn't that highly sought out.

Judd: I saw a scene from it where it was at a party, the magician and he's doing—I think flying through the air and disappearing, it was very strange.

Harry: I wasn't involved in the whole film, so I'm not sure. Was it the boy doing it? Or was it—

Judd: It was a man.

Harry: A man? Well that's probably the uncle because what I did, I did the water torture stuff, the escape that Houdini did. The water.

Judd: Did you do it for real?

Harry: Oh yeah, I did it thirty times for real holding my breath in six hundred gallons of water, yeah.

Judd: Oh my God.

Harry: Yeah, my God.

Judd: And is that how your character dies?

Harry: I'm dead throughout the entire thing. Actually, he's killed attempting a prison escape. A guard shoots him. And the kid's aunt and uncle explain that he was shot accidentally while he was staging some publicity stunt but the kid finds out that his father was actually not a real well man. He was pathological. He couldn't stand locks and he would open any lock that he came across. And he was arrested for breaking and entering, essentially, and tried. Once he was in prison, he tried to escape because he couldn't take locks and was shot trying to escape. And so the boy tries to duplicate his father's feat and it's all very convoluted. It was a real confusing film, which is why it's going to be on cable any minute now.

Judd: So you didn't see the whole film?

Harry: I've seen it on American Airlines but I fell asleep.

Judd: That must say something for it.

Harry: Well, you know. Off the record—no, not off the record, forget it. That's the only film I made. I've read for a couple of films but I haven't been taken on by them. I'm doing this very slowly. I don't want to bite off more than I can chew and end up looking foolish.

Judd: So you're just doing your act?

Harry: Well, my act and I'm breaking into acting very slowly. *Cheers* was a good first step because I got to write my own material.

Judd: On *Cheers*, you basically played yourself.

Harry: Yeah. And in *Night Court* my name is still Harry and I'm—my best friends are still three-card monte workers and I still have spring snakes hidden everywhere and joy buzzers, but I'm the judge.

Judd: This is a new sitcom called *Night Court*.

Harry: Yeah, it's by the guy who wrote *Barney Miller* for the last three seasons. Reinhold Weege. And it feels very much like *Barney Miller*. I'm the judge in a New York night court, and it's the starring role.

Judd: Do you think you're going to get tied down if it's a successful series?

Harry: I wouldn't mind. If it becomes a success, it will be a real joy to do it because it's a quality show. I wouldn't feel tied down at all. I would feel employed, you know.

Judd: So for *Cheers*, they just spotted you and just saw your act?

Harry: I'm not sure how it happened. I think somebody related to one of the Charles brothers—I took him at the shell game years ago. I got twenty bucks off him or something. He remembered that and he saw me on *Mike Douglas*. But it is a very natural situation for a con man: a bar. Well, actually, when they brought me in, their suggestion was they wanted me to be an aspiring magician and I suggested, "Well, wouldn't a con man be more natural in that setting?" What was unusual about it was, Harry on *Cheers* actually takes money from people and there's something to despise in that and so making him likable—making a guy who is in essence a likable thief—there was the question of trade and practices. Can you present that kind of role model on TV? But then the poker episode really redeemed him because it showed that he would take a nickel here and a dime there, but when somebody's in trouble, there's enough Robin Hood in him that he will help people out. When he leaves with the money at the end of the game, you think, *What a jerk*.

Judd: I did, I said I couldn't believe—

Harry: But then he comes right back and that's the trick. A con like that is just an elaborate magic trick or a swindle. It's bringing people to the wrong conclusion and then surprising them.

Judd: You sound like you've done that trick in the bar.

Harry: I've done that plenty. I haven't paid for a lot of drinks in my life. I've run some scams, yeah. But fewer and fewer as time goes on, which is good. I'm finding more legitimate ways.

Judd: Like acting?

Harry: Yeah. As I grow older and I don't run so fast, I'm not so eager to get myself in situations where I'm going to have to run.

Judd: How would you describe your act? Are you a magician who does comedy, or a comedian who does magic?

Harry: It's a character, it's a guy. It's *a* Harry, as opposed to Harry Anderson. He's a guy who knows magic but doesn't respect it much. I have an attitude about people and it's very tough to analyze. I've tried several times. It's easier to do than to analyze. He's a little ill at ease up there. And he's a little ill that everybody's staring at him and he can't believe that people are buying this. *I can't believe I'm thirty and I'm doing this*. You know. One of the things I love to do onstage is insist that people talk and participate. "It's a live show, folks, come on, come on," and as soon as they say something, I tell them to shut up. You know. Because it pokes fun at the whole theater situation. People are very ill at ease when a performer talks directly to them. Knowing that and then playing with it—he eventually doesn't feel ill at ease. You poke at him long enough then eventually it doesn't matter anymore and he's just laughing right along with everybody else and bringing him to that point where their egos kind of go away and the way to do that is, is I make myself look like a jerk. It's an old Elizabethan idea. The fool is the only one who is allowed to make fun of the king because he is a fool. I can say whatever I want about anybody else because I'm just an idiot talking—I'm not insisting that I'm any smarter than anyone else. It's satire.

Judd: A lot of the tricks that you do, sometimes people think they see what's going on and then you just like turn the whole trick around so it's, like, it looks like you did something but it's nothing.

Harry: It's bringing them to a false conclusion, and then pulling the rug from under them. Giving them the feeling that they know what's happening—and then telling them they've been manipulated. That's part of things like three-card monte, and the shell game. You give them the impression, with a bent corner on the card for example, when you're tossing the cards, the money card seems to have a bent corner so everybody's now betting because they see the bent corner, and how that bent corner is no longer on the money card, but another card altogether. Those are sucker gags. You let them think they've got you—and then you pull the rug from under them.

Judd: And that's the card you have the money riding on.

Harry: It's toying with them and doing what a swindler would do when he's taking their money, only there's no harm, there's nothing to be lost. You can poke somebody in the arm, and it can be affectionate. You know it could be a "How ya doing?" A friendly gesture. Or you can hit them, and it hurts. Same gesture, different intent. This is tricking people but to no bad end—just to make them laugh. That's what I'm going for.

JAMES L. BROOKS
(2014)

I interviewed James Brooks on the morning we all found out that our friend Mike Nichols had passed away. When Jim walked into my office, I could see in his face that he was devastated—and I wasn't sure whether we should even bother doing the interview or not. But in this raw, grief-stricken state Jim became reflective about Mike's work and his decades-long friendship with this man we respected so much. Which then led to an interesting conversation about comedy and life—the man is truly wise in these ways—that could only have happened on a terrible day.

Judd Apatow: Awful day with Mike Nichols, huh?

James L. (Jim) Brooks: Awful fucking day. I got up at five this morning. I just happened to wake up and I saw the news of his death, and—I was alone, and I just went over and started reading this horrible *New York Times* obituary that I'm sure will be gone by tomorrow.

Judd: Really?

Jim: Horrible. Just a list of hits and misses.

Judd: Mm-hmm.

Jim: Have you ever seen the sketch he did with Elaine [May], "The $65 Funeral"? You've seen that?

Judd: Not in a long time.

Jim: It's killer. You see him making fun of death and stuff like that, right there, and you laugh. And then you start reading some of the crazy, open, honest stuff he's been saying of late and—he's never to be equaled. It's literally impossible to beat him. Impossible. And, I've just been—I'm still in a fog, because of the enormity of it.

Judd: Yeah. I just knew him in the last few years, but he showed *This Is 40* in New York before it came out. He presented it onstage.

Jim: Wow.

Judd: And he was so nice to me. Scott Rudin set up a screening of *This Is 40* for twenty-five people during the day in New York, and Mike came up to me afterwards, and he was crying, in the most beautiful, connected way. Then he wrote letters to each of my children, talking to them in great detail about what they had accomplished in the movie. To my little daughter, he said, "One day you're going to realize that you kind of captured life." It was so kind, and he was always like that.

Jim: For a long, long time. Extraordinary generosity. He sent out love, he did. And the most acerbic wit. Don't ever be chopped up by Mike Nichols. You'll just never recover from it.

Judd: What do you think it is that he did for actors? Why did they love him so much?

Jim: I know what he did for them, because I've asked so many of them. The bottom line is, it was never put better than: When you do something wrong, he says it's his fault; when you do something right, it's the most glorious thing God ever created. Richard Burton, who—I mean, drunk, mean guy—once said, "It's not like he's directing you. It's like he's conspiring to make you your best." Mike was a great director of actors. I don't have that tenderness and generosity.

Judd: Did he read your scripts? Was he one of the people you would go to?

Jim: He was. I was talking to him a lot about the one I'm writing now. He was very there for it. I didn't want him to read it yet, but he had heard me talking about it and it was special, the way he told me he wanted to "be there" for it. It's so important who your buddy is. He was like, Let me be your buddy on this.

Judd: There's very few people in life who you feel like you can talk about this type of work with.

Jim: Yeah. By the way, here's a question. Tell me who else holds up like Mike and Elaine, where the work is still so vital and vivid, and doesn't lose anything.

Judd: It's very different, but I think a lot of what George Carlin was talking about in the last five years of his life will hold up for a long time, when he got really angry and cut right to the heart of how he felt about everything. And I've been listening to the old Pryor stuff, and although it is of its time—I mean, if you listen to Pryor 1976, as the bicentennial is coming, talking about what's wrong with America? I forgot how militant he was. I don't think anyone talks about politics like that now. No one has the guts to do it that way anymore.

Jim: Yeah.

Judd: What do you think Mike's purpose was in his work, and how does it relate to yours?

Jim: Oh, I don't think like that. There really is a word for what he did: *inspirational*. It just is good for your internal ethos. Anyway. How did you get started interviewing comedians?

Judd: When I was a kid, a high school kid, I had a radio show and I just started talking to all these people. I interviewed fifty people. Leno and Seinfeld, but back when they were just guys on *The Merv Griffin Show*. Paul Reiser, Howard Stern, John Candy—

Jim: (*Whistles*)

Judd: I even interviewed Lorenzo Music and Jim Parker, writers from *Mary Tyler Moore* and *The Bob Newhart Show*.

Jim: (*Laughs*) It's funny because I did that with my student newspaper, too. Not with comedians, though.

Judd: You interviewed Louis Armstrong, right?

Jim: Yes. I talk about that all the time, Louis Armstrong, because I asked him a great question. I said, "How do you keep your lips going?" And the answer was at least nineteen minutes long. And he showed me his lip ointments and the process for when they go in. It was great.

Judd: (*Laughs*) Who else did you interview?

Jim: Singers. Some of them were big names. I was nobody. But my picture was in the high school paper every week, standing there with the person I was interviewing.

Judd: (*Laughs*) Yeah, the kids at your high school hated you.

Jim: They loathed me.

Judd: (*Laughs*) They turned on you. That's funny. The funniest thing, to me, is when a kid thinks, *I've got to get out of here.* I had that sense.

Jim: You knew you would get out? Did you feel like you had the power to get out?

Judd: Well, yeah. I thought, *These comedians are all from Long Island, and I'm from Long Island. I'm not that different from them.* I'd just sit with Seinfeld and go, "How do you write a joke?" And he'd walk me through a routine.

Jim: Wow. Wow. That was back when?

Judd: Nineteen eighty-four. Anyway, I think so much of why people get into comedy is out of some sense of feeling abandoned. When I was a kid, my parents got divorced. My mom left—

Jim: Your mom left, not your father?

Judd: Yeah. She moved out, and that was the thing. As a kid I thought, *No one's mom leaves. The dad always leaves. Why would she leave?*

Jim: You were how old?

Judd: Thirteen. But then the rest of your life, on some level, you feel that sense of inadequacy.

Jim: Did your mom maintain contact with you?

Judd: Yeah. But she had a bit of a mental break after the divorce. She claimed that she thought she was going to leave and come right back, and my dad immediately moved his girlfriend in. Right before she died, she told me, "I always thought I was going to come right back. I always thought it was going to be a couple of weeks."

Jim: Wow.

Judd: She called one day and asked me to read her the number on my dad's credit card, because she needed it for something. But really, she was just angry—and she blew thirty thousand dollars that they didn't have. It all went downhill from there.

Jim: Jesus Christ, Judd.

Judd: So I figured I needed to get a job. And that made me want to get into comedy, and to get to know comedians. It made me think, *If I start five years before everyone else, I'm going to be safe.* So, a lot of the need to be productive is the terror of things falling apart. Do you feel like that's a part of your thing?

Jim: I'm staggered by your story.

Judd: (*Laughs*)

Jim: You drop that and then turn it into a question? Are you kidding? It's a life experience here, that story.

Judd: As I said to someone recently, I'm trying to fuck my kids up *just* enough so they'll want to get a job.

Jim: (*Laughs*)

Judd: I'll tell you another funny thing. I lived alone with my dad. My sister lived with my mom, and then my sister and my brother both moved in with my grandparents in California. So, I'm alone with my dad, and when I left for college, on the way to the airport—I was on my way to USC film school, which was a big achievement for me—my dad tried to convince me not to go. He was begging me to open up a video and CD store with him. Which is the worst business. It's like—

Jim: It's been eradicated from the earth.

Judd: My dad almost ended my entire career and life. He begged me to stay and open this store with him.

Jim: Jesus. Jesus.

Judd: But that's the drive, I think. It's fear. I don't know how you feel about this, but I always say, when a movie comes out, I don't get that much satisfaction when it goes well. I feel comfortable in process, but when it's over, I don't actually get—I enjoy being in the middle, working towards something, because there's a feeling of safety. I feel like I'm doing something.

Jim: When I'm writing, and I go through all the stuff you go through, the one thing I got is: It's worth it. Writing is worth it.

Judd: Yeah.

Jim: You know? Someone says, "What do you do for a living?" and it takes you so long to say, "I'm a writer." I'm working as a writer, and so I always— that really calms me. Even when I'm going nuts with it, even when it's impossible, I say, Boy, this is a legitimate thing to be. This is worth going nuts about.

Judd: Yeah.

Jim: Directing is a different story.

Judd: It is.

Jim: But I think of it as an extension of writing. And it's fun to discover that when you leave the movie you had in your mind when the process began, that's always—I think Mike Nichols said it best. He said, "Every day there's a surprise, something you didn't expect. And that's the joy of making movies."

Judd: But do you feel the work, for you, comes from a healthy place or—

Jim: I think everything is great. Any kind of movie you make is great, you know. It's wonderful, wherever it takes you. But to me, the golden ring is when you get to do a movie *and* self-express. More and more, the process of making a movie has become: Don't you dare complain.

Judd: Yeah.

Jim: If you have that going for you, don't you breathe.

Judd: If they don't throw a superhero in it, you've won.

Jim: Yeah.

Judd: Do you notice common themes or things you're trying to work out, when you look back at what you've done?

Jim: You know, I mean there's—I guess self-consciousness. People use the word *ego* all the time, but self-consciousness kills. You can't do your best work when you're self-conscious, when you're conscious of yourself. So the most I get is every once in a while I'll read over something, and I'll recognize, *That's my shit. That's what I do.*

Judd: That's me.

Jim: Right. And then I try not to feel good about that, but I do.

Judd: Sometimes I think that's as close as I get to a spiritual moment. The moment of creation is the closest I feel to a godlike experience of connecting with something larger.

Jim: I think the whole thing with writing—generally, you push and push and push and then, come on already, when do you pull? At a certain point, it pulls.

Judd: It comes together?

Jim: No, I mean it's pulling you forward and you're not working so hard. You're not laboring. You're serving. Laboring becomes serving.

Judd: I remember hearing you talk once about serving the characters and honoring the characters, and I had never thought about it in that sense before. As if your characters were real people and you were trying to do right by them, as the writer.

Jim: And the constituency they represent.

Judd: Yeah, that was the first time I heard it framed that way, and that had a big impact on me. Like, *Oh, wow, this stuff is important.* I think a lot about your work, and what I connected to when I was young, because I was born in '67. What year did *Mary Tyler Moore* come out?

Jim: Nineteen-seventy.

Judd: And what year was *Room 222*?

Jim: Two years earlier.

Judd: Did they overlap?

Jim: Yes. *Room 222* was running the first three years *Mary* was on.

Judd: Wow. For me, those shows—and this was at a time when the whole country was watching ten or twelve shows—they programmed my mind. Your shows and Norman Lear's shows, Larry Gelbart: Those shows, those characters, had a big effect. They were a part of your day, the struggles of those people, and the humanity of those shows. It's like building neuropathways for morality and compassion. I remembered when *Rhoda*—was that the first show that had a gay character on it?

Jim: No, we did an episode of *Mary*, and we made one of the characters gay, and it was a big deal. I had a thing where one of our jobs was, you know—we were doing this during the feminist revolution, which everything seemed to be centered on, and everybody wanted us to say this, or say that, and you're just slapping hands off the wheel. I'm very much against proselytizing, unless it comes from the characters as an expression of who they are. I mean, Norman Lear did it—that's who he is—but that's not who I am. He broke down barriers. Things were so tightass then.

Judd: Yeah.

Jim: And we followed his show, which was the best thing that happened to us.

Judd: You were on right after. So that night on TV was *All in the Family* and *Mary Tyler Moore*, *M*A*S*H*, *The Bob Newhart Show*, and then *Carol Burnett*?

Jim: It was a great night.

Judd: A perfect night.

Jim: The last big Saturday night.

Judd: It's completely different now, because no one's watching any show in those kinds of numbers. The biggest night of *Breaking Bad* is half of what *The Mary Tyler Moore Show* would get.

Jim: I had a show canceled with a thirty-five share. (*Laughs*)

Judd: How do you think that changes the culture, the fact that we're not watching the same things together anymore?

Jim: Well, it's changed it enormously. Look at sports. Or *American Idol*, a few years ago. These are the only kinds of things that bring people to the watering hole now, you know? We all come and talk about it the next day. We're all bound together. We all had a common experience. All of that is changing. There's a price to that.

Judd: Yeah.

Jim: But television is still the greatest job. We agree on that, right? Television is the greatest job?

Judd: Yes. Yes. So, was *Mary Tyler Moore* eight seasons?

Jim: Seven.

Judd: Seven seasons, and it went right into *Lou Grant*.

Jim: Yes.

Judd: That was one of the great transitions of all time.

Jim: Yeah. When is a spin-off not a spin-off?

Judd: I used to love that show.

Jim: You know what was so great about that? We got our stories from the newspapers, literally.

Judd: And so after *Mary Tyler Moore*, you went into *Taxi*?

Jim: Mm-hmm.

Judd: What was that like, working with Andy Kaufman?

Jim: He'd always be in character. He was great. I tell Andy stories all the time. How can you resist Andy stories? He invented performance art, just amazing, bizarre stuff. But when you gave him notes, he'd be in that character, and you'd give him notes and it would be like he was Latka with an American talking fast at him. And then he'd do the note. He'd always do the note.

Judd: But he was in character the whole time he was on set?

Jim: Yes.

Judd: Did you have private moments with him when he *wasn't* in character?

Jim: My favorite private moment with him was when he was hospitalized after the wrestling match, and I found out it was all a fake.

Judd: Who told you?

Jim: We had been really scared. We were running the tape and then we froze up and we saw—he did a very difficult physical stunt, a brilliant physical stunt. There's no way a stuntman could do that stunt better than he did. That's how good Andy was. And I was pissed off because—

Judd: Because he scared everyone?

Jim: This was on front pages! Yeah. And I said, "Do you know what it's like to think you were seriously injured?" And he says, "Do you know what it's like to be in traction for a few days?" (*Laughs*)

Judd: (*Laughs*) For no reason. Where were you when you had that conversation?

Jim: I was in my office and I think he was still in the hospital. I don't know.

Judd: And so when he would make a joke like that, what was his tone like? Did he ever talk about what the purpose of it was?

Jim: He'd talk like a guy who just came up with a good bit.

Judd: To him the bit was just riling people up? There's no point to it, really, other than isn't it funny that you're going to get upset about this?

Jim: He was inventing an art form, for Christ sake. He was an original talent.

Judd: You spent years around him, but there were very few moments when he would drop it and say, "The reason I'm doing this is because . . ."

Jim: It was deeper than that. And it's not even a question of dropping it. He was *in* it.

Judd: Writer-wise, *Taxi* was like the all-star team of all time. Has there ever been more great writers in the same space at once?

Jim: We had a great time. We really worked. It was great. The Charles brothers. David Lloyd. It just worked. And the cast was great, too. We had fun. We had a party every Friday night. And this was in the days when —

Judd: When everyone was on that lot?

Jim: Yes. And it was literally segregated. Television people used one entrance and movie people used another. At that time, nobody who ever worked in television got a movie job. But you know that.

Judd: You couldn't be a movie star *and* a television star.

Jim: You couldn't get a job. You couldn't get a writing job. Nobody was interested. You did television. You were lower order.

Judd: Even as a writer, you couldn't cross over?

Jim: There were a few people who made it over the fence in the early eighties. But the fence was still up — which was great, because you not only had a job you loved, and were making terrific money, but you also got to feel like an underdog. (*Laughs*)

Judd: While you were getting rich.

Jim: It was bliss. It was just bliss. Yadda, yadda, yadda.

Judd: And was that the great moment for you? I feel like, in my life, there was a brief moment where we were all together and then people started splitting off and doing different things, but still, there was that one moment where everyone is around each other for a while. Was *Taxi* your special moment, where everyone was at the perfect level of their career to bond and not be behind their gates and split off?

Jim: Yes, it was perfect. It was a community, a real community. Everyone's working. Everyone's having fun, doing something. I mean, that's it, you know?

Judd: And that's about when you started directing movies, right? With *Starting Over*?

Jim: Yes.

Judd: That was a big movie in our house. My dad and my mom really looked at that as one of the great, hilarious movies. They talked about it a lot.

Jim: Jesus.

Judd: Maybe because they were on the verge of breaking up, but they would talk about Candice Bergen singing that song, and it was one of their favorite moments of all time. But is that why you asked Burt Reynolds to do *Terms of Endearment*, because you had just worked with him in *Starting Over*?

Jim: No, I wasn't quite that foolish. (*Laughs*) I couldn't get *Terms* made. I forget what the budget was, but it was modest, and I couldn't come up with the money. But then Burt said he'd do it, and that made it happen. And then I'm revving up, doing the rest of the casting, and his publicity agent calls me and says, "Burt's not doing your movie, but he wants you to know he loves you." He'd taken another role.

Judd: Did the whole thing kind of fall apart at that moment?

Jim: Yeah.

Judd: So who became the great supporter of *Terms of Endearment*?

Jim: Grant Tinker, who had gone over to NBC, and pre-bought it for television.

Judd: I've never even heard of that.

Jim: That gave me the final million.

Judd: That's a good friend.

Jim: Great boss. A great boss. My obsession with the movie was that it was a literal comedy.

Judd: About cancer.

Jim: I wanted to do a truthful movie, but—I went through arguments with the Golden Globes where the studio had to put a muzzle on me because

I classified my movie as a comedy and they classified it as a drama, and it was the whole point that I was doing a comedy. I lost that one and I won drama—but then, afterwards, when people didn't see it in theaters, the solitary experience, I think, is, you know, it's not a comedy. It's in a completely different tone because you're watching it alone, I think.

Judd: Because in the theater, it murdered.

Jim: Yeah, it did.

Judd: Why do you think it has transcended? I think a lot about culture, how quickly things disappear now. There's so much new stuff, but these shows and movies, they're timeless, whether it's *Mary Tyler Moore* or *Terms of Endearment*—they are surviving. What do you think they have in common?

Jim: I don't know. Humanity?

Judd: What do you think you did right as a parent?

Jim: Oh, God. It was an awful house my kids grew up in.

Judd: Yeah?

Jim: I don't know. (*Laughs*) Would anybody ask what your parents did right to produce you?

Judd: Well, I think it's always a combination of your parents love you and you watch their mistakes and some kids take some things from the mistakes, and some kids are injured from the mistakes—

Jim: That's true. Jesus, why does everything you say sound so good? (*Laughs*)

Judd: I'm just trying to calm myself down.

Jim: Can you heal, do you think?

Judd: I notice with my friends' kids, some of them crash early, and then they pull out, and they're kind of awesome and funny and interesting. Other kids seem kind of great, and they have trouble later, and it's fascinating how parenting relates to this environment—you've written a lot about it—in *Spanglish*, which is about how money and doing everything right doesn't always make a great kid—

Jim: My whole goal in *Spanglish*—I had this kind of thing in my mind. I wanted to show the father as the saving parent instead of the mother as the saving parent. It was a big deal for me, because I was so tired of those things where Dad learns to feel.

Judd: Yeah. (*Laughs*) Yeah.

Jim: I spent a lot of time as a parent thinking it was my duty to give my kids the lessons of being poor when they weren't.

Judd: Yeah.

Jim: It took me so long to stop—you know?

Judd: They're never going to appreciate it like you did.

Jim: It took me so long to get off it. I want them to be from New Jersey, and they're from Brentwood.

Judd: You think, *Can my kids do well if they're not embarrassed that they didn't grow up in pain and poverty?*

Jim: I think, in some ways, the worst thing I did as a parent is that I passed on the embarrassment of riches, as if they should be embarrassed.

Judd: I have that, too. As a kid I always said, "I want to leave this town," but there's no moment where my kids are like, "We've got to get the fuck out of Brentwood." Why would you leave? My daughter, it's time for her to get a car, and I think, *My dad didn't get me a car.* It wasn't even discussed as a possibility. And you think, *How spoiled—am I teaching her a lesson by getting her a shitbox? But I want it to be safe.* And you're terrified that somehow it's going to ruin her.

Jim: Yes, yes, yes. A shitbox with a five-star rating.

JAY LENO
(1984)

When I was a kid, Jay Leno was hands-down my favorite stand-up co-median. He wasn't the host of anything yet, of course. He was a semiregu-lar guest on *Late Night with David Letterman* and I went to see him several times at clubs in Long Island during high school. He was a master. He would tear down the house. His act worked so well because he was a pure workingman's comic. He was real. He talked about the things that annoyed him, he had brilliant observations, and it was all just about as good as a stand-up act in a comedy club can possibly be.

I have gotten to know Jay a bit in the years since our interview, and he's been nothing but nice to me, for reasons I still do not understand. He did this interview with me when I was in high school, first of all. Then, when I was in college, I sent him a whole list of jokes to see if he'd buy them for his *Tonight Show* monologues. And one night, not long after, my grand-mother knocked on my door and said, "Jay Leno's on the phone." I didn't believe her. But I went to the phone anyway, and this voice said, "Hi, Judd. I read your jokes. They're not quite there yet. They're close, but they're not quite there," and then he proceeded to explain to me what, exactly, was wrong with my jokes in the kindest possible terms. He was so generous and encouraging, I didn't even realize that I was being rejected. That's not easy to do, to call a kid and tell him that his jokes aren't good, and the way he did it just made me want to work harder. It also made me want to treat people kindly, the way Jay treated me.

Then, much later, when I started directing my own movies, Jay would always book me as a guest on *The Tonight Show*. I never told him that one of the main reasons why I started making movies in the first place—why, from as early as I can remember, I wanted to get into this business—was so that I could one day become successful enough to be a guest on *The Tonight Show*. For me, *The Tonight Show* was the endgame, period. Sometimes I think movies were just a way to get there.

Jay Leno: Is there an interview, or am I just talking?

Judd Apatow: Well, yeah, you're talking to me. That kinda thing. Okay, um—I know it's hard to get going, but once you get going—

Jay: Okay.

Judd: Where are you right now in your career, if you had to describe it?

Jay: Ah, about twenty-five miles outside of New Jers—outside of New York. I guess I'm in Jersey right now. Where am I? I have no idea. I mean, the last two years or so I've been doing the Letterman show a lot and that seems to have helped an awful lot. You know, the clubs are kind of full on Wednesday now, instead of just the weekends, so that's nice. But I don't know, I'm too close to it. I can't tell.

Judd: You're a draw, but you're not pulling like Universal Amphitheatre or anything.

Jay: (*Laughs*) No, but—I really can't tell. I mean, I like this stage of my career. Because I'm at the point where I know if the stuff is still funny. The audience is still at the point where, unless it's funny, they don't laugh. They might like you going in, but if it's not funny, they don't laugh. Sometimes when you get real big, they laugh at stuff that's really not that funny and you don't know anymore.

Judd: Are you happy doing the clubs or would you like to play the larger audiences?

Jay: I like doing the clubs. Two hundred to four hundred seats is about the maximum for ideal comedy, where you play with the crowd and all. I mean, obviously the big rooms are nice because there's more money. But performance-wise, the smaller rooms are more fun to do. I mean, it's like anything else. I like this. I'm happy where I am now, and—you know, the

This interview took place in the office at Rascals Comedy Club in West Orange, New Jersey, in 1984.

whole idea is if you keep coming up with new ideas and new material, everything else just falls into place.

Judd: Who are the people that you've opened up for?

Jay: Oh, everybody. Everybody from Stan Getz, Mose Allison, Rahsaan Roland Kirk, Chick Corea, all the way to like John Denver, Tom Jones, Perry Como, Kris Kristofferson. All kinds of people.

Judd: I thought I saw you once on *Laverne & Shirley*.

Jay: Oh!

Judd: What is the point of doing that show at this stage in your career?

Jay: Well, the point of doing that show is the same point of doing this show. Somebody asks you to do it, and you go, *Well, why not? I like Penny and Cindy and all those people, they're good friends.* People ask you to do the show, and it's nice. I mean, okay, the show is not exactly *King Lear*, but that's all right.

Judd: But it's the kind of thing you make fun of in your act.

Jay: It is. Sure it is. But I'm not above doing something I make fun of in my act. I also eat at McDonald's and all those other things I make fun of. That's all a part of the business, you know. I do *Hollywood Squares*. I do whatever people ask me to do. Unless it's something which is just totally, oh, I don't know, I mean, sexist or racist or something of that nature. But when you do those kinds of shows it just helps, you know. When I'm on TV, I'm either on *The Tonight Show* or the Letterman show, which is on after eleven-thirty at night in most parts of the country. Consequently, there's a whole generation of people that never see you or know who you are. So when you do a show like *Laverne & Shirley*, it gives my relatives a chance to see me on television.

Judd: Would you want more people knowing you? Is that something you want?

Jay: That's something every performer tries to get. It's like anything else: You do your work and the more people you can please with it, the better it makes you feel.

Judd: What prompted you to go into this?

Jay: Oh, I don't know, it seemed like a fun way to make money at the time. I was in college, and I used to do ah—all those college shows, you know, like in Boston there are two hundred or three hundred colleges. So consequently every Saturday the cafeteria would become the Two Toke Café or something like this. And there would be nineteen-year-old folksingers with guitars ODing on the stage, and I used to emcee some of this stuff. And I would ah—you know, I would say, "That was so-and-so." Boo, get off the stage, man you stink, get outta here. The audience was terrible, I was terrible, the acts were terrible. But it was fun being onstage and screwing around and—I started going around other coffeehouses and things like that and getting onstage. I was making five bucks, six bucks a night, which is what friends of mine who were waiters and waitresses were making at the time.

Judd: When you were in college?

Jay: Yeah. Colleges. I used to work strip joints. All kinds of places like that.

Judd: Strip joints? How did that work out?

Jay: Oh, your eyes light up, huh? Well, there were no comedy clubs.

Judd: What year is this?

Jay: Seventy-three, '74. Most of the comedy clubs didn't come along until about '77, so the only place you could work was strip joints. You know, I had read Lenny Bruce and Milton Berle and all those people, and they all seem to have gotten their start in strip joints. So I used to go in and do strip joints. They were terrible. I was like nineteen, with long hair. It was terrible. But I thought it was fun.

Judd: What kind of reactions did you get?

Jay: Terrible. "Get off the stage, you stink." I had a guy jump me with a Heinz ketchup bottle once. Split my head open. I got eight stitches on that one.

Judd: Why'd he do that?

Jay: (*Laughs*) Why? Why did he do that? I don't know. Why do people beat up grandmothers and rob their purses? You want a rational explanation for why a guy came onstage and hit me on the head, and knocked me out? I don't know. If I knew why, I wouldn't have done it.

Judd: What did you study in college?

Jay: I don't know. My mom has the degree in the living room. Ah, speech therapy. I went to college and I said, "What requires the least amount of studying?" Speech courses had—at the end of the year you had to give a talk. I figured, well, I can do that. So I get up and give my talk and get a C and then get out of there.

Judd: So you're doing comedy at that point, at the end of college. You knew that was what you were going into?

Jay: Well, I was also a Mercedes-Benz mechanic at the time. I didn't have any expenses. I didn't have any lifestyle to maintain. I liked doing it. I would drive hundreds and hundreds of miles to work for free for four or five minutes. I didn't know if I would ever really make a living at it. It was just a fun way to screw around. I'd make thirty bucks a week or forty bucks a week at best. But that was enough to live on. I had a junky car, and it was fun, you know. But that's the whole key. You gotta keep moving. You gotta work every kind of job there is. I used to do old people's birthday parties for the state. Which is *real* depressing. I had a friend who worked in social services in Massachusetts, and I'd get like eight bucks to drive out to Duxbury, to an old folks' home. And it would be like, (*quietly*) "Bessy, we have a comedian here, you know." Oh, it was real. I mean they were nice old people. And they would kind of look at ya. It was sad. Real bizarre.

Judd: You sound like you've played, like, any kind of place where people congregate anywhere.

Jay: What do you mean, I still do.

Judd: What are the other strange places?

Jay: Everything. Indian reservations, any kind of job I could get. You know, that's it. You learn from the bad jobs. You don't learn anything from the good jobs. When you go into a club and everybody's happy to see you and you do your jokes, and the jokes that normally don't work, work, you say, well, this is terrible. Give me a place that's awful. Like I was in New Mexico a while ago at an Indian reservation, just a very strange setup. Nice people, but—and they laughed. So I said, Okay, this stuff is gonna work on the Letterman show.

Judd: And how did you progress to better places?

Jay: Well, what happens is you get better money after a while. The places don't get any better. You know, it just depends how much respect you get.

Judd: How did your comedy change over the years?

Jay: How? Well, I don't know. I mean, you just get better the more you do. The real trick is to listen to it and throw out everything that's not funny. You've interviewed a lot of comedians, you've seen a lot of comedians. I'm sure you've seen a lot of new people, too. And I'm always amazed when I go to clubs and I see new comedians, and night after night they do the same jokes that don't work. If a joke doesn't work, you just get rid of it and do something else. Better you do eight minutes of really funny stuff than sixteen minutes of hit-and-miss, you know. That really seems to be the whole key to it. You bring a tape recorder, you tape it, you say, *Gee, every night, this kind of gets a laugh, but not really.* Well, get rid of it. It's not etched in gold, you know.

Judd: And when did you start doing talk shows like *Mike Douglas* or *Dinah Shore*?

Jay: First show I ever did was *Merv Griffin*. Then about a year and a half went by where I didn't do anything. Then I did *The Tonight Show*, and that's where everything really started moving. *The Tonight Show* kind of officially puts you in show business, you know.

Judd: Is acting something you want to do?

Jay: I like doing this better. I mean, doing films is fun. I'm not as—when I do a scene in a film I have to stop and say to somebody, "Is that any good? How was that?" Whereas in comedy, I hear the laugh, great, I know it worked, thank you, goodbye, I'm outta there.

Judd: Right now you're doing *Letterman* every month. Is he someone you knew before?

Jay: Yeah, I knew David years ago in L.A. We both used to write for Jimmie Walker.

Judd: You wrote for Jimmie Walker?

Jay: Yeah, yeah. We both used to write comedy. Jimmie was great. Any struggling comic, Jimmie would pay them a hundred bucks a week, and we'd meet once a week at his house, and throw jokes around and ideas, and—it worked out pretty good. He was real good to a lot of people that way.

Judd: What about comedy albums? Have you ever wanted to do that?

Jay: I don't buy comedy albums myself, and I'm a comedian. So no, I don't have any interest in them. I mean, if I was gonna take every joke I've ever done and never do it again, then I might put it on an album and sell it. I know, as a kid, I would get annoyed if I buy a comedy album and then go to a nightclub and see the guy and for an hour, I hear exactly what was on the album. I'd rather do it this way, kind of door-to-door comedy, and do my act.

Judd: How would you describe your comedy if you had to? It's a little sarcastic and observational—

Jay: (*Laughs*) That about sums it up. Sarcastic and observational. I don't know. I try not to—you know, I don't even say I'm a comedian onstage. I just do it and let people form their own opinion about what it is. To sit and pontificate about the wonder of it all is a bit narcissistic. You just do it. As you move along with the business, you get a little bit more experienced. Like now I can go into *Letterman*, think of a joke that day, and do it on the show and there's a ninety-nine percent chance it'll work. Whereas the old days, you kind of had to go over the routine more and more. Working with an audience is like being an animal trainer. If you go in the ring and you're a little bit nervous and your hand's shaking, the animals sense it and they rip you apart. Same thing with audiences. If you get up there and go, "Well, hi, everybody . . . ah, how you doing . . . ah, ah, ah . . . ," people go, "Get off the stage!" They're not gonna laugh. But if you use a little bit of authority and kind of take charge . . .

Judd: Is most of your humor worked out on the stage? Some people work it out on paper, and they think about it—

Jay: Oh no, I don't have anything on paper. I've never written anything down. I suppose I should. Everybody says, Oh, you should make notes. I seem to remember the funnier stuff and forget the stuff that isn't that funny. Once in a while I forget a funny one, but no, I don't write anything down.

Judd: Why do you think in the last couple of years, tons and tons of clubs have been opening up all over the place?

Jay: It's like anything else. Tons and tons of clubs are closing all over the place and a few good ones will remain. I mean, I think it's great. It gives everybody a chance to work. There's good and there's bad sides to it. The good side is everybody gets a chance to work. The bad side is people that probably would not be in the business are still around.

Judd: Right now, you know, it's like—there's hundreds of people getting into it—

Jay: There's thousands. When I used to audition at the Improv—you know, the Improv in New York would have audition nights, same as Catch a Rising Star. And we would go there and there would only be four people auditioning. Suddenly there are thousands. You go to the Improv on the audition nights and they're lined up around the block.

Judd: So how do you keep it from getting boring?

Jay: It's a job. You have to do your work, you know. It's not a hard way to make a living, it's a fun way. You make a lot of money for having a good time. And if you can't get up for it, well then get out of the business. You know people say, Well, gee, what happens when you're just not in the mood? Well, I mean, the worst I ever had was a bad hour. You know, most people have a bad day. If I can't fake it for an hour . . .

Judd: But don't you ever get bored of it?

Jay: I get a kick out of doing it. I change it a little bit on a nightly basis, try out new jokes and whatnot. The whole idea is to keep coming with new things and new ideas. No, it doesn't get boring for me. I really like it.

Judd: A lot of your act is about television. Television commercials. What do you think about television? Do you think it's really bad, because it seems like you really just—I mean you must watch it—

Jay: No I don't. I mean, again: The whole trick to being a successful comedian is to make fun of the things you like. Occasionally when I really go after something I don't like—it can come off vicious. People sense a hostility. I'm an average person, I watch a lot of TV. Admittedly, there's a lot of stupid things on TV, but I have to watch it to make fun of it. And the fact that I'm talking about a show like *Manimal* or some incredibly stupid program like this—everybody laughs. They must have seen the show, too. So you find a common bond with people. The whole thing to do in comedy is finding a common bond with people in the audience. Everybody has a TV, so you talk about TV. If everybody had elephants, you'd talk about elephants. If you go right to television, old, young, right away everybody understands where you're coming from.

Judd: Once, on *Letterman*, you just took out a *TV Guide*.

Jay: Yeah, that was the last time. I started reading about shows that were on.

Judd: And you just opened it, 'cause it looked like you were just—

Jay: Well, I had looked through the *TV Guide* earlier that day. That was an example of what I was talking about a minute ago. The real trick to doing the comedy, the real trick to knowing if you're growing or not is— like, when I look at my first *Tonight Show*, there were a lot of jokes in it. I mean, *joke* jokes. Then one day I was sitting in a restaurant with a bunch of comedian friends, after a show, and everybody's talking. And I was telling some stupid story about something that happened on the road. It's one of those stories that didn't have a beginning or an end. It just had a lot of—a lot of middle stuff. And everybody's laughing. And I see, *Gee, they're laughing harder with this than anything else I do in my act.* So the next night onstage I just got up and started talking, telling that story. You know, I said to the audience, "This doesn't have a beginning or an end. I went into this store . . ." And everybody was laughing the same way. And I real- ized, *Ooh, here is a major breakthrough for me. Because here's a chance to just talk and be funny as opposed to sitting down trying to think up a rou- tine and how to* structure *it.* And that's how you grow.

Judd: How do you handle hecklers?

Jay: The trick to working with hecklers is to give them enough rope so they hang themselves. I like a good heckler. Somebody who's intelligent, who I speak to and they speak back, and I say something to them, and they say something to me. Everybody gets *yeah yeah*—those kind of hecklers. And those are awful, but the real trick is working in inverse proportion to the heckler. For example, if I have a guy that says, "Hey, what are you doing?" You know, some real dumb-sounding guy. Then I go, "Well, ex- cuse me, ladies and gentlemen, obviously an English professor here to- night." Boom, boom, boom, boom. You just work the opposite. You try to throw them off guard. And most hecklers will back down. The second time you say, "What's that, sir?" (*Timidly*) "Oh, ah, I just want to say you're a jerk." I like to have fun with them. I'm never hostile with anybody, un- less it's somebody who is just totally abusive. Then you can go for the throat.

Judd: What would be your strangest experiences in comedy?

Jay: My strangest experiences? Oh, I don't know. God, I mean there's thousands of them. I used to work the Playboy Club in New York and they would give a report card after each show. You know, like have a guy like Vinny from the Bronx: "Hey, you get a D tonight. I didn't think you were that funny." And they would tell you how they would mail these to Mr. Hefner to look at, you know, that kind of thing. So I'm working there one time and they—you know, they get tour groups in there—and they've got three hundred Portuguese and two interpreters. Nobody tells me they're Portuguese. You know, I don't know. So I go out there and I start my act, and I hear these two guys going, "Heh, heh, heh." I hear two guys laugh- ing and the rest of the audience is just staring at me. I said, "How you folks doing?" And they would smile and nod. But they didn't speak English or anything. So I'm out there, like, this is unbelievable at this point. Finally one of the interpreters yells out that they're Portuguese. So I come offstage and Vinny the room director says, "You get an F." I said, "What're you talking about?" He says, "You get an F, pal. Nobody laughed tonight except them two guys." And I said, "Come on, they didn't speak *English*." He goes, "Well, you shoulda done Portuguese material." I said, "Yeah, you're right, it's my fault." And I have to sign this thing that says F on it. It was the stupidest experience of my life.

Judd: So, where do you want to go with this? You're working a lot now. Is there something else that you want to be doing?

Jay: No, I like doing this. I enjoy it. I have a good time with it. If something else comes along and someone offers something else, I'll try that for a while. But there's nothing I enjoy doing more than this. I find it as challenging as anything else you can do. And I really haven't reached a peak where I'm famous enough to go, Well, everybody's seen the act, let's try something else. When that happens, maybe I'll try something else.

JEFF GARLIN
(2013)

In the late eighties, when I was on the road as a struggling stand-up comedian, I had the pleasure of opening a few times for a young guy named Jeff Garlin. His act was loose and weird and improvisational in a way I could never hope to replicate. He looked so happy up there. He seemed to enjoy getting huge laughs as much as he enjoyed creating awkward moments. And when you're on the road with somebody, going from club to club and town to town, you get to know that person pretty well. And nobody's more fun to be on the road with than Jeff. We would be driving down some small-town street and there would be a fast-food restaurant on every single corner, and Jeff would say, "I wonder if there's a fast-food restaurant around here?" We would drive some more, and there would be seven banks in a row, and Jeff would say, "Do you think they have a bank in this town?"

Jeff, of course, would go on to be one of the minds behind *Curb Your Enthusiasm* and one of the stars of *The Goldbergs*, but to me he'll always be this special individual who is somehow able to make something new happen every moment you're with him.

Judd Apatow: Is it important to you if your kids are smart?

Jeff Garlin: No. I mean, yes, I hope they're smart and self-reliant so they can enjoy life—but they'll probably be more miserable if they're smart. If they're stupid, they're going to have a great time. Because really, everything is created for stupid people. Books, movies, TV shows for the most

This interview originally took place in front of a live audience at the Largo in Los Angeles for Jeff's podcast.

part—they're for stupid people. So, they would be much happier if they were stupid. But I think both my boys are going to be miserable just like their father.

Judd: So they'll be smart and miserable.

Jeff: Well, they go hand in hand.

Judd: Yeah.

Jeff: Do you know any smart people who are just, like, chill? Really happy? No, seriously, do you know any smart people just, like, "Hey, weeeee!" You don't, do you?

Judd: I don't. I mean, I don't think I'm smart. But I think I'm beginning to think I'm smart based on how miserable I am.

Jeff: That's a good way to measure it, by the way.

Judd: Yeah.

Jeff: But I know you and I'm telling you: You're smart. You're really smart.

Judd: They say certain people aren't good soldiers because if they're in a foxhole all night—you know, if you're creative and smart, you're thinking about all the different ways someone is going to blow your head off. But if you're not that smart, you're just like chilling out. And I feel like that in life. I'm just in the foxhole all fucking day thinking about everything that's going to go wrong in every possible way.

Jeff: And that's why you're prepared.

Judd: The preparation is not helpful at all, really.

Jeff: I'm equally miserable but—by the way, we're having a conversation here. It's kind of rude if you don't look at me.

Judd: I know, but why do you need to look at me?

Jeff: Because I'm talking to you.

Judd: You know, when I was first dating my wife, she said to me one day when we were talking, she said, "Dude, what are you looking at?" And I said, "I'm looking at your mouth." And she's like, "Why are you looking at my mouth?" "Because you're talking, and I want to know what you're saying." And she said, "You know, when you talk to people, you're supposed to look them in the eye." No one had ever said that to me before. I was twenty-eight years old and I thought—

Jeff: Did you really go through life up until twenty-eight—I mean, did your parents tell you when you were a kid that you were deaf?

Judd: Like, I mean with—

Jeff: Like, "Look at the lips, it's very important."

Judd: Right now, I am having to make an extra effort to not look at your mouth.

Jeff: That's crazy.

Judd: It is crazy and it makes me wonder how I was parented. Where was my mom looking? Was she looking at my mouth? It makes me realize what my damage is, and why it's hard to connect with people: because I'm a mouth looker.

Jeff: So you say mouth looker, and that makes sense, but I never heard of that before.

Judd: Someone told me you exercise now.

Jeff: I've been exercising for a while. I do Pilates, for Christ's sake.

Judd: Really? Like you slowly lift your legs with pulleys, every morning?

Jeff: Not every morning, but often enough.

Judd: With an instructor?

Jeff: With an instructor. I do privates.

Judd: You do privates?

Jeff: That's one of the luxuries I actually partake in. I have to have privates because the thought of me being in a Pilates class—that's goofy.

Judd: There's nothing about Pilates that won't make one of your balls fall out of your pants.

Jeff: By the way, nothing. You have to prepare for that ahead of time. I'm a big boxer-brief guy. With boxer briefs, you get no ball fallout. And then, I try to avoid—

Judd: You do Pilates in boxers?

Jeff: Boxers?

Judd: Didn't you say boxers?

Jeff: Yeah, but underneath my sweatpants. With sweatpants, my balls aren't going to drop out.

Judd: I don't like that flexibility. I need it compact.

Jeff: No, boxer briefs hold everything in. You know what boxer briefs are?

Judd: No. I thought it was brief *or* boxers. I didn't think it was the same.

Jeff: Boxer briefs are like longer briefs—like, they come down to here. You never worn those?

Judd: I have like tighty whities.

Jeff: Is that what you wear?

Judd: I don't need the extra shorts aspect of it that you seem to like.

Jeff: Do you really wear tighty whities?

Judd: What does this do for you?

Jeff: There's a certain confidence—I would have to drop my pants right now to show you. But I would not look like an idiot, whereas you, my friend, you wear tighty whities and we would be laughing at you.

Judd: The idea with that is that you have a bigger dick than me.

Jeff: I would wager everything I own that our dicks are the same size.

Judd: Really?

Jeff: We got the classic, average Jew dick. I see my dick all the time; I know it's not big. It's very normal size. It's not like a tiny festival. But I don't wear the boxer briefs because I have an extraordinarily large dick or small. My penis has nothing to do with it. It's just a nice—it's a very comfortable loungewear.

Judd: Okay. I was listening to an interview with you recently, and there's a long section where you're talking about what a good guy you are. Now, is that because you are a good guy, or like you're such a murderer that you just say that?

Jeff: One of my favorite comedians of all time is Jack Benny. But besides being my favorite comedian, he also had a reputation of being the biggest supporter of other comedians and the nicest amongst comedians, and I really want to be known as, if not the nicest, then one of the nicest comedians.

Judd: Are you a people pleaser?

Jeff: No, I could give a shit about that.

Judd: There was a letter that someone showed me once—Jack Benny used to write letters to this television producer—but what made me laugh is that they were kind of dirty. And you don't think of guys like Jack Benny as dirty.

Jeff: Right.

Judd: He was talking about how he loved a lot of the shows that year, but his favorite one was called "My Mother the Cunt."

Jeff: Jack *Benny* wrote that? Wow. Because he really was clean and adamant about being clean.

Judd: So he likes that kind of joke but he thinks it's wrong to do the "My Mother the Cunt" joke to America—like we can't handle it?

Jeff: They *couldn't* have handled it back then.

Judd: I just mean they all had a different sense of humor that they didn't share with the public, like Milton Berle taking his dick out and putting it in a hot dog bun. But then when these young comedians like Robert Klein started showing up, they were all like, Oh, this is out of line!

Jeff: Let me ask you a question. You're busy. We don't spend a lot of time together but I look at you as a friend. J. J. Abrams is the other person who you remind me of in this way. And that is, I call you, I email you, anything, and right away, you respond: "What's going on? How are you doing?" It's not like two weeks later. But I, even being one hundredth as successful as you, don't get back to people ever. I just wonder how you pull off being a great dad, a great husband. You're this successful producer. You make movies. You're producing a TV show for HBO. I mean, how do you do that?

Judd: Does this also relate to the fact that you have to keep saying you're a good guy? When in fact you're like the asshole who never returns emails?

Jeff: By the way, isn't it true that when you don't return someone's email, they think there's something wrong? Whenever I do write people back, their response is always: "Oh, I thought you were mad at me!" What? If I'm mad at someone, I tell them. But how do you pull this off? I don't know.

Judd: For a long time, people thought all my emails were angry. Because they would be very simple.

Jeff: Informational.

Judd: Yeah.

Jeff: I'm totally good with that.

Judd: But you know what helps? Exclamation marks. Now I've adopted an email personality that is not anything like me. I'm like a fourteen-year-old girl who puts exclamation marks after everything. Because people kept thinking I was mad at them. Well, I don't think answering emails correlates to any positive qualities that I, or anyone, has.

Jeff: No, what I want to know is—

Judd: What's probably happening is, like, one of my kids is choking on a bone and I'm not helping them because I'm so obsessed with answering your email. So maybe I'm a prick who cares more about your email than my children.

Jeff: I really want you to answer this.

Judd: I'm being honest.

Jeff: Really?

Judd: I'm saying, why the fuck am I answering your email? Honestly, I have a lot to do.

Jeff: That's my point.

Judd: I'm busy. I have children. They need help with their homework and why am I checking the fucking email?

Jeff: Oh, stop it. I'm saying as a *person* here. The point is, you're thoughtful. You always take time to be present. I don't know how you do that.

Judd: I know, but you're wrong. It's an addiction. It's a modern addiction. The email and the Twitter. It's distraction. There's better things I should be doing with my time and I'm not present at all. I'm staring at your mouth.

Jeff: You don't want to take credit.

Judd: I think I'm a nice enough person. But unlike you, I don't brag about it.

Jeff: I was a virgin until I was twenty.

Judd: You were? How did that work out?

Jeff: I actually lost my virginity to a heckler.

Judd: You did?

Jeff: I swear to God. I did. It was on the beach, South Beach. There was a comedy club. I was hosting a show. This woman heckled me unmercifully and later on that night some guy goes, "My friend wants to buy you a drink." We were on the beach, you know, at this place called the Carlyle. And she called me outside. She said come outside, and then she kissed me. I didn't stop her. I was twenty. She was thirty and a lawyer, and she ran on the beach ripping off her clothes yelling, "Follow me!" So I did. And then, in a lifeguard stand, she was naked and as soon as my penis went in it could have ended because I was like, *I'm not a virgin!* I didn't enjoy. It was like, I wasn't even thinking about it at all. It was like in, done. And then my clothes had fallen from the lifeguard stand into the sand and there was a bum walking up the beach to take my clothes, and so I jumped up naked with a boner, and ran down and fought off the bum for my clothes and then I went up and she was, like, *angry* at me. I was like, I'm not going to lose my wallet to a homeless man. And we continued. She was really nice. It didn't last long.

Judd: The first time I had sex, it was a ski trip senior year.

Jeff: High school? See, you're way more advanced than me.

Judd: Yeah. It was, you know, brief. And then afterwards, as a joke, I said, "Was it good for you, too?" And she said, "Well, I guess it'll get better."

Jeff: She was a girl you were dating.

Judd: Yes.

Jeff: Did she hang around to see if it got better or was that it?

Judd: She found out that it was not going to get better for about six months or so. She tested it out.

Jeff: I loved the way you said six months or so. You were a slow learner.

Judd: Well, because that's, like, a first love, someone you've done everything for the first time with. The two of you had this experience that this is what sex is, the way we do it, and then I think she just went off to college and went, *Oh, we've done it all wrong the whole time.*

Jeff: My high school years were filled with unrequited love. One after the other. I was the guy the girls talked to about the guy that they're fucking who is an asshole. I was the guy they talked to about that.

Judd: I mainly had that, too. Most of the time that was the situation. I don't have many road sex stories, either, because I was very uncomfortable with that. But I remember being out on the road—my first road sex story—in San Luis Obispo at some comedy club opening up for Rick Wright.

Jeff: I remember him.

Judd: And this nurse hit on me.

Jeff: Was she wearing her nurse outfit?

Judd: No, but she was very nursy.

Jeff: She showed nursing qualities?

Judd: Yeah, and I'm at the club in the hotel. It's like the perfect setup. And I thought, *Well, I should do this.* So we went back to my room.

Jeff: What were you? Like, nineteen? Twenty?

Judd: I was twenty years old, and I'll tell you how long the sex was. Okay, ready, and . . . we're done. And I think, *Well, I'm young. We'll just have sex again and the second time will be better.* And . . . we're done. And I remember the look in her eyes, the shame. Like, *Why am I fucking this boy? Who can't even fuck me correctly?* I'm very embarrassed and I remember sitting in bed and watching, on television, while I was praying for a third shot—*Jo Jo Dancer, Your Life Is Calling* was on cable with Richard Pryor. And it was terrible.

Jeff: You didn't like it?

Judd: It was terrible. It's the kind of thing that puts you on your heels.

Jeff: You didn't like the movie, you mean?

Judd: No, the sex.

Jeff: Oh, okay, because I got the indication that you didn't like *Jo Jo Dancer, Your Life Is Calling*.

Judd: Well, there is—

Jeff: It's not great. But there's good stuff in it. And it's Pryor playing himself, which is awesome.

Judd: I need to watch it again. But did you ever become the guy trying to get laid after the show?

Jeff: You know the answer to this one. We were on the road together a lot as young comics. No fucking way did that ever happen to me.

Judd: How many times did you get laid on the road?

Jeff: I have someone who keeps track of that for me. Unfortunately they're not here tonight. Otherwise I could—I'm guessing, I mean, I can think of two. In twenty-nine years.

Judd: It takes a lot to be a road comic and not get laid.

Jeff: Yeah, it does. Because you're surrounded by it. You're surrounded by girls who would fuck you under normal—if you knew what you were doing. Anyway. You have two children, and you don't want another kid, do you? I'm too tired.

Judd: I have two girls and I think it feels like the right amount with the potential of a very dangerous foster child in my future.

Jeff: Your daughters, by the way, are so adorable, and talented. When you sit down to write a movie, are you thinking, *I've got to have them in it*, or do you start writing and they pop up?

Judd: I just don't like other people's kids and I don't want to be around other people's kids.

Jeff: Let's take a step back for a second.

Judd: Yeah.

Jeff: Okay. Young actors—kid actors—are, for the most part, so frightening. A couple things happen: Number one, the parents come with them. And they're always scary. It's all about them, really. It's like parents of Little League kids—you know how they overcompensate and all that. That's how it is with stage moms. I've had times when a seven-year-old goes, "Oh, I saw your show last night." "*Curb Your Enthusiasm*?" "Yeah." And then the mother goes, "He loves it." Wow. My younger one is eleven and still has never seen it. He won't see it for a while, either.

Judd: Why?

Jeff: Because it's inappropriate.

Judd: Eleven? There is literally zero chance that your son is not spending at least one or two percent of his time watching blowjobs on the Internet. It's impossible. There's no scenario—

Jeff: One time my wife and I found—this was like maybe a year ago. He was ten. He had googled "big bosom." It turned out that his friend told him to.

Judd: And you think it ended there?

Jeff: I do.

Judd: The other day, my daughter said that in the second or third grade, she was so into American Girl dolls that she decided that she wanted to see what an American Boy doll looked like. And googled "American Boy doll." And saw—

Jeff: A penis?

Judd: Graphic sex.

Jeff: Graphic sex under "American Boy doll"? I'm just trying to think how that goes together. By the way, you can google the word *candle* and the first thing that pops is—

Judd: A candle in someone's ass, yeah.

Jeff: So I'm thinking, *American Boy doll . . . I guess there's a boy, he's a doll?*

Judd: You think your eleven-year-old can't handle Susie Essman cursing?

Jeff: I don't know if it's Susie Essman's cursing as much as "I'm going to fuck the Jew out of you, Larry."

Judd: Why is that hurtful?

Jeff: When did *hurtful* pop up? Did I say I want my children to avoid all hurtful things? No. It's inappropriate because he's not quite going to get "I'm going to fuck the Jew out of you." There's certain—

Judd: Why are you underestimating him?

Jeff: I don't know. I just, I just tend to—

Judd: Does he beg you to watch *Curb Your Enthusiasm*? Does he say, "Can I please watch it, Dad?"

Jeff: The truth is, he doesn't even want to watch it.

Judd: Yeah, or he's seen every episode at his friend's house. My kids would be like, "No, I don't want to see *40-Year-Old Virgin*. I don't want to see *Knocked Up*." And then it just, like, hit me: *Oh, they've already seen it.*

Jeff: You worked with one of my heroes, Albert Brooks.

Judd: Yes, I did.

Jeff: So on the first day of shooting, he's doing a scene and you're directing, and you've got to give him a note.

Judd: Yes.

Jeff: What are you thinking? Because I know you love Albert like I love Albert.

Judd: Well, it's scary. But the process actually starts much earlier than that. You know, I wrote the part with him in mind and then gave it to him hoping he would do it. It would have been bad if he said no because I put in a lot of time thinking about him in the part, and then a lot of rehearsals so by the shoot, we're comfortable. I mean, I was still nervous. But it's not like I'm sweating it out.

Jeff: Well, if I'm suddenly directing Albert Brooks, it's going to be a bit freaky in my head.

Judd: Yeah, well, that is why I do a lot of rehearsals.

Jeff: Did you do rehearsals just to be calm with Albert?

Judd: Well, I actually did a lot of rehearsals with Albert because I wanted him to rewrite all of his scenes. We would improvise. I would say throw out the script but get to the same information and then we would play and I would chuck out more ideas.

Jeff: Did you videotape it?

Judd: I did. And then he would email me better jokes at night. He'd start thinking about it, like, *What I can say is this.* And so there was a great six-month period of getting pitches from Albert—all of which were great.

Jeff: So, let me see something here. Oh, you know what? We're almost at an hour.

Judd: How long are we supposed to talk?

Jeff: There's no "supposed to," but you know.

Judd: Like two?

Jeff: By the way, that's a question I want to ask you. What do you think about when you hear that Dane Cook or Dave Chappelle do like twelve-hour shows or whatever the hell it is? Have you heard about that?

Judd: I have, yeah. Never seen it, though.

Jeff: I haven't seen it, either. You couldn't pay—I mean, God bless both of them, but I don't want to see—

Judd: Actually, I saw Jim Carrey do that in like '89 or '88.

Jeff: What did he do?

Judd: We were at the Comedy Store. He's not megastar Jim Carrey yet, but he's solidly in the *Living Color* career Jim Carrey, and Sam Kinison comes in and does thirty or forty minutes—you know, an unannounced bump of Jim. "Jim, you have to go on later, Sam Kinison's here." And then Andrew Dice Clay comes in and does forty-five minutes and Jim is so mad that he keeps getting bumped and now it's eleven, eleven-thirty at night and he was supposed to go on at like nine forty-five. So he decides that he is going to go onstage until they have to close the club. And so he does two hours straight, and the comedians are screaming because there are people who were supposed to go on after him.

Jeff: That's awesome.

Judd: It was awesome. I think that was the night he came up with Fire Marshal Bill.

Jeff: Yeah, because in those moments is where he'd come up with stuff.

Judd: He started just doing the burnt-guy face and complaining about how all of the electrical outlets weren't safe and he did that for thirty-five minutes to kill time. It was a great thing to witness.

Jeff: You came over to my apartment one day, when I was living on Genesee, and you said, "You have to come down to Comedy Magic Club with me tonight, to see Jim Carrey." And I go, "The guy who does Sammy Davis and stuff like that?" And you're like, "Yes, but he's changed everything. He's going to blow your mind." You were adamant and so I went and it was ridiculous how great it was and—what was the opening that he did? He did some sort of thing where he pretended to be opening and then kept going and going until—he was Andy Kaufman–like in what he was doing back then.

Judd: Well, you know, he had done impressions for a long time and then decided that he didn't want to be an impressionist—but he had no act. So he would go onstage with nothing, and do a set every night. After a year or two, he developed an act. But for a while, you would see Jim Carrey with nothing go onstage, searching. They were the best shows I've ever seen. He was just so interesting.

Jeff: Okay, here's the reason I said earlier, "We've been here for an hour," was not to stop things but—

Judd: I have nowhere to go.

Jeff: You're committed.

Judd: I like to be here until people really want to leave. But that's kind of how I am as a person. That's why my movies are too long. That's why I eat too much.

Jeff: Where would you find that your movies are too long?

Judd: Where would you find out?

Jeff: Do your friends tell you, "Your movie was too long"?

Judd: Oh yeah, everybody.

Jeff: Well, a couple of things on that. First off, I remember going to see a screening, an early screening, of *Talladega Nights*. You were there, I think.

Judd: Yes.

Jeff: Okay. You were there. It was at Sony. Did you produce that movie?

Judd: Yes.

Jeff: Okay. So it's one of those screenings that you guys do. I found a lot to laugh at, but I had to go to the bathroom at a certain point. So I walk in the bathroom, and there's Adam McKay.

Judd: Not watching his own movie.

Jeff: Peeing. And I said to him, "What is with all these movies being so goddamn long?" And I didn't realize, I mean I knew that he directed it but I forgot who I was—I was just speaking frankly. And he looked at me like, What? I think all these comedies should be ninety minutes. I remember when I saw a rough cut of *40-Year-Old Virgin*. I saw like a two-hour-and-forty-minute cut.

Judd: Yes.

Jeff: No, I really did, though. I really did. I don't know if you remember me saying to you, but I told you in no uncertain terms: "Cut it down to ninety and it'll be a huge hit."

Judd: Yeah.

Jeff: I still wish it was ninety. By the way, loved it. But I would have loved it more at ninety. You know, Groucho Marx came to see Second City one time and I said to him, "Groucho, what did you think of it?" And he goes, "Make it shorter, and make it funnier." That's sort of my attitude about comedies. All Woody Allen: ninety minutes or less. You can't watch a fucking short movie anymore. I understand if—what's his name, the guy who directed, like, *Lawrence of Arabia*? David Lean? If it's a David Lean movie—all right, two and a half to three hours. But a comedy should be shorter.

Judd: I don't subscribe to that.

Jeff: I know you don't. And by the way, I love your movies, I really do. But I would love them more if they were shorter.

Judd: You're probably right. *The 40-Year-Old Virgin*, I think, was like an hour and forty-seven. And then I put seventeen minutes back on the DVD, which is a lot. But I like showing people the other things that we did that I was proud of. I feel like people's attention spans are getting so short that I want to make them suffer.

Jeff: I am with you on that. I remember going to your apartment once and watching that movie about the workers on strike. The train people—

Judd: *Matewan*?

Jeff: *Matewan*, yeah. You're like, "You've got to see this movie, it's amazing." And that's a long movie. By the way, I'm all for long movies, but—

Judd: Not funny ones, right. You don't think you can sustain joy or laughter over the long haul. See, when we were doing *Funny People*, I literally thought, *I'd like to make this the longest comedy ever made.* I wanted people to suffer through parts of it where you think it's going to go happy, and then it goes to a more painful place, and the length is part of it. It's like, *Fuck, when will this end?*

Jeff: *Fuck, when will this end?* I love that as an aspiration for a filmmaker.

Judd: You're probably right, though, about length. But when things are good—you know, I'm not, like, upset that *Pulp Fiction* is so long.

Jeff: I am.

Judd: And there's two *Kill Bills.* I'm excited.

Jeff: I'm very upset. I'm not very upset but—

Judd: Really?

Jeff: I mean, I'm done. Because I feel like *Lawrence of Arabia* is *about* something. It's filling me. *Kill Bill* is just too fucking whimsical to be nine hours long. You know, if something is really, really, you know, *whoa*, then yes, I'll sit there for the whole fucking thing. But if it's—

Judd: What about Harry Potter?

Jeff: I've never seen a Harry Potter movie. It all goes on too long.

Judd: I get mad that people will sit through Harry Potter for two hours and forty minutes and not give me two hours and forty minutes.

Jeff: By the way, I'm so with you. What makes you think that Harry Potter should be—

Judd: You haven't even seen the first one to judge the Potter movies. It's not like you saw the first one and you went, "That sucks, fuck Harry Potter." You've watched no Harry Potters.

Jeff: I have never seen a Michael Bay movie, either.

Judd: But maybe you would be the biggest Michael Bay fan in the world if you saw one.

Jeff: No I wouldn't.

Judd: How do you know?

Jeff: I just know. I know it's a difficult place to argue from, I know.

Judd: You don't enjoy action and comedy hybrids?

Jeff: I love action and comedy hybrids, yes, but not Michael Bay's. I'll never see his—it's a matter of pride.

Judd: Okay, well, who's the funniest person that made you laugh? Who made you laugh the hardest?

Jeff: Let me think about that. Watching their work?

Judd: Yeah, not just hanging out. But their work.

Jeff: Can I do both?

Judd: Yes.

Jeff: All right, so their work: I guess Peter Sellers, *The Party*. I laughed harder with him than anyone. And then on a personal level: Amy Sedaris.

Judd: I was also thinking of stand-up. You're talking about movies.

Jeff: Stand-up? You know who used to kill me when he was at his peak? Kevin Meaney. He used to destroy me. Night after night, the same exact act would kill me.

Judd: Chris Farley, in person, was one of the funniest people ever.

Jeff: Yeah, but he's not a stand-up.

Judd: I'm changing the rules. When I think about stand-up, there's so many that it just becomes ridiculous. I mean, my favorite thing used to be watching people write their acts onstage, free-form associating to come up with the next thing. There were days, when I first started, when I really used to laugh. I don't laugh anymore. I'm dead inside.

Jeff: It's much harder now, stand-up-wise, to get a laugh out of me. Even after someone's done, I'll go, "That was a good set." You know, and I'll mean it but I didn't laugh once.

Judd: Yeah, that's sad. I mean, Chris Rock's act is crazy. Like, to see him really on his game?

Jeff: You know what's sad? When you see Chris Rock at midnight at the Comedy Store working out his act and what he's working out is better than anything you've ever written. It's just so sad and frustrating and you're laughing, and you're going, *You fucker. You're that good.*

Judd: There were so many people, when we used to go on the road, who would just kill so hard. I never did. I was never that good.

Jeff: When we were on the road together—one thing, by the way, somebody said they saw our names up on the wall at the Improv in Addison or Dallas, you know, wherever it was, and everyone's names and the date they played there are on the wall. And it was you and I opening for someone. I'm not going to say who it was because they haven't gone on to anything and they—well, they weren't a nice person but, uh, they weren't so fuck them but I'm not going to say their name. It's just mean.

Judd: But you'll slam a guy like Michael Bay? Who you've never met?

Jeff: Yes.

Judd: But the guy who was mean to you, you will not call out?

Jeff: Yes.

Judd: Is that because he doesn't have Michael Bay's money? Like where, what's your line?

Jeff: My line is Michael Bay better be able to take it. Not even because of money. Fuck him for making those shitty movies. Fuck him for wasting America's time. Fuck him. Fuck him. And by the way, Albert Brooks's speech in *Broadcast News* about lowering our standards: Michael Bay does it at a rapid pace. He's not like slowly chipping away with each movie. Immediately upon first movie it's a punch in our face to make us stupid. I'm sorry. You just got me on a rant. I apologize.

Judd: You say this and you've never seen any of his movies. What are the top three or four jokes that, even for you, are uncomfortable?

Jeff: I never—generally, I'm thinking about what's for lunch. Uh, the only time that I am offended is when something is not funny. Trying to be shocking, and if it's not funny, you know, like whatchamacallit, who played Kramer?

Judd: Michael Richards.

Jeff: Michael Richards. You know, I've seen things worse than that, and you have, too. Horrible, horrible things. And if he was funny that night, nobody would have been pissed. But he wasn't funny. Hall of Fame not funny.

Judd: But was it offensive?

Jeff: What? Him saying what he said about the fork and shit like that? Yeah!

Judd: I've seen people do things like that. I felt bad because I felt I kind of knew what he was trying to do.

Jeff: He was trying to provoke a response. Do you know that when he came offstage, he said—I think it was Tom Papa, who was going up next. He walked over to Tom and goes, "Yeah, weird crowd." Having no idea that his life was about to change. People freak out like that. Not every night, but it happens. Anyway, we're done. And thank you. I thoroughly enjoyed my time with you. You're a good man. You should take more credit for being a great guy.

Judd: Thank you, Jeff.

Jeff: You're welcome.

Judd: And I'm going to tell that to my good friend, Michael Bay, when I see him.

Jeff: You can tell Michael Bay. Michael Bay, by the way, I wish him nothing but happiness. I really do. I want him to be happy, have a good meal. I hope that all things are good for Michael Bay, but I want him to stop making movies. That I do. If it brings him joy, let him make movies—but don't put film in the camera.

PART TWO
J–M

JERRY SEINFELD
(2014)

I couldn't wait to talk to Jerry Seinfeld again for this book, thirty years after our first interview. Jerry is someone I have known a little bit for a long time. Whenever I'm around him, though, I usually don't speak much. I'm still a little bit intimidated. The truth is, most comedians don't understand why he's so happy when they're so tortured. But I look up to him more than ever, and every conversation with him is an opportunity to learn. You'd be a fool not to take advantage of what Jerry Seinfeld has to offer.

When we did this interview, I had just started doing stand-up again, after a twenty-year hiatus, and it seemed like a perfect moment to grill him about his current joke-writing process, and to soak up some of his stand-up wisdom. And, once again, he lit a fire under my ass—no one else has his work ethic or his clarity of vision, his passion for the craft. But I also had the opportunity to ask him questions about how he raises his children and his spiritual life, which is something I always wanted to do. Also, this being a few decades after our first interview, it was fun to remind him of what his dreams were back then, and to ask him how it feels to have made every single one of them come true.

Judd Apatow: You know how, back in the day, I interviewed you for my high school radio show?

Jerry Seinfeld: Yes, it's still resonating.

Judd: Well, I thought I'd start out by talking about that interview, back in 1983—which I remember and you shouldn't.

Jerry: No, I do remember. I do. It was an odd thing.

Judd: We did it at your apartment in Santa Monica. Do you remember that?

Jerry: I mean, I'd never had a kid come to interview me with a tape recorder before.

Judd: I remember you had a funny look on your face because I don't think you knew a child was coming. The tape recorder I used was literally straight from the AV squad at Syosset High School—this huge green cassette recorder.

Jerry: How old were you when we did this?

Judd: I was fifteen. But I was aware of you, I think, from your earliest TV performances. I was watching way too much *Merv Griffin Show* for a kid my age. I saw you on TV before you ever did *The Tonight Show*.

Jerry: Wow. Boy, those were the days.

Judd: Is that the greatest moment in a comedian's life, doing *The Tonight Show* for the first time?

Jerry: Yeah.

Judd: Do you remember it?

Jerry: Well, Leno recently told me that he came to my first *Tonight Show*—which I didn't even remember.

Judd: The other thing that I remember about our interview is that your apartment had nothing in it. Like, it was *not* decorated.

Jerry: Oh, I was a minimalist from the beginning. I think that's why I've done well as a comedian.

Judd: No distractions.

Jerry: If you always want less, in words as well as things, you'll do well as a writer.

Judd: That whole high school radio show thing happened because a friend of mine decided he wanted to interview rock bands—we were like fifteen or sixteen years old—and then he goes off and interviews R.E.M. one day.

And it occurred to me: *Maybe I could use this high school radio station to meet my heroes and ask them, like, "How do you become a comedian? How do you write jokes?"*

Jerry: Wow, that's great. Not to take you off track here, but I heard that you were doing some stand-up at the Cellar recently. Is that true?

Judd: It is true.

Jerry: I want to know what that was like.

Judd: Well, I was interviewing Pearl Jam for their last record and as I was writing questions—you know, I think about them a lot because they're my age and they've had, in a way, a similar experience to us in the arc of their careers. And I just kept thinking, *These guys get to write songs, and they spend their lives singing them and enjoying themselves. But I make these movies, and there's all this stress and then, when the thing comes out, I'm not a part of the experience at all.*

Jerry: I understand.

Judd: So I was making a movie with Amy Schumer, and she kept talking about doing stand-up and I finally said to her, "You know what, I'll do a set and see how it goes." I hadn't done it in twenty years. And the first set went well and I went on every night, after we would finish shooting, for the next three months. I've been doing it ever since and it's literally like I spent my entire life directing movies just so I could get better spots in comedy clubs.

Jerry: It's really fun. You find that you're this breed, you're a dog breed. I always thought it was weird that dogs would bark at other dogs. They should be barking at everyone else. And that's the way I see comics. I didn't feel comfortable anywhere until the day I walked into a comedy club. But where do you think you'll go with your stand-up, Judd?

Judd: I have to say that I am loving the fact that there's no career goal connected to it. It's purely for the joy of trying to get good at something that I was just okay at back in the day. It's unfinished business. And it would just be great to figure out how to tear the house down consistently.

Jerry: Right.

Judd: It's been so much fun—oddly, way more fun than anything else I've done.

Jerry: Now, why would you say that?

Judd: Because it's immediate. I mean, I'm sure you had this experience making *Bee Movie*—you spend your whole life in meetings and editing rooms, isolated and alone, arguing about budgets and time frames. And there's that moment you share with an audience, where they relate and a joke works, and it brings you so much more joy. But you don't always get that from a movie. If it's the first time you show a movie and the place goes nuts, that feels great, but still: not as great as a good stand-up set. Also, it only happens once or twice per movie and each movie might take four years. So you're getting two hits off of four years' work.

Jerry: *Bee Movie* was a very unhappy experience, from start to finish. I remember standing in the back of the theater and it wasn't great, but it was decent and, and I remember listening to the laughs and thinking, *These laughs are shit*. That was not worth it.

Judd: I completely relate to that.

Jerry: And does the audience react when you are introduced? Do they know you?

Judd: I thought a lot about how you always say that buys you about ninety seconds.

Jerry: Yeah.

Judd: It buys me like thirty seconds. But I think they feel like they know me a little bit from the movies, so it's as if they have a head start understanding my point of view. But I couldn't enjoy it more. I'm fully addicted to performing again. I put as much time into my stand-up as my movies.

Jerry: Good.

Judd: I always remember you and Larry Miller saying that to be a comedian, you have to sit down and write. That's the job. How much time do you spend at a desk?

Jerry: I just finished wrestling with a bit, actually. I couldn't stop. I do it compulsively. I write with a pad and a pen. I like a big, yellow legal pad. And once I get that pad open, I can't stop. It's kind of like free-diving, you know. You have a certain amount of air and then you just have to come up. I'm good for an hour or two and then I collapse on the couch and sleep.

Judd: Do you have a legal pad organizational system?

Jerry: Oh, it's very complicated. I have the legal pad and then I have one of those accordion folders with a different slot for each letter. Once I'm done with the bit, it either goes in the garbage or the accordion folder. Those are the only two destinations. And then it's in the air. It has to survive on its own. Bits are like turtles right after they hatch, running to the beach.

Judd: Have you ever had a period where you were sick of it?

Jerry: No. No. No. Never.

Judd: Not even for a second?

Jerry: If this is something you have a gift for, it's going to suck you along into it. All you have to do is transition from looking at your phone to putting the phone down and opening up the pad where there's nothing going on. There's no light hitting your retina. So, no, I've always found it to be—I just see something and I write it down and I go, *Gee, that almost worked. That kinda worked. Maybe* that's *the good part. Let me get rid of the bad part and write a different intro to the idea.* And the next thing I know, the day is gone.

Judd: Do you feel like your act has changed in a substantial way? Has your work become more personal, now that you have kids?

Jerry: No, it's just—you know, I'm still mud wrestling with a pig.

Judd: Is there a line for how personal you will go in your work?

Jerry: I'm doing a thing now about dadness—you know, when you reach dadness fully, no one in your family can hurt your feelings anymore, because you don't *have* feelings anymore. Feelings are too much of a problem to have, so I just got rid of them. That's true, you know. That's a true thing about becoming a dad. But you get to a point where—if my wife or children insult me in any way, I'm just like, "I don't care. I don't care if you like me. I don't care what you think of me." When you start out in this family thing, you're a human, and then, as you go along, you realize that you're an android. I'm doing this bit now, I have this thing in an episode of *Comedians in Cars*, where I'm driving a Ferrari and I describe it as a machine that stirs, you know, that stirs deep, human emotions, and that I really need that because I don't have any. I guess that's personal, but I don't feel like I'm revealing anything. I'm a person that denies emotions very strongly. I'm only interested in what gets a laugh. I often get the "Why don't you talk about politics or talk about this or that?" stuff. I'll talk about anything that I think is funny or will get a laugh. If I could get a laugh with politics, I'd be doing politics.

Judd: I find that everything about a family is drama and emotions and tears and yelling. How is that for you as somebody who doesn't live his life that way? How do you deal, in the middle of the madness of kids, when someone wants something so badly they will scream and push you emotionally until you crack to get it?

Jerry: My kids never get me to crack. It's because of my stand-up training. Like, "You're nothing compared to the Comedy Cellar."

Judd: That's so funny.

Jerry: "You think you're tough?" My kids said something to me last night, and I said, "That line is so weak, give me my last name back. You don't deserve it."

Judd: I have the opposite thing with my daughter. She said to me the other day, "Dad, all those things you say that you think are jokes are not funny."

Jerry: Oh, my son had one even worse than that. We were making up words as a game at dinner one night and I said, "You know, I've made up a lot of words that people actually use as words." And my son said, "Uh, really, like what? *Unfunny?*"

Judd: That's brutal. I do feel like there's no larger pride than in seeing your kid get funny.

Jerry: No larger pride. Do you think they pick it up around the house or do you think it's genetic?

Judd: It has to be genetic but I think that as they watch us reacting to things, over and over again, and see how we look at things, they also just pick it up. But Leslie and I, you know, from day one, the second our kids started terrorizing us with their emotions, we would crack immediately. Like when they cried because they wanted to sleep with us, we would always wind up sleeping with them.

Jerry: We were the same. I just meant, my kids will never get me to yell. I will not yell.

Judd: You'll give in, though?

Jerry: I'll give in, but I will not yell. Nor will I show any emotion.

Judd: How old is your oldest child?

Jerry: They're fourteen, eleven, and nine.

Judd: So you're in full puberty mode.

Jerry: Not quite. I'm an inch away.

Judd: Because I'm in the mode where suddenly boys are calling and boys are around and when they're in the house, I have this very primal hatred of all of them. They're all scared of me. I think I'm being nice, but I'm not.

Jerry: I am going to try my darnedest to avoid all those clichés. I'm going to be fine with the boys, fine with the mischief. It's just too cliché to be, "So you're interested in my daughter, huh, young man?" I don't want to be that.

Judd: Well, it's also that all the boys are so unamusing, it bugs you. If they were funnier, you might like them. They just have so little to offer.

Jerry: But don't you think there's just going to be just a natural, powerful editing process that goes on? Your daughter is not going to be able to hang out with unfunny guys forever, right?

Judd: That's an interesting thing I've noticed. Because of my job, my daughters have gotten to hang out with some of the most interesting, funny people around—and it makes them think less of their friends.

Jerry: That's good.

Judd: They think they're so uninteresting and so not funny.

Jerry: They're right.

Judd: They actually have a problem with it sometimes. They don't like what their friends talk about, or what interests them.

Jerry: That's a great contribution you've made.

Judd: What was your family situation like, financially, growing up?

Jerry: We were fine. I grew up straight middle class.

Judd: I'm interested in how you approach having money and raising kids and making sure you instill some sense of values.

Jerry: We talk about it a lot and we make a big deal about it and they have absorbed it. They understand the natural, obnoxious vibe that people are going to have of them—that they'd better watch it, you know, because they're going to be hated for this.

Judd: "Everybody knows what we have, so you'd better be cool."

Jerry: I have cars. And my son, when I pick him up at camp, says, "Dad, you better not come in a different car. No one's impressed with your cars. Come in the same car every day so no one knows you have more than one car."

Judd: I find myself saying to my kid, "I earned this money, not you." I'm allowed to enjoy it, but you go make your own money.

Jerry: I say that, too. "You're not getting any of it."

Judd: Do you subscribe to the Warren Buffett theory? Are you going to give your kids nothing?

Jerry: No, I don't. I wish I subscribed to that theory, but I don't. I honestly don't even know what to do about that. Let them fight over it.

Judd: For me, I wanted to be a comedian and I wanted to work from a very early age because I was afraid of being broke. What was your core motivation?

Jerry: To never have to do anything else. I learned very young in this business that you bust your ass or you get thrown out of the kingdom. My motivation was not wanting to leave the kingdom. Plus, I just love the life of it. I love my independence and the joy of hearing laughs and making jokes. It's as simple as that.

Judd: Does the TV show seem like this weird little dream that happened in the middle of your stand-up career?

Jerry: That's a very good description of it.

Judd: Like this odd distraction for eight or nine years and then back to real life?

Jerry: Obviously, after the show, I saw there were many other avenues available for me. I missed the solitude. I missed the griminess and the simplicity of the life. I remember working it out with a friend of mine, James Spader. I said, "What do I do with my life now?" And he said, "Well, what has been the best experience that you've had so far?" And I said, "For me, it has been performing for live audiences." You kind of get to do that on TV, but TV is so much work and the pipeline is just too long. In stand-up, you get addicted to that intensity: You have an idea for something, and then you're onstage that night and people are reacting to it. That's very intense.

Judd: How did you handle the grind of doing the show, with scripts coming in and not being good and having to deal with fixing them and everything? At *The Larry Sanders Show*, we did fewer episodes than you per year—you know, we would usually do thirteen. I think there were two seasons where we did eighteen. But by the end, everyone was decimated by it.

Jerry: Decimated.

Judd: And we didn't do it anywhere near as many years as you did *Seinfeld*. How did it feel to be in the center of that storm?

Jerry: We were killing ourselves and the reason why I stopped the show was I literally physically couldn't go on. We were doing twenty-two episodes a season. And then once Larry [David] left, I was doing all the rewrites—to rehearse all day and then to do all those rewrites and all the editing and all the casting, it was just . . . I was lucky the show happened when I was young and healthy. You're strong in those years and you're pretty smart. I couldn't have done it before or after.

Judd: People don't understand how it grinds you down. They don't understand why people who have done it don't ever want to do it again.

Jerry: Right. "Why did you stop doing the show?" I don't have a good answer for that. I can't explain. You can't explain what that is.

Judd: There's no way for people to understand what you give to a show like that.

Jerry: Yeah, and when your name *is* the show—I mean, it was the best possible experience in that medium, but you can't do it forever. And the thing is, are you willing to compromise quality to keep it going? Of course, the answer to that was no. And that's why the show ended when it did.

Judd: Sometimes, when I think about my career, I think of it in this weird way. I had this show that was a financial failure, *Freaks and Geeks*, which didn't even last a full season. But in my head, I have tricked myself into believing it was a major accomplishment. I tell myself, *Well, at least I accomplished that.* And then I look at the rest of my life and career as post–*Freaks and Geeks*. Whatever I do, it doesn't matter because I pulled it off once and that was enough. I look at the rest of my career as gravy. Do you look at like your career in a similar way, as post-*Seinfeld*? When something so enormous is accomplished, does it just reframe everything?

Jerry: Mostly, it just frees me from having to do press. And I travel in comfort. That's what it gave me. No, I mean, it gave me everything, and that was always my thought when I was doing it. If I sacrifice every cell of energy that I have doing this, the rest of my life will be pretty good. So I just died on the shield. I went to the point where I thought, *If I keep going, I could lose my sanity.* That was how far I took it mentally.

Judd: I had that at the end of a season of *The Larry Sanders Show*. I took a job punching up *Happy Gilmore* right afterwards, and I stressed myself out so much trying to do a good job that I started having these crazy panic attacks. Which was my body telling me, you need to lay down.

Jerry: This is one of the great perils of the job. You can work yourself to destruction. Because the work is interesting and exciting and all these opportunities are rare and wonderful and hard to resist.

Judd: Two years ago, I took my first Transcendental Meditation class. Just to get centered.

Jerry: Oh, really?

Judd: You started doing TM in college, right?

Jerry: I started doing it in college. While everyone was at lunch, I would go back to my room and do a TM. I did it once a day. But about a year ago, I was talking to a TM instructor, and he started telling me, "You know, if you do two a day, it's a lot more powerful." So I just recently started doing that and it has completely changed my life. I honestly will do four a day sometimes. I pop them like Tic Tacs.

Judd: How is it possible that, in all those years, no one told you that most people do TM more than once a day?

Jerry: All I think about now is what the experience of the show might have been like if I had applied this as the real antidote, which is what it is. It's the antidote to that difficult life.

Judd: Is there any part of you that thinks that a certain level of bad energy and exhaustion helps you reach some other comedic place?

Jerry: No, I don't believe in that.

Judd: One of the funniest things I've seen is on a DVD extra of the *Larry Sanders Show* DVD, you and Garry Shandling debating whether or not you need pain to be funny. And you're saying, "Well, what about talent? Some people just have a God-given talent." And Garry says, "Why are you so angry, Jerry?" But I agree with you. I think the TM thing is very powerful. Sometimes I actually have a phobia of feeling good. I resist it because I'm not used to feeling that way.

Jerry: I don't fall prey to that.

Judd: Do you think your general disposition comes from a place of spirituality, or were you like this from the get-go?

Jerry: That's a tough question. I was drawn to a lot of Eastern thought, a lot of Zen stuff. I've always been drawn to Eastern philosophy and religion more than Western or Jewish, I guess. Which is why I took to TM so quickly. No question. But going back to our thing about emotions, I just don't accept irrational emotion as part of my behavior. I'm not going to act on an irrational emotion. So I think that's probably built in, but reading some of the Zen stuff I've read over the years and doing all the TM has definitely shored it up. Now I'm this guy, whoever that is.

Judd: I read a lot of Zen but it ultimately makes me unhappy because I don't want to be one drop in the ocean.

Jerry: I do.

Judd: How do you get over that hump?

Jerry: You look at some pictures from the Hubble Telescope and you snap out of it. I used to keep pictures of the Hubble on the wall of the writing room at *Seinfeld*. It would calm me when I would start to think that what I was doing was important.

Judd: See, I go the other way with that. That makes me depressed.

Jerry: Most people would say that. People always say it makes them feel insignificant, but I don't find being insignificant depressing. I find it uplifting.

Judd: Insignificance is a hump I have trouble getting over, but maybe that's because my parents were crazier than yours.

Jerry: Maybe. Or maybe you think this is your only life, and this is the only stuff you're ever going to do. Which, you know, I don't subscribe to that.

Judd: What do you subscribe to?

Jerry: That this is just one chapter of thousands of chapters.

Judd: My parents never mentioned spirituality or God or anything. The only thing they would say is "Nobody said life was fair." That was my entire religious upbringing.

Jerry: Nobody said life wasn't fair, either. Nobody is in charge of saying what life is and that's what it is.

Judd: But generally, your parents were cool, right? You had a good relationship with them?

Jerry: I wouldn't use the word *cool*. I would say they were . . . highly independent. My father's mother died giving birth to him, and my mother grew up in an orphanage. My father was out of school probably by sixth grade, on the street. And they didn't marry until they were in their forties so they were very, very independent people, and I just folded right into that place where you won't need anybody.

Judd: That didn't make you needy?

Jerry: It made me feel free. You don't need people. They're unreliable.

Judd: It's such a different type of a comedy upbringing. I feel like most comedians have broken parents who don't know how to mirror you; they want you to take care of them. So you spend your life trying to please other people and thinking that you are significant because you can change the world or change things, but you find out that you really can't, and then you're miserable.

Jerry: Pleasing people is fun. It's never been an emotional nutrient for me. It does make me happy when people like something I made and it makes me unhappy if they don't like it, but that's not my *nutrition*.

Judd: You're a lucky man in that respect.

Jerry: It's allowed me to play the game for what it is. I look at everything as a game.

Judd: I recently watched that speech you gave about advertising, at the Clio Awards, or whatever. I really enjoyed that.

Jerry: Oh, thank you. Boy, you see everything. You know, I wrote that because I was so regretting that I agreed to accept this stupid award, I thought, *Let me at least give myself something to do there so it's not just torture.* The premise of that speech was that it doesn't matter if the product is good because I so enjoy that moment before I find out. I enjoy getting sold, and I enjoy thinking that I'm going to get this great thing. That's all I need.

Judd: That's maybe the greatest lesson you can teach a child.

Jerry: I've always loved getting sold. That's true of all good salesmen. All good salesmen love to get taken in by a pitch.

Judd: Are you just loving doing your show, *Comedians in Cars*?

Jerry: Yeah. I love it because it's a completely free canvas, like stand-up. Nobody cares what I make. As long as the audience likes it and I like doing it, that's the end of it.

Judd: Looking back at the shows you've done so far, what were the ones that had the biggest impact on you, or that surprised you the most? Because you have people on that show that we don't see in that format, ever. You don't see Howard Stern talking as he does in life, ever. You don't see Letterman do that.

Jerry: I think people enjoy that. I never know what the show is going to be. Somehow I get in there and I can make it into whatever I want. It's a can of Play-Doh. You just make stuff. I don't deal with any executives, on any level. It's just me. It's just like stand-up. I go, "Here's something I made for you." And that's it. I wanted people to see what the life of a comedian is like: Ten percent of it is being onstage, and ninety percent is just like hanging out with these great people. And that's really made my life.

Judd: Just the joy of that.

Jerry: I wanted to show that. I thought people would get a kick out of seeing what it's really like. This is the fun part.

JIM CARREY AND BEN STILLER
(2010)

One of the most intense experiences I've had in this business was the creation of the film *The Cable Guy*. In 1995, Jim Carrey, Ben Stiller, and I were all just beginning to make a name for ourselves in Hollywood — well, Jim was having a little more success than Ben and me in this department. The movie happened at a moment when Jim Carrey truly could do anything he wanted. *Ace Ventura: Pet Detective* and *The Mask* had just come out, and he was on fire. What he decided to do was a dark, strange comedy starring a needy, media-addicted man with a lisp — and by doing so, he basically announced to the world, "I'm not only going to make hilarious, silly comedies, I'm also going to challenge you and myself." We all loved the movie, but when it came out, it was not the mega-blockbuster that the business demanded. In fact, we went quickly from having one of the best, most rewarding experiences of our lives to getting the shit kicked out of us by the press for daring to attempt to blaze a different trail. For some of us (especially me) it took a fair amount of time to recover our footing. Looking back, that movie was the moment that dictated what the three of us — and so many of our friends — would do with our careers. This commentary for the tenth-anniversary release of *The Cable Guy* on video was the first time we sat down to talk about how it all went down and what it meant. It's been twenty years now since we shot *Cable Guy,* and the prevailing feeling I'm left with is a sense of pride about what everybody in the film has accomplished — both in their careers and as people.

Ben Stiller: Let's introduce ourselves.

This interview was originally featured on the DVD of The Cable Guy *and appears courtesy of Sony Pictures Home Entertainment.*

Jim Carrey: Okay.

Judd Apatow: Who are you?

Jim: I'm—Orson Welles! My name is Jim Carrey.

Ben: And I'm Ben Stiller.

Judd: I'm Judd Apatow, and I guess we should talk a little about how this movie got started. There was this script, *The Cable Guy,* and I knew that you were doing it, Jim, and I desperately—

Jim: And you jumped on board and rode my coattails all the way to the top.

Judd: Yes! And here I am, looking down. Actually, I made a very brief play to direct, which got rejected by the Sony people in about fifteen minutes.

Jim: Really?

Judd: Then it was like, well, who else?

Jim: "Judd Apatow will never direct a movie."

Ben: Yeah. Dream on, buddy. Dream on. So, what should we talk about?

Judd: Well, we could talk about—that me and Ben went and visited Jim when he was shooting *Ace Ventura: When Nature Calls* to discuss what to do with this script. And Jim had very specific lisping ideas for his character.

Jim: I wanted to do the lisp because—you know, the more money people pay me, the more I want to rebel.

Ben: Yeah, I remember. We went to Charleston. I remember you were shooting a scene from *Ace Ventura* where you were—was that the scene where you're coming out of the—

Jim: The rhino's butt.

Ben: Yeah, the rhino's butt.

Judd: But it was hot out! It was like a hundred and five out!

Jim: Yeah! People were dying out there. People were falling apart. And the producers were asking them to drink less water.

Ben: Couldn't afford the water!

Jim: Yeah, and we spent a couple days, just brainstorming.

Judd: I have those notes still, from the hotel: It just says, like, (*stilted voice*) "Push tit against glass. 'Oh, Steven!'"

Jim: That's right. But that's one of the most sublime scenes ever, in a movie. Oh my gosh. Can't believe we got to do that.

Ben: And then you got to—you sort of rewrote the script—

Judd: I went and rewrote the drafts.

Jim: You cut your teeth!

Judd: Lou Holtz is the credited writer on this film; I did a pass on it. I think if I said more than that I'd get kicked out of the Writers Guild. But this was post–*Ace Ventura: When Nature Calls*. It was a white-hot Jim Carrey madness at that moment.

Jim: Yeah. And I was just about to destroy the industry as we know it.

Judd: You were paid twenty million dollars. What'd you do with all that money?

Jim: I'm still living off that twenty million dollars.

Ben: And they made a big deal of it—the studio *announced* it, I remember. They were like very excited about it.

Jim: Yeah, they stuck their heads right out there. Into the guillotine.

Ben: It put us out there, right from the beginning.

Jim: It really did expose us.

Ben: "Let's get our money's worth!"

Jim: "Oh, yeah. We'll be *real* happy for them. We're rootin' for 'em!"

Judd: I remember they said forty-million-dollar budget, twenty million to Jim, and then if we ever asked for more than forty million dollars they'd get very angry.

Jim: (*Watching movie*) Hold on, I'm caught up in this. I'm so good at this.

Judd: At this moment in time, when I was doing my work, I was very, very lonely. I was lonely, and so the idea of the desperation of this was not a big leap for how I was feeling at the time.

Ben: I was coming off a big breakup, too.

Jim: We're all disenfranchised. It's all about abandonment, man. Every role I do is about abandonment. How about you guys?

Ben: My life is about abandonment.

Judd: I remember every aspect of this—we could not have laughed or enjoyed the ideas of this or the shooting more. But then, when you watch it years later, you do think, *That was completely crazy.*

Ben: I think a lot of the issues with the movie are about the *context* of the movie being made as this sort of mainstream, summer, hopefully comedic blockbuster type of movie. But really we were making this dark, pseudosexual tale of two men who become obsessed with each other.

Jim: With homosexual overtones!

Judd: This is the first bromance.

Jim: Yeah. But I think it was important! I still think so. This movie is what's wrong with *everything*.

Ben: I don't think the studio ever—they were sort of afraid to *question* what was going on.

Jim: Well, I don't think you should. I think it's a great movie, man!

Ben: But if it had come out on Halloween or something, or if they hadn't put it out there as—

Jim: I remember they took all the psychodrama craziness out of the first trailer and I got worried right then. I went, *Uh-oh. They're trying to mask this thing.*

Ben: The trailer was a little ridiculous, in terms of the oom-pah-pah music.

Judd: We wanted the trailer to be a little more, like, *Cape Fear*.

Jim: I wanted me attempting to put my drill into Matthew Broderick's head or something like that. I wanted it to just be out there.

Ben: Judd, you said that the experience was fun, and it *was* so much fun—up until the day it came out.

Judd: I remember at the premiere, literally at the premiere, someone handed me two faxes—the *Time* review and the *Newsweek* review—and they were both bad. And I was like, *What's happening?*

Jim: I knew. I *knew* we were in trouble, financially. The wolves were at the door at that point. But I also *knew* that we were doing something interesting that, in retrospect, we were gonna look back on and—

Ben: I remember that you never ever had any question about where you wanted it to go. I blame you.

Jim: I would take it further. I would.

Judd: At the time, it felt like you were throwing down the gauntlet, that you were announcing that you wanted to do things other than big, broad comedy.

Jim: It was a complete rebellion.

Judd: It kind of set up people to know that *The Truman Show* and *Eternal Sunshine* were coming. This one was the first time they were like, "Oh my God, this is *not* what his other movies were like."

Jim: How they speak about it still is so strange to me. It's like, "And then he gave the audience something they weren't ready for. . . ." They talk about it as if it was some murderously dark thing and I think it was just funny, and the need of the character is hilarious, but our sensibility, you and me—you love to go to that place.

Ben: Were you thinking of that at all when we were doing it, though? In terms of how audiences would react to it?

Jim: No, I always follow what I think is funny.

Ben: Your character is funny to me because he's just so needy, and he's so—he just wants a friend. I mean, he has a very clear motivation. He's pure.

Judd: And it took an insane level of commitment. Jim, you had limitless energy: It was never like, "I'm tired. Can I go home?" It was always like, "Grr, how many more? Let's go, let's go!" (*Growling sound*)

Ben: I think we were sort of all at that place in our lives where we sort of had nothing else going on except our work.

Jim: We had nowhere else to go.

Ben: I just wanted to be there all the time.

Judd: I remember when—I used to have panic attacks around this time from smoking too much weed and working too hard. And I'd have to go into these meetings with the head of Sony, Mark Canton—

Jim: Everything was on the line for Mark at that point.

Judd: And I'd realize that this meeting is going to take two hours and I'd have a panic attack. Or we'd be at page five of a hundred and five and I'd know that I was going to have a panic attack for a hundred and fifteen pages but not *look* like I was having a panic attack.

Jim: Wow. I didn't know you were going through so much, Judd.

Judd: Here's something: Jim, you make sweet love to my wife, Leslie Mann, in the movie *I Love You Phillip Morris*.

Jim: We go at it! We go at it like bandits. Like bandits! My God, my forehead was bleeding from the headboard.

Ben: Now, what was that like?

Jim: It was insane. Unbelievable. I dislocated her hip.

Judd: I don't mind when it's friends! Between friends, it's okay. The only person that bothered me was Owen Wilson.

Jim: Well, of course. Because you figure, like, that could be something real.

Judd: I just want to be apologized to before you do it—like, "Sorry, Judd, it's the job." But Owen was just like, "Hi, Judd." Then just did it. Anyway, Jim, was this the weirdest character you've played? Or Ace Ventura? Like, what's the top three weirdest Jim Carrey characters?

Jim: I don't know. I don't think they've happened yet. But yeah, Ace was definitely an out-there character. And suddenly I got this big paycheck and stuff, and I didn't know what to do with myself. My first terror went through me—*Oh my God, you're getting paid a lot of money, you're gonna get safe*—and so my reaction is always to do something outrageous.

Ben: Well, it worked well for you until this movie.

Jim: Till I started chasing penguins around and kissing up to the public. No, this movie *rocks*! I don't care what anybody says. I don't care what the masses say. This movie is dear to me.

Judd: How do you feel about the movies you've made since then, about your canon?

Jim: It won't be complete, Judd, until you do your best work with me. Seriously, we have to reteam. It has to happen. I mean, honestly. I think the world is ready for this.

Ben: They're clamouring for *Cable Guy 2*.

Judd: That *would* be awesome.

Ben: This time we'll have a hundred-million-dollar budget.

Jim: And I should get paid fifty of the hundred million! That would be amazing.

Judd: For all the film students out there—are they learning anything about film right now, listening to this?

Ben: I never know if these things are supposed to be entertaining or informative.

Jim: I don't know what they're supposed to be.

Judd: This is your first commentary.

Jim: I feel so virginal right now.

Judd: I kinda feel like you should do some impressions, since we're on audio now.

(Jim does an impression.)

Judd: Now do your Clint Eastwood face!

Ben: Come on, dude. I was just watching that on YouTube. There is this incredible YouTube video of you doing all the impressions, from the early days—

Jim: Well, yeah, I was on the Johnny Carson show. Remember him?

Judd: You were on with Johnny? Did you meet Johnny Carson, or—

Jim: I was on twice with Johnny. He was awesome, man! I loved him. He was on something, for sure, but—

Judd: He had questionable years of sobriety.

Jim: I don't know *what* he was doing, but he had energy to burn. It was crazy. Between commercials he'd just be looking at you out of the corner of his eye and drumming with the pencils or something and going (*giggles manically, sniffs*). Just, like, going like the hounds of hell. He was like a child. A man-child.

Judd: I remember Ben and I being somewhat shocked at your energy level, too. Take after take after take—it literally threw me as a person that it was possible.

Jim: I'm a desperate human being.

Judd: Do you feel like you're needier now or then?

Jim: I'm definitely in more pain now than I was.

Ben: Me too! I'll join you there.

Judd: Does success bring about peace and calm, or more pain?

Jim: When you start to realize that peace and calm are not actually gonna help you in the business—that they'll actually be bad for you—that's when the real divide happens. When you go, *Oh, I could work towards peace, I could find bliss, but I won't have a career*. It's all about abandonment, it's all about need, it's all about worthlessness. If I remain worthless in my own mind, I will be the king of show business.

Ben: The building blocks of success.

Judd: I remember John Cleese—he *knows* he's not as funny anymore, but he says he doesn't care because he's happier now. But I have to say, he seems pretty pissed lately and he's been pretty funny. He got divorced recently.

Jim: Oh yeah, there you go.

Ben: Pain and humor go together.

Ben: There's David Cross! Left side of the frame.

Jim: David Cross! We love David Cross. How many people were in this movie? We started the industry!

Judd: Sometimes when I watch this movie—I always thought it was going to be some kind of wild roller-coaster ride that'd also be, like, super-fun and delightful. But then, it has true madness in it.

Ben: I think it was a roller-coaster ride, it's just that it was going *down* the whole time. The big drop.

Jim: I disagree. I think it's sublime.

Ben: No, but it's a fun drop.

Judd: I remember when Jim said at the end of the movie, "I have to die. I need to jump off the tower and die."

Jim: Yeah.

Ben: Well, you should have died, that's the thing.

Jim: I really should have. When you go halfway, it never works.

Ben: That's my fault. I take responsibility.

Judd: They weren't going to let us kill you.

Jim: People don't understand, truly, how warped you are, Ben. They haven't even scratched the surface. Your iceberg is large under sea level there.

Judd: Ben, this was the second movie you directed, after *Reality Bites*, but did you feel like, *Oh, I'm not getting as much acting work at this time, so that's why I'm gonna direct?* Or—how do you decide how much acting to do? It takes so long to direct.

Ben: Well, this was a weird period in time. I sort of had a career as an actor but not really—

Jim: (*Pretends to wake up from snoring*) Sorry, guys!

Ben: Let's go back to the beginning—when I was about fifteen I played with the idea of becoming an actor.

Jim: You didn't direct for quite some time after *Cable Guy*, did you?

Ben: Well, nobody was banging down the door. Let's call it—basically I got a new agent. And he said, "Okay, you can't do anything for about six months."

Jim: Hide under the porch.

Ben: And then we'll see where we're at. It's so obvious in show business. When a movie doesn't make a lot of money, people don't call.

Judd: But then you did *Zero Effect*, and then right into *Something About Mary?*

Ben: I did—after this, I did *Zero Effect*, *Something About Mary*, *Permanent Midnight*, and *Friends and Neighbors*. I could keep going, Jim—

Jim: No, I'm loving it.

Judd: But I remember when you got *Something About Mary*, that was big, because your star had not risen—

Ben: It was a break. Huge. The Farrelly Brothers gave me a chance because they liked *Flirting with Disaster*.

Jim: Which is one of the classic comedies of all time, by the way. That was a genius movie.

Ben: But it was a weird time, where I didn't know what I was going to—

Jim: When you kiss Téa [Leoni] in that movie, did you *really* kiss her?

Judd: Versus how *you* kissed her, in *Fun with Dick and Jane*?

Jim: It was crazy! It was crazy what was happening outside the frame.

Judd: I just remember once, we were at a restaurant after *Something About Mary*, and you were saying, "It's really weird, because people keep walking up to me with their hair gelled up, like with semen," and I was like, "Really? Nooooo." And then a girl walked up to our table and said, "Can you come say hello to my friends?" And you walked over and came back and said, "One of the girls had her hair gelled up, like the—"

Jim: It's a nice thing! That's nice.

Judd: It's nice having catchphrases, visuals, that people yell at you.

Ben: But this was your reality, Jim, when you were making this movie. It had already been like that for a few years. What was it like?

Jim: It was odd.

Judd: I remember being in the mall with you, Jim. We were in a bookstore and suddenly people started walking up to you, and then more people, and more people, and then we realized every single person in the mall is headed to you, and then it got sort of dangerous for us to get out and became a *Hard Day's Night* moment.

Jim: No, exactly. And that's why I'm a martial artist. That's why I'm a weapons expert.

Judd: How emotional do you get now when a movie does well, or badly? Like after having made a lot of movies, how emotionally connected are you?

Jim: My entire self-worth is wrapped up in it.

Ben: I find it hard to totally disconnect from that stuff.

Jim: I want to go to a place where they hate me personally, and I have to win them back. It's odd, because some of them—when a movie doesn't work, you know, it's because it had something of gravity in it, and actually there was something that was not going to appeal to everybody, and it spirited people away in the other direction.

Ben: It's a complicated thing. Because how do you disconnect from that, but not make it about yourself, too?

Jim: Whenever you try to do something serious, you're gonna lose people. Certain people. Because they want you to be a certain thing and—

Ben: There is that thing with comedy. People can take it very personally if you're not there to be *funny*.

Jim: On Twitter, man, every once in a while, every fiftieth person is like, "Who do you think you are? You better not be dramatic anymore. Don't you be dramatic!"

Ben: I'll tweet something about Haiti and there'll be someone who'll tweet back, "Be funny! Who cares about Haiti!"

Jim: "Who cares about Haiti? Put your penis in your zipper and shut up."

Ben: "I'm unfollowing you, you're not funny. You just care about Haiti."

Judd: I get that for retweeting your Haiti things! "Stop retweeting Ben's Haiti things!"

Jim: "Who do you think you are, funnyman?"

Ben: Judd, how do you feel when your movies come out?

Judd: I have those moments where—

Ben: I'm looking for some insight here.

Judd: Where I'm so proud . . . and it doesn't do well. Like this movie. This blew my mind—I didn't recover like you guys. This one threw me for years because I loved it *so deeply*. Like, how come—I loved this work so much, what Jim's doing, what Ben's doing, and how come it didn't do well? It threw me because I thought I was in tune with what the audience liked.

Ben: See, I've never felt like I had any idea about what the audience liked. It's always like a crapshoot, really. (*To Jim*) We were talking about it—you only do what feels good to you, right?

Jim: Yeah. Only what feels good.

Ben: Yeah. How can you figure out what twenty million people will like?

Jim: Well, it's the Emerson thing: What's true for one man isn't true for all, and—

Judd: I went back to TV after this. I retreated.

Ben: I didn't direct again for four years after this.

Judd: It's true.

Jim: I still marvel at where everybody went. It just blows me away. It's hard for me to even be in the room with you guys.

Ben: (*Laughs*) Honestly, though, Jim, just to put it in context, when we did this movie, you were giving us a shot—right? I mean, wasn't Jim giving us a shot?

Judd: We were all giving each other a shot, but in weirdly interwoven ways.

Jim: Judd was like pumping me back when I was in the clubs and stuff, and no one was watching me.

Ben: I remember going to your young comedian special, in Phoenix, with David Spade.

Jim: Judd actually opened for me.

Judd: And I thought, *I gotta quit. Because I can't do that.*

Ben: So what did you think, Jim, when you said to everybody, "I want Judd to produce it," and then Judd said, "I want Ben to direct it"?

Jim: You know, this is the thing—

Ben: You had the power to do that.

Jim: No one really knows anything about comedy. We know a little bit about what we're doing, but as far as the industry—the exec branch—they don't know how it happens. It never comes to you prepared and ready to go, you always have to work it to death till the last second, in the moment and whatever. And I don't know what the hell I'm trying to say right now.

Ben: I think you're saying that they don't know, so they let you go with your instinct.

Jim: Exactly.

Ben: If you're the guy in the power position, they'll listen to you.

Jim: A lot of the comedies, you find yourself having to take shots with people, because they have that kind of—not a lot of experience, but they have that kernel of brilliance, that you go, like, "A good brain's a good brain, man. Let's go."

Judd: And they don't know to be scared. I mean, we weren't scared when we did this and in a lot of ways that's what makes it pure. Really, it's like a pure comedic thought.

Jim: There's not somebody trying to fit it into a shape or a form that's *known* to be successful.

Ben: And I don't think we knew enough about the context of the "business" to know whether or not it could hurt us.

Jim: It's too bad that my money got in the way of all the fun. But you know, I'm just not going to look back with regrets. I'm just not. It was fun. Such a fun movie. We really had a lot of *fun*. And I can't believe that the three of us can't find the time to come together again and do something creative. Seriously, I hate you guys.

Judd: We've all priced ourselves out of the business.

Jim: You guys got huge kingdoms. I can't even get inside.

Judd: I'll work for free. I'll say right now, I'll get it going.

Ben: Get my assistant, okay? She'll hook it up.

Judd: Call my assistant's assistant.

Jim: We really should do something, because this is not enough. We just cut our teeth on this thing.

Judd: It'd be fun now that we know more. But do you think we're scared now?

Jim: I'm not scared.

Ben: Fear is part of the experience, but—I'm beyond fear now.

Judd: I paid off my house, I'm okay.

Jim: You can live forever.

Judd: Is that where we stop?

Ben: I'm glad we did this. We've wanted to do this for about ten years, right?

Judd: Ten years.

Jim: Well, I'd never done this before. How'd we do, by the way? Did we do okay?

Ben: We can always come back and do it again.

Jim: Let's start it over. We're going to do it again. Turn it over and I'll be you this time, Judd.

JIMMY FALLON
(2015)

I don't understand Jimmy Fallon. He's fast, witty, handsome, musical, inventive, a confident performer, a great listener—and he is definitely having more fun than the rest of us combined. I always thought comedy came from pain. I thought the people who created it were drawing from some bottomless well of existential angst. I thought it was impossible to do it well if you are also an enthusiastic, hopeful, energetic person. Most talk show hosts are fun to watch because they seem so miserable, but Jimmy is the opposite. He is more of a Steve Allen or Martin Short type of guy. He is exactly what he seems to be when you see him on TV—a warm, chipper, funny guy. A good person. I wanted to speak with him to figure out how he became this way—with the secret hope that it would help me shed some of my old, boring, neurotic, my-pain-is-so-old-I-don't-even-remember-where-it-came-from BS. I think I got my answer but I am not sure I can make it work for me. (I think he is happy because he is not a Jew.)

Judd Apatow: I had the loveliest time with your wife at the wedding the other night.

Jimmy Fallon: She just got back. She's like, "Thank God for Judd Apatow. He was fantastic."

Judd: I was a stand-in for you.

Jimmy: Did you do all my bits?

Judd: Yeah. If she didn't look over, she may have thought that you were there.

Jimmy: Was it fun or was it just a wedding?

Judd: It was great. When you go to a wedding and Lionel Richie comes out and sings "I'm Easy," what more do you want?

Jimmy: Goose bumps.

Judd: He was really funny, too. I always get annoyed when someone like that is funny.

Jimmy: I know. What did he say, "I only do this if I get paid or invited," or something?

Judd: Yeah. (*Laughs*) I was—I wanted to say, "Hey, I used your song 'Hello' in *The 40-Year-Old Virgin!*" But then I realized I used it in the sequence where Steve Carell prepared to masturbate.

Jimmy: That's why I don't go out anymore. Because I'll see somebody— "Oh, hey, I just talked about you. I talked about your bad plastic surgery. Sorry!"

Judd: That's your biggest conflict. You have no choice but to be nice to their face, and then take them down in the monologue.

Jimmy: (*Laughs*) What a big tough guy I am.

Judd: Someone told me a funny story about the *South Park* guys—they had, I guess, torn Janeane Garofalo apart in something, and then they were in a restaurant and saw her across the way, and just ran away before they could be spotted.

Jimmy: Did you ever hear the story about Wayne Newton punching Johnny Carson?

Judd: No, no.

Jimmy: There's a story that Wayne Newton got pissed off that Johnny Carson was making jokes about him, so he stormed into his office, past his secretary, grabbed his collar, and said, "You say one more joke about me and I'll fucking knock your block off." I don't think Johnny mentioned him ever again.

Judd: I love people almost getting in fistfights over jokes.

Jimmy: What is wrong with people?

Judd: Your show seems so well run. I guess my first question—as some-body who had to run shows when I didn't know how to do it—would be how, in the beginning, did you know how to set up your show, not only for it to work comedically, but for it to be a place that was happy and func-tional?

Jimmy: We just went in knowing that we might get canceled. And if you're going to go down, you have to go down doing what you like doing and what's fun for you, because I don't ever want to do something painful and then have everyone go, "Hey, that works. Keep doing that painful thing for years."

Judd: *SNL* is famous for being a survival-of-the-fittest atmosphere. It's al-most built for people to turn on each other because everyone is under so much pressure to get on the show. But all these other shows that Lorne produced seem like happy places.

Jimmy: It's so—I watch *SNL* all the time and I see a new cast member, and I think, *Oh, man, no one's going to write for that person next week.* Because they scored too hard.

Judd: (*Laughs*)

Jimmy: Got to take them down a notch.

Judd: You're very close to Lorne. What is the thing you think people don't understand about him?

Jimmy: Maybe that he does not care about money. He's very successful, so he doesn't need money, but it's like—if it was anyone else, they would have made some contract deal where they would get five percent of every person who leaves to become uber-famous. Will Ferrell would be giving Lorne five percent after the next *Anchorman*. But Lorne doesn't care. He's proud of the people who do something else off the show. It makes him happy.

Judd: What was exciting about *SNL*—well, I'm a little bit older than you, but when *SNL* was originally on, it was before the VCR was something that most people had. And when *SNL* was on, you really thought, *I may never get to see this again*. You had to watch it because there was no way to know if you would ever get another shot at it.

Jimmy: I taped every *Saturday Night Live* as soon as I could afford videotapes. I taped every episode that I could tape. Then I would go to my friend's house with the tape and show them the best sketches—you got to see Chris Farley and stuff like that, you know. I was like the human Funny or Die.

Judd: Where did you grow up?

Jimmy: Saugerties, New York, which is Woodstock.

Judd: Did you have friends who loved comedy? Because I was totally alone. No one gave a shit.

Jimmy: I had a good crew of maybe like five to ten kids I could watch the tapes with. They'd have a party and sneak booze in the basement or something and I'd come in with a tape and show a couple of funny sketches, and they'd all laugh, and we'd just hang out and listen to music and stuff like that. I was really into it. And then my dad bought a VCR, because he wanted the video camera that came with the VCR that attached with the wire—

Judd: Yeah.

Jimmy: —and you had to carry around a box.

Judd: (*Laughs*)

Jimmy: He used that to tape home movies, but I used it to tape *Saturday Night Live*. They had like a weird rerun thing of *Saturday Night Live* that was on in the eighties. I taped *Saturday Night Live* as well, but they also ran old ones from the seventies.

Judd: I remember that.

Jimmy: And so I used to tape them, but I couldn't always play the tapes back because that was the only VCR we had in the house, so what I would do is play back Richard Pryor's monologue, and record it on a reel-to-reel that I bought at a garage sale. Then I would go up in my room and play it and lip-sync Richard Pryor's monologue in the mirror.

Judd: Oh my God.

Jimmy: I did Steve Martin, too. I would do all of their bits and lip-sync them like they were songs.

Judd: I'm always fascinated what draws people to doing any of this, but you seemed to have super-cool, healthy parents.

Jimmy: They're not healthy, but they are definitely—

Judd: You liked them?

Jimmy: They were great. I had a great childhood.

Judd: Are your parents still around?

Jimmy: Yeah, I talk to them almost every day. They are great. They belong in a mental institution, but besides that, very nice people.

Judd: (*Laughs*)

Jimmy: They were funny people. We were an Irish Catholic family, so we'd have parties. My dad loved to listen to music, so we always had the radio on, and so they would have parties and people came over and after a couple of hours people would stand up in front of everybody and sing a song. And then everyone clapped and then someone else would go, "No, *you* sing one," and then someone would sing "I Left My Heart in San Francisco," and then someone would sing "When Irish Eyes Are Smiling," and then my grandfather would get up and sing last, some song, and everyone would start crying because it was a really sad Irish song. And that was the end of the night. But we'd all have a good laugh, my grandmother did bits—my grandparents lived right next to me, almost in my backyard, in a little guest house almost. They kind of helped raise me. I really got a lot of my sense of humor from watching them do bits, but we would listen to comedians on Sunday mornings. They would play this channel, an AM radio station that would play comedians, and we would listen and—it was fantastic. We used to listen to the radio and just laugh, and go, "Oh my gosh." And then I started getting into it. I really loved comedians, so my dad would buy an album like Rodney Dangerfield, *No Respect*, and he would—I remember this—he would take a key and scratch out any of the dirty words, so that when I played the record, it would skip over the curse word.

Judd: That is hilarious. And you were never a dirty comedian.

Jimmy: I never was a dirty—no, I never was.

Judd: But your show now, in a way, is like sitting around, singing songs at the piano, enjoying people. Is that how you see it? I mean, the idea of my crazy Jewish family sitting around, singing a song, is unfathomable.

Jimmy: This was a weekly event. This would happen all the time, and everyone would get involved. My sister wasn't as into performing as I was, but we would play "King Tut" and come downstairs in my mom's dresses— the ones that looked kind of Egyptian—and we would dance and lip-sync "King Tut."

Judd: See, I did all that and no one cared and I was alone.

Jimmy: (*Laughs*)

Judd: It's like we have the same story—if everyone ignored you and you just watched *Love Connection* alone in your room every day for seven years.

Jimmy: I look back, I mean there are tapes of me doing Pee-wee Herman and impressions of people, Michael Jackson, Eddie Murphy—

Judd: I remember meeting you when you first got to *SNL*, I remember seeing you there. And I remember you did an impression of Adam Sandler.

Jimmy: That was my breakout episode. Ben Stiller was hosting.

Judd: That's right. It was the Stiller episode. That's why I was there.

Jimmy: It was a Halloween episode, Ben Stiller hosted, and I remember Ben said to Higgins, "Hey, this kid does a great Sandler." They go, "Yeah, yeah, we've seen it, but Adam doesn't have a movie coming out, so we'll wait until something—" and Ben goes, "No, it doesn't matter. You should have him do it." So we wrote up celebrity *Jeopardy*, where I did Sandler and Ben did Tom Cruise and Daryl did Sean Connery. That same episode is when I played guitar and did guitar impressions with Colin Quinn on "Weekend Update."

Judd: Yeah. Wow.

Jimmy: Usually, if they know that a bit is going to kill, they'll put it at the end of "Update," but they didn't think I was going to work that well, so they put me in the middle—and I crushed. It was a good bit. I did impressions of Alanis Morissette and all this stuff and no one knew—I was brand-new. It was my third episode, I think.

Judd: That's the biggest moment, when you realize you've found something that will make you break out a little bit.

Jimmy: And that was it. I was the impressions guy. It all started happening from that one episode.

Judd: You try so hard to figure out what will make people notice you—

Jimmy: I remember I called Adam before I did it, because I wanted to make sure I had his blessing. They called him and put him on the phone with me, and I was so nervous. I was like, "Hi, Adam." He goes, "How ya doing, man? Let's hear it." I go, "Okay." I go (*making funny sounds*), I go, "All right, I talked to my mother the other day and she said, "What is wrong with you? There's something wrong with you. . . .'" And I was doing this whole bit, and he goes, "All right, that's good. That's good. You gotta do it." He was awesome.

Judd: That's because no one ever calls or shows any respect in that situation. I remember Dana Carvey did Shandling on *Saturday Night Live*. It was really mean, and not a great sketch—I think Carvey called Shandling up after and was like, "Oh, I'm so sorry," and Shandling wasn't thrilled about it. Garry just said, "You know what? We're going to do a *Larry Sanders* episode about it." And then they wrote an incredible *Larry Sanders* where Larry was mad when Dana Carvey guest-hosted—he did an impression of him and tore him apart.

Jimmy: I remember that. It was a great one. Out of all the things I watched to get ready for this job, *Larry Sanders* was the ultimate—

that's the ultimate piece of advice I'd tell anyone to watch if you're doing a talk show. It's so real and so well done. That's how a show gets made.

Judd: It seems like effortless, the way you generate all this material.

Jimmy: Well, I think you have to keep trying and keep swinging and get up to bat and try a different type of joke, because you don't know which one is going to connect. We try a lot of stuff that doesn't work, and you go, like, "Wow, that one did not work," but we tried it. And that's what you have to do. I remember—it was the first season of *Late Night*, and you were nice enough to come on the show and you go, "This is great, this is fun, but honestly, remember these years because you will not be doing this much pre-tapes and stuff down the road because you guys will burn out. There's no way." And I really took that to heart. Every time I'm like, "We don't have time to do that," I think, *No, you know what, I'm going to make Judd Apatow proud and I'm going to stay late, I'm going to stay till two in the morning.* I swear to God, I think about it all the time.

Judd: Because Letterman, there was a moment when he just stopped going to New Jersey and knocking on doors, doing bits.

Jimmy: But that was the best part.

Judd: It was. It was incredible. And I felt a deep sadness when I heard he was not going to do remote pieces anymore.

Jimmy: He was the best at it.

Judd: It must have been odd to go up against Letterman, since he's the one that made us all want to be funny.

Jimmy: Yeah, but it's just the way it worked out.

Judd: Do you ever interact with him?

Jimmy: I don't. You know, we started joking back and forth a while ago. He would say—he would try to tweet me. Almost like he didn't understand Twitter. He's like, "I'll tweet Jimmy Fallon!"

Judd: That's funny.

Jimmy: It was a funny bit. Then, I would try to teach him how to tweet through Twitter, and then I think CBS asked him to stop.

Judd: (*Laughs*) He was sending too many people to your Twitter account.

Jimmy: Yeah. They were like, just stop saying his name. I think they have a blanket rule, CBS isn't allowed to talk about me or something. So silly.

Judd: Everyone in late night right now is great. It's a weird moment, as a fan of comedy and good things: You go, *What am I going to do, get up every morning and watch five hours of talk shows?*

Jimmy: You can't do that. That's a waste of your day. But the bummer for me is that I can't watch anyone else now because I don't want to take any of their bits. Being an impressionist, I imitate everybody, so if I watch Letterman every night, I would start doing him in my show, and if I watch Kimmel, I'd do his bits, you know. So I get nervous and I just can't watch anyone.

Judd: Is there a part of this job that still blows your mind? For me, watching your show, when you're standing next to Bruce Springsteen singing a song and doing a bit, I think, there must be a feeling of nirvana in that moment that I can't even imagine.

Jimmy: But when it's happening, you don't feel it. The *idea* of it happening—it's almost happening, it's about to happen—that's the excitement. Once it's happening, you just don't want to screw it up and embarrass him and I want to make sure he's having a good time, so I'm really kind of nervous and just want to focus and do well.

Judd: The one that made me laugh was when you were singing with Paul Simon, and I realized, oh, there's no joke here. Jimmy just forced Paul Simon to sing a song with him.

Jimmy: (*Laughs*) I will never do anything like that again. I did that once and I sang "With a Little Help from My Friends" with Ringo, and that was the last time I'll ever sing.

Judd: No, you have to keep doing it. It just made me laugh so hard. This is a fun moment in late night. I would watch *The Tonight Show*, I never felt I was like Johnny Carson, but it's funny for me now to have almost all those late-night slots filled by people I'm friends with or know a little.

Jimmy: Yeah, you know them, and you're like, wait, what?

Judd: You can't imagine Carson being as excited about doing his show as you are and we are. Like I don't think Carson ever thought, *Oh my God, I can't believe Dean Martin was here tonight.*

Jimmy: (*Laughs*)

Judd: Those shows were driven by such darkness. Carson was funny, but he also looked like there was so much more going on here, which we didn't understand. And I guess Letterman is that way, too. We were fascinated to see how these guys would interact with people because, on some level, we thought they were miserable.

Jimmy: Yeah, well, you could tell when Dave hated somebody or when Johnny hated somebody.

Judd: I think that people are generally struggling, and a lot of people are having a hard time and are miserable. To watch someone who is genuinely enjoying themselves is an elixir, and it shocks people. I think they watch you and think, *I wish I was that fucking happy*, and they get a real—it gives them a break. I think we watch Letterman out of our angry side some of the time.

Jimmy: That's not my style, so I'm not good at that.

Judd: It taps into the national neurosis in a way, where people are so happy to not be unhappy. You know, we all want to be around the piano, singing the song.

Jimmy: I don't know if you had this, but I always wanted to please everybody. I always wanted to make everyone proud of me and happy.

Judd: Yeah, but what is different for me is that, when I go home, I feel shame at the need to make people happy in order to feel good. I don't know how you are afterwards, but it doesn't feel like you have the bad aftertaste.

Jimmy: When it's the TV show, I don't really, no. But if I'm at a party or a wedding and I have to get up and do some bit that I think is funny—and if it goes well—I just go like, *Why did you have to do that at the guy's wedding? Can't he just get married without you being the big star?*

Judd: How is the social part of this life for you, where you get to know all these people that you look up to?

Jimmy: It's odd, but you get used to it after a little while. I don't know, all of this is fun and surreal, and it's just been getting crazier and crazier.

Judd: And now you have two kids.

Jimmy: I do.

Judd: You have two girls?

Jimmy: Just like you. I'm like, I finally get it now. It's like, this is why you're doing what you're doing. This is the future. And also, God, it's so worth it. It's just the greatest feeling in the world. The little arms, they hug you and it's like, ugh, it's a crusher and I'm a mush. I'm an Irish emotional mess.

Judd: You understand how people get needy with their kids because you're like, "You're still going to talk to me when you leave, right?"

Jimmy: Totally. It's so embarrassing. And you always say, "Well, I won't do that, I'll be the cool parent." But you can't help it.

Judd: You can't and you just—that balance of how do I give them rules, which they want to fight me on, and guarantee they want me to be their best friend at the same time is impossible.

Jimmy: You invented this human, so you're like, *I made the best human I can make. This is my Sistine Chapel, and I should be able to appreciate this. Not someone else.*

Judd: And then there's that weird moment—and everyone tells you about it your whole life and you think, *No, that will never happen to me*—where, for a year or two, your kids tell you to fuck off.

Jimmy: Yeah. It does happen. Right around twelve or thirteen is what everyone's telling me.

Judd: That little kid who's just, like, "I want to show you the teddy bear I bought"—twelve years later they're like, "Get the fuck out of my room!"

Jimmy: "Get the fuck out."

Judd: I have the thing with my daughter where I hate any boy that comes by—like, in my bones, I hate any boy that is circling.

Jimmy: Yes.

Judd: But there's one kid that is like a super-goofy, nerdy kid, who I realize, *Oh, that's me. That's exactly who I was in high school.* And I'll say, "What about dating that guy?" And she's like, "Oh, he's such a nerd." And I'm like, "You don't understand him. He's special. He's going to fill out one day. He'll show everybody."

Jimmy: (*Laughs*)

Judd: I'm like, "How come you don't want to date my doppelganger?"

Jimmy: But she will date someone like you.

Judd: That's the scary part. I wish I had self-esteem so she would like a guy with self-esteem.

Jimmy: I'm going to be so bummed out because my daughter is going to marry some feminine guy that laughs at himself too much. And I'm going to go, *That's me. She did it.*

JON STEWART
(2014)

I've known Jon Stewart since we were both young comedians. After his first attempt at a talk show on MTV, he took some time off to write and act on *The Larry Sanders Show*, where I was working as a writer, and we spent a lot of time together. As great as he was on that show—his acting was fantastic and he was a force in the writers' room—I always felt like it was a rest stop on the way to something bigger. He was like a lion taking a nap before going out on the hunt. After *Larry Sanders*, of course, he went on to anchor *The Daily Show*—and, you know, change the way comedy and politics intersect forever.

There are certain people I've known for a long time that I feel an odd sense of pride in knowing, because I simply can't believe how brilliant their work is and what they've accomplished. It shocks me that I used to sit in the back of clubs with these people, and they went on to speak to presidents and influence people in such a profound way. Jon is one of those people. He makes me proud to be in the world of comedy.

Judd Apatow: I am going to ease my way into this with you, but how much stand-up are you doing these days?

Jon Stewart: You know, these past couple of years I have not done much, but before that, I was going out one weekend every month, every other month, something like that. I try to keep it to that.

Judd: And are you still writing new material for your act?

Jon: I keep it just stale enough so that the rote memorization I had of my act was still, you know, mindful to some extent.

Judd: I just started doing stand-up again about four months ago. I hadn't done it in twenty-two years.

Jon: Holy shit.

Judd: But one of my strongest memories from my stand-up career was the night you and I were auditioning at Stand-Up New York for the HBO *Young Comedians Special*. And you went on and just smoked it. And got the special. And me, I had invited all of my high school friends to come watch, because I was still in my early twenties and still did things like that. Most of them had never seen me do stand-up, and I went up and ate it so hard. I still wake up in the middle of the night and get a shiver thinking about it.

Jon: How much do you love to bomb, though?

Judd: Uh.

Jon: Oh, I love the bomb. You have to *embrace* the bomb. And the bigger the moment, the tastier the bomb.

Judd: Is there one in particular that wakes you up in the middle of the night?

Jon: I think maybe the most pleasurable bomb was—you know, when you're bombing young and you're in the Cellar. Those are the most volatile bombs. Because you haven't quite established a baseline of confidence yet. So you really feel the sting of it. Like, *I can't understand why those Dutch sailors don't find this amusing,* you know. You don't realize the fragility of the atmosphere in the room.

Judd: Yeah.

Jon: I remember this one time. I had already been on TV for a bit by this time. They were reopening Radio City Music Hall, so this is probably the largest crowd I've played. It must have been five thousand people. And it's a big night of big stars—there's Billy Crystal, and they're raising him up on a platform through the stage floor, like he's Michael Jackson. He's leading the charge. Fucking crushing it, destroying the room. Ann-Margret is in the audience. This is like some big return to glamour for Radio City Music Hall, and I come out and there is some confusion in the audience as to why I am there. I can feel it. Six minutes into the bit, and it had not in any way dissipated. What was impressive about it was, you would think the law of averages says that if you have a room full of five thousand people, *some* of them are going to laugh at some point at something, even if it's just something they whispered to their friend. You know what I mean? But it was total silence. Impressive in its discipline. At a certain point you think, like, *Doesn't anyone here have a cold? Isn't anyone here going to sneeze? Shuffle their feet?* No sound. I really felt like there was a moment of silence at some point for something; I just didn't realize what it was. I'm coming offstage and it was truly shocking, in its unanimity and uniformity. And I turn and look and there's Shirley Jones. She's backstage. I don't know Shirley Jones. She looks at me and doesn't say anything; she just opens her arms up to give me a hug. It was one of those, like, *There, there, poor boy.*

Judd: Wow. I had one where—well, I didn't perform but it *felt* like I had performed. I went to the AFI tribute to Mel Brooks, and I was supposed to get up and speak and I got really nervous.

Jon: You can't win that.

Judd: The place is packed and I'm with my daughter. I'm usually with my wife at these things, because she will encourage me and say, "Don't worry, you always do great." But my daughter is as scared as I am. She's sixteen and terrified for me. So I would say to her, "I'm really scared," and she'd be like, "Oh my God." And then the show starts. Martin Short does a medley of Mel Brooks songs. Tears down the house. Billy Crystal comes out with the most heartfelt, hilarious anecdotes. Tears down the house. Sarah Silverman comes out and does some variation of what I was going to try to do, only better. *Decimates* the place. I turn to my daughter and say, "I'm really scared. I don't know if I can do it." And she goes, "Don't do it. Don't do it." I walk over to the first AD and say, "I'm not going to speak." That was as bad as it gets.

Jon: You actually defused the bomb with, like, ten seconds to go. You fucking pulled the plug, man.

Judd: I totally pulled the plug, and then people just kept killing. The funny end of it is that special won the Emmy for best special and I thought, *That's because I ran for my life.*

Jon: You know what you did? You sacrificed yourself. To give them the Emmy.

Judd: I knew Mel didn't need me. He had enough love.

Jon: It's always stunning how the old-school showbiz guys can crush anywhere, anytime. You realize that what we would consider the gauntlet of stand-up—the shitty clubs, the one-nighters in Jersey, the hotels in Rochester, all the shit you go through—is like a sanitized private school compared to what these guys did.

Judd: I asked about stand-up because it strikes me that you're basically doing a fifteen-to-twenty minute stand-up set every night on your show—and one that you've never done before.

Jon: The show is such a different animal, though. It's structured differently and written differently, and you have all the creature comforts of television to fall back on: The over-the-shoulder graphics, the montage, the willing audience. It's *such* a different experience. It doesn't feel analogous to stand-up in any way, actually, and maybe that's why doing stand-up still feels pure to me. It's like when bands get a little more established but they still want to go back and play the clubs they grew up in. Stand-up is such a visceral, direct experience.

Judd: When you think about your post–*Daily Show* days, do you hunger to be doing more live performance or—

Jon: I hunger for a nap.

Judd: I know. I watch the show every night and I have the same reaction every night: *How does Jon keep up this level of enthusiasm?*

Jon: I always have this sense, with the show, that it is a beast that just wants to get the hell away from us. And so the effort and energy that it takes to corral the beast every night—that is where your focus has to be. That being said, I guess I don't look at the forms as exclusionary. It's really a function of time, and I think that when I stop doing this, I will want to do stand-up. I just don't think I'll do it to the exclusion of other things, the way that we used to. The single-mindedness of it when we were younger is probably something I won't return to.

Judd: Here's the part that I am most impressed by: When I go to work in the morning, I'll usually have someone bring me breakfast. I get somebody to make me—

Jon: Do you really?

Judd: Yeah, and I'll—

Jon: What do you have for breakfast?

Judd: An egg white omelet of some sort.

Jon: Look at you, with the egg white omelet.

Judd: And that'll take me—

Jon: Maybe a little spinach in there, a little tomato, a little feta?

Judd: I'll have a little—uh, yeah, spinach mainly.

Jon: Nice.

Judd: And I'll sit and I'll eat that omelet and I'll take an hour. I'll watch your show. I'll watch Colbert. Okay, so there's an hour where I've gotten no work done. And then I'll just kind of wander around and chat with everyone at the office and make a couple of calls. I can easily kill until one o'clock that way. But you have to hit the ground running. Hard. Every single day.

Jon: We work in an office. You know, it's funny. People always say to me, Ah, man, you guys—it probably must be so much fun, sitting around! And it's like, Yeah, our morning meeting starts at nine. We have to pitch out our ideas—and in some ways that is the challenge of a show. It's to create a factory that doesn't kill inspiration and imagination. You try to create a process that includes all the aspects of a mechanized process that we recognize as soul killing while not actually killing souls.

Judd: That is the invisible genius that the world will never understand. We worked at *Larry Sanders Show* together as writers, and we've had friends who have worked on many shows. And I find that, on most shows, the result of a very difficult process with high standards is that everybody hates the head guy. The head guy is not a beloved figure—whether it's Garry, Roseanne, or Cosby.

Jon: See, here's where I disagree. I think that's not necessary. When I was working on those other shows, I felt like there were aspects to it that didn't need to exist in order to maintain the creative excitement. It didn't need to be Machiavellian. You could get everybody to have common cause, and do it in a way that maintained a certain humanity. I always look at it like: Think of how much energy it takes to fuck with people. What if you try to use that energy to get the show done faster and better and get everybody out by seven? If I go into the morning meeting and I have clarity, and I can *articulate* that clarity, everybody's day is easier. If that doesn't happen, it's my fault.

Judd: How often does it happen that something heinous happens in the world, and you walk in and say, "I have no take on this whatsoever, it's so horrifying. I have nothing to say."

Jon: Well, then that's our take. And that's where the stand-up background comes in. What's the audience feeling right now? Let's just articulate back to the audience what they're feeling so at the very least, they get a recognition laugh as opposed to bringing them some sort of analysis. None of us may have a take, but if you maintain your ability to recognize a good idea, at the very least you know everybody is up for it. We'll sit in those meetings and we may come in with nothing, but at some point, it's sort of like it's a refinery. We've been here sixteen years, so we've sanded out every rough aspect of the process. Any extraneous energy that would be spent on things other than trying to make the show good have been removed.

Judd: I just always felt, and I don't know if this is your take on things, but when we did the last-season *The Larry Sanders Show*, life got very stressful.

Jon: It was tough.

Judd: It was tough for many reasons, but a big part of it was that the show was so personal to Garry. It was hard to crack what he would like, and he was acting so much that he needed the staff to come through for him so he could have time to sleep and do his work. There was a tension that couldn't be removed, which is: You were never going to nail it and it was always going to be painful for Garry because then Garry would have to say, "Okay, just come to my house on Sunday so I can rewrite the script." There was some pain to that. But as I've watched the evolution of *The Daily Show*, I thought that something about the experience of being at *The Larry Sanders Show*, and being around Garry, as complicated as it was, must have inspired you in some way.

Jon: No question. Well, first of all, Garry is brilliant. The biggest thing, and this is not necessarily what comes through on *The Daily Show*, but the biggest thing that I picked up from Garry was the difference between character and caricature. That idea of, you know, it would have been very easy for us to solve almost any story problem we had with Hank walking in and calling someone a cocksucker. We knew that would kill, and it would move, but it would reduce everyone to two dimensions. Garry also taught me about intention. Intention is a really big thing at this show. We always want to know where's the intention and, now, let's find a path to that intention. Those were positive lessons. But then, there were the negative lessons, too—it's where I learned the importance of trying to create an atmosphere that was maybe slightly less volatile.

Judd: Yes, well, there was always that—the struggle that comes when certain people are trying to please their boss. My approach was always: This is an impossible job for Garry. I'm just going to try and help him in any way I can. But other people, when they would pitch a joke that didn't get through, would get angry at Garry. And that was destructive.

Jon: It's so important to remove preciousness and ownership. You have to invest everybody in the success of the show, and to let them feel good about their contribution to it without becoming the sole proprietor of a joke. There has to be an understanding that that may be a great joke, but it might not serve the larger intention, or the narrative, of the show. You have to make sure that everybody feels invested without feeling that type of ownership. The other side of it is doing twelve episodes is a very different process from having to set up something that can serve a hundred and sixty episodes, and I think you can get away with more volatility in that other environment.

Judd: And the storytelling requires that people go to some deep place, emotionally, which makes them vulnerable and raw. And on a show like *Larry Sanders*, you had the sense that the episodes are going to hang around for a long time, and be seen more over and over again, so you really can't bear to have a crappy one.

Jon: Correct. The fact that *The Daily Show* is ephemeral makes the process so much more forgiving. The idea that you're crafting twelve unique, careful episodes is very different than the feeling of, like, *Okay, well, that one sucked, but who's on tomorrow?* It gives you a cushion you might not have elsewhere.

Judd: Looking back, one could say that the final season of *Larry Sanders* is almost perfect, in its story line, with the young guy, played by you, pushing Garry out.

Jon: It's *All About Eve*.

Judd: And it is exactly what happened with Leno and Conan.

Jon: We created this template. People used to say to me, *Larry Sanders* is a satire on the dark underbelly of show business. And I always felt like, *Oh, you have no idea*. You have no idea of the darkness of the underbelly of show business.

Judd: How has the way that you look at *The Daily Show* changed over the years? Do you have a different sense of its purpose now?

Jon: I never think about its purpose. I think about its process, and that has changed dramatically. In other words, the evolution has been less about: What is our job here, or what is our purpose of being here? It's about: How can we make the show better, more distinct, with different voices? The two areas where I think the show has evolved the most are through the integration of new technologies, obviously—you know, search engines that didn't exist when we started, and that help us find material. When we got here, we used to cut the show in an online room. You could use maybe five rolls for an act and if you cut that montage and you got one of them wrong, you had to go back and start again. And I also think we have a better understanding of the diversity of voice. We've moved it from more of a strict, periodic structure into something that could become more essayistic.

Judd: Was there ever a moment when you realized, *Oh shit, people are actually paying attention to my point of view a lot more closely than I thought they would be?*

Jon: There were two moments where that occurred, in some measure. One was winning an Emmy. That got in my head a little bit, feeling like I suddenly had a responsibility, that we had to live up to this thing even if I couldn't fully define what that thing was.

Judd: Sometimes I liken it to Chappelle in the sense that, for some reason, the responsibility of the show took him away from the idea of having fun, and enjoying himself.

Jon: The sense I got from Dave was it wasn't so much the responsibility as he wasn't sure if the show was being received in the way it was intended. I think Dave felt a responsibility, as a black performer, to live up to a responsibility and to not give people—you know, it's sort of what we call the bucket-of-blood laugh. George Carlin and I used to talk about that a little bit because he would do those shows where he'd be like, "You know, we only bomb brown people. We only bomb brown people except when we bombed Germany they were white people and that's because they were going, you know, because they were bombing people and that's our fucking job. That's our fucking job." It's a great bit but you definitely felt, in the audience, that there were some people going, "Yeah, that's our fucking job!" And for George, it created this sense of "Oh they're not taking this in the way that I intended it." And in some ways you have to let that go because it's something you can't control. You can only control the intention of the execution, but I think for Dave it became more complicated than that.

Judd: I get it, too, because every time I do stand-up, I wake up the next morning and I feel this shame that is so intense, like I was drunk all night and I don't remember what I did.

Jon: Really?

Judd: I feel embarrassed at even having had an opinion or a thought.

Jon: But isn't that the whole—I mean, there's a certain arrogance in us entering this business. There's an arrogance in the idea of saying, *Where's that spotlight shining? Oh, it's up on the stage? Well shit, why don't I walk up there? What's in here that's going to amplify my voice? Is that a micro-phone? All right, so I got a light shining on me, and my voice is amplified and you're all looking at me. Well, let me stand here and give you some-thing worthwhile for ten minutes.* But I don't think it goes much further than that, if that makes sense. After that, it becomes a question of, does it resonate?

Judd: What effect does raising your kids have on the mechanics of getting all your work done and presenting your point of view with the world? How old are your kids now?

Jon: Ten and eight.

Judd: I have one about to turn seventeen and one about to turn twelve.

Jon: Oh dear, do they still like you?

Judd: They have to act like they like me because they still need me for some driving. But we're right at the end of that.

Jon: A little gas money might still keep you in the loop.

Judd: Maybe. But in some way, you must have perfected some sense of balance between your time at home and your time at work—which seems impossible, given how demanding your show is.

Jon: I have done my best, but it's still not satisfactory, especially as the kids get older. It's different when they begin to share and experience things that are more complex. It's one thing to, you know—I have this letter up in my office. It's something my daughter Maggie wrote to me. It says, and this was after we were down the Jersey Shore, bodysurfing. I think I tanked it and smashed into the sand. It says, "Daddy, I know you are a good writer. You're a good surfer, too. When you got on that big wave, you got hurt bad. I know you saw a lot of nature. You're a great dad. Love,

Maggie." That is, like, beautiful. It's simple. But now, they're older and they are beginning to articulate things in a much more complex way, and you need to be there more. And nine-to-nine is a shitty schedule for that kind of thing. So I'd like to say that I've achieved that balance, but the truth is, I probably haven't.

Judd: The conversation I get into in our house is: "Dad, we have money, so why don't you stop working so much?"

Jon: Because I'm an obsessive weirdo?

Judd: And what if Ebola happens in a much larger way and we really need to get the compound solidified?

Jon: Exactly. You are just preparing. I also think, to some extent, you are where you came from. No matter where you end up, no matter what you achieve, on some level, you feel like you belong in a basement underneath a Middle Eastern restaurant telling jokes. That's never out of you. Leno used to have this. He'd always say, "I never spend any of my stand-up money." He'd been doing *The Tonight Show* for like twenty years, and he'd say, "I don't spend my stand-up money. That goes right to the bank because you don't want to mess with that. You never know what's going to happen." And you're like, "Yeah, I guess the collapse of Western society maybe, but I think you're in pretty good shape." It's a psychosis more than anything else.

Judd: I know that when I started doing stand-up again, and I would get eighty dollars for my Saturday night spot at the Comedy Cellar, I held on to that money with a joy that I don't get when the *Drillbit Taylor* residuals come in.

Jon: Because we're psychotic and, at some level, not living with a real sense of things. But also, you know, I like working, man. I just wish I was better at it. One of the nice things about doing this show versus stand-up is that there is a moment of Zen at the end of it. There's a good night. You're done. With stand-up, you're never done. You always feel like you've got to keep that notebook by the bed. And so you stop experiencing anything. You just exist purely as an observer, constantly trying to figure out if I'm going to be able to work a bit out of this. It's a different way of approaching life. It's exhausting.

Judd: How is it that your family's not angry at you?

Jon: You'll have to talk to them. I think there's a certain normalcy. My kids have never known me not to have this schedule.

Judd: Do you enjoy work in the same way after all these years? Has the pleasure of it changed? Because what I find most shocking, as someone who burns out—I mean, we did thirteen episodes of *The Ben Stiller Show* and I literally prayed for cancellation in my room at night—I can't believe how vital and alive your show is, and with no sense of burnout.

Jon: It's hard. In some ways, I think it's cyclical. I liken it to batters in a slump. Sometimes you just have to simplify, return to basics. You know, *All right, well, I'm not hitting right now.* That's when I feel the worst, when I feel like I can't—the inspiration's just not there or you feel like you can't solve the problem with the joke. You can't elevate. That's when you feel the shittiest and so, in those moments, you just have to think like a baseball player: *Okay, if I'm not hitting, at the very least I'm going to run out every ground ball as hard as I can. Or I'm going to do the best I can in the field. I'm going to try and make up for my lack of creativity until, hopefully, I hustle my way out of that slump.* But I will say this: Through it all, I have always retained the ability to feel the joy of the funny. When somebody comes up with something really funny or we hit a jag where it's clicking, that still feels like that wave you've been chasing. It can still make me jump up and down like a little kid. That's what you chase.

KEY AND PEELE
(2014)

Whenever I sit down with Key and Peele—which is fairly often, and we're usually talking about a screenplay we're working on together, and who knows if we'll ever finish it—I think: *I wish I had a Key or a Peele in my life*. The only two people I've seen who seem as close in their friendship and sensibility are Seth Rogen and Evan Goldberg. I mean, where's my Peele? Where's my Key? Why the hell am I sitting alone in this room?

Anyway, these guys are hilarious and, maybe more important, they seem to be having the best time in their work, and with the fact that they get to do it together. They are funny and sharp on all subjects, but I can't think of anybody who has been better on the subject of race in America. They have found that magic formula of making people laugh until they shit themselves while also saying things that need to be said right now.

Judd Apatow: So you've just finished shooting the show, and you did two seasons *at once*?

Keegan-Michael Key: Yeah, pretty much.

Judd: That's crazy. Was it a nightmare? Two-thirds of the way in, did you go, "This is a terrible decision," or did you not hit that level of suffering?

Key: Some things fell through the cracks. We'd be on set, trying to fix things, but then we'd have a hiatus week, and then we'd have to shoot something for Comedy Central on the hiatus week, but while that's happening there's always still a stream of emails that come through saying, "Here's the second version of this cut, of this episode," or, "Do you guys want to give notes on this?" And there's just no time to weigh in on all that stuff.

My parents, Maury Apatow and Tami Shad, either exhausted
at the end of their wedding, or pretending to be. 1964.

Me dressed as Harpo Marx for Halloween. Never been happier. 1975.

With Jay Leno backstage at Rascals Comedy Club in West Orange, New Jersey. 1984.

Interviewing Jerry Seinfeld at his West Hollywood apartment. Notice the lack of decor. 1983.

Me being way less funny than Robin Williams on *The Tonight Show* with the great Jay Leno.
(Paul Drinkwater, © 2010 NBCUniversal Media, LLC)

Dennis Miller before hosting the *Paul Simon Live in Central Park* HBO special.
Notice my green shorts. 1991.

Steve Allen waits to speak into my gigantic tape recorder. 1983.

Martin Short and me. One of us is aging badly (not Martin). 1984, 2013.
(Photo on right courtesy of Justin Bishop)

This is how comedians dressed on the 1992 HBO *Young Comedians Special*. (*Clockwise from top left:* Bill Bellamy, Nick DiPaolo, Judd Apatow, Janeane Garofalo, Andy Kindler, Ray Romano, and Dana Carvey) (*Photo courtesy of Andy Hayt*)

A bunch of idiots trying to get stage time at the Improv. (*Left to right:* Judd Apatow, David Spade, Allen Covert, and Adam Sandler) (*Photo courtesy of Tony Edwards, 1990*)

My first gig writing for the HBO special *Tom Arnold: The Naked Truth*. I now weigh more than Tom. 1991. (*Left to right:* Judd Apatow, Tom Arnold, Roseanne Barr, Martin Mull, and Pete Segal)

Traveling with Jim Carrey to London for the *Liar Liar* press junket. 1997.

Me, Ben Stiller, and "Saul." 1993.

Kenan Thompson at sixteen. Me at twenty-seven with mullet. 1994.

Leslie Mann and me on the set of *The Cable Guy*.
(Melinda Sue Gordon, © 1996 Sony Pictures)

Rip Torn, Garry Shandling, director Todd Holland, and me
(looking on while wearing a free *Larry Sanders* shirt).
(Photo courtesy of Larry Watson, 1997)

Me and Busy Philipps's head talk to (*right to left*) Linda Cardellini, Paul Feig, Seth Rogen, Jason Segel, and James Franco—holding his usual thick book.
(*Photo courtesy of Gabe Sachs, 1999*)

Jon Stewart at my thirtieth birthday party.
I've only aged thirty more years in the last seventeen. 1997.

This photograph of the cast of *Anchorman* on a hot day is the best photograph I've ever taken. 2003.

Adam McKay and Will Ferrell invite me to join the Funny or Die team.
(Gemma La Mana, © 2008 Columbia Pictures)

GQ Man of the Year shoot. It took five of us to equal one man.
(Photo courtesy of Danielle Levitt, 2007)

Interviewing my heroes Mel Brooks and Carl Reiner at a Twitter event.
(Jerod Harris, © 2013 Getty Images for Viacom)

Laughing with James L. Brooks at the Motion Picture Academy.
(© 2007 Academy of Motion Picture Arts and Sciences)

I copy everything from Harold Ramis, including his poses.
(Suzanne Hanover, © 2009 Columbia Pictures)

The cast of *Girls* laugh at me, again.
(Dimitrios Kambouris, © 2013 Getty Images)

Me wearing a nicer suit than Paul Feig at the *Bridesmaids* premiere.
(Alex Berliner, © 2011 Universal City Studios, LLC, courtesy of Universal Studios Licensing, LLC)

At the end of *Late Night with Jimmy Fallon*, for some reason
Eddie Vedder thought we should square dance.
(Lloyd Bishop, © 2015 NBCUniversal Media, LLC)

Jimmy Fallon and me. Ew.
(Lloyd Bishop, © 2015 NBCUniversal Media, LLC)

Four completely sober men on the set of *Pineapple Express*.
(Dale Robinette, © 2008 Columbia Pictures, Inc.)

Amy Schumer, Bill Hader, and I pretend to laugh for the photographer.
(Mary Cybulski, © 2015 Universal Pictures, courtesy of Universal Studios Licensing, LLC)

The Apatow-Mann family, modeling our asses off at the *This Is 40* premiere.
(Kevin Winter, © 2012 Getty Images)

This looks like the Apatows at home, but it's actually the set of *Knocked Up*.
(Suzanne Hanover, © 2007 Universal Studios, courtesy of Universal Studios Licensing, LLC)

Jordan Peele: No, at some point you've just got to go—

Key: Yeah, you've got to delegate. Trust people and delegate.

Judd: Do you have people that you could trust with a full episode? Could you say, "I'm so burned out, I am not even going to watch this one," and have faith that it's going to be solid?

Key: Yeah. I've watched episodes on TV with my wife at night and I'll see little cuts of things and go, "Oh, that was a nice little touch."

Peele: There was an episode where an old edit got used by accident, though.

Key: Oh, shit. That's true.

Peele: Something got by and I didn't . . . I was so pissed. They're fixing it now for all the future airings and stuff, but I couldn't blame anybody because I didn't screen it.

Judd: Yeah, you remember those things forever. What level of control freak are you guys at?

Peele: I feel like, in the beginning, I wanted to be part of every single stage of the process. There was a fear that it wouldn't go right. When I was at *MADtv*, it was crazy. I felt like I was putting good work in and then it would somehow get corrupted: Some edit would get made or a sketch I wrote that I thought was genius wouldn't get picked. That whole mentality made me a real control freak. But you know, like we were saying, this time we had no choice but to let go of the reins a little.

Key: I'm—to my detriment—a very trusting Pollyanna, and that can lead to times when a piece of work suffers, so I try to be a little bit more of a control freak. But my thing is—and this is not necessarily the best process—but, once we get on set, I know Jordan and I can fix anything. We can fix anything on set.

Judd: In the writing?

Key: Yeah, the writing, but even in the performance.

Peele: With this double season, when they requested twenty-one episodes, I think our first response was, like, *We're going to kill ourselves. We're going* *to kill ourselves working this hard.* One fear we had—and we had a serious discussion about this—was that we've been designing the whole process of this show so we kind of can't fail, but all of a sudden we're doing twice as many episodes. And one little dip in quality at this point is, I think, a legacy-affecting dip. Same thing if we get better. Plateauing, we're okay with, but it's not great. So that was the big thing: What is the show going to do? Dip, plateau, or get better? And I still can't tell what it is.

Judd: During the last season of *Kids in the Hall*, it felt like they had so burned through their ideas that they went to some other crazy, absurd level. It was definitely hit-and-miss, but there were things in it that were so insanely funny—things you could only have written if you were burned out.

Key: Right, exactly. And to be honest with you, I actually think the second half of our fourth season, we will not plateau. I believe that it's going to be better. Because when you've been working with someone for eleven years, you get to a place where there's going to be something only you can do. Like Steve Coogan and Rob Brydon. They're at a place where only they can do something that way, and I feel like we have things only we can do, and so it will excel and it will grow. It will grow.

Judd: It must be a big trial by fire for you guys, as friends, to be under that much pressure. Especially with this season getting so much positive attention, and you guys being on the cover of *Time* magazine and everything. That's a lot to have on your plate at once.

Key: It's been interesting. There are fellow writers who were early adopters of the show, people who have been on board since day one. But more interesting to me are the regular people, who don't have anything to do with our industry, who have gotten on board. I want to meet those people. I think a lot of those late adopters are probably biracial like us and said, *Oh my gosh, here is a show for me.* That's why the quality has to stay up, because you've got new people watching the show now. It's like a series of tidal waves—and in the midst of it, you keep walking up to podiums and receiving awards and just going, "Thanks," and then: "Oh, I've got to get back to the office now."

Peele: It is weird, but all the cool accolades have really beaten the *enormous* paychecks in coming to us.

Judd: Right. You're not making as much money as your accolades would suggest, and eventually, you just get pissed at everyone.

Key: Just steaming, staring at your Peabody Award, like, *Those fuckers. This system is not working.*

Peele: Cosby's made so much more money than we have. And it makes the accolades feel like some kind of weird accident. But I think the next couple of years, it will continue to sink in. Like: *Oh, this was a crazy time for us.*

Judd: What really sticks out?

Key: The Peabody Award, don't you think?

Judd: That's a great award. Your program shows that prejudices and the way people were and are ignorant are ridiculous and should be mocked. Like my daughter, she's mad that we even have to talk about homophobia because she doesn't understand how anyone would feel that way. She actually gets upset. But that's because her generation grew up saying homophobia is stupid, racism is stupid, and so it's not even in their heads. I think comedy has helped affect that. Do you get that sense?

Peele: Our target demo was teenagers, and so we were forced to make a show that was relevant to them. A lot of the work we did in that first season was really about: What *is* this show? Every sketch we chose had to help us define what the whole point of this thing was. We are doing sketches that could only be done today, things that wouldn't have been relevant several years ago. It's like what you're saying: Racism still exists, and it's ridiculous, but there are still parts of the country where the youth have just a completely different view of race, and we want to bring that conversation into the larger culture.

Key: That's really the biggest, most significant paradigm shift: Kids don't look at race, they look at culture. I don't think they know that they're looking at culture, but they're co-opting each other's culture and it's starting to mush together, whereas for me or for someone older than me, everything was always about the color of your skin.

Judd: But now it seems like it is a little bit more about class?

Key: It does. And when I say culture, I mean class. As in, you can afford to be part of a certain culture. For a lot of people, their culture is defined by where they are socioeconomically, and for decades, rich kids have co-opted poorer kids' cultures because they were bored or whatever.

Judd: My daughter is at this nice private school, but there are a lot of scholarship students there, too. She says that the school is very aggressive about wanting everyone to hang out with each other. And when they don't, they assume it's because of race, but she says it's because of class, that it's uncomfortable for the kids who aren't living at the same economic level to integrate. And that kids from similar class backgrounds tend to hang out together.

Key: Yeah. My wife and I drove out to Riverside yesterday to watch my best friend's oldest son play for his Pop Warner football team. They lost the game by a field goal, and it was a heartbreaker. My friend is from Rancho Palos Verdes and all the kids on the other team were from San Bernardino, and as we were driving home, my wife said, "Well, those kids really need it. Good for them." And I feel that all the way. You know, I'm from Detroit. It doesn't matter when New York City wins a sports championship. But when Detroit wins a sports championship, it actually *means* something. We need the money for infrastructure, we need the boost. This is the same thing. The majority of those kids were African American, and they're from some really bad, downtrodden school district in the Mount Baldy area. It's different than kids from Rancho Palos Verdes. And they're out there, screaming and running around the field and jumping up and down. It means something for them.

Judd: I think it means so much whenever you see somebody that you relate to in whatever way kicking ass and succeeding. I'm so interested in this with the president, and how people look at him.

Key: Yeah, and trying to figure out what box to put him in. You have to understand that if you're going to put him in a box, you should put him in the child-of-a-single-mother, lower-middle-class box. That's the box he belongs in. You know, as Jordan has said in the past, I sometimes think we have a show because Obama got elected. That pushed these issues to the forefront, and people have had to address it. What happens when a person's mixed?

Judd: The country's completely mixed, but you still see the last vestiges of some things—

Peele: There's such a diversity of experiences, and having a sketch show now has been a great way to explore it all, because there's no single comment to be made that's going to sum it up. Often we'll make a sketch and go, "You know what? You know who's going to love this sketch? Hispanic break dancers are going to love it." And then this one, "This one is for the black people in Ferguson that need this story told as a reminder to everyone else."

Key: Right, that this is going on, and that we know that's going on, and that everybody else needs to know that that's still going on. Whenever people stop to talk to me on the street, I'm always like, "I'm sorry, I'm so curious, you're going to have to tell me what sketch hooked you in. I want to know what demographic you're coming from."

Peele: In the beginning, we really latched on to being biracial as something that made us similar to the president, but also as the thing that made us relevant and hadn't been explored. As the show has gone on and progressed, though, the more important thing is that we're able to tell the stories of anybody. We can get away with going anywhere because we've gone everywhere.

Key: This is so lofty, but it feels like we ended up writing an American show.

Judd: Absolutely. And not just where America is now; it's also where America's going.

Peele: Part of the interesting thing about this whole conversation is the fact that I think we consider ourselves kind of like modern-day jesters. Our job is to be a mirror for everything that's going on, and I think that if people had the sense that we were just purely in the president's pocket or whatever, we'd lose credibility.

Judd: I love that your comedy doesn't seem to come from insecurity or self-hatred. I could be completely wrong—you may hate yourselves—but my sense of humor came from feeling like I was not like all these other people and it sucked. It made me mad at the world. But I don't get the sense that you guys came from the same type of emotional experience. What was the thing that made you funny?

Peele: I think we both had success early on that probably helped us not have a disgruntled vibe. But I think our ability to be chameleons comes from an early sense of identity crisis.

Key: I agree. That was our survival mechanism.

Peele: Keegan grew up in Detroit and I grew up in New York, both fairly cosmopolitan places. But we both still lived in a culture where being a black person who sounds white is a recipe for a beating.

Key: I mean, if you go way back—primordial, right—as human beings, we have had to categorize things to stay alive. Eat the brown one, don't eat the green one. So some of that primal stuff kicks in for people and they go, You're not fitting in my box. And that's why you get beaten up, because you scare them and they just happen to be bigger than you and know how to throw a football. But I think for me, humor is definitely borne of the insecurity in being adopted and being biracial and saying, "I just got to figure out what the gig is that will allow me to feel good emotionally and survive the beatings."

Peele: You know, the beauty of a show like *Freaks and Geeks* is that anybody who is left to create their own identity because they don't fit into the "cool" ones, or the ones that are already in place, can get working on this creative business early. All the main characters on *Freaks and Geeks* would be wildly successful today.

Judd: Yes, they would. The ones that aren't in jail.

Key: Something that has always been positive for me, in our working experience, is that we're trying to figure out that puzzle in different ways.

My mom had to keep nudging me and nudging me until she finally kicked me out between the curtains and onto the stage, you know: "That's where you belong!" I was painfully shy in grade school. I was the most well-spoken kid and experienced the most emotion and I was mesmerized by all the school plays—*Annie,* and *Godspell*—but my brain said, *You can't do that. Why would you think you could do that?*

Judd: Who told you you couldn't do it?

Key: Nobody. This is my pop psychology theory: I had a complete, profound, horrible sense of self because, even as a nine-year-old, you can comprehend the idea of, *Why would a woman have a baby and then give the baby away? Why would you do that? There must be something wrong with me.* So I could sense how amazing it would make me feel if I got out onstage, but I wasn't allowed to do it because there's clearly something wrong with me. But my mom kept on pushing. She was pushing so hard, like, "This is where you belong. You just need the confidence to know that it's going to be okay."

Judd: That's why I stopped doing stand-up for so long. The same psychology: *There's no reason why anyone would ever want to listen to me.* Then I read somewhere that the best gift you can give other people is your story, and it just hit me, like, *Really? That's the whole thing?* And then I thought about who I liked, and how they were going about it.

Key: Like with Bill Cosby: all he's done his whole career is tell his story.

Judd: Or part of it!

Peele: Yeah. But I want to get back to being a chameleon: So much effort has been put into becoming other characters and becoming other identities. I remember the first time I faced this was when I went to iO [formerly ImprovOlympic] in Chicago, maybe fifteen years ago. And improv is a totally different form. The playing around was fun, but the monologues were so hard. Right before we started doing the show, I tried stand-up for the second time in my life and I realized that if I didn't have a sense of who I am, the show would just be these empty characters—and they wouldn't connect. So I started piecing together a few short bits that exemplified my place in the world, and that was the missing element that is so important and has really helped us in the show. Especially with the car segments. Four years ago, I don't know if I would have had the ability to say, "All right, just be yourself with Keegan. Just do what we would do in a car." And that was such an important lesson.

Judd: I think those segments are more revealing than being in front of a crowd.

Key: For me, the big challenge is that I am still in this place where I care about what other people will think. It reminds me of something you said, Judd, that has been working inside of me: *I* have life rights. So I'm going to write this character and Albert Brooks is going to play the character and I know it's my dad. And I don't care because I have life rights. It's my story. I'm trying to find a way to install that idea into me.

Judd: That you're allowed to do that.

Key: Right.

Judd: These things also get complicated when you feel abandoned. You worry that if you talk about your life and your family that people will abandon you again.

Key: And how can you navigate that? Yeah, it's tricky. This is why I didn't go into stand-up. When my dad was still alive, I said, "I want to do stand-up like Eddie Murphy. Maybe I could do that." And he was like, "Well all right, but don't tell any jokes about me." He just straight-out said to my face, "Don't tell any jokes about me." Nigga, you *are* the jokes. You're like seventy percent of the jokes!

Judd: I sent my dad the script for *This Is 40* and said, "It's fabricated, but it comes out of certain aspects of our relationship." And he said, "Well, as long as he's likable. Just get someone funny to play me." I'm like, "Albert Brooks is doing it." And he's like, "All right."

Key: He signed off on it? That's great.

Judd: What made you think you actually could do comedy as a career? Jordan, you were in New York and went to a nice high school, right?

Peele: Yes, I was at the Calhoun School but I was the artist kid, very quiet. My mother would have never guessed that I would have gotten into this. But when I was ten years old, I saw this play at this place called Tada, a children's theater, and it was amazing. I thought: *I have that, I can do that.* So I went and auditioned. I sold the fuck out of this audition. They asked me to sing "Happy Birthday" and I sold it. I got down on my knees and—

Judd: You went James Brown on them?

Peele: Total James Brown.

Judd: How old were you?

Peele: Ten. And I got the coolest part in the play and very quickly I realized that I loved doing it. It was like, *Okay, I actually have a knack for this,* and they saw something in me that was probably just that love of what I was doing coming through. From that point on, I started auditioning for commercials. Didn't get any parts, which disheartened me and left me with this feeling of *Maybe I don't really have a place in this. I don't know what I'm selling.* It was intense.

Judd: I wanted to do commercials as a kid, too. I got head shots made like in seventh grade but I got the chicken pox and had these terrible scars, and they refused to heal. They were red and full of pus and then I actually shoved poison ivy up my nose to make my friends laugh—

Peele: Oh, fuck.

Judd: So I got poison ivy all over my face, plus the chicken pox, and I didn't know what to do, so I put poison ivy medicine on the chicken pox, which made them blow up like ten times the size—which caused these horrible scars and the pus. And so my dream of acting was over.

Peele: How old were you?

Judd: Between seventh and eighth grade. But that's what I wanted to do, was go out for those Jack in the Box commercials.

Peele: That's a really fucked-up time to be selling yourself, too.

Key: The most fragile time.

Peele: I remember one audition I went on, for some kind of fast-food spot. I got in and homeboy was like, "All right, dance." Oh my God, I busted out and danced. I danced for about sixty seconds. He was like, "All right, great, great, great . . ." And then you don't get the gig. I just went there and danced on cue.

Judd: Oh my God. I just found this old tape—a recycled three-quarter-inch tape that I was putting my stand-up act on a long time ago to use for getting gigs and whatever. And apparently it had also been used as the audition tape for a dance party show on MTV. I started watching it and my roommate, Adam Sandler, shows up on the screen. It's his audition! They put music on and he's dancing, walking up to other dancers, asking them questions, dancing the whole time. It was as humiliating an audition as you could ever imagine. "Hey, buddy, where ya from? You like this song? Yeah, I like Tiffany, too."

Key: "I like Tiffany, too." Oh that's awful.

Judd: But how did that—all the early acting stuff and the commercials—lead to becoming aware of improv and Second City?

Peele: For me, that didn't happen until college. I went to high school and did a couple of plays, got into college, Sarah Lawrence. I was interested in theater. My thing was doing puppetry.

Judd: Getting laid a lot?

Peele: Did not get laid as much as I would have liked to. But the need to be liked by girls was a huge motivator. Just to try and make something beautiful because I never had any wild man machismo. I never had any of that shit that the girls like, that X factor. And so.

Key: Well, you have, like, the *Beautiful Mind* X factor.

Peele: Yeah, but when you're young, that's worth nothing.

Key: When I was fourteen or fifteen, I used to listen to that 1977 compilation *SNL* cassette and warped it in my dad's van. Warped it because I just listened to it all the time, and that's how I first found out about sketch comedy. Then I saw an NBC special about, like, the biggest star in the world right now is John Belushi, and they showed clips from *Neighbors* and an old Samurai sketch. And I just started reading about everything John Belushi did, and about how he started at Second City, but it felt like there was no way to get there, you know? There was no conduit. I didn't know about improv until a guy I went to college with at the University of Detroit said, "I'm going to start an improv group called New and Improved," and I said, "I've got to jump in here and audition for this."

Judd: Were you studying theater at all in college?

Key: I was studying theater, yeah, and I did this improv group, went off to graduate school, and then, after graduate school, joined the Second City in Detroit and was there for four years.

Peele: I was hosting at Second City so I was taking classes there but really the best thing I did was sit there and watch the main stage.

Judd: Were those the Adam McKay–Tina Fey years?

Peele: No. This was right after, with Stephnie Weir, Rich Talarico, Kevin Doyle, Susan Messing, Tami Sagher, T. J. Jagodowski—just unbelievable, night after night. It's so important to see the best. That's how you know how good it can be.

Key: And you're like, *Can I do that?*

Peele: I remember feeling like, *Oh no, I can't do that. I just watched some* magic *right there.* It was a gut-wrenching feeling.

Key: So many people have the same journey. I remember being a first-year in graduate school, sitting in the room where we did all these showcases that nobody watches but the other students, and the second-years were doing their Greeks final. And it's all like the Trojan women and everybody's been fucking raped sixty-five times and the husbands have been killed and babies have been chucked off the side of mountains. There was just so much raw emotion taking place in these four actors in front of us. I remember looking at my roommate and another one of my friends and saying, "I'm getting kicked out. I'm getting kicked out of this program. I'm never going to be able to do that." But then you get the tools, and one of those tools is the confidence to say, "Of course I can do that." It was so important for me to be able to get that foundation.

Judd: When I first started doing stand-up, I was watching the highest level of it with Jim Carrey and Sandler and I just thought, *I'll never get there*. It was almost like it was unfair. It was like if Brando was at your college and you were watching him while you were taking your first acting classes.

Peele: One of the breakthrough moments for me was realizing that, you know, you can take all the classes you want and learn and practice and get all the advice from other people, but it's really like learning an instrument that has never existed until you were born. No one can tell you how to play that instrument. There's a part of that journey that you have to figure out for yourself.

Key: And then there's putting your own spice on it.

Peele: Yeah. When I moved to Chicago, I was like, All right, I want to be a sketch comedian and my power is going to be in the fact that I'm going to dedicate myself completely. There's not going to be a fallback, you know? I'm going to watch people give up and I'll still be there, learning from it all, and if I stay with it, I'll be successful. That was everything.

Key: Part of Jordan's X factor is that nobody out-hustles him. You can try, and you will fail. Which, of course, makes your job easier if you're working with him. So even if you're excelling, he's there taking the pressure off. He's the anchor.

Judd: I always wanted to be that guy, too. Like, no one is going to do more than me. You see so many people who are great but they don't go that last twenty-five percent in effort. It's what Seinfeld talks about, how he just gets up every day and writes for two hours. Every day, he sits alone in a room with a legal pad. And I guarantee you that one percent or less of comedians do that.

Peele: You know, after ten years in Hollywood, you really see the system is set up to sap money from people who are trying to get into the business. It's just set up that way. There's so many things that people are told they *must* do. You must get representation. I mean, the number of people that sit by idly in this town saying, "I just need to get an agent or a manager," and you're like, "You've been here what, eight years? Dude, just make a show."

Judd: A lot of people ask me, "How do you get people to read your scripts?" And I'll go, "Did you *write* one?" "No, but I was wondering how you get someone to read one." You know, there's no great script in town sitting in the stack that people don't know about. There's no insanely funny person that can't get attention or get an agent. That's not going to be the hard part.

Key: Yeah. You've got to just do the show first. I mean, that's the way it's always worked.

Judd: So now that the sketch show is ending, do you guys have a vision for the next phase of your career?

Key: Yeah, I mean, in my mind—and I think I have probably said this to Jordan in some form or another—it's almost like, boy, wouldn't it be great if we could be the next Pryor/Wilder? You know, go off and do maybe three projects that fulfill us, and then come home and see each other? I think we have the ability to do that.

Peele: We're never going to have another version of this.

Key: We'll never have another version of this.

Judd: You really have very few people in life you get along with, especially in a creative situation. Some people are great together but then they just can't stand each other because every time an idea is accepted or rejected, there's so much on the line emotionally or self-esteem-wise. When you find people who make it work, it's that much more important.

Peele: Absolutely. Before I met Keegan, I could spend a week with my best friend in the world before getting sick of him. But because we've got something more important than us that we're working for, it has put us in this category where we could spend years with each other and always have this positive working relationship where we're trying to make each other laugh. It's a special thing.

Key: The love—our love—is wrapped up in the work. There's this goal that we're always trying to achieve together. We know we can't achieve it alone. It works because of a mutual respect for each other.

Judd: It doesn't seem like it takes you two a lot of effort.

Key: No, it doesn't, and I think that's because, as different as we are energy-wise, we're very similar in a lot of other ways. Our backgrounds are similar. We're nonconfrontational guys. You know, I don't believe in the idea that conflict must exist for creativity to flourish. That's such a false thing. For us, it always goes back to the respect thing. It's just releasing the ego. I just hold his hand and we jump off the cliff. He's got me. If he says, "This bit is going to work," it's gonna work.

Judd: That's just so rare. In the world of comedy, so many people are so damaged that even though they say, "I got you, no matter what," a fair amount of time they're really like, "Well, fuck you, I'm doing it this way." So for two people who are healthy to say to each other, "I got you"—and to believe it—is a beautiful thing.

Peele: The best moments I've ever seen in improv are funnier than the best stand-up bits that I've ever seen. There's something that can only happen between two people collaborating, and I just think that two people with the same vision is better than one.

LARRY GELBART
AND JAMES L. BROOKS
(2007)

In 2007, the Academy of Motion Picture Arts and Sciences asked me if I was interested in putting a panel talk together. I said yes, but only if I could invite James Brooks and Larry Gelbart, and spend an hour talking about comedy. I knew I had no business being on the same stage as these guys; nobody does. I was simply thrilled to have the opportunity to sit there and talk to them, and I knew at some point that a photograph would be taken of the three of us onstage, which I would cherish for the rest of my life. So yes: I did it for the picture.

Why did I pick James Brooks and Larry Gelbart? Because two of the most formative shows of my life, the shows that trained me in comedy—not to mention how to be a human being—were M*A*S*H and *The Mary Tyler Moore Show*. The work these men did was emotional and hilarious and, I felt, spoke to the best part of human beings. I mean, M*A*S*H was the highest-rated program in the history of television: More than 100 million people watched the finale. James Brooks has won nineteen Emmys, for shows like *The Mary Tyler Moore Show*, *Lou Grant*, and *The Simpsons*. And I'd like to point out that *Freaks and Geeks* lasted eighteen episodes.

Everything flows from these guys.

Judd Apatow: There's an enormous amount of pressure here right now. This is a pressure cooker.

Larry Gelbart: For the record, dying is harder.

This interview originally took place as a panel hosted by the Academy of Motion Picture Arts and Sciences.

Judd: Oh, yeah.

James L. (Jim) Brooks: This means I have to go.

Judd: Anyway, it's exciting to be here. It is an honor to share the stage with the two men who are the primary reasons I wanted to be involved in comedy, and I also feel bad about your being here, which clearly demeans you. I was looking at everyone's credits on Wikipedia last night, and it was embarrassing. I felt bad. I read them and thought, *I should not be here.*

Jim: You've done more pictures than I've done this year.

Judd: Oh, Jesus. Anyway, when I was a young man and, you know— M*A*S*H, *The Mary Tyler Moore Show, Taxi*, these were what made me want to do this. So this is very exciting for me—not so much for you, but for me. We are going to show a few clips tonight. We're going to start off— each of us has picked a clip from a film that influenced us in some way. The first clip is mine, from *Punch-Drunk Love*. It's a Paul Thomas Anderson movie, and Adam Sandler is one of the stars. This is a scene where you see him with his family and all of his sisters, who don't treat him very well. I was working on *The 40-Year-Old Virgin* simultaneously, but this struck me as the much better way to do it, so I wanted to show that.

(Clip from *Punch-Drunk Love*: Barry is uncomfortable at a dinner party with all of his sisters.)

Judd: I really like that movie. It's a great, strange movie with a tone that's all its own. Whenever I'm working, I get nervous when there aren't laughs—I'm always trying to figure out what that balance is: How do you deal with the question of how funny should it be, and is there a moment when things become too funny and you lose the humanity?

Jim: It's a great clip and it's a great question.

Larry: And here's a great answer: You are your own gauge for what is funny and what is not. *You* have to decide. If it gets to you, it's good enough to be put in the script. Too funny? It's too funny if it's not character-driven or situation-driven. If it's just funny for funny then it's not worth keeping.

Jim: Great answer.

Larry: Thank you.

Judd: *(To Jim)* Well, the next clip is your clip.

Jim: Can we just show it, and then talk about it afterwards?

Judd: Okay. I hope it's one of my movies.

(Clip from *There's Something About Mary:* Mary mistakes Ted's semen for hair gel.)

Judd: You just went blue. You went blue.

Jim: I think the unfortunate expression is "seminal joke in motion picture history." I think it changed movies a little. And I think the film itself had about as many tens in it as anything I've ever seen—just huge, huge jokes. But everything sort of pivoted off of this one joke.

Judd: And the masturbation sound effect was good work. Good sound work there. I think it might have been Ben Stiller but someone was telling me about having to do a scene where they masturbated on the screen and they said that what's embarrassing about it is that in a way you're revealing to your crew how you masturbate. *Ah, so that's how Ben Stiller does it. . . .*

Jim: There was a very forlorn masturbation scene in *Punch-Drunk Love.*

Judd: That's right, the phone sex sequence. You know, when we were working on *The 40-Year-Old Virgin* there was a masturbation question, which was: Does the forty-year-old virgin masturbate? And of course, it's a very important issue because you're trying to decide how sexualized he is. So I brought in a team of the great comedy writers to help me with this question and Garry Shandling cracked the code on it. Garry's pitch was, you don't see him masturbate. You just see him *prepare* to masturbate. You see him put on his pajamas and brush his hair. And I thank Garry for that. Okay, now, Larry, do you want to say what your clip is?

Larry: *To Be or Not to Be.* The original version. I used to think that anybody who wanted to write screen comedy should see this picture once a year. It's just a marvel of construction, casting, and wit on an impossible subject, the Nazis. Let's show it.

(Clip from *To Be or Not to Be:* Ehrhardt stalls Professor Siletsky while running to manage his acting troupe in the next room.)

Jim: Larry, Jack Benny was singular, don't you think?

Larry: I think it's his only successful film. He was in a string of terrible movies, but this worked for him.

Jim: But his energy just—

Larry: Amazing. It was amazing. The story of this film was that Carole Lombard, who co-starred with him, was touring the country selling war bonds and she died in a plane crash and so they did not promote the picture. They thought it would be in bad taste to have her laughing on screens all over the country when, in fact, she had died. Mel Brooks redid it, of course, with his wife, Anne Bancroft, a number of years later.

Judd: Larry, how did you become a good writer? Where did that transition happen?

Larry: I learned the difference between good and bad and I opted for good.

Judd: That will help all aspiring writers. But was there a moment, as you transitioned from writing jokes for comedians and sketch comedy to storytelling, that was seminal for you?

Larry: The stage play A *Funny Thing Happened* was the transitional period—I had to write something that was more than twelve minutes long, like a Sid Caesar sketch, and they didn't pull up the scenery every night afterwards. It was an education in construction, and the teacher, of course, was a Roman playwright named Titus Maximus Plautus, who did his best work in 253 B.C. It's wonderful working with dead authors because their lawyers are dead, too—and their agents. But that was the transition for me.

Judd: (*To Jim*) And what about for you?

Jim: Well, I had television, and there's nothing better than to do a show every week. That was my college: I learned from the actors on *The Mary Tyler Moore Show*. You know, I had been writing for just a relatively short time and Allan Burns and I were able to do what we wanted and we had a great boss. We were too dumb to know how rare it was.

Judd: There's so much depth in the work, though. Was there someone that taught you about that early in your career?

Jim: I don't know how that happened. I remember there was a writer named Leon Tokatyan, who was on the *Lou Grant* series, and he used to love writing these long speeches. He made me just want, in every script, a place where I could pull off somebody talking for a page, a page and a half. If I could make *that* work, if I could make people sit for that, it became a big deal for me. He was a direct influence on me, I think.

Larry: The worst thing we had to accustom ourselves to was self-censorship—not the censorship that we all know about, but *anticipating* the censorship so that you knew certain areas were strictly out of bounds and that's, you know, the death in a sense of some part of your creativity. Knowing you can't say something or do something.

Judd: And now look what's happened.

Larry: *There's Something About Mary*.

Judd: Which obviously was a big influence on me because it's a sweet story but it also has some very broad set pieces. That's always fun to do—

Larry: You have an ability to mix the crude with the sweet, which is amazing. People talk about laughing one minute and crying the next, but to be repulsed one minute and then enchanted the next? That's a gift.

Judd: I remember watching episodes of *Taxi* where there would be big, broad comedy and then it would land on something very emotional or sweet and seem to go back and forth with ease. I always think of the episode where Judd Hirsch was addicted to gambling.

Jim: It's so weird. We were just talking about that today, and I got so messed up, being so heavily nostalgic about it because I—that was the best job of my life. There was nothing better for me than *Taxi*.

Judd: In that scene, Judd Hirsch wants money so badly that he steals it out of Reverend Jim's pocket and then slowly you realize that Reverend Jim knows that he did it and shames him. It's a really powerful moment. Those kinds of turns were very influential to me, in what I try to do. Okay, now we're going to show some clips from our own movies. Do we want to see that?

Larry: Sure. I'm tired of watching them at home.

Judd: I guess, you know, the first one is mine—

Larry: That's amazing.

Judd: Well, then it can be topped by yours. You see, if I'm last then I don't look good.

Larry: Of course. We'll do it according to our gifts.

Judd: Exactly. So this is a clip from *The 40-Year-Old Virgin*. It's a fight scene between Catherine Keener and Steve Carell, where she realizes that they've had twenty dates and it's time for them to have sex for the first time, and he's trying to get out of it. There's some improvisation in here, which is why it seems real—they really went at it for a while.

(Clip from *The 40-Year-Old Virgin*: It is Trish and Andy's twentieth date.)

Larry: Good stuff.

Jim: Were you nervous about that scene? Was it always looming for you?

Judd: Well, when we hired Catherine Keener we were all a little scared of her. It was amusing that she was there, every day, and going really hard-core Method with our movie. We tried hard to make her scenes good, mostly because I thought that she would yell at us if they weren't. For this scene, I wasn't sure how funny it would be. There was a script but then we let them go to town on each other, and then they ended up with this weird Einstein run. A moment like this only works because you're really getting a sense of how Catherine Keener fights in real life.

Larry: She must have had a great time, right?

Judd: She seemed to enjoy that day. I have to say, she fought well. When that scene worked, it surprised me that it could get dark and the laughs could continue. I was really excited by that because it worked in a different way. Okay, now we're going to go to the next clip, which is from Mr. Brooks. Can I say where it's from? Do you want to introduce it?

Jim: Which one is it?

Judd: *Broadcast News*.

Jim: Oh, yeah. The reason I picked this is because I think of anything that I've ever done—you know, what I got a chance to say in this scene, and it's always a little dangerous to delve into that territory, was and is enormously important to me. So that's why I wanted to show it.

Judd: I know it well and I'm excited.

(Clip from *Broadcast News:* Aaron tells Jane how awful his time on the desk was, and that he's in love with her.)

Judd: That was amazing. A perfect scene, and a perfect movie. It really is, as is *Tootsie*. They are two movies that just function perfectly in every possible way. What was it like working with Holly Hunter? What was that process like with her?

Jim: It was great. First of all, she and Albert both did four years in acting school, totally trained actors. They both went to Carnegie Mellon. Which is interesting because not a lot of people assume it about Holly, and not everybody knows it about Albert. She's a very dedicated actress. Well into the shoot, I finally said to her, "Am I allowed to talk to you about making something funny?" And she really thought about the question. She took it seriously and then she said, "Yes, you can."

Judd: What is the gestation period like for one of your screenplays?

Jim: Seasons pass, years fall away. I take a long time.

Judd: And what about you, Larry?

Larry: First comes the phone call—you know, I'm the odd man out here because you guys get to direct what you write. I get to defend what I write—and not always successfully. I've had every kind of experience, from terrible to rotten, and no two are alike.

Judd: What was the worst?

Larry: We are about to see a clip from *Tootsie*, which was a difficult process.

Judd: A very painful process. Even though it's combative to make a movie like *Tootsie*, can you enjoy the final product and see that something good came of it? Or do you watch and think, *There are still things that are wrong*?

Larry: I know things are wrong. There's one scene—I don't know how it got past continuity, but it depicted a night that was at least four weeks long. That kills me.

Judd: So *Tootsie* irritates you? It delights us and irritates you. Should we skip the clip? What do we do?

Larry: Oh, I don't care. You can play it or not.

Judd: What specifically about the process was so painful?

Larry: It was a battle of egos and wills and I just withdrew from the combat—which is to say, I was fired. It's better left undiscussed.

Judd: All right, well, let's watch it. Do you want to watch it?

Larry: I'll sit here and look at it. I'll watch it.

(Clip from *Tootsie:* Michael Dorsey tells his manager, George Fields, that he needs to get off the show.)

Judd: We love it.

Larry: I didn't say it wasn't wonderful.

Judd: What was your reaction the first time you saw it?

Larry: I saw it in a screening and I whispered to Sydney Pollack, "Can you get Jessica Lange out of the picture?" She went on to win the Academy Award, of course, which shows you how smart I am. It was a mix—it's still a mixed bag of feelings.

Judd: Who are other comedy writers-directors that you admire who are currently working today?

Jim: I just always think, whenever I see anybody else's work, how tough it is to get it right. It's so hard to get the opportunity these days to do a film you care about—that you want to make and somebody lets you. Anybody who gets that, for starters, I like. And when it's pulled off, it's just extraordinary.

Judd: I remember there was an event at the Museum of Television and Radio where you talked a little bit about honoring your characters, and I found that inspiring as I was heading into writing *Knocked Up*. Can you speak a little bit about that, the characters you're creating?

Jim: When I just saw *Tootsie*—you know, I understand it's genuine and deeply felt, but it's a mountain of a picture. It's one of the greatest films ever. And the fact that people walk away not all feeling wonderful shows how tough it is all the time. Almost everything we're discussing here is about indelible character. I don't think there's been a clip where that hasn't been true. I think the relationship, when it's allowed to happen, between writers and actors is just—it's what we're all there for.

Judd: How much do you think of the audience when you're writing—or do you primarily write for yourself and not worry about what they'll get?

Larry: I don't worry about what they'll get. I write for myself on the assumption that there are a number of people who have similar sensibilities and will appreciate what it is that I thought was good enough to present, not to them but to me.

Jim: Well, on the ride to the preview, any thought of writing for yourself leaves me. Let me tell you the greatest story about people who genuinely work for themselves: John Cassavetes did a picture called *Husbands* and *Time* magazine called it the greatest film ever made, and you can certainly make the argument for it. They had a scene that took place in a john, which maybe was twenty minutes long. It was Peter Falk, and Cassavetes and—

Larry: Ben Gazzara.

Jim: Ben Gazzara. They were pals and they basically started independent film. They were standing at the back of an audience—and I heard this from Cassavetes, this story—and people started leaving the theater during that scene, considering it so awful. And they clapped each other on the back and said, "We did it." That's a true story.

Larry: That's wonderful.

Jim: That's as pure as it is.

Judd: Larry, can you talk a little about your time working on *Your Show of Shows*?

Jim: And can you say who was on staff, too, Larry?

Larry: The truth is, I was never on *Your Show of Shows*. I was on *Caesar's Hour*, which was the next thing that Sid Caesar did after *Your Show of Shows*. At that time, among the writers were Mel Brooks, Mel Tolkin, Neil Simon, and Woody Allen later on. Carl Reiner sat with us every minute. Sid was there, too. What was it like? It was like being in a great jazz band and having these other guys to bounce off and, uh, knowing that you were with the best, knowing you were on the New York Yankees.

Judd: So you could feel it every day, that this was an all-star team?

Larry: The individual successes came later, but we just knew that we were the best around. Fame and celebrity were not part of it. It was just know-ing you were with a great bunch of guys. There was one woman—Selma Diamond on *Your Show of Shows*, and a woman named Lucille Kallen, who was one of the original writers—but basically it was a boys' club and it was thrilling but it was tough. I mean, the show was broadcast every Saturday night. We had Sunday off, and Monday morning we said, "What do we do next week?" A season back then was thirty-nine weeks, not twenty-two.

Judd: How long was the show?

Larry: Too long. It was an hour live, in front of an audience, of course—no laugh track, no sweetening.

Judd: Was that the most fun of all the experiences that you had?

Larry: Well, it was the most fun of that kind of fun.

Judd: What's your writing schedule like? How do you work?

Jim: Why do I experience every question as if I have to confess to some-thing? It's, uh, I have an erratic daily routine. I always hope for three hours in the morning. I rarely get it.

Larry: I get up very early, four, five o'clock in the morning. It's just a sneak-ier way of living longer, really. And I just sit down at the keyboard and work on several things. It's probably better to work on one thing at a time, but you have to keep feeding the beast and hopefully, an outline—yes, I have to outline. I may deviate, you know, find myself inventing a dozen off-ramps, but I have to have a map to start with.

Judd: I haven't figured it out. Before I had children I would get up about noon and watch the *Real World: Vegas* marathon and then I would eat some chicken marsala with pasta and then I'd get in this really weird, like almost-high kind of funk from it. And then slowly I'd pull out of it and I'd get like the greatest forty-five minutes of writing done.

Larry: Things like peeing with a boner?

Judd: Yeah, all the pride I feel. Let's go to another clip. We're closing in on the end of the night so we're going to go to a clip right now from *As Good as It Gets*. Any introduction?

Jim: This is a very odd clip, and Mark Andrus, who wrote it with me— Mark wrote the original screenplay and it brought me into a kind of situation that I would never have brought myself into. And this scene is very odd because when you see it you're not sure if you want any laughs. I hope there are jokes in there, but I'm not necessarily going for that.

(Clip from *As Good as It Gets*: Melvin tells Simon the only reason the dog prefers him is because he keeps bacon in his pocket.)

Judd: At the time, I heard you did a lot of research on OCD but you also did a lot of work with the idea of the dog and the dog's personality. Would you like to speak to that?

Jim: I'm a nut on research. I get very obsessive about it.

Judd: How do you know when you've accomplished everything you set out to accomplish in a film?

Jim: I don't know if that's happened to me yet.

Judd: Larry, what about you?

Larry: Now we get into the writer-writer as opposed to the writer-director. As the writer, I'm rarely around at the end of the picture, including the wrap party.

Jim: Have you seen pictures of yours without wanting to fix something?

Judd: Well, I shoot an enormous amount of film, and when I'm shooting what I think to myself is, *If I hated this scene in editing, what would I wish I had?* And so as I'm shooting, I'm shooting many permutations of the scene. It might be different lines or alts. If it's too mean, let me get something a little less mean. If it seems sentimental, I might get something edgy. I usually have like a million feet of film that in my head—I've edited every permutation and I'm just flipping things in and out so at the end of it I'm reasonably happy. But I have to say, when I watch it a year or two later, I start seeing issues that haunt me. I don't think anyone's ever completely satisfied. Have you ever been completely satisfied? Is there an episode of a show where you think—

Jim: Sometimes in *Taxi*, yeah.

Judd: When you watch *Terms of Endearment* now, what bugs you?

Jim: I haven't seen it in a long time, but I get knocked out by actors. The thing that keeps me from really hating the experience of seeing these pictures again is that I get lost in the acting.

LENA DUNHAM
(2014)

I remember the day someone handed me a DVD of a movie called *Tiny Furniture*. This was during a phase of my life when I was beating myself up for being bad about watching things that people said were important to watch, so I went home and watched it right away, not knowing that the woman in this movie had also written it, directed it, produced it, and shot most of it in her parents' apartment for forty-five thousand dollars. The movie was hilarious and heartfelt and weird in all the right ways.

Afterward, I emailed her immediately. "Hey," I wrote, "if you ever need someone to help you screw up your career, call me." The next day Lena emailed back, thinking that I was one of her friends goofing on her. I soon found out that she had just begun to develop a television show for HBO with my friend Jenni Konner. They asked if I wanted to come on board and help, which led to one of the greatest creative experiences of my life: working on *Girls*.

Lena Dunham is one of the few people on earth who I have never gotten into a fight with. Even in the throes of a production, when deadlines are looming and people are exhausted and unpleasant, every moment with her has been a joy.

Judd Apatow: So.

Lena Dunham: So.

Judd: I wanted to ask you where you feel like you're headed, after accomplishing so much at such a young age. You're in this position of getting to say a lot with your show and your book and everything else you're doing. How do you feel about what you've been able to express so far?

Lena: It's mind-blowing to me. And because so much of the stuff I've been able to make is so personal, there's always the fear that you're going to run out of gas. But in the past few years, to my surprise, I've become more politically and historically engaged, which has given me this whole other area of human stories to explore. I have all this stuff percolating in my head now which, for the first time, isn't just about me — and that's an exciting feeling. All of the projects I'm thinking about now, none of them are about a twenty-seven-year-old girl who's pissed at her mom. They all share my concerns, in a way, but on a different scale and in a different time period. I'm excited by the idea of moving out of super-confessional stuff.

Judd: When you started, it almost felt like you were writing about your life in real time. But then your actual life started veering pretty dramatically from the character you were writing about.

Lena: Totally. And my life also became my work, which is the thing I'd always wanted — to be a person who worked so much that I wasn't even available to go to dinner. It's not like I'm out on the town every night, collecting crazy new experiences, but I am expanding my brain. I feel so hungry for information. I go home every night and I read like half a book and three magazines and some old articles from the Internet. It reminds me of college, when I would go into the library and check out ten Criterion Collection movies and then watch them all over the weekend. I remember coming out of those weekends, feeling like, *I'm a radically different person than I was on Friday*. . . .

Judd: What do you think people have taken from *Girls*? Do you allow yourself to think about what kind of impact it may be having?

Lena: It's impossible for your own brain to comprehend that other people are seeing this stuff, translating it, analyzing it, outside of your own bedroom or whatever. But I guess the thing that's most exciting to me is when men, particularly fathers, tell me that the show has allowed them to understand their wives or daughters better. That, to me, is a really moving compliment.

Judd: I imagine that's especially true for parents whose daughters are going to college.

Lena: Yeah, and who feel like, *What is happening to my child? Is she ever going to have a job? And what does her sex life look like?* In a way, my work gives them more things to panic about, but it also gives them a sense, I hope, that she's part of something. I also like when women tell me that the show made them feel more comfortable and strong both with their body and in their relationships, that it has given them more authority.

Judd: We thought, in the beginning, that people would have debates about the show, for sure, but I don't think that we thought there was much of a political statement being made. I first realized the debate would happen in the second episode, when we were talking about whether Jessa was going to get an abortion.

Lena: Yeah.

Judd: And I said, maybe she shouldn't have an abortion in the second episode.

Lena: Your quote was, "There's Jerry, there's George, and then there's their crazy neighbor Kramer—and you're having Kramer shoot someone in the face in the second episode. And I'm not saying abortion is like shooting someone in the face, but I am saying we're asking a lot of the audience if Kramer gets an abortion."

Judd: Right. But then, after the first season, when you realized that people were dissecting it and debating it and trying to figure out your politics, it never felt like any of that got in your head or affected your writing. One thing I always tell people is that, when we're in the writers' room, all that talk doesn't affect you negatively. It doesn't impact the creative process. Why do you think that is?

Lena: I think it's because the writers' room is the place where I feel most comfortable. That's the safe space. And so I think I was always determined not to lose that. I wish I could be the person who never reads reviews, but I totally check out what's happening online and I have a pretty good sense of the dialogue around the show. But at the same time, you can't internalize it. That is just gonna kill whatever is exciting or thrilling or organic about the process. There were definitely times where you and I talked about trying to respond to criticism that we found frustrating, but doing it in kind of a wink-wink way.

Judd: Like when we had Donald Glover on the show and you revealed to him that, on some level, you liked dating him *because* he was black.

Lena: It was thrilling and it added to her image of herself as a liberal woman who came to the city to have certain kinds of experiences.

Judd: I don't know if I ever quite landed on what my official position was about making the show more multicultural. Some people say, Well, New York is multicultural but there are plenty of people who go to school and, if they're Caucasian, they have mostly Caucasian friends. Whether that's healthy or not, it's not misrepresenting the world. But what's really wrong with television is that African American show runners are not being encouraged to create shows. What some networks do is try to make themselves feel better by jamming some "diverse" characters into their shows.

Lena: What I always say—and it's kind of my stock answer because I think it's the true answer—is that I'm grateful that the conversation around diversity is happening, period. We've introduced characters of color, and we've done it in a time frame that makes sense to us. What was hard is when people were saying, "You're racist and your family's racist and look at you and your racist show." Being assigned a label like that, especially when you consider yourself to be a liberal person, is distressing.

Judd: I didn't expect Chinese filmmakers to represent the Jewish nerd experience on Long Island.

Lena: And you shouldn't! But what's interesting is that what people were also responding to—which is a real criticism and one I take seriously—is that, if you look at the show, it doesn't look like the New York I know. So we've been more attentive to that, trying to look at each neighborhood and go, Okay, who lives here and what would it look like and what feels real?

Judd: So much of the conversation about diversity on TV should be about subscribers and advertisers. If the networks thought they could make more money creating shows with diverse casts they would do it in a second.

They've clearly decided there's not enough money it. Every once in a while they throw a bone to the idea of diversity, but it's not a high priority.

Lena: It's awful and distressing. But as you proved with *Bridesmaids*, the conventional wisdom is often wrong: Women are going to come to movies. And obviously, black people and black women want to see strong characters who reflect them on television, too. And the industry is lagging way behind on what people's needs are. You have much more of a relationship to the financial and business angle of the industry, because I work at HBO, where there are no ads and I can do whatever I want. But you've had the experience of having to satisfy a studio, a network, do test screenings. You understand the machinations behind it.

Judd: I remember working on a black cop movie.

Lena: Which one?

Judd: I shouldn't say because of the story I'm about to tell. But there was a black character—a gigantic star—and in the movie, he had a romance with another black actress. And I noticed that they never kissed in the movie. I asked about this and the producer said to me, "Yeah. Internationally, people don't like to see black people kiss." And you could tell that the black star understood that as well. They were all pandering to cultural prejudices or what they *thought* were cultural prejudices. Which was bullshit, but my jaw still dropped.

Lena: That is one of the most upsetting things I have ever heard.

Judd: Yeah, and if you think about it, it's very real. It's all of those prejudices—like people say comedies don't work in Asia. So you're saying that Asian people don't laugh, they only want giant robots? It's all driven by money, ultimately.

Lena: Because of what HBO's value system is, I feel like I've been able to avoid the part of the job where those awful truths are revealed to me.

Judd: Has it ever hit you that, in terms of the nightmare of television and development, you haven't had to suffer?

Lena: I think about that all the time. Every time I meet someone who is going through the network TV process. They seem so beaten down. And your stories about your own career when you were younger—I have all these moments where I'm like, I am never allowed to complain about anything ever in my life because of how easy I've had it.

Judd: But it's also, I think, one of the main benefits of your show. You are not reacting from the place of someone who has been beaten up and, as a result, is flinching and making choices based on having been beaten up on other projects. Your lack of history is what makes the show feel pure.

Lena: I feel so lucky because I've never had to take a note that I didn't agree with. I've never felt like my vision has been diluted. And that's a crazy thing to be able to claim. Judd, I have a question I have always wanted to ask you, but because this recorder is turned on, I feel emboldened to do so. Do you think people are scared of you?

Judd: Scared of me?

Lena: Yeah.

Judd: I, uh, I don't know. David Milch said something to me once, which I'd never considered before: He said executives don't want to give notes and don't want to stand behind their opinions. Executives want *you* to have enough power or reputation so that if you screw up, it's your screwup, not theirs. The whole thing is inverted. Executives are looking for ways to *not* be responsible. And when you achieve a certain level of success, you'll notice that some executives disappear because they have deniability about the process. "Of course I trusted Judd, he's had enough success that I should let him do what he wants to do." It's actually harder for them to work with young people, because then they have to be responsible.

Lena: That's so interesting.

Judd: As soon as I made people money, some people went away, but I never felt anyone being afraid of me. It was more like, "Oh, everything he does seems pretty solid. I'm going to let him do his thing." Everybody told me you get five bombs before you go out of business. You can withstand five. Your budget will get lower every time you have a bomb. If you have three bombs in a row, then your budget's going to drop to like eight million dollars. At five, you're done.

Lena: Five bombs in a row?

Judd: Five bombs in a row, and you're done.

Lena: Have you had five bombs in a row?

Judd: I've had things that are a wash. Nothing I've done has been a *bomb*. At the end of the day some of the more difficult movies, like *Funny People*, probably will lose a little money, but not a lot. Sometimes you make things and, the whole time, you're aware that it might not make money, and yet it's what you should be making at this moment in time and you hope it will connect in a big way because it is unique and personal. You have to try to do things that are more challenging to the audience. Those often become the biggest hits. Sometimes they don't make a ton of money. I mean, you have to take your swings. As you have, with *Girls*. Do you think much about what you want to do, beyond the show?

Lena: I want to make more movies because it's something I love doing. I love the format. But TV is the best. When we first started, James L. Brooks said to me, "If a TV show is working, it's the best job you'll ever have." And he was totally right. But there are stories I want to tell that aren't serialized stories. Let's see. I also want to write a novel. That's something I have always wanted to do and then, at a certain point, kind of thought to myself, *Well, that's going to go by the wayside. . . .* It's funny when you want to dabble in new things, and you must feel this sometimes, you get this realization: *Oh, there are people who have spent their whole lives figuring out how to do this, and the thing I make will never be equivalent to what they're doing.* Are there any genres that you want to explore, that don't seem like a natural fit for you?

Judd: I guess I'd like to experiment with having more drama and a little less comedy in some films. But I don't sit around thinking, *I want to make a science fiction movie or a period drama.* It never occurs to me because I'm so confused by modern life already that I never feel satisfied that I have figured anything out. I don't need a metaphor for what I do.

Lena: What do you think about the trend of comedians being obsessed with the idea of becoming dramatic actors? I was just rewatching a Joan

Rivers documentary, and in it, she's crying because she says no one's ever going to take her seriously as an actress and being a comedian was just a thing to do. Do you relate to that?

Judd: I think comedians are interesting when they have other facets. Sometimes I feel like a goofball—I just feel dumb and want to process all my thoughts through humor. Every once in a while, it's a way to make things less painful. But then you begin to feel like you're always trying to filter life through funny and you wonder: Is this insincere on some level? Sometimes I feel like I'm making jokes because I'm uncomfortable with my own thoughts and opinions. I feel this need to make it entertaining for you. I think that's one of the reasons why so many comedians want to do dramatic acting. At some point, you get the urge to drop the cover and just be real.

Lena: It's less so now, but sometimes, when I had a serious thought, I would almost say it in a goofy way—like, I'd take on a weird voice so I'd be like (*in a weird voice*), "You know, I think women have to be able to get free access to abortions!" It was this strange defense mechanism. But as I've become more confident, I'm more comfortable having a serious thought and owning it as a serious thought.

Judd: When you were in college or when you were making *Tiny Furniture*, did you have any thoughts about becoming a public person?

Lena: As a teenager, I had a whole idea of what my life would look like. I wanted to live in Brooklyn. I wanted to have a dog. I wanted to have a cute boyfriend with glasses. But in college, I thought I was going to make weird movies, be a professor of women's film at not that good of a college, and just have a cool, weird life where I met interesting people and organized events. I guess my model for a creative life was much more of an artist's model and much less of a Hollywood model, if you will. So the past few years have been strange. I'm still navigating the difference between what's happening now and what I thought my life would consist of.

Judd: You don't seem like you're shutting down emotionally from it all, though. I'm sure a lot of it is that you're happy and in a happy relationship so you're not fully exposed, and some part of you remains intact.

Lena: And I have a partner and a fun life and we are always working, so it feels like a safe place to be. But it definitely seems like this business gives people a weird chip on their shoulder: *I feel defensive and everyone wants something from me.* It can seem so corrosive and dark and divorced from reality. You've watched a lot of people get famous, so I'm sure you know what I mean.

Judd: I've seen people burn out and people lose touch with why they work. I've also seen people who satisfy so many of their dreams that they just become lost. That's what *Funny People* was about: a guy who didn't have any substantial relationships and who has all of his movie and comedy stardom dreams come true, and he is left with this feeling of emptiness. Because he never figured out that other part of it. In a way, that character is almost the reverse of you. His experience is the exact polar opposite of yours.

Lena: Something that strikes me about your work, every time I rewatch it, is that there's a real morality to it, a sense that we're all supposed to treat each other kindly. A sense that we're all here to take care of each other and to serve a purpose in the world. There's this real message of hope. I find it comforting.

Judd: But you also notice the repetition of that at some point. And so lately, I've been thinking of writing about sacrifice. I've never written anything about people who are willing to sacrifice for other people. We'll see if I can pull it off, but I'm very aware that I've been writing in a certain vein for a while now, and that I could keep rewriting those ideas in a million different ways.

Lena: That's why watching you reengage with stand-up is exciting. In a similar way, what writing the book did for me was allow me to—it's not like I'm talking about experiences in the book that I haven't talked about in the show. I'm talking about sex. I'm talking about growing up. I'm talking about being female. I'm talking about my body. I'm talking about my family. But now I get to talk about these things from this super-personal place. By reengaging with your stand-up at this point in your life, you're getting to come at the topics that matter to you from a totally different angle.

Judd: Yeah, and switching modes forces you to really slow down and think things through. Because you go through life in a haze, staring at your phone and watching *The Bachelor* and being reasonably happy, but you never really break it down. You never stop to think about what's going on in your mind and what you're struggling with. Early on, someone said to me, "The greatest gift you can give is your story," and that, for me, was the turning point. That became the premise of my work. That's when I realized that maybe the things that I think are boring about myself are interesting to other people. Hearing what's in your mind truly makes people feel less alone and gives them hope for things that they want to do and get through things that are difficult.

Lena: That's the reason I make things. Some people make stuff because they want to provide escapist entertainment and blow up cars. Some people make stuff because they want to put out a message of social justice. For me, the seeds of what I do were planted by sitting in my room, reading confessional poetry, and listening to Alanis Morissette and thinking, *I need to find a way to translate all these feelings, which are so like explosive inside of me, into something else.* There are always people telling you that your experience doesn't matter, that it's navel gazing or unnecessary. "We don't need to hear about twentysomething girls who feel like they're ten pounds overweight. We don't need to hear about forty-year-olds getting divorced." But we do need to hear it, because that's who so many people are! I mean, it can be the difference between someone feeling like they have a place in the world and someone feeling they don't. I'm not saying we're here to stop school shootings, but I am saying that art has a place in making people feel less alone—and that, to me, is what's intoxicating about it.

Judd: What about your work as a director? What has surprised you about doing so much of it, and directing so many different actors?

Lena: I love it so much, and I came in thinking that my first two loves were writing and acting. Directing was the thing that I could take or leave, but now, after four years of doing the show, it's like my fiendish obsession. I've had such a steep learning curve. Blocking, camera, lighting, and also getting to engage with all these actors, who approach it in a totally different way. I'm realizing how malleable you have to be and how open you have to be, if you want to meet an actor on their level. I'm eager to direct something that I'm not in. The next step in honing the craft would be totally removing myself as an actor so I can get super-focused on someone else's performance, to really get in there with them.

Judd: What's your relationship with Adam Driver like? Because, to me, in addition to building an incredible relationship with all the women on the show, you have stumbled into this magical pairing with this incredible actor. He's truly headed toward world domination now, but, you know, it started with you and him together, and the work you guys did creating this bizarre, unique person, a character that I think is unprecedented on television. That relationship seems to keep morphing.

Lena: I love Adam so much, and I know for a fact that I didn't know what I was doing as an actor until I met him and he forced me. I'm not saying I'm brilliant now, but he forced me to stop and take stock of what was happening when I was in a scene. He forced me to slow down and pay attention.

Judd: He's so present.

Lena: He's so present, he won't let you do anything else. If he thinks you're not present, he'll fucking slam his fist into a wall to elicit some adrenaline reaction within you. I feel, in many ways, that Adam was my teacher and also that we worked together to figure out what those first scripts *were*. It was such a powerful relationship. There's almost something mystical about it, when you meet someone who brings that out in you. I wouldn't presume to say that I bring anything out in him, but I would say we figured out a groove together.

Judd: Do you think he connects to you in the same way, or is he having a different type of experience?

Lena: I don't know. I only know what he's thinking when we're working. When we're in a scene, I feel like I have a really good sense of what he needs and where he's coming from. But when we're just like eating lunch and having a conversation? I have no fucking idea.

Judd: You've had a similar relationship with the women of the show, and, you know, we talked before about how, in television shows sometimes, the cast gets crazy after a few years. At a certain point, everyone comes to dislike each other. But for you, it has evolved in such a positive way. I mean, you've known Jemima [Kirke] forever.

Lena: Twenty years now.

Judd: And Zosia [Mamet]. What's that been like, having that bond with all of those women you work with now?

Lena: I think I assumed just because girls can be so annoying, it was somehow going to devolve into one massive catfight. Like you said, that's what you always hear about television shows: By the end, nobody's speaking and everyone's arguing about who gets the best hairdresser. But we all have been through this thing together and we've stayed connected. We're all really different but we support each other's decisions and there's a real beauty to it—we're not best friends, going out together every Friday night, but I know that if I needed something, they would be there in a second. There's an essential net of support. I also have so much respect for like how each of them is navigating their career in a really different way but totally owning it. Each girl is totally carving her own destiny. Zosia's writing a feature and Jemima's making paintings and Allison [Williams]'s playing Peter Pan and they're each doing their thing and it's crazy. Allison's getting married now. Jemima's married and a mother of two. Zosia and I both bought homes with our boyfriends. It has been this weird journey to adulthood—and by the time the show's done, we could all be carrying babies around.

Judd: Maybe that's when the show should end.

Lena: Totally.

LESLIE MANN
(2012)

It's always fun to do an interview with my wife, Leslie, because she's always hilarious and we're often right on the edge of getting into a real argument the entire time. It's such a tightrope walk when you do personal work—let alone work that involves your wife and kids, and is inspired by your life—and then have to talk about it with journalists. The problem is, Leslie and I have different ideas about how we want to portray the level of truth involved in our movies. I probably lean—out of pure laziness— toward talking about it as if it mostly comes from our lives, or at least an emotionally truthful place. Leslie prefers to say that the majority of what we do has been fabricated. The truth is probably somewhere in the middle, but this does lead to some tricky moments when we try to talk about our work with other people.

Leslie is my muse in ways that people don't fully understand. When I have an idea for a movie, she's the person that I kick it around with. When I'm outlining a screenplay, she's the one who says, Well if you're going to do this scene, then why don't you do that scene, too? Many of the scenes I've written were Leslie's idea, but I won't get more specific than that here because I want people to think they were all my idea. If any of our movies resonate with people in any way, Leslie's courage to explore these difficult, emotional areas is the reason why. She never thought of herself as a comedian—comedy is just something that seemed to happen to her. Which I am eternally grateful for, because there is no one I love working with, or being with, more.

This interview was conducted by Olly Richards and originally appeared in the March 2013 edition of Empire *magazine.*

Empire magazine: How did you broach the idea of making a movie about—I was going to say ups and downs, but it's really just downs—of marriage at forty?

Judd Apatow: Well, there's nothing funny about the ups. That's the whole point.

Leslie Mann: Every other movie is about the ups. Or the end.

Judd: I was just thinking about doing something about family but I hadn't thought of an idea. Then I thought about how I liked Pete and Debbie in *Knocked Up* and you could make a whole movie about them. . . . So I told Leslie I was thinking about it while we were on vacation in Hawaii.

Leslie: It was a tense day. The kids were being pains. So it was maybe not the best time to talk to me about it. But we talked about whether it would be a good idea, whether it would be good for the kids.

Judd: You resisted the idea of using the kids.

Leslie: No, I resisted that on *Knocked Up*. I knew we'd have to use Maude and Iris in this because they were our kids last time. I didn't want to use them originally.

Empire: What convinced you?

Leslie: Nothing. Judd manipulated me, lied to me, and steamrolled me. He told me he was auditioning kid actors while I was busy doing something, then: (*stage whispers*) "If it doesn't work out, maybe we could use the kids. . . ." Three days before shooting he said, "We had no luck finding kids, so we're using ours."

Empire: How do you establish what from your personal life can go in the film?

Judd: I think naturally we steer it. There's way more that could be in there. . . .

Leslie: But you would want to slit your wrists if you saw that version.

Empire: Who decided there should be a scene in which Leslie fondles Megan Fox's boobs?

Judd: I don't remember. At some point someone must have pitched the idea. . . . Maybe Megan.

Leslie: Oh, I doubt it. It was you, and you're trying to put it on someone else. I'm sure Megan would not push the boob touching.

Judd: I would not have pushed it.

Leslie: What is wrong with you? You're like a dirty man.

Judd: Is that scene dirty?

Leslie: No, I don't care. But a lot of people seem interested in it. . . . It was your idea. Admit it.

Empire: You two met when Leslie came in to read for *The Cable Guy*. Judd, you said you liked her straightaway. Leslie, were you aware?

Leslie: Nuh-uh. Jim Carrey wasn't there, so Judd was reading Jim's part. I don't remember Judd at all.

Judd: I had little birds and hearts floating round my head and she didn't even notice.

Leslie: I had a bit of a crush on Ben Stiller, so maybe that's why. I was focused on my work. I'm professional. Also, Judd was talking like *The Cable Guy*. He had a lisp. It wouldn't have been very sexy. . . . He would send his sister —

Judd: This is a lie!

Leslie: It's true. He would send his sister to my trailer to tell me about all these dates he was going on.

Judd: She just likes me, so she says nice things. I didn't send her.

Leslie: He *sent* her. What was your move?

Judd: I just forced you to be around me more than you wanted to be. It was subtle stalking.

Empire: Do you find the same things funny?

Judd: No.

Leslie: Yes we do! Are you serious?

Judd: We'll agree on some things. But there's some comedy I'll love that—

Leslie: Like what?

Judd: You wouldn't sit and watch Monty Python movies with me.

Leslie: I love Monty Python movies. What are you talking about?

Judd: But I'll watch weird comedy all day long and you'll want to watch *Dateline Mystery.* . . . I think maybe it's not that we like different things but I have a higher tolerance for mass quantity. Leslie might want to watch one episode of *Louie,* but I'll happily watch nine more. She'll want to switch to *Psychic Kids.*

Leslie: That is a good show.

Empire: Is there any comedy you vehemently disagree on?

Judd: I don't think so.

Leslie: I thought you said we didn't have the same sense of humor?

Judd: I think maybe you're not drawn to spend as much time with it as I am. I'm fascinated by how it works or *why* something's funny. I watch endlessly. Leslie is faster to switch off.

Leslie: You don't know me at all. You seriously do not know me. You are so self-involved that you have no clue who I am.

Empire: What are your favorite comedy movies?

Leslie: *Harold and Maude.*

Judd: I thought you hated that. I'm joking! Come on, our daughter's named Maude. So we're in tune there.

Leslie: Are we in tune or out of tune? You keep changing *your* tune.

Judd: I'm trying to make this interesting! I'm shaking it up.

Leslie: Shake it up by leaving.

Judd: What are your favorites?

Leslie: I have three: *Harold and Maude, Broadcast News, Terms of Endearment.*

Judd: Okay, we're in tune.

Empire: Paul Feig, co-producer on *Freaks and Geeks*, described you as "a shouter," Judd. When did that change?

Leslie: Right after that. It was his back.

Judd: I herniated my disk right after *Freaks and Geeks*, due to bad posture, a car accident, and general stress. Then when *Undeclared* went down, I was fighting the studio because they wouldn't let me direct a pilot I wrote. . . . But I realized I was treating this executive like my mother and the other person who wouldn't let me do it like my father, and I was projecting all my issues onto them. As soon as I made that connection, everything changed.

Empire: You had rave reviews for *Freaks and Geeks* and *Undeclared* but terrible ratings. How do you deal with the knowledge that you're making something good that nobody wants to watch?

Judd: It felt so bad. I had a rebellious streak that it was better to be a cool, indie geek than a mainstream rock star. *The Ben Stiller Show* was canceled after twelve episodes. *Cable Guy* didn't do well. I was doing punch-ups on some movies that were successful, working uncredited on a lot of things that were doing well. I knew what it took, but I didn't necessarily want to do it in my own work. I got really depressed and kept switching back and forth between [TV and movies] when I wasn't succeeding commercially in either. At the end of *Undeclared*, I asked Will Ferrell to play a meth addict who will write your term paper for money. He hadn't had a big movie yet, just some supporting parts. I thought, *This guy should be a movie star but I can't get a movie made with him, so let's just put him in an episode.* He had a good time, so he brought us *Anchorman*, which he wrote with Adam McKay.

Empire: Leslie, what was your point of view, watching your husband go through that?

Leslie: It was awful. He was really stressed out and that put a lot of pressure on me. We had a new baby. He was such a nightmare. Just kind of on another planet, stressed-out and unavailable. Obsessing about work . . . But he's kind of still like that. I'm really tired of it.

Judd: I could talk for hours about *her* being miserable about work.

Leslie: Do you know what I did? When his back went out, I went to New York and did this little film with Jeff Goldblum and I had my first love scene with him. So I was really enjoying myself and I felt terrible about it. Judd was literally being operated on—

Judd: On my spine.

Leslie: And I was in bed with Jeff Goldblum! And Jeff is very Method and he wants to rehearse—

Judd: But this as a business can just consume everything. When you have a family, you're worried. And for Leslie, you're always auditioning and waiting to see if people like you. Eventually we thought, *We should just create our own work.*

Empire: So tell us about *The 40-Year-Old Virgin* and finally getting that success.

Judd: We got shut down after two days. They thought Steve Carell looked like a serial killer.

Leslie: They thought Paul Rudd was fat.

Judd: They thought I was lighting it like an indie. They literally shut it down in the middle of the day. They didn't even wait. . . . I decided not to yell. That was a turning point. I decided just to listen and not react at all. I didn't tell them it was insane to shut down a production and cost themselves half a million dollars when they could just call me at night and discuss it. Because I didn't yell, it resolved itself much quicker.

Empire: How did it resolve?

Judd: We started up again two days later. It was really silly.

Leslie: You made some adjustments. Paul went on a diet. He literally stopped eating. What did you change with Steve?

Judd: Nothing. Steve decided the character would be a little more Buster Keaton–esque. He was low-energy and everyone else was spinning around him. Everything we shot in those first two days became some of the funniest stuff in the movie. It was the speed-dating sequence. So there was no purpose to it.

Leslie: If you look at Paul Rudd in the speed-dating sequence compared to the rest, he's, like, ten pounds heavier. Then in the rest of the movie his hair looks cute and he's thinner.

Empire: Then *Knocked Up* happened. . . .

Leslie: *Knocked Up* is the story of when our daughter Iris was born.

Judd: Almost beat for beat. From the doctor not showing up to getting the doctor you rejected earlier and asking him to deliver the baby and him being mean to you. We knew it was a crazy story. The last third is almost exactly what happened. Leslie goes into labor and I call my doctor but he's out of town.

Leslie: But we saw him about three hours before that and my water broke. He said, "No, your water didn't break, you can go home." He wanted to leave town and go to a bar mitzvah in San Francisco. So I think he lied to me and said my water didn't break, which is really dangerous. But he's such a stupid fucking asshole and I hate him. So we wound up with this guy who had giant hands, like Shrek. And there were complications and he was mad at us and he reeked of cigarettes and it was just horrible. But it made a good movie.

Empire: When did you both first realize that you could make people laugh?

Leslie: I would audition for dramatic parts and people would laugh at me—not ideal at the time—so slowly I realized the comedy world is where I belonged.

Judd: I wanted to be funny more than I was. I realized, when I worked with people, that I could write in their voices. So I could write jokes for *Roseanne* or *Larry Sanders*, but I didn't have my own voice.

Empire: You started as a stand-up. Was your intention to become a performer or writer?

Judd: I probably thought I could become Eddie Murphy. . . . But I didn't do any of the acting side because I was confident that I was terrible. Even when I did stand-up, I was smart enough to know that I had no life experience or real opinions. So it was more fun for me to write for people who had really strong opinions, because I didn't care about anything but being a comedian.

Empire: Was the decision to move to writing a conscious one or driven by circumstance?

Leslie: It was a decision made by Jim Henson.

Judd: I auditioned for him for this reality show where he gave cameras to a couple of comedians who traveled round the country. I auditioned with Adam Sandler and David Spade and Rob Schneider. Jim Henson said he wanted to buy all my ideas but didn't want to cast me because I lacked warmth.

Leslie: From the guy who created the Muppets.

Judd: From the guy who taught you how to *read.* It hit me hard. . . . But the fact he wanted my ideas was important. I realized Adam Sandler was really fun to watch and be around and I knew I wasn't like him. I was just a normal guy with some good lines.

Empire: You've now worked together many times, but *This Is 40* was the first time Leslie was the lead. How was that different?

Leslie: It was just more tiring, but he protected me from all the stresses from the outside world. I don't know what the budget is or what the politics were. It was just a safe world for all the actors. I was so grateful for that. Thank you, honey. I kind of like you a little bit more again.

Judd: See, we've gone full circle. She hated me and then she likes me again. This is my day. This is my life.

LOUIS C.K.

(2014)

Louis C.K. is one of those people who are so brilliant and funny and uncompromising that sometimes I need to avoid their work. When I was writing *This Is 40*, I made a point to never watch his TV show because I was aware that it was, on one level, about a middle-aged guy with two daughters, and if I watched it, and loved it, I would probably feel like there was no need for me to make my movie. (Only after I locked my film did I go and binge-watch it. I couldn't love it more.) I also make a point of not watching too much of his stand-up, because he's so prolific and covers so much ground. Watching him makes me feel like there's nothing left to talk about, and that everything has already been done, as well as it can be done, by Louis. He has raised the bar for all of us.

It is worth noting that we conducted this interview in Louis's kitchen in New York City and, as we spoke, he made me a delicious dinner of steak and beans. For a moment, I felt like I was one of his kids, and I came away thinking, *They have a pretty good situation there.*

Judd Apatow: I was reading an article about you recently and I saw that you had an experience a little like mine—as a kid, I worked at a radio station, and you, somebody got you a job at a TV station?

Louis C.K.: Yeah.

Judd: I had a guy like that, too. He ran the high school radio station and treated us like adults. He was the cool guy. He would curse and he went to NYU with Martin Scorsese and taught film at the high school and he made me think that you could do anything, even as a little kid. So I had a radio show and interviewed all these comics. And I'm wondering what that was like for you to have this teacher who said, I'm going to hook this kid up.

Louis: In junior high school, I did nothing but drugs. I got in trouble all the time. I was a messed-up kid. And then in my first year of high school, I stopped all that and became a good student, but the problem was, by then, all my friends from junior high school had dropped out—like, every one of them. Five of my friends dropped out of high school after one year. And there was this kid Neil who lived a block from the high school and everybody would be there, at his house, partying every day—from nine in the morning, when his parents left for work.

Judd: Where did Neil's parents think the kids were?

Louis: They couldn't control it. Both parents worked. I mean, everybody I knew was getting high and nobody could do anything about it.

Judd: Did they assume the kids were going to get jobs when they were that young?

Louis: Everybody had jobs. I had a job. Sophomore year of high school, I worked at Kentucky Fried Chicken. Everybody worked at fast-food places. So all these kids were told by their parents—the parents got together and said, Just get out of school and work. The idea was that they were all going to come back to school a year later and try again. Anyway, all of a sudden all of my friends were getting high every day and I couldn't resist, so I just stopped going to school.

Judd: What grade is that? Tenth?

Louis: Tenth grade. And before that, I was a great student. I was getting A's. So there's this meeting with all my teachers and my mom came and they told her: "Your son's not coming to school." And my mom, who thought we were out of the woods, was like, "God damn it." It was a great meeting because I felt like I was able to be honest with it all. My mom and I had been through a lot together, and I said, "I'm having a hard time staying here. I get depressed in school and it's hard." And one of my teachers—he was my homeroom teacher—he just said, "Well, you can't do *nothing*." He said, "You don't have to go to school if it's not for you, but you can't do nothing. What do you want to do?" And I said, "Well, geez. I'd like to make TV shows and movies." And he said, "If I can get you a job in that area, will you do that?" I said sure. And he came up to me the next day with a card and he said, "This is the number for Continental Cablevision, the local cable company." They had a TV station. He said they hire interns and it doesn't pay anything but you can go there and you can learn about television. And so I went to this place and there were these people making television and it was pretty good equipment and they had a news show and sports and little art shows and stuff. So they explained, If you come here, we'll teach you how to use all this equipment and you can do whatever you want. And I couldn't fucking believe it. I stopped going to Neil's house immediately and I thought, *I want to get back into school.* I had a direction in my life. So I started going to the station and it was all grown-up people. I was the only kid there.

Judd: Would you edit? Did you work the cameras?

Louis: I just started doing everything. I sucked in the learning. I would sit and watch the news editor. I learned how editing worked, and I was very good with machines. I could fix cameras when they broke and stuff. So I became the kid everybody trusted. They let me take the equipment home. If you could fix it, nobody cared. So I became a pet there, and everyone treated me like a grown-up.

Judd: I did the same thing at Comic Relief. When I was in college, I saw on TV that they were planning to do Live Aid but with comedians. It was called Comic Relief. I called up and said, "I will do anything." I was eighteen. "I'll do anything, just let me help." They said, "Well, we don't have anything," but then three months later they called back and said, "Come in and help us." I started putting on benefits around the country at all the clubs. But it was the same attitude: I am going to be your go-to guy. And that's what you want your kids to have. It's hard, I think. I talk about this all the time with my kids. The reason why you do that is because you can see your demise if you *don't* do it. Our kids, though—they don't have that fire on their ass because when I was a kid both my parents went bankrupt. It was very chaotic for a while and so, when those opportunities came up, I was an animal because I was afraid that I would be homeless at some point. I used to think that all the time. Jim Carrey always used to say that when he saw homeless people he would have this image of the guy patting the ground going, "Here, this spot's for you"—and that's what drove him. And he was homeless as a kid. His dad was an accountant who lost his job and never got an accounting job ever again and they became janitors at a factory. The whole family had dropped out of school. They would all clean together.

Louis: Wow, yeah, I don't know. Who knows what's in store for our kids. It might not stay like this forever. I always say that to my kids. I probably lay it on them a little too much. Someday they might be saying to their friends, "My dad used to have a house on Shelter Island, and he had a boat." I mean, for Jim Carrey's climb and everything that happened for him—the massive success—he's looking for work. You *always* end up looking for work.

Judd: When things started going really well for you, were you able to enjoy it?

Louis: Oh yeah. I remember the first time I did *Letterman*. I had all these thoughts reeling in my head that I had to do this or that, and then when I got on, right before I got onstage, I thought, *Don't forget to enjoy this because you're going to fucking kill yourself if you don't enjoy this.* And I've always remembered that. It's all very fleeting, you know.

Judd: That's the big thing about it hitting a little later in life. You're wise enough to realize: *Oh, this is a big moment.*

Louis: I've never had all-at-once successes. I've never had any big leaps, the rags-to-riches thing. Everything has been one foot in front of the other, one step at a time. So many times I heard, You're up for this thing, this is the one, and it's going to be huge. And it never happens and then it's back to coming down to earth. You get blue balls from that, you know—like, *This is going to be it!* And you start thinking about how you're going to change your life.

Judd: What was the big one of those for you?

Louis: I met with these people at Good Machine, which was an indie film group. They were making some great stuff, and they repped this movie I wrote called *Delicious Baby*. It was this fucked-up movie about a woman who moves to a small town and everybody worships her and meanwhile she's been eating all the kids. And, uh, nobody wants to believe it because they love her and a robot ends up choking her to death. So they read it and they took me to lunch. They sat me down and they said, "We have some big news. We're making *Delicious Baby*. We have a green light." And that feeling was incredible. What an amazing feeling. Anyway, we made the movie and it won an Oscar.

Judd: End of story.

Louis: Yeah, no—so it didn't get made, obviously. And I had to come down from that. Oh, that fucking hurt. That was brutal. There were a few of those kinds of things. I thought I was going to be on *The Tonight Show* with Carson. I got a call saying I was going to be on *Letterman* when I was nothing, a club comic. At the time, Frank Gannon booked the Letterman show and he told me he was going to put me on—and then he retired. I was really young then. A shot at *Letterman* could have totally changed everything.

Judd: In a good way or bad, do you think?

Louis: I'm glad I didn't get it. I'm glad for every single thing I didn't get.

Judd: I always felt the reason why I was interested in comedy was that I was on some level hostile and looking for answers. When you look back, what do you think was the fuel for your work?

Louis: I think comedy is a freeing thing. It's not even an escape. It just feels good. You know what I mean? My parents were divorced around the same time as yours—I was in fifth grade, ten years old. Those were formative years. I was awkward and I couldn't quite score the way everybody else did. I didn't feel like I was succeeding as a kid. I was bad academically, always behind, always in trouble. I had friends and stuff, but I didn't feel like I was winning in school. And comedy was this amazing thing because comedy is like saying the wrong things—when you see a grown-up do it and they succeed at it and get applause . . .

Judd: When did you tune in to what comedy was?

Louis: My first love was Bill Cosby. My friend Jeff had a whole stack of his records; we would just sit and laugh. I loved the sound of it. I loved the sound of his voice and hearing the audience and the nightclub feeling and how it sometimes felt like a concert. I used to listen to how the record *sounded*. Oh my God, I just like—it put a real lust in me.

Judd: What's the thing that Cosby did that you wish you could do?

Louis: I wish I could control myself like he did. I wish that I could . . . talk . . . like . . . this . . . on . . . stage. Respect the negative space. Respect the silence, let it alone. I wish I had that kind of control. I came up in the Boston clubs scene where—

Judd: It's combat. You learn it as combat.

Louis: And I still—whenever I'm watching my opening act on the road or if I'm in a club, I'm like, *They're all gonna leave. They're not going to be there when I get out there.* Like, *I need to get on right now.* I always closed the show because I was too dirty and too loud. No one wanted to follow me.

Judd: It all changes when the crowd is there to see you. How many years has it been for you where they're really there to see you in a big way?

Louis: I had done *Lucky Louie* and it got canceled, and then I did this special called *Shameless*. It went on the air and I got a call from the guy at HBO: It's good, it's good. Anyway, I had built some shows, booked some touring clubs, and one of them was in Philadelphia. I had a week booked there—you know, you do Tuesday through Sunday. You have two on Friday, three on Saturday. Any other week I go and nobody is there on Tuesday. Fifty people Wednesday, a hundred Thursday. Friday and Saturday are packed if the show's any good. That was for years, you know. For like twenty years I had done things like that. But anyway, I got a call one day. This was in January and I had Philly booked in April, and they say, "We want to add a show on Thursday in Philadelphia." And I said, "Why? Why the fuck do they want to make me do another show?" And he said, "Because they're all sold out."

Judd: Three months in advance.

Louis: And I was like, "What the fuck did you say to me? They want to start *adding* shows?" It had never happened to me. That's a big fucking deal. That was a big thing, to suddenly go to clubs that were sold out well in advance—they're all there to see you, and you're taking the door, and the club that you've been working for and has abused you is suddenly, you know, "sir" and "please" and "thank you." It's a weird thing. I started doing theaters in 2007 to 2008, seven hundred and fifty to fifteen hundred seats.

Judd: Does it change your act?

Louis: It's a huge amount of pressure. 'Cause you have to be really great. When you're the headliner at some club, you're just the last guy. You do forty-five to an hour, close strong, and make people feel like they had a complete eat. When you do well as a headliner in a club, people are like, "That guy was good, that guy was good." But in a theater, there is an enormous amount of pressure because this is their choice for the night. So you want to deliver. And I get anxious about that. Once you're doing twenty-five hundred seats, five thousand seats—there's a whole other thing there. It has to be phenomenal.

Judd: And you're turning the whole act over, too. Carlin would turn it over, but he did it over a few years. . . .

Louis: He did a gradual thing. But for me, it was more interesting to do it this way, to think of each year's act like a different book that I wrote.

Judd: Are you aware of how much that's changed comedy? How everyone else is looking at their acts because of you?

Louis: I'm not aware of that. I know that some people don't like it that I say . . . Look, when I started doing a yearlong tour and a stand-up special, the next time I would tour, it seemed natural for me to let my audience know it's a different show. You're seeing a different show. I never was bragging to other comedians. Some comedians got pissed off because they thought I was bragging. I don't give a fuck what they think.

Judd: I do feel a sea change from it. It seems to have inspired people to work harder, to evolve who they are on a daily basis. I used to work with Larry Miller at the Improv, and he was incredible, and he had this polished act. He was the one who urged me to write more. To treat it like a job. He'd do his Thanksgiving bit, and it could be one of the best bits of all time, but now I feel—in the best possible way—that comics feel the pressure to be in the moment with what their life is, with their act.

Louis: I think it's better. Chris Rock taught me a lot about this kind of stuff, but I really learned it from Carlin. I remember I was in the parking lot of the Yang—what's that Chinese restaurant in Boston that does comedy?

Judd: The one that Steven Wright was discovered at?

Louis: No, not the Ding Ho. The Ding Ho was gone. I can't believe I'm blanking on it, 'cause I did so many gigs . . . I opened for Jerry Seinfeld there. But anyway, I was sitting in the parking lot and feeling like shit and listening to this interview with Carlin. And he said that he gets done with his jokes and moves on. And I thought, *God, if I only had the fuckin' courage to get rid of these jokes. I've been doing them all my life. And I hate all of them. I hate every joke I tell.*

Judd: But you stuck with them.

Louis: Yeah, you stick with them. Because you don't need anything else. I got all these tools, I know how this bit works, I know how this bit works. So I started thinking about that and then, years later, I was talking to Chris Rock and he said, "If you do *Letterman* or you get the big shot, don't go back and do your classic five minutes. Do what's exciting you *today*. Do what's really turning you on in the moment." And that was a great piece of advice. Chris said, "If your audience sees you're special and they think you're funny, and they go see you live and it's a totally different show from last time and it's great, they will never let go of you. You will never lose that audience. They will never let you go." That's how he put it. What an interesting way to think of an audience—and that's Chris's audience—they just hold on to him. So that became my endeavor. I thought, *I'll go out, do another hour. Creatively, I've got an empty vessel, nothing in it. How do things cluster together?* I thought about these things scientifically, like this documentary I saw, when you snap your Achilles' tendon they put like a fiber on there and your body starts to coat it with tendon material. . . .

Judd: And it grows around it?

Louis: Yeah, it grows around it. Because something's there, when there's nothing there. So I thought, *How does that apply to my act? How do I build an hour when there's nothing there?* And so I would go onstage with five minutes of improv, ten minutes, now I've got a really strong twenty. So stop doing it and start at five again and build another twenty, and I've got forty minutes now. I can do forty minutes. I'm not doing the L.A. clubs anymore, I'm going to Horatio Hornblower's in Ventura, or the Wolf or whatever it is. Those clubs, you know, people are eating steak, there's a little more pressure. And try to turn that forty—it's like the way they make yogurt, they take a lump and put it in milk and it fills it up, fills it up. Go onstage with not quite enough time and with the pressure of headlining, and forty turns into an hour just out of necessity. I've got an hour now, I can do an hour. Make it great. And then decide that that hour is shit and I need twice the material. Do a second hour, fold it in. I worked so hard on that stuff. I don't know if I have the balls to do it that way anymore.

Judd: That's not how you do it now?

Louis: I do. I mean, the last hour I did, I feel like it's my last one for a little while. But it's like, how many of these things do you need to do? Also, I love club comedy. I miss it. I miss fucking around on the club stage.

Judd: Is that what you want to do now?

Louis: Well, my TV show has me in the clubs. Sometimes when I'm filming my show, the Comedy Cellar is a location, so if I have extras hanging around, I bring them downstairs and do a set and they'll kind of chuckle and I'll use it on the show because I'm able to do weird little bits that don't quite make any sense. But I'm getting into different-sized things these days. Like, I just did *SNL*, and I got obsessed with the monologue. I thought, *Geez, if I can do a great SNL monologue—*

Judd: It was a dark monologue, the one you did.

Louis: That was a fun thing because I got into it as its own project. I thought, *I want to do the stuff that I do at SNL*—and luckily I had done the show before. The great thing about doing something twice is—you know, when I came out to host *SNL*, the rehearsal audience is cool. They're cool people and they feel like they're in on something so there's a cool feeling. And then you come out for the live show and you're like, *Wait, these people are fucking tourists and a lot of them are kids. There are families. People are here with their parents and they're not cool.* And so, the second time I thought, *I want to do a really interesting monologue that's like its own piece of performance,* and I thought, *They're not going to like it.*

Judd: I mean, you don't usually hear people talk about religion and death—

Louis: No, not at all. That's the stuff that I've been doing, and I was saving it for the series but I thought, *Let's take my best right-now material and use it. The audience is not going to like it but it doesn't matter on television because if you don't let it get to you, nobody can hear.*

Judd: It played really well. I mean, watching it on TV. It sounded like it was all going well.

Louis: I trained for it by going to really shitty places. I never worked so hard on a set in my life, certainly not a four-to-eight-minute set. I did a lot of bad places with open mics where it's all, you know, bitter comedians and no audience. I remember one place there was literally water leaking on the floor next to me and there's a guy in the front row on the phone and I was like, *This is perfect.* I just played. I thought, *I need to be able to play this without any support,* and I got really good at it and I got a great fucking crowd. The *SNL* crowd loved it. It was totally unexpected.

Judd: Is dress rehearsal the first time Lorne sees the monologue?

Louis: Yeah, Lorne really helped me because I did the first show—you know, the worst thing that can happen in an important show is when the rehearsal goes well. It just hurts you. You need caution and an alert mind to do this kind of thing. And I came out for dress and I did twelve minutes and I fucking killed. And nobody had seen it. Nobody had seen the material because I had been running out at nights to do it. So we have the between-show meeting and Lorne—my manager had said to me, "Don't let Lorne cut a single minute. Do twelve minutes like you did in the room," and I was like, yeah. After all this work I did do to humble myself, I was really jacked up. So I go into the meeting and I'm like in this big, leather chair and Lorne says, "Have you had any experience at *SNL*?"

Judd: I haven't worked there but I know the moment you're talking about.

Louis: Everybody's there. It's like meeting the president. It's, like, very important. And he says, "So you did twelve minutes in the monologue. How much do you want to do on-air?" I said, "I want to do all twelve." And he goes, "You're not doing twelve." He goes, "It was good but there was a lot of air in it, a lot of stopping and starting. I know there are cuts in there." My faced turned red. I was angry. I was like, "Well, I don't know. I thought it was pretty good. And fuck you." I was really mad. And then later this woman comes in and says, "Uh, we're one minute under." And so I go, "Then I'm doing twelve." And Lorne turns to me and goes, "Calm down." I was really insulted. He said, "I'll give you seven and nobody's ever done seven." And I said, "What if it goes long? What if I go over and I end up doing ten or more?" And he goes, "Then we'll know that you're very un-disciplined and that you're unprofessional." And everybody laughed. So I said, "I want to see the monologue from rehearsal." And he goes, "Show it to him." My point was to prove how great it was. And I watched it and I was like, *God damn, it's not that good.* Tons of air. And a lot of stopping and starting. I had a whole fart thing. A whole thing about farting on a baby that fucking killed, and he was like, "You're winning without it. I wouldn't do it." So I realized the farting on the babies was stupid and it's going to ruin the monologue. So I got Michael Che, who writes for the show, and asked him to sit with me. It's the most vulnerable thing you can do is ask a comedian to help you cut your material, but I was like, "What do you think?" And he was nervous, he was like, "I don't know." He didn't want to make a wrong decision. But I cut it down. I cut four minutes out as we're ticking off time to get on the air.

Judd: And you have to act and work the other sketches, too.

Louis: Yes, it was high pressure. Very high pressure.

Judd: How do you remember it all?

Louis: Well, because you fucking better know it. You fucking better know it. I mean, I had to switch the order. I had to change stuff. I just told my-self, *Don't try to remember this. Make these decisions and they'll be there for you when you hit the moment.* I loved it. This kind of thing to me is the most worthwhile life experience. I'm standing at the door to *SNL* after all that shit, and Gina the stage manager is counting off and my hands are on the door, and I just started chuckling. I was like, *This is fucked up. This is live television. This is fucked up.* And I went out and it just—it was all there for me and I was able to sail. The audience was at the right place. They looked a little critical but I felt like, *It's going to be okay. I'm going to bring this material and you're going to like it.* Fuck, did that feel good.

Judd: And that was the day that you realized Lorne knows what he's doing.

Louis: He knows exactly what he's doing. He's so smart, but he scared me. And I needed to go in scared.

Judd: You *like* being scared?

Louis: I remember when I was a kid, Billie Jean King was doing that Battle of the Sexes thing—I don't remember if it was happening when I was a kid or if I saw a show about it. But I was so impressed with her. She reminded me of my mom and I just thought she was the coolest person and I hated Bobby Riggs because my mom was a single, working mother. They toured together and did these interviews together, and he was always going, like, women should just go back, put on a tight shirt, and make me a steak. He said this amazing shit and she's just sitting there with a smile on her face. And they turned to her and they say, "How do you feel about all this?" And she says, "Well, all this does is put pressure on me. Everything he says just means that I have to beat him." She gets this big smile on her face and says, "I love pressure."

Judd: Wow.

Louis: And I never forgot it. I was like, fuck that. That was such an interesting notion—that pressure, give me, give me, give me, because all that's going to do is make me better. Like, eating pressure. Having it be fuel. I like that. Whenever I realize, *Uh-oh, this is fucked up, I don't feel ready, this is going to look bad if this doesn't go well,* I get that physical feeling. I don't like that feeling, but I like the whole arc of it. You need the whole arc for it to be good. When you win and you do well, it feels great.

Judd: Was that an historic moment for you, hosting *SNL?* Was that one of your dreams?

Louis: When I worked at *Conan,* *SNL* was right next door and I used to go through *SNL* to get to the commissary, just walk through the studio so that I could smell it. I loved the fucking *smell* of the place. I didn't want to be a sketch performer or anything, but the idea of hosting it? I never thought that I would be that guy. I was very happy to get the shot, terrified to get the shot.

Judd: I can't imagine how scary that is.

Louis: I was really scared.

Judd: Like, *How am I going to learn how to talk off of these cue cards?*

Louis: Yeah, everything. Everything. *How am I going to do any of this?* I thought, *I've got to get a writer to help me. I've got to bring a guy in. Everybody does that.* But then I was hanging out with Amy Poehler a lot and she said to me, "Don't bring somebody in. Just give yourself to the process." So I just showed up and said, "What do you guys want me to do?" And I let them lead me through it. But the second time I did it was the best because I had the benefit of experience and I was so excited to do it again and I knew a lot more about it and all the people were junior. There were all these young kids and I found myself teaching some of them, and that was a nice feeling. Anyway, it is fun to be part of old hallowed things.

Judd: How long do you think you can do your show for?

Louis: I don't know. I feel like I have to take it year by year. This year was a totally different experience than last season. I didn't do it like a job. I decided I don't need to go and try to make movies or anything. This show was a good job. It's a good thing to be doing creatively. I had this thing that I was going to make a movie. And I'd been saving it and I said, *Fuck it. I'll make an episode out of it.* So I cut it into two pieces and I made it an episode and it's a whole flashback thing.

Judd: There's a type of storytelling, and movies are not hospitable to it. It's a miracle when shows fall together and you feel like, *Oh, this is the right idea for the right person and shit's about to go down.*

Louis: TV shows are about getting the right tuning. It's like trying to crack a safe. Once you get it, it starts paying off like a slot machine creatively— like, I created a machine that makes paper cups, you know. I just sit there and stack them. And it keeps running as long as people want paper cups.

Judd: Whose voice is in your head that's wise?

Louis: A collection of people. My mom is a big part of that for me. She's got a calm and thoughtful approach to things and, yeah, it's her, it's me — I feel like I've invented a lot of that for myself. Sometimes it's friends like Chris Rock, who is one of the smartest people I know. It's different people who have said stuff to me and then things I've learned.

Judd: My mom was very manic and up and down — you know, super nice but also super screaming and crazy. You get that implanted in your head. Like, if you have the solid mom implanted, moments come up like *SNL* — like, *Here we go, you're walking out onstage.* And that's the voice that takes you out there.

Louis: That's right. I mean, it's funny. Chris Rock is a lot of those for me. I remember when I did *Lucky Louie*, I was really scared. That was my first series, my first real job. And right before I went out I thought, *This might not go good.* And I called him and said, "I have a feeling this might go badly," and he said, "You're damn right it might. It's very likely to go badly and all those people are working hard and you better fucking step up. You better do something to not let that happen." And I was like, *Shit, that's right.* There's a few people like that. Paul is another. Paul Kozlowski, this comedian that was in Boston when I was coming up. And I had a kind of doldrums moment once, on the steps of a comedy club, and I said, "This is really hard. This is hard. I hardly ever get on the stage and when I do the crowds suck." And he said, "So get out, then. There's too many comedians. Get the fuck out. Quit."

Judd: "We don't need you."

Louis: "Quit." I had a few moments like that. But once I had a kid, I remember thinking, you know, *I want to show up for this,* and I remember thinking that stuff of like not being able to sit alone with myself. That's not a good thing about me. I wanted to change and this was a good reason to do it, and I remember sitting alone with my daughter a lot and breathing and going, *Just cool it, you know, be here for her.* She was a great target for my better intentions. I remember telling myself, keep being part of it and change as many diapers as I can and also try to get the kid away from my wife so I can have my own set of parenting skills. So I wasn't just her assistant. I put a lot of thought into that. It was a big deal for me. Uh, I don't know how we got here.

Judd: What are the things that you're trying to say on the show about being a parent?

Louis: I always try to show that I don't have any control as a parent, you know what I mean? I did this thing with the little one on the show and I'm telling her this thing about don't look into your neighbor's bowl unless it's to check if they have enough. I try to teach my kids this kind of thing. The reason why we cut sandwiches in half is so you can offer somebody a piece of your sandwich. You don't need the whole sandwich. Everybody in your line of sight, you offer it to them and if nobody wants it, then hey, you get a whole sandwich but you're only supposed to eat half. I tell them these things.

Judd: Do they believe you?

Louis: Sometimes.

Judd: And you don't know what sticks or how it sticks, because I'll say something to my daughters and I'll think they don't care at all, and then a year later, in conversation somehow it comes up that they remembered that.

Louis: Yes, that's right.

Judd: It's interesting to me because I have two daughters. And it really does change your reality when you spend an enormous amount of time only with women and little girls. It's a very sweet, intimate relationship. Like my daughter—I know you hate all the cellphone stuff, but she'll text me all day during school and tell me, like, "I just cried during Spanish class because the teacher asked me a question and I didn't know the answer and I cried and I'm in the bathroom right now."

Louis: Isn't that nice that she's reaching out to you that way? I don't hate the cellphone stuff, by the way. I think you have to—

Judd: No, I agree with everything you say about it. It's a battle to figure out how to manage technology with kids.

Louis: Yeah, it is, but it will be a battle for them for their whole lives, too. I mean, when I'm at my best, I leave my phone around without looking at it and I only use my computers to write or edit or whatever. My favorite part of the year is when I'm editing my show because I can't touch the Internet; I'm using my computer to edit. Because it's a sickness. Like right now, because the show is on the air, I'm reading shit about it and about myself and I'm tweeting because I never tweet. I don't partake in that back-and-forth thing, but when I do because I'm tweeting to promote and then I'm like, *Did anybody respond, why didn't anybody respond?* And *Oh, fuck that guy. Should I say something, fuck, maybe I'll direct-message him. Fuck you.* It's a sickness. I can't handle it. So the thought occurred to me: *I need to help my daughter figure out how to do this.* I think I've done a good thing already, which is that she'll be the last one of her friends to get a smartphone. And because she's watched all her friends change since getting them, and I've watched them change, too. I know all of these kids. I know the parents and I know the kids. I've known them since they were little. And I see these kids who suddenly are seized by this thing. When they come over—like, my daughter had a sleepover party recently and I made her friends check their phones at the door.

Judd: They start shaking.

Louis: They itch, they shake, they can't listen to each other—it hurts them to not have their phones. And she's observing this because she's not one of them. It's a big caution for her. So when she does get one, she'll have a better shot than I have and that her friends have had.

Judd: What's hard is that they are afraid to drop out of this mass communication. But like I've said to my daughter, "Maybe you should be known as the kid who is hard to reach."

Louis: That's right. That's the coolest possible thing you can be. But it's pollution. It's pollution. You need time by yourself. I was watching *Rocky* with a friend of mine. And there's all these scenes of him sitting on this dirty mattress, alone—the guy is so alone, it's beautiful how alone he is. Nobody's alone like that anymore. Nobody. You know, cops on the beat in New York are staring at their fucking phones. Airline pilots are on iPads. Fucking hell. It's crazy.

Judd: When I'm working sometimes, I have this book of Cassavetes interviews at hand. He just has so many quotes about doing things differently — one of the quotes is something about, I don't care if people like the movie, I just hope, in ten years, it's still stuck in your craw somewhere. Like, they're still thinking about it.

Louis: You want it to be compelling, that's all. The likable thing is not really worth much. It's a low-wattage bulb, you know. I remember when I did *Pootie Tang*, it was such a fucking disaster and John Goldwyn was the head of Paramount at the time. And he was so mad. He watched the cut and brought us in. Me and David Gale, who ran MTV Films, Sean Daniel, who had been the head of Universal who was now running the company [Alphaville, a production company on *Pootie Tang*]. All these people, and I was the director, and I remember they all walked in and I stood back a little and John Goldwyn was holding the door, and he went, "Come on." He told me to come in and his voice was shaking, he was so upset.

Judd: Had he read it?

Louis: I don't know. Somebody actually brought that up: Did you read the script? "Because," the editor said, "we kept to the script pretty much. Did you approve this movie?" And David Gale said, "I think something's lost on you. I think you're not getting something." "What am I not getting? What am I not getting about you taking four, by the way, *million dollars* of our money? This is an irresponsible, wasted effort." He hated it so much. He said, "Why would Pootie Tang make that beautiful woman drink milk from a saucer on the floor, and yet he throws himself at this whore?" And I remember when he said that I was like, *This is fucking great. This means I did something right because he's so upset.*

Judd: Oddly, those are the ones that people keep watching and talking about.

Louis: No, that's right. And I think I'm able to do that on the show because the show doesn't have an obligation to tell a whole story. Sometimes we tell two in one episode. I had an instinct that I should try to be as bold as I can about how I play with the format because I'll chase away everybody who doesn't like it and then I'll get fans who do like it. If the net number is high enough, I'll keep the job. And if I keep the job this way it's a great fucking job. I never cared if I got canceled. That's the only thing that makes me do this stuff well, is I was willing to let the job go any day.

Judd: I always heard that from Larry David. That was his big inspiration. He was willing to walk away from *Seinfeld* when they would give him bad notes.

Louis: You have to be willing to say, "Let's not do this show. Let's not do it."

Judd: Do you notice a common theme when you look at the show, or is it too soon to tell? For a lot of people, when you see their body of work, you realize there are certain things that concern them. They make mirrors of their lives. Do you notice that for yourself?

Louis: I don't know. I don't know if there's a common theme. I guess I'm always trying to figure something out on the show.

Judd: Is it self-discovery?

Louis: I like to put myself into fucked-up situations and make mistakes and deal with it. I like to do that over and over again on the show, and maybe I like to do that in my life also. I read in some places that the women on my show were all crazy. They didn't say that for the first couple of seasons, but people started to go, "These women are all fucking nuts." For me, it's because that's an interesting problem, that's all. It's an interesting story.

Judd: I've gotten in trouble for having strong women or angry women or dealing with those types of problems that people would say, Oh, you're being a misogynist. Even Katherine Heigl said, "Oh, you're making the women out to be shrews."

Louis: *Knocked Up* is the best thing she ever did. The best thing she ever did. The fact that she was unhappy is amazing, but for a man, a woman is a problem. She's a mystery and she's a choice. The women in our lives are a list of choices that we've made and decisions that we've made. And it's the same for them.

Judd: Are you a therapy person?

Louis: I used to go to therapy, but I can't do it now because it's been too long. It's like not going to the gym for a long time. I don't want to start all over again.

MARC MARON

(2010)

I've done a fair amount of interviews in my life, but the one that people mention to me the most is the one I did for Marc Maron's *WTF* podcast. In addition to being an incredible comic, Marc is an insightful interviewer and empathizer and therapist of sorts, and we connected in a deep way about so many aspects of our journey. At one point, as I was talking about my pain as a kid and how some of those issues have persisted into adulthood, his eyes welled up with tears—and it made me extremely uncomfortable. I thought he was going to start crying right in front of me, so I changed the subject slightly, because I wasn't sure I could bear to see him lose control. Looking back, I regret having done this. I probably should have kept going just to see what happened. I could have destroyed him. For those of you interested in hearing my story, this would be it.

Judd Apatow: All right, I'm holding the mic. Is it happening now?

Marc Maron: Yeah, sure.

Judd: This is it.

Marc: I am in Judd Apatow's war room. Is this the war room?

Judd: This is the situation room.

Marc: Ah, the situation room. So this is your office? A lot of boards, things being outlined. It's like—I can't read your fucking writing.

Judd: Well, part of the reason why I have bad handwriting is when I used to do stand-up comedy, I would write jokes on planes and I was always

This interview originally appeared on the WTF with Marc Maron *podcast.*

embarrassed that the person next to me would see what I was writing about.

Marc: Is that true?

Judd: Yes. And so I found a way to have terrible handwriting that only I could read, so if I was writing some joke about impotency or something, it would be unreadable.

Marc: You did it by design?

Judd: I did. And I still do it now, so if my wife sees any weird notes or joke ideas or things that might be offensive, there's no way she can read it.

Marc: Because I'm sitting here thinking, like, *Man, I got the scoop.* There's a whole Apatow movie outline on that board but all I can make out is— I think down on the lower left, does it say "sperm issues"?

Judd: It says "sperm issues." Yes, it does. But that would be in all of my movies.

Marc: And then it just, the rest is undecipherable.

Judd: Exactly. And it shall be until America gets to see this.

Marc: So I just watched *Freaks and Geeks* for the first time.

Judd: Oh, wow.

Marc: It's nothing personal. I miss a lot of things. And the interesting thing to me is—the scene that resonates almost more than the rest to me is when Bill is watching Garry Shandling after school. It's one scene, but, for some reason, I was like, *That was beautiful.*

Judd: There's a scene in the show where Bill Haverchuck, played by Martin Starr, comes home after school and you can tell he's a latchkey kid and no one's around and his mom's a former stripper. And he looks really sad and he watches Garry Shandling on *The Dinah Shore Show* while making a grilled cheese sandwich and eating chocolate cake. And he goes from being really sad to laughing his ass off. After we made it Jake Kasdan said to me, "That's the most personal thing you've ever done in your career. And it's the best thing you've ever done, too."

Marc: That scene?

Judd: That scene. And that was probably the turning point for my whole career, realizing that the little moments that I thought were boring or just not interesting to other people are actually the things that people would be most interested in. I always thought I was a bore. That's why I quit stand-up comedy.

Marc: Was your mom not around?

Judd: I lived with my dad after my parents got divorced. And I just didn't do any after-school activities. I just went in my room and closed the door and I was in my fantasy world, watching, you know, Michael Keaton do stand-up on *The Mike Douglas Show*, and I couldn't have been happier. I look back on it as a great time.

Marc: I had that same experience. Because one of them—like I still remember one of the moments I decided to be a comic was watching Jay Leno. I don't know if it was on *Mike Douglas* but I remember the joke— they were cutting away to a commercial and he was on that ridiculous set and he said, "What happens now, does the chair fold up into the wall like we're on a game show? Am I going to disappear?" And it was just a moment. It was a beat. But I remember thinking it was the most hilarious thing I had ever heard in my life.

Judd: I remember going to see *The Merv Griffin Show* being taped. That's how into it I was.

Marc: In New York?

Judd: In Los Angeles, when I was in high school. Dr. Ruth was the other guest, and she's taking calls, giving sex advice, and Jay Leno realizes that this makes no sense because the show doesn't air for a month and where are the calls coming from? Like, is there someone backstage doing this? He calls her on it, like, "These are not real calls. Where are these people coming from?" And I thought, *That is the coolest guy in the world. I want to be that guy.* I couldn't get enough of it. I've looked back on it and wondered, *Why did I like it so much? What was it that I was attracted to?* I was obsessed to the point of highlighting the *TV Guide* so I knew when the comics were on.

Marc: Did you read "My Favorite Jokes" in *Parade* magazine? Maybe you're a little younger than me. But in *Parade* magazine, on the last page, there used to be a thing called "My Favorite Jokes" where they just had comedians' jokes written there.

Judd: I used to transcribe *Saturday Night Live*. I would record it on an audiocassette.

Marc: How old were you?

Judd: Ten. I have the transcriptions of Bill Murray's Oscar picks bit from "Weekend Update" in notebooks.

Marc: Why did you do that?

Judd: I don't know. I think that I was in some way trying to figure out how to get into that world—how does it work? I wanted to break it down somehow. It wasn't conscious.

Marc: Did you used to do that with stand-up as well?

Judd: I didn't. I did it with *Saturday Night Live* sketches and some *Twilight Zones*. And then Steve Martin hit in '76, '77, '78. Richard Pryor, Monty Python—I was losing my mind with comedy nerdness.

Marc: You were an original. Comedy nerds didn't exist yet. You were just a kid who was precocious in a sense. I was the same way in that I related to these comics. They made me feel better. They had a certain amount of control, it seemed. They could handle shit.

Judd: They had a stance on why the world didn't make sense, and they would call everyone on their shit. I couldn't get enough of those people.

Marc: I'll tell you something Harry Shearer said to me, and I want to get your opinion on it. He said the reason why people are comedians is to have control over why people laugh at you.

Judd: I look at it this way: When someone is laughing, I know they don't dislike me. I don't know if they *like* me, but I know that in that moment they don't *dis*like me. And that's why I get the need for constant approval, because if you're smiling I know you don't hate me. You know, *Why do I*

*need that much approval? Is there any point where I get enough approval
and I'm full?* And I've realized that there is no point.

Marc: Really?

Judd: I once received a call from Steven Spielberg. Steven Spielberg, who
I used to work for at DreamWorks, was trying to reach me to say that he
liked *Knocked Up*. And I so wanted a letter from him. Paul Feig got one
when we made *Freaks and Geeks* and I was so jealous that he got a letter
from Steven saying that he loved *Freaks and Geeks*. So I didn't return the
call and I told my assistant, "Can you say Judd's out of town and is it possible that he could write a note just so I can have the letter?" He sent me
the dream letter, the beautiful letter with nothing but kindness. You know,
a great guy. It's just what you want. And I have it. But what happened afterwards is I thought to myself, *This is the best you can do. Who else do I
want to compliment me? How many of these do I need to feel good about
myself?* And, *Why doesn't it last?* The wound is still there.

Marc: What is the wound? Because I know I have it.

Judd: You know, I'm not sure exactly. I've had therapists who say everything that happened to you happened in the first three years of your life—

Marc: Yeah, let it go.

Judd: It may have just been the way your mom looked at you. I mean, who
knows?

Marc: You believe that?

Judd: I don't know. I don't know if that's true. I do know that in every situation that I walk into I feel like the weirdo. I feel like that awkward guy picking up my kids from school. I feel that way on the sets of my own movies.

Marc: Uncomfortable in your own skin?

Judd: I never feel like I own the moment, you know.

Marc: You feel like you're a *victim* of the moment?

Judd: I just feel like a punch could come from any direction even if I'm
everyone's boss. And the thing is, no one ever punches me. What I'm

realizing is, *Okay, that's how I'm wired, and if I just acknowledge it, some of it will disappear.* That's a little bit of what *Funny People* was about—he gets sick and says, you know, What was the point of all this? I'm here in this house and I'm all alone and everyone outside likes me and I don't have any strong relationships. Why did I do this?

Marc: A lot of that movie was drawn from your early career with, you know, I mean in the sense that Garry Shandling was your mentor, right?

Judd: I had a bunch of mentors. People were very nice to me when I was young. Shandling hired me to write the Grammys for him in 1990.

Marc: How old were you?

Judd: I was twenty-three. And then he hired me on *The Larry Sanders Show* and, and has been helpful to me on everything I've ever done. I used to write jokes for Jim Carrey and I worked on some of his movies. So I had to fabricate a character that was an amalgam of a lot of people but slowly you realize, *Oh, it's just me. It's the worst part of me.* And then suddenly it all makes sense: Here's me at my worst. Here's me at my angriest.

Marc: Here's me as a pregnant woman.

Judd: Exactly. Here's me at my neediest. Here's me screaming at the crowd. I mean, your thoughts are coming out in different ways. And some of it is observations of other people. Some of the rants in *Funny People* were based on me watching Rodney Dangerfield yell at the crowd at one in the morning, you know. One night he was in his bathrobe or something. He gets onstage at the Improv and he just didn't do his act and it was fantastic. He said to the crowd, "Yeah, sometimes life makes perfect sense, and then you cum." There was a woman there and he says, "Oh yeah, yeah, you're beautiful. You're beautiful. You'd be different. You'd love me for me." It was brutal. It was brutal to watch. And it was fantastic to watch. I've just seen a bunch of people have that meltdown, where it's one in the morning and they drop the act and they tell you what they're going through. That's my favorite part of comedy, when you go to that next place.

Marc: You don't see it as much as you used to. I mean, in the clubs. I don't know how often you go out there anymore, but there was a time when that generation—there seemed to be a little more freedom and a little less eyes on everybody. There was a time in the eighties where the meltdown was fairly commonplace.

Judd: Those moments between midnight and one-thirty in the morning at the Improv—that's where a lot of the great things happened.

Marc: How many of that generation have sort of disappeared, or no one knows anymore? Are you ever saddened by that?

Judd: I did go into Best Buy once and a comic who was hilarious was a salesman there. That was rough. That made me sad because I thought, *I was never as funny as that guy. That guy used to kill.* But at some point you can't go on the road anymore. If you want to have a life and kids, you can't be on the road thirty-five weeks a year.

Marc: But is it that that same sort of wound that you're talking about can also swallow people? And the fact is that you were able to manage your talent and be political and ambitious enough to get what you wanted to get done, done.

Judd: I was very lucky that part of my dysfunction as a person is a terror of bankruptcy—financial bankruptcy, not emotional bankruptcy. So as a young person, I thought ten years ahead. I had a show in high school where I interviewed comedians like Leno and Seinfeld and John Candy.

Marc: How did you manage to get hold of them?

Judd: I used to call their publicists and say I was from a radio station in New York, and they were too lazy to look it up and figure out that it was a high school radio station. I was afraid that I was going to not be able to take care of myself in my life, so in my head I always thought, *Well, what do I need to do? Okay, I'll interview comedians and they'll tell me how to be a comedian. They'll tell me how to write.*

Marc: Were you freaking out inside, talking to Seinfeld? What were you really trying to do there?

Judd: It happened right after my parents got divorced and I just thought, *I got to get something going in this life. I really need to take care of myself.* Because when your parents get divorced they just make terrible mistakes and they fight and you see that adults have very real flaws. And I think my instinct was, *Oh my God, maybe they're wrong about all sorts of stuff they keep telling me. And if my mom thinks my dad's the devil and if my dad's enraged at my mom, then maybe some of this advice they've been giving me is wrong. I mean, I don't think he's the devil. He's very nice to me.* And it just completely threw me—like, it's important that you believe your parents. So when you see them at a terrible moment, screaming at each other—my reaction was, *Nothing is true. I don't believe anything. I can't rely on these people because they can't rely on each other and they've bailed on each other, and, like, "Our family isn't important enough for you guys to just figure out how to get along?"* It was terrible. Now that I'm older I realize it was much more complicated than that.

Marc: You were sort of in crisis mode.

Judd: I was *totally* in crisis mode. I was losing my mind. I thought, *I need a job,* but I also had a sense that my parents were not going to be able to afford college because they were having financial problems. And so I thought, *Why don't you jump right into your dream, just have the balls to do it.* Anyway, when my parents got divorced, my mom moved to Southampton and we—my parents used to own a restaurant, and the bartender there was Rick Messina.

Marc: Oh my God.

Judd: Rick Messina is the great manager who went on to represent Tim Allen. Back then he managed the East Side Comedy Club on Long Island, which was the first comedy club on the Island, and a bunch of other clubs. So when my parents got divorced, my mom got a job seating people at her former bartender's comedy club. I mean, this was the dream situation for me. This was ninth grade, and it's the summer, and my mom is seating people at a comedy club. Every weekend, I would go watch every show—Leno, Paul Provenza, first show I ever saw of a young comedian. And years later I thought, *That's really kind of the worst job ever. What could Mom have gotten paid to do it?* I'd like to think that she did it because she knew I would like it. And my dad was great. He would drive me to comedy clubs a few times a week and was a big supporter.

Marc: That's sweet. So okay, you saw Leno, you saw Provenza. This was 1980 . . . what?

Judd: This was '82 or '83, and then I got a job at Rick Messina's comedy club as a dishwasher so I could see the comedians. Then I realized that I can't see the comedians, I'm in the fucking kitchen. So I switched to a busboy at East Side Comedy Club. Eddie Murphy used to come in, and Rosie O'Donnell was just starting at that time. I would watch the comedians, and I thought, *I don't have the balls to tell these people that I want to do this.* It may have been obvious to them but I couldn't even tell anyone, I was so scared. In my senior year in high school, I finally got up at open-mic nights and was awful, so awful.

Marc: It's terrifying.

Judd: And John Mulrooney's hosting the open-mic night. And he just, I mean, it was pandemonium. He would kill and insult the crowd—

Marc: I remember him.

Judd: And he was fantastic. But to go on after that, when you have no idea what you're doing and you're seventeen years old? There'd be twenty comedians who'd all get five minutes. And you never knew if Mulrooney was going to do twenty minutes between acts and so you might get on at eight-oh-five, or one in the morning.

Marc: You are the real deal. You came from a real comedy background in a way that none of us did. Many of us who started on those open mics didn't watch comedy until we were stuck in those rooms and we *had* to. But you were actually just compelled to be there as a busboy. What were you, sixteen?

Judd: From the earliest time, I understood that people got onstage with mics. I never had any interest in doing anything that I'm doing right now. It was not part of the dream. If you listen to those early interviews I did, it's all about joke writing. It's not screenwriting. I'm not talking about how I love movies. I want to understand the mechanics of a dick joke. That's my vision quest. When I interviewed Seinfeld the first time my brother was with me and you can hear him laughing. He's laughing in the background, and to us, it was like being in the room with Paul McCartney. It was. I think, to some extent, we had a vision for what Jerry Seinfeld was more than Jerry Seinfeld had a vision of what Jerry Seinfeld was. It was like being in a small club seeing R.E.M. in Athens, Georgia, in the early eighties and knowing what they would become.

Marc: A really small club. Just you and your brother.

Judd: Exactly. And the great thing about it was most of those people were very, very nice and so it also made me feel like, *Oh, this is a world of strange people who might accept me one day.*

Marc: In retrospect, have you brought it up to Leno and Seinfeld and Shandling that you interviewed them when you were sixteen?

Judd: I've mentioned it and none of them remember it—and they don't seem very interested in it, either.

Marc: But these guys gave you a blueprint for your life.

Judd: Yes, they did. And they don't completely get the significance of it. Because they might be having that effect on a lot of people.

Marc: I find that hard to believe, because if somebody writes me an email or even says that I've changed them in any way, not only does it make me feel good but I have to fight the urge to go, like, *How? What did I do?*

Judd: Maybe they do get it. Maybe it's just something that—it's hard to express or connect about because it is such a powerful thing. It's weird to look someone in the eye and say, "You've changed my life." You know, I treasure when Seinfeld sends me a note and says he likes *Funny People* or something. It means more to me than he could ever know because I literally thought about him as I made it. And I thought, *One day Seinfeld's going to see this. I better not fuck it up.*

Marc: All right, so at some point you come out here. I met you briefly. The first time I met you was at a party at Stacey Nelson's house. She was a publicist. I was dating her. I was being held hostage at her house. I think it was 1989. I met you at a party and you insisted that I was never going to leave L.A., and I left.

Judd: Really? Why would I say that?

Marc: It was one of those weird moments where everyone's hanging around and you go, "So what are you doing here?" And I'm like, "I'm staying at her house, you know, I've got to go back to New York." You said, "Oh you'll be back. You'll be back." It was almost ominous. But I left. There was that whole crew there at that time. You know, it was Ben Stiller and—I imagine that's around the time that you guys were working on *The Ben Stiller Show*. Was that '88?

Judd: The show was '91. We probably started working on it in '91 and it aired in '92.

Marc: And that was your first real TV job?

Judd: I wrote stand-up for a few comedians and when they did specials I would be a co-producer or something. I wrote with Roseanne, I wrote for Tom Arnold. Then I met Ben at an Elvis Costello concert and we both knew that HBO was looking for a show—a sketch show—and we thought of something in two weeks and sold it. People thought we had been friends forever, but we had known each other for fourteen days.

Marc: In *Funny People*, there was footage of you and Adam and Janeane Garofalo.

Judd: Yes, and Ben.

Marc: And you were all in—what year was that, '89 or '88?

Judd: That was '89 or '90. And in the footage in the beginning of the movie, you see Adam making a phony phone call, which I actually shot in our apartment back then, and Ben Stiller and Janeane Garofalo are there laughing, so you see them very briefly in the opening credits. At the time, Adam was so funny but had no outlet so he would make funny phone calls for hours and hours. I thought it was so hilarious, it didn't make sense *not* to record it. I felt bad that they would disappear and never be heard again, so first I would audio-record them and then video-record them.

Marc: Do you have all that stuff, too?

Judd: I have all of it. When we were doing *Funny People*, I found hours of Adam Sandler making phone calls. He was always calling Jerry's Deli and complaining about the roast beef and saying that it made him sick. And they would always be so nice and then he would be, you know, an old lady and he would negotiate getting a free sandwich. It was always like, "Could I get a free sandwich for my trouble?" And they would say okay. And he would say, "Well, I had turkey but I don't want to get hurt again, this time could I get the roast beef?" He would keep them on the line for twenty minutes, negotiating a sandwich. As a comedy nerd, I knew: *That's the guy. Adam's going to hit. There's no way this doesn't happen.* He just delighted us. He made us laugh so hard.

Marc: You keep using that term, *comedy nerd*, but back then it didn't exist. You were just a guy who loved comedy.

Judd: I remember moving to L.A., and I started doing stand-up at this place called the L.A. Cabaret in the Valley, in Encino. And I started meeting comedians for the first time, personally, not just interviewing them. And I realized, *They're all like me. They all like the same stuff. I finally can talk to people about Monty Python and the Marx Brothers.*

Marc: This is a recurring theme with you. These socially awkward, alienated guys that have to group with each other and sort of have this different type of strength to get through things.

Judd: Cocky nerds. My wife and I always talk about it. It's people who think they don't think ill of themselves—they actually think that there's something special about themselves but no one's noticed it. And so the characters on *Freaks and Geeks*—the geeks look down on the people who beat on them, but they still are terrified of them. And that's what makes them interesting. They have an air of superiority as they're getting pummeled.

Marc: You and Ben Stiller really created this community of comedy nerds in some ways. Do you feel that?

Judd: I think that Ben in a lot of ways is the beginning of much of what's happened in modern comedy. He did *The Ben Stiller Show* on MTV with Jeff Kahn, which was a *Larry Sanders*–esque show, where it was behind the scenes of a sketch show where Ben played kind of a jerk. And I met Ben after he did that. So when we created *The Ben Stiller Show* [for Fox] together, I didn't know what the hell I was doing. Ben knew how to make short films. I was just the guy trying to figure out how to not have Ben realize I didn't know how to do anything but write stand-up jokes. So I'm just keeping my mouth shut and listening to Ben because he was already brilliant and had a vision for what this was, and slowly I figured out how to run a writing staff and edit, but I was faking it. I was faking it for a long time.

Marc: Isn't that what everyone does for the first couple of jobs?

Judd: Yeah, but I was in charge of the writing and editing of the show. And so it was not like faking it as a staff writer. I was twenty-four or twenty-five years old with no background at all. And I hired people with Ben who were brilliant, like Dino Stamatopoulos and Bob Odenkirk and Brent Forrester and David Cross, and so in a lot of ways it was trying to manage these personalities who were bursting with energy. I mean, Bob was the funniest man in the world. The energy he had during *The Ben Stiller Show*—when he didn't like someone else's sketch, he would be like, "Oh my God, you can't do that. Who *wrote* that? Your unfunny uncle?" I was so intimidated because I wasn't anywhere near as strong as Bob but I also had to pick what sketches of Bob's we would shoot on the show. And then David Cross came on for the last few and you felt like, *Oh, this guy is in a whole other world with Bob.*

Marc: Then you went on to do *Larry Sanders*, which is another defining show for comedy nerd-dom. I mean, that's an amazing show.

Judd: That's where I learned how to write stories. Garry was nice enough to hire me on that show after *The Ben Stiller Show*, but I had never written a story before.

Marc: You wrote sketches and jokes.

Judd: I knew how to write "Legends of Bruce Springsteen" but I didn't know how to write about *people*. I was there, on and off, for five years and Garry ultimately allowed me to direct an episode and that's how I started directing. But it was an amazing place to be. And also scary because it's

Rip Torn and Jeffrey Tambor and they're brilliant and terrifying. Imagine having to walk up to Rip Torn and give him a note to change his performance. I mean . . .

Marc: How did that go?

Judd: It didn't go well. It didn't go well at all. I mean he, he was a blustery guy. But correct most of the time, and a wonderful person who would always wind up doing what you were trying to get him to do, but if you walked up to him and said, "Rip, I think you need to play it a little nervous here," he'd say, "I'm not *nervous*! I'm in *charge* of the place!" "Okay, Rip, I'm sorry. We'll just do it the way you want to do it." Then, three takes later, he might give you one. And then he'd walk up to you: "Come on, did you like the one I did the way you wanted me to do it? That was all right." I felt like I was watching some of the greatest actors of all time. Certainly some of the greatest comedic actors of all time. When they did the last scene of *The Larry Sanders Show*, where Jeffrey Tambor goes off on Rip and Larry and says, "There's a book being written about Hank Kingsley and you are not in it, and you are not in it, and fuck you . . ." I forgot the exact words, but they did it in one take and wrapped the series. That's ballsy. They were at the top of their game. It was fun to learn from them.

Marc: Do you think Garry is an underappreciated comic?

Judd: He's the best. I mean, what he did with *The Larry Sanders Show* is an achievement that's impossible to even explain. Imagine having to write a show. He's the head writer. And then you have to rehearse it for three days and then shoot the entire show in two days. So seventeen pages a day while punching up next week's script and editing two shows.

Marc: But also the idea that it's not just the work ethic. All guys who do well work hard. But to create a cast of characters who work within show business that are pathologically selfish and narcissistic and not great people is, uh, difficult. It's challenging to find heart there. And Garry clearly did—on that show, he did. You find heart through the weaknesses of all these extreme narcissists and lunatics. And I think that in some ways, in *Funny People*, that was your quest as well. It's hard to sell show business as being a reasonable place for human beings to work.

Judd: That's true, and Garry used to always say, *"The Larry Sanders Show* is about people who love each other but show business gets in the way."* I've always thought that's true of any story. With *Funny People,* I thought what gets in the way for George Simmons is that he's so funny and people love him so much on a grand scale that it allows him to never grow up. Only when life is about to end does he realize, *I'm alone here. I paid a massive price to be this guy.* We all know people like that.

Marc: When you look at the comedy movies that come out now, I admire the direction you're going because I like—I like to *feel* things. Because I don't do it in real life. I watched *Butch Cassidy and the Sundance Kid* the other day because it was on a British Airlines flight. I was coming back from London and they had it in the collection part. And it was great! I laughed and I cried and it's *Butch Cassidy and the Sundance Kid.* You know, it's not supposed to make that happen. But it was this weird moment where I realized that I don't experience much joy in life and that there are things like movies—and like what you're talking about comedy when you were a kid—that's part of experiencing joy in life. I admire your angle on it, but I have a harder time. It seems like there's a trend in comedy movies now that you might start with a pretty good story that seems kind of human, but out of some weird fear or overcompensation it just goes into fucking ridiculous-land.

Judd: Yes.

Marc: You've produced movies like that, no?

Judd: I've produced some movies that are better than others.

Marc: I'm not putting a judgment on them.

Judd: There are movies that are a little more premisey and there's movies where you're sticking very close to the truth, and sometimes when you reach for a joke—I always call it *sweaty.* It's brutal when things aren't organic and also sometimes you see movies that you could tell that nobody is passionate about. It's just a project. It's a way for people to get paid. You know what those movies are. When you see a movie that Sean Penn directed, you realize he's not fucking around. It's like listening to a Nirvana record or something. This is not a job. They have something to say. And in comedy, the people that we like the most, when they score they have something to say that's important to them. And to me, that's what I'm always looking for.

Marc: In your mind, what is the perfect comedy that you judge all others against?

Judd: There are a few movies I always go back to. I always go back to *Fast Times at Ridgemont High*. It pulls off a couple of things at the same time. One is that it has this really hilarious, broad humor with Sean Penn, as Spicoli. But Jennifer Jason Leigh gets pregnant and has an abortion in it and it's played straight and he's able to be incredibly truthful. That has always been one of the main models.

Marc: Because of the emotional variation?

Judd: When you can do that well, it's a big deal. *Terms of Endearment* I always go back to as a movie about something very serious that's hysterically funny. All the classics like *Annie Hall* and *Dr. Strangelove*.

Marc: How about *The In-Laws*?

Judd: Oh yeah, *The In-Laws*—all the old Albert Brooks movies. Anytime you talk lists, you feel terrible because there's ten more behind every one you could mention.

Marc: But it's interesting to me that for the most part, outside of appreciating it as a classic, Woody Allen is not an inspiration for you particularly?

Judd: Well, I never mention Woody Allen because some of his stuff is so great you feel like a fool even mentioning that you're even in the same business as him. It just feels awkward to say I do what he does. But also, I think probably when all that stuff happened to him, and his family and the stuff with his kids, there was a part of me that disconnected. Maybe after I read the Mia Farrow book I just was like, I got a little creeped out. And my incredible worship and affection got dented. I don't know where I stand on any of it. He's stranger than I thought he was. And darker than I thought he was. So I don't connect to it in the exact same way as when I was a kid watching *Take the Money and Run*. I know too much now.

Marc: When I read *Please Kill Me*, about the punk rock scene in New York, about Lou Reed, as shitty as those—I knew they were all drug addicts and everything else, but you know, Lou Reed was such an asshole, it just fucked it up for me. I don't read much about comics because I know how filthy we all are.

Judd: You don't want to know too much about anybody. I mean, if you read a Groucho biography, you'll be like, *Oh God, sometimes Groucho was a prick.*

Marc: Yeah. Now, do you do Marx Brothers?

Judd: I'm obsessed with the Marx Brothers. They were on TV all the time, and I have to say they were the first comedy act that I connected to. I think it was because it was so rebellious. Groucho was basically saying, "This is all bullshit," and for some reason I couldn't have taken to it more.

Marc: Did you feel that because you're not that aggressively, you know, "Fuck you"? Do you feel—

Judd: I never felt that way enough to be super-funny, quite frankly. There were comedians when I first started out who were working, like Kinison and Bill Hicks, and those were the guys that were the best guys when I first started. They were hilarious because there was such rage and self-righteousness and they thought they had the answers for everything. I never felt that way about myself. I never thought I had any answers for anything and I wasn't as mad as them. I was just trying to meet a girl and to get to second base. As I've gotten older I really do believe that life is about finding ways to connect to other people, and I'm more attracted to a James Brooks sensibility, where all of these stories are about how people finally come together.

Marc: I think that's where the joy is. That's where humanity is. I think there's sort of the "Fuck you, I'm better than you" or "I know more than you" or "Life is fucked." I come from that mold and now that's all melting away.

Judd: That's why I made *Funny People*. I mean, it's exactly that. He has a moment where it melts away, and then suddenly he's better, and *What do*

I do? I swing back and forth all the time. I think, *Well I've done a lot of what I wanted to do, so why am I even doing it now? What's left to say that I haven't said?* You don't want to be working just to work. And so I don't know. I just want to go deeper and more personal every time to the point where you start writing and you think, *Can I even say this? Who will I hurt if I express these ideas? Am I giving up too much of my experience?* But there's no way to dig it out without going to the places you would normally hide from everybody. So it's just about going deeper.

Marc: To push it a little further.

Judd: I've listened to your show a lot and you talk a lot about your family and what makes you feel separate from other people, and that's what interests me now: Why do I feel separate? Why am I still in my room watching TV? In my mind, I'm still in that room and I'm not as connected to other people as I want to be, so I'm trying to do that. But even when I'm doing it, if I'm at a party or I'm at school, there's a part of me that wishes I could run out and sit in my room and watch *The Merv Griffin Show* alone.

Marc: Why are we so afraid of joy?

Judd: That's the question. And I've thought about it a lot, and I think it's because we think right behind joy is a knife that will cut our throat if we really feel it. It's almost like a laugh—your chin goes up and your throat is exposed. *If I laugh too loud, someone will slit my throat.* That's the terror of joy.

MARTIN SHORT
(1984)

I spent a fair number of my teenage years sitting alone in front of the TV late at night, watching *SCTV*, which came on after *Saturday Night Live*. *SCTV* was a sketch show from Canada. It was not done in front of a live audience; everything was shot on tape. (*The Ben Stiller Show* was heavily influenced by *SCTV*. Ben and I used to say, "We're like *SCTV* if they'd had money to work with.") The cast was epic—John Candy, Harold Ramis, Rick Moranis, Catherine O'Hara—but the person who made me laugh the most was Martin Short, with his impressions of Jerry Lewis and Katharine Hepburn and the epic characters he invented, such as Jackie Rogers Jr. and Ed Grimley.

I showed up at his hotel in New York, where he was promoting a new season of *SCTV*, to conduct our interview. Of all the people I interviewed in high school, he was probably the nicest. God, did he indulge me. I've gotten to know him a little bit since then, and it all makes sense now: This kindness and warmth is just the way he lives his life.

On the night that Steve Martin won his lifetime achievement Oscar in 2013, I was lucky enough to wrangle an invitation to go back to Steve's house for a celebration. There weren't many people there. For a while, it was just Steve Martin, his wife, Anne, Martin Short, Tom Hanks, Bill Hader, and me, and as a group, they were as funny as anyone I have ever been around in my life. Just a shocking level of intelligence and humor. That night, I went home and thought: *Martin Short was the funniest person in that room; ergo, Martin Short is the funniest person in every room.*

Judd Apatow: When did your comedy career begin?

Martin Short: In 1972, I did a show called *Godspell* in Toronto, and it was my first professional show. It was an interesting cast, because there were a lot of talented people in it who were doing their first professional show, too. Gilda Radner, Andrea Martin, Eugene Levy, Victor Garber. Paul Shaffer was the piano player. Everyone became good friends and it was great. We were just out of school, glad to not be in school. We did it for a year.

Judd: And what did that lead to?

Martin: It led to just kind of continually working in Toronto. Canada is a great place to work, because you're not pigeonholed. There's no star system. You're not put in a kind of "He does that and that's all we'll ever ask him to do" role. So, you can do commercials and Shakespeare for radio and musicals—you can do anything, if you get the job. I did all that for about six years, until '78 or so, when I joined Second City. Then I did that for a couple of years and then did it in the States and did a series called *The Associates* and then—

Judd: *The Associates* was highly acclaimed, but that also got canceled.

Martin: The story of my life.

Judd: How does Second City work?

Martin: It works in a—it's very organized. The set show is from nine until ten-thirty and then there's a break and there are improvisations. They are free, so if you're arriving at eleven you can watch them, and they are based on suggestions from the audience—they fall under different categories of places or current events. Then you go backstage and you put up this piece of paper with all the suggestions and you have about ten minutes to come up with a scene. You might give the lighting guy a cue, like, "Okay when I reach this line, cut it" or "We're going to go in this direction." Sometimes the lighting guy is very important—he might look at a scene and take it out earlier, let it go. The scenes are taped, so four minutes later when it's time to write another show, the main bulk of the show, the part that people pay for, you sit around saying, "Wait a second. There was a scene I did one night, an improvisation—what was that scene about a cabdriver?" And then they pull out the tape—when I was there, they were audiotapes, but now they're audiovisual tapes—and you look at it and you remember what you said. Then you start rewriting and building it.

Judd: You have ten minutes to do fifteen different pieces. How do you handle that? Does it always work or—

Martin: No, often you bomb. You bomb bad. But it doesn't matter because the audience knows you're improvising, and so they're kind of with you. I mean, it's fun.

Judd: How does it work [on *SCTV*]? Is it all cast writers? Do you have additional writers other than the cast?

Martin: Yes, we do. The cast writes but there are five additional writers. You come up with an idea, you write it out, and you take it into weekly or biweekly meetings where everyone sits around in a circle over a big desk and reads the material. The material is voted on, whether they wanted it in the show, and sometimes, very few times, a sketch is totally thrown out. Usually what happens is suggestions are offered from everyone in the room about how it could be better, and that sketch is taken away and improved, and read again, and passed, and put up on a bulletin board, and through that a show is assembled.

Judd: Do you have an audience?

Martin: No.

Judd: Does that help the show, you think?

Martin: For the kind of show *SCTV* is, yes. You know, *Saturday Night Live* has the advantage of that energy that it gets from being live, but it has the disadvantage, too, of only being able to do a take once.

Judd: Do you have a laugh track?

Martin: Yes.

Judd: And do you think that hurts the feel of the show? Because sometimes those are not so good.

Martin: It's like anything: If it's done well, it doesn't. If it's done badly, it does.

Judd: Anybody that we would know who you worked with on Second City?

Martin: You mean, onstage?

Judd: Yeah.

Martin: Well, Catherine O'Hara and Andrea Martin, John Candy, Eugene Levy, Dave Thomas . . .

Judd: They were all doing that at the same time they were doing *SCTV*?

Martin: Some had left and some would come back for a month. That's what was great about Second City. You could go back if you wanted.

Judd: How do you become part of Second City? Isn't there an audition where they make you do characters?

Martin: There is a system. There's an audition where you have to do five characters coming in a door and then you leave and you come through the door again as another character. If you're good at that, you usually get into the touring company, and you do resorts up north, like any touring company. From there, you go to the main company.

Judd: Did you ever do stand-up comedy, like in a club?

Martin: Yeah, I played with that a little bit in California, but it's just not as much fun. When I was doing *The Associates*, I would go down—Robin Williams was a friend of mine, and he was doing *Mork & Mindy* in the next studio and he would go down every Monday and join the Comedy Store players at the Comedy Store, and so I started doing that. It wasn't the greatest improvisational atmosphere, because the Comedy Store is primarily for stand-up comics, so I would watch, and tried it a couple of times, but it was just not as much fun.

Judd: You like the challenge of bombing?

Martin: No, I don't like bombing.

Judd: Or the challenge of knowing it could go down the tubes?

Martin: I'm not crazy about risking it, except it does feel great when it succeeds.

Judd: Were you funny as a kid? Class clown?

Martin: If you call this funny, I guess. I fooled around a lot, yeah. Some teachers thought I was a saint, others a nightmare.

Judd: The ones that thought you a nightmare: Why would that be?

Martin: I would just constantly fool around.

Judd: Did you go to college?

Martin: Yes. I graduated as a social worker. I was—I originally went into premed and then I realized I hated science. I did two years of premed. So, I switched to social work, and that's where I met Eugene Levy and Dave Thomas—I went to school with them.

Judd: What do you think about Rick Moranis and Dave Thomas making— I guess they just finished their movie *Strange Brew.* What do you think about, like, all of a sudden, two characters from *SCTV* becoming national characters?

Martin: Oh, it's great. It's great.

Judd: Is that strange, when a little skit turns into a big hit?

Martin: Yeah. Dave is a good friend of mine and he is constantly amazed, too.

Judd: Okay, so when you're doing impressions in the show, do they write sketches for you and then say, "You're going to have to do an impression of so-and-so," and then you have to develop it?

Martin: Well, a lot of the impersonations, you write yourself. I'm trying to think. There's a few instances where someone will say, Will you play this person? And you'll try to figure it out.

Judd: How do you develop the impression itself? Do you just wing it?

Martin: I look at tapes. Makeup can take three or four hours, so I sit with a Walkman on and listen to the voice, and sometimes I'll get certain phrases that the actual person—when I was doing Huntz Hall, there were phrases he would use and I would lift those phrases out and put—even if it was just a word or two words together, a certain sound, you know—I'd put them into the script. You can mimic that.

Judd: You also did a Robin Williams impression. You did all the different little characters that he does, and it was amazing. How did you develop that?

Martin: Well, I know Robin, so there's all different things—there's his "ha ha," a laugh which he rarely does on television, and I—that was from seeing him on *The Tonight Show* and he just never sat still, so I came up with the premise for Tang, the guy trying to get the answer out of him, and Robin wouldn't do it. You just get into the voice, you know? I did Paul Anka one week and I could not get him at all. I was sitting in that makeup chair and I was trying—I kept staring at the makeup job they were doing and listening to Anka with my Walkman in my ears, and the longer they did my makeup, the more I become like him or sound like him. Sometimes it just evolves.

Judd: Do you have any idea what you want to do after *SCTV*?

Martin: My dream is to do a Broadway show. I've always wanted to do a Broadway musical. I like doing television. I get terribly unhappy if I'm not doing something comfortable, and if I don't think it's particularly good.

Judd: Are there any skits from *SCTV* that you're particularly proud of?

Martin: Um, I guess the one—there are two sketches that—there are three sketches—no, there's four, eight, twelve sketches that I feel strongly . . . No, I guess like a sketch called "Oh That Rusty," which was about a child star who had been playing an eight-year-old for thirty-one years, and now he's real old and fat; but he would wear a wig, and they would have to build the set real big to make him look young and to make the show relevant in the seventies, they fired his mother and hired a seven-foot-two black guy to play his father so he would look short in size.

Judd: I liked "The Boy Who Couldn't Wait for Christmas."

Martin: That's a strange one. That's just a short little piece about a guy who can't get to sleep before Christmas, and that's the kind of piece that you write and you kind of—it's real personal, so you write it alone in your office and you hand it in and go home because you're assuming that people are going to say, "How does this happen?" "Well, look, he's tired." You know? Then you get a phone call that says, "We like it." Oh, good. Okay.

Judd: How much rehearsal time goes into something like that?

Martin: Not a great deal. But there's a Sunday rehearsal, where we'll sit and discuss with the director how we like things done, and he'll say to us, "No, it'd be better this way," and you work out the scene. Then you rehearse a couple times on the floor, two, three, four times. I like to do lots of takes.

Judd: What do you find funny?

Martin: There are not many things that I *don't* find funny. I think the Three Stooges are great, but if they're not on top of it, they're not funny. Woody Allen is fabulous, but if he's not on top of it, he's not so fabulous. There's no one kind of comedy that is synonymous with my comedy. I like physical comedy. And comedy that comes out of nowhere — unexpected twists are the most interesting to me. It gets boring if it becomes predictable.

PART THREE

M–S

MEL BROOKS

(2013)

When I was growing up on Long Island in the 1970s, one thing was
understood: Nobody was funnier than Mel Brooks. Yes, we all enjoyed
our Woody Allen movies and our Blake Edwards movies, but there was
never any real debate: Mel Brooks was the king.

He is the original gangster of comedy. His work dates back to Sid Caesar and Carl Reiner, for chrissakes. He is the 2,000 Year Old Man. He's
responsible for, at minimum, two of the top ten comedies of all time,
Blazing Saddles and *Young Frankenstein.* (There is a legitimate argument
to be made that he is responsible for more than half of the top ten.) One
could say *Blazing Saddles* is still the edgiest comedy ever made; scream-
ingly funny and original, yes, but all in the service of important thoughts
about race. I'm not sure it could be made again today.

I hesitate to use the word *important* when talking about comedy, or
movies in general, but Mel Brooks is important. His movies are important. And even now, in his late eighties, he's as funny as funny gets—and
a hell of a lot quicker than the rest of us.

Mel Brooks: So, what was it before Apatow?

Judd Apatow: What was it before? It was Apa-toe.

Mel: Okay, not such a big move. I mean, people from Europe, they made
really big moves.

Judd: Oh, you mean before they shortened it? I think it could have been
Apatovski.

This interview was originally part of Sirius Radio's Town Hall series and took place with a live audience.

Mel: Yes, it could have been that. You have no idea?

Judd: I think it was Apatapatovski. There's this strange man that keeps sending me information about my history and I'm not even asking him to do it. He recently sent me a photo of my great-great-grandfather's cemetery plot.

Mel: Where, in the Bronx somewhere?

Judd: Brooklyn. He said, "I just happened to go to the gravestone of your family member." Should I be nervous?

Mel: No, there's a lot of people like that. They don't mean any harm. There's a guy that sends me stuff on my Uncle Louis. His people came from Poland. My people came from Kiev. I don't know what they're talking about but anyway, I had an Uncle Louis. My real name is Kaminsky. K-A-M-I-N-S-K-Y. Danny Kaye's name, too. A lot of talented guys named Kaminsky. I think Hank Greenberg's name was Kaminsky. Anyway, so he was telling me about my Uncle Louis, who was a zealot. He was a rabbi and a zealot in Poland. And it's where we just keep moving. We move, you know, they arrest us, and then we move. And so Uncle, Great-Great-Great-Great-Uncle Louis, my grandfather's uncle, was always getting arrested. I asked the guy, "Well, why?" He said, "Well, on Saturday he would pick up a brick and break windows and they'd say, 'Louis, you know we're Protestant, we're Catholic, we're open for business. We're not Jews.' He said, 'Nobody should be open on Saturday.'" So I come from that stock. You can see a lot of that in me. I'm a bit of a zealot. I'm a zealot when it comes to bagels. I have never eaten—I think I've eaten two or three bagels in California and I just break into tears. It's the water.

Judd: You're not on that non-gluten kick.

Mel: No.

Judd: You're full gluten. Well, I should do this introduction of you because it's a long one.

Mel: Really? Why don't you do the highlights of Mel Brooks? Go ahead.

Judd: Well, according to this—

Mel: Like the highlights of *Hamlet*.

Judd: Okay, ready? (*Reading*) "In every medium through which entertainment could possibly pass, Mel has made people laugh all over the world." It says here, you are one of only eleven people in history to win an Emmy, Grammy, Oscar, and Tony award.

Mel: Right, I also got other awards. I have a fifty-yard dash from PS 19. I have many awards that I just don't brag about. But they're important to me.

Judd: Are they, though? Do you care? Like, do you care that you won the Oscar?

Mel: You know, when I was younger, I really did. It was thrilling. But then as you get older, you're more interested in your cholesterol.

Judd: When a bad movie wins an Oscar, do you get mad because you're like, *That kind of ruins my Oscar*?

Mel: No, no, no. I forgive and forget. It's not good to have a grudge against anything.

Judd: Actually, I disagree. There are a lot of reasons to have grudges. I'm mad at everyone in this room right now. This is quite a crowd we have here.

Mel: We have a good crowd.

Judd: These are fans. These are hard-core fans.

Mel: And they've washed.

Judd: Yes.

Mel: They're all clean. I'm smelling, they all smell good.

Judd: Well, our first question here—people are going to stand up and read questions.

Mel: Sure.

Judd: Steve Bugdonoff. Glendora, California. Did I say it right? How did I do with my pronunciation?

Steve: Horrible.

Judd: Oh no. Let's hear it. Let's hear what it is.

Steve: It is Bogdonoff.

Judd: Bogdonoff, see, that is not the way anyone says that name.

Mel: You are the only one who would say Bogdonoff. We have Bogdonovich. We have ways of saying Bogdonoff. But most of us would say Bugdonoff. Even though it's your own name, I think you're in the minority. I mean it.

Steve: First of all, Mr. Brooks, thank you for this opportunity. As a longtime fan, my question is: Classic comedy like *Blazing Saddles* probably couldn't be made today and—

Mel: I agree. Probably couldn't. The N-word couldn't be used as frequently and spiritlessly.

Steve: Yet the film so perfectly lampoons bigotry, so my question is: How do you feel about today's standard of political correctness?

Mel: I think that word in and of itself is pale and kind of weak. And jejune. I'm very bright. Jejune. Jejune—you'll have to look it up—but it's just timid and I don't think anybody really covers racial hatred the way it should be covered. I agree with you. I agree with you even though you say your name wrong.

Judd: How did people react to it at the time?

Mel: At the time, there were letters. There were many letters from many people that said, How could you *say* that word? You're hurting so many people with the using the N-word, you know. And I had hired a very dear friend of mine who was working at the Vanguard in New York at the time when I was writing the movie. Richard Pryor, probably the best stand-up comic that ever lived. Man, he was the best. I said Richard, "I want you to write this movie with me." He fell in love with Mongo. He wrote a lot of Mongo. So anyway, I would say when the little old lady with the bonnet is walking down the street in Rockridge and Cleavon Little greets her and says, "Good morning, ma'am, and isn't it a lovely morning?" And she says,

"Up yours, nigger." Boom, you know, it's like, wow. Everything gets silent. But then we kind of save it a little bit. He goes into the jailhouse and he's in kind of tears and talks to Gene Wilder, who was the Waco Kid, and Gene says, "Well, what did you *expect*? 'Come home, marry my daughter'? This is 1874, this is, these are people of the land. These are pioneers. You know, morons." And that kind of took the edge off. But, you know, that was a tough one. John Calley—God bless him, he died last year—ran production for Warner Brothers at the time. So I said to John, "Can we beat the shit out of a little old lady? Can we actually punch a horse? Can we use the N-word? Can we?" And Calley said, "Mel, if you're going to go up to the bell, ring it." And I never, that was early in my career and I never forgot what he said. I've gone, you know, uh, with the caveman masturbating in the *History of the World*—I was ringing the bell. I never forgot that advice.

Judd: The next question is from Richard Walden.

Richard: It's an honor.

Mel: It's a pleasure.

Richard: Who was the funniest celebrity you know? And I don't mean someone who is funny on camera, but someone we might not think is funny, but in real life—

Mel: Carl Reiner is a seriously, seriously funny guy. He lost his wife, Estelle—she was a great singer, great person, great friend of Anne and I, just a wonderful person. Carl is still alive, he's ninety-one. He's a great comedian to this day. Estelle used to just rifle through magazines to buy things. She bought things through the mail all the time. She'd pick a dress, she'd pick a thing. She'd pick an iron. If there were Ginsu knives, Estelle had them. So anyway, the doorbell rang after she had passed away and a guy came and said, "Package for Estelle Reiner," and Carl wondered what it was and he took it and he said, "It's not a package for Estelle Reiner; it *is* Estelle Reiner." It had come from the Neptune Society and they, you know—but I mean, *the guts*. That's a brave comment.

Judd: You and Carl are as funny as ever, but do you find that other funny people you hang out with have stayed funny—or did some people lose their sense of humor? I mean, why is it that you guys are always current and hilarious and it didn't fade at all, in any way?

Mel: Yeah, there's a couple. I don't know, even someone like Shecky Greene, one of the funniest guys that ever lived, went through a dark time. He had stage fright and suddenly he wasn't funny for three or four years. I think he's back doing everything well. Unless he's dead, I don't know. But people go through different periods and they're assaulted by different memories or psychic problems or just physical maladies and they just don't feel *funny*. And you know, but I have never—God bless me, I'm knocking wood. I feel good. I have salmon and tomato every day. I like cucumber soup. It's cold but I like it. But I feel well and I have never given up my joie de vivre. I just love being alive and being in comedy, you know. But it happens. It happens to people.

Judd: Was it a big deal for you to make yourself a star of your movies?

Mel: It was. You know, I would have been a star ten years before I became a star. There was a great, great star, a great actor-comedian, Sid Caesar. And had I not run into Sid Caesar I probably would have gone from the Borscht Belt—"You're looking at me, ladies and gentlemen, I met a girl who was so thin, this girl was so skinny you can't believe it. I took her to a restaurant, the maître d' said check your umbrella. That's how skinny this girl was"—and, you know, those were the kind of jokes that I used to do. God bless. Anyway, I ran into Sid Caesar and I realized, you know, this guy's truly a genius, because he'd be in a sketch with Imogene Coca and she would go on and on about a car that was wrecked because it backed into the drugstore and then it smashed into the candy store, and he—Sid thought it was somebody else and he was laughing. The greatest laugh you'd ever heard. He was just on the floor spitting with laughter, and then, little by little, he realized that Imogene—it was his car. It was the family car. And then he just got quiet and more quiet. And then without asking him, without rehearsing, without directing him, she kept on with the story and tears ran down his eyes. You know nobody came with glycerin. He just cried. And the audience went bananas. The greatest sketch ever. I was one of the writers.

Judd: But did that delay your feeling like you should be the star because you were watching the greatest?

Mel: No, I was seeing stardust and I was seeing magic. And I was seeing real comedy and that was enough.

Judd: All right, the next question is from Don Moore.

Don: Yes sir. I was just wondering, Mel, you've had such a long career in show business and a successful career, does it bother you on any level that your legacy will be that of funny guy, comedy writer?

Mel: Strangely enough, I've always been just a little irritated, perturbed, upset that I have never been recognized in this business by my peers—by my fellow directors—as a director of movies. I have never been saluted or, really, thought of. I've been thought of as, you know, a funny writer, a producer of funny stuff and a performer, a funny performer, but I've never been considered . . . Kubrick thought I was a good director. Hitchcock thought that I should have won the Academy Award for *Young Franken-stein*. Just for the backlighting, he said.

Judd: When comedies work, they feel effortless, so I think people get no sense that it took so much more work than making CGI dragons fly. They don't really give people credit for that.

Mel: You're right. They see what's green screen and think, *How did they do that? Look, the wings look so* real.

Judd: I think that's always been the case with the Oscars.

Mel: Well, Woody won for, you know—

Judd: *Annie Hall.*

Mel: Yeah, *Annie Hall*, but there was a lot of heart and warmth in *Annie Hall*. I should have won for *The Producers*. It was crazy.

Judd: Well, they think misery is harder to create.

Mel: I think to make people sad is easier than to make them laugh. I do. I mean, they're both hard, you know. Dickens did them both. Nikolai

Gogol. Those are two guys you should read if you want to do sad some-times and you want to do comedy sometimes.

Judd: I think there's nothing harder to do than make a movie that is tear-down-the-house funny. It is harder than any kind of movie to make. To figure out a way to get that kind of momentum, that kind of joy from the crowd—to create tension and release, tension and release, for ninety min-utes? I mean, I saw *Young Frankenstein* when they played it here in Santa Monica a few years ago and it was the biggest laughs I've ever heard in a movie theater. Every moment of the movie. There wasn't, like, you know, the moment that kind of resets—it just kept going and going. It's almost a miracle.

Mel: Well, look at the cast. You had Peter Boyle. Cloris Leachman alone could have carried that movie. Gene Hackman, without money, without— you know, we gave him some billing at the end, you know, to play the blind man and pour boiling soup on Peter Boyle's crotch. I mean, that was so—

Judd: See, I wouldn't think he would be funny, Gene Hackman. How did you know Gene Hackman was that funny?

Mel: I like comedy that just strays an inch from reality. If it strays an inch to the right or left then it's really good because you don't, you feel it so real, you don't expect it to explode. Gene Wilder does that for me every time. He's very sincere. He's very emotional. He cares so much. You couldn't ask for a better real actor to play Dr. Frankenstein.

Judd: Wilder is your De Niro.

Mel: He's actually my Alberto Sordi. If you know anything about movies, Fellini—Alberto Sordi was his leading man, his comic leading man, in those early pictures. He went on to Marcello Mastroianni for *La Dolce Vita* and other movies, and he was always amusing and lovely and, you know. Fellini went on to a handsome guy and I never would have done that. I would have stayed with Alberto Sordi until I died.

Judd: What about Marty Feldman?

Mel: Oh, Marty Feldman is . . . I don't know. God put him together. We had nothing to do with it. The only way to hide from Marty Feldman was to put your nose against his. And then he can't see you because his eyes, his eyes go out the sides, you know. But we used to, I mean, Jesus, it's so wonderful. It was thrilling making that movie because Madeline Kahn, the funniest, the funniest, most moving—I mean when she did Lili Von Shtupp in *Blazing Saddles* and she leaned against something and missed and she . . . I'm a composer. I know a lot about music. She did a strange one-third off harmony with the melody. They had to carry me out.

Judd: Our next question is from Maria Markarian. How did I do on that one?

Maria: Very well, actually.

Mel: You're in my next picture, Maria.

Maria: Let's do it.

Mel: Just your name. You may not do a lot, but I like the name.

Maria: So my question is, aside from Carl Reiner, who has inspired you the most in your career?

Mel: I guess, you know, that's a good question. I don't know. It could be Buster Keaton. It could be Charlie Chaplin. Those guys inspired me. I was about nine years old and I used to go to Feltmans and Nathan's in Coney Island and Feltmans would have these silent movies. You'd have a knish or a hot dog for a nickel and maybe three cents for the root beer. It was incredible. And then you'd see, they'd show Harold Lloyd, you know, *Safety Last*, or Buster Keaton, *The Navigator*, *The General*. Or *City Lights* with Charlie Chaplin. I was just lost in it. It was so funny it made me cry. I had a lot of early influences way before people of my time told me, in no uncertain terms, what is really funny. What is really human and what is really funny.

Judd: Okay—

Mel: That's my answer.

Judd: Our next question is from Cindy Kapp.

Mel: Spell Kapp. K-A-P-P?

Cindy: Yes.

Mel: Oh gee, how do you like that? You know there was somebody in music — Kapp Records.

Cindy: Yeah.

Mel: Do you know that? Are you related?

Cindy: Kapp was shortened from Kappulski.

Mel: Oh, Kappulski. Well, good shortening. Tell the family well done.

Cindy: Thank you. All right, my question is: What movie or project are you most proud of, and if you could go back and do something differently, what would you change and why?

Mel: You know, it's hard. It's like children. It's hard to pick. But I do have some favorites that I am really proud of. I'd say an underrated movie that I've done that I'm proud of is *The Twelve Chairs* because it's that perfect — for me, it's that perfect combination of having something really important to say about the human condition and human behavior and, and flights of fancy and comedy. It's a wonderful mélange of comedy and, I don't know, bravery. I do like it. I'm very proud of and I'm very good in it. I have a small part, but I like it. But I'd say *Twelve Chairs* is overlooked.

Judd: Are you writing a musical of *Blazing Saddles*?

Mel: I am working on a few tunes. I don't know if it'll ever come to, you know. But finding Broadway was a thrill for me after sixty years of fooling around in TV and films. When *The Producers* opened on Broadway, it was a thrill of a lifetime, and then when it opened in London, and they stood on their chairs and screamed? I said, "This is British reserve?" But anyway, I love the payoff. I really do. I've got to be honest with you. You don't get that payoff in film. And you get even less payoff on television, because you could be there alone watching it, and there's no communal, you know, Let's laugh together. Let's be together and enjoy it. You get goose bumps and you cry. I mean it's the most fulfilling thing that could ever happen to any kind of creative artist.

Judd: Are they doing it around the world now still, productions of it?

Mel: They did "Springtime for Hitler," they did *The Producers* in Berlin. I didn't go. I was afraid there would be a guy in the balcony with a rifle, but I mean, what a thrill that they did it in Austria, and in Berlin in Hitler's theater. You know, that box. They invited me to be in that box. No thanks.

Judd: Yeah.

Mel: It's in Akron, Ohio, now in some high school. I swear. I mean, if I'm needy, I could go see a couple of high school kids do *The Producers* and it would be a little bit of a thrill for me.

Judd: Oh, absolutely. Our next person is Miriam Kavas from Panorama City.

Miriam: Well, first of all, thank you for the many years of enjoyment that you've given everyone. My question—

Mel: This is good. I'm enjoying myself here. This is wonderful.

Miriam: Which of your productions have given you the most satisfaction?

Mel: *To Be or Not to Be*, with my wife. Every day, I couldn't—I liked it so much I couldn't get enough of her. We did "Sweet Georgia Brown" in Polish and there's no greater joy than singing with my wife "Sweet Georgia Brown" in Polish. It was very moving. I mean, that was the most enjoyable making of a movie for me. I wasn't worried about money or art. Every day I would come in early to make sure the set and everything was right, and I'd have a breakfast burrito with rice, beans, scrambled eggs, chorizo, and a kind of green tomatillo sauce and a big cup of coffee. I loved that. I loved my breakfast burrito and my big mug of coffee, and Anne was there already getting her hair done, so we'd hang out. We would hang out for, like, twenty-four hours. And that was, you know, how many people could stand their wives for twenty-four hours? But she—I could cry now. She was easy, let me tell you. She was easy. She was fun.

Judd: I realize that is one of the many ways I've imitated you, by working with my family, and with my wife, Leslie.

Mel: That's great.

Judd: Do you have the best memory of anyone you know?

Mel: Uh, yes. I think I do have the best memory of anybody I know. Because I want to remember more than anybody I know.

Judd: Do you currently have a writing schedule? Are you writing or are you just doing work?

Mel: I have an office and I go every day and make notes. I have a little upright piano, and sometimes I compose a little bit, but I don't know. I don't know if anything will happen but, you know, I try to stay interested.

Judd: You're open to inspiration.

Mel: I'm open to it. I'm desperately waiting for it.

Judd: Can we talk about me for a bit? I have to say as a young, young man—I remember when the VCR was invented and we had, we had *The Godfather* and *Blazing Saddles* and *Young Frankenstein* and *The Producers* and *Annie Hall* and *Sleeper,* and that is what built my brain. Those are the movies that made me want to do this.

Mel: How old were you then?

Judd: I was born in '67. So you know eight, nine, ten. I must have watched those movies hundreds and hundreds of times, and it's always fun to go to a theater and see them with people. If anyone gets a chance to see them in a movie theater with a lot of people, there's no experience like watching *Blazing Saddles* with three hundred people. It's complete madness and—

Mel: I know. The thrill is seeing it communally. Seeing it in a movie house on a big screen. And that's, you know, television is wonderful and DVDs, they're wonderful, but they are really a disservice to movies. I mean, you enjoy somebody cackling from the balcony. You enjoy people around you joining you in the laughter.

MICHAEL CHE

(2014)

When I dipped a toe back into the world of stand-up comedy in the summer of 2014, one of the people performing in the clubs with me almost every night was a thirty-year-old man named Michael Che. At the time, he had just left *Saturday Night Live* and was dedicating himself to working on his stand-up act. I would go on before him most nights and then come out and watch him perform, and I was just blown away by his confidence and poise, by his facility with language and the sophistication of his jokes. He had that easygoing air of somebody who is clearly on his way to comedic greatness. And sure enough, before the summer was over, he'd been hired as a correspondent on *The Daily Show*, and then, just a few months later, *Saturday Night Live* hired him back, stealing him away from *The Daily Show*, to be one of the anchors of "Weekend Update." When you're that strong, that's how it goes.

Judd Apatow: Well, you're in the thick of it, aren't you?

Michael Che: I'm definitely in the thick of it.

Judd: Belly of the beast?

Michael: Absolutely.

Judd: You're kicking ass, though. You've taken to "Weekend Update" so quickly. Does it feel that way to you?

Michael: You never feel that way. You always feel like there's more shit to do—and you need to tighten and tighten and tighten it. Hopefully, by the second half of the season, things start to feel a lot smoother as we get a better sense of what we can do and what we can get away with.

Judd: As an outsider, it seems like you've found your angle on it. And you and Colin Jost—the pairing works so well. It's exciting to watch it come together so fast.

Michael: It's definitely the hardest thing I've ever had to do in comedy. It's exciting to know that it can still get better and go further, you know.

Judd: It works because you guys are so different.

Michael: We're completely different. We answer questions different. We dress different. Everything about us is different, but nothing's forced. It's not like they like put us together like some buddy cop movie, but it totally could be.

Judd: In the beginning, Colin seemed so anal and tight, and you're so loose and confident, it seemed like you brought something out in him that helped him discover what his point of view on the news is. The interplay between you was fascinating. I felt like I could see you guys figuring it out.

Michael: They wanted us to be different than what Seth was doing. They wanted it to be fresh. You know, Norm Macdonald's update was nothing like Dennis Miller's and Dennis's was nothing like Kevin Nealon's and Kevin's was nothing like—you know, everyone's different. Then, Jimmy and Tina. The one thing that really jumped out to me about them was that there were no runs, really. There was mostly just headline punch lines. I wanted to do something where we could go on a run with the story and inject more personality and opinion. That's what makes *The Daily Show* and *Colbert* so great. You're excited to hear what their take is going to be on a certain thing as opposed to them just having something witty to say when they find out about a two-hundred-year-old turtle that got arrested or whatever.

Judd: I think the only person who did anything close to what you're doing was Norm Macdonald.

Michael: Every generation has their "Update" host, you know, the way the people have their Johnny Carson or their Jay Leno or their Jimmy Kimmel. Norm was the "Update" guy when I was a kid, so he's the one that will always seem the rightest to me.

Judd: People forget that Norm was fired for making O.J. jokes after NBC told him to stop. [*Editor's Note: Norm says that is a stalking horse. They just had it in for him and were looking for an excuse.*]

Michael: People don't even know that.

Judd: He also did an enormous amount of aggressive Michael-Jackson-is-a-child-molester jokes.

Michael: Super-aggressive Michael-Jackson-as-child-molester jokes. Super-aggressive Germans-love-Hasselhoff jokes, too. It was edgy stuff, but it's just not the same climate today. Now it's this whole thing of you are what you tweet. I could know you for twenty-five years, I could have followed your whole career, but if you tweet something I don't like, that means you're just this kind of a person and you should never have a job again.

Judd: Treacherous waters.

Michael: Oh my God.

Judd: At any moment, some joke you make in the middle of the night can end your career. It's a very different time for humor because you have to assume, with any great joke, it's going to anger a certain percentage of the audience—and those people now have a way to communicate their rage. You can unleash the lunatics no matter what side of the issue you are on.

Michael: And it's so passionate on Twitter. But if someone recognizes you on the street, it's like, "I'm your biggest fan." Everybody I've ever met is my biggest fan and everybody on Twitter thinks I suck and shouldn't have a job. Obviously these people are not my biggest fans and obviously these people don't hate me. But it's a strange thing that people do.

Judd: Twitter's just this place where the twenty percent who hate what you do will just let you know, and then it feels like eighty percent hate it. I don't love Spanish rock and roll, but I'm not on the Internet trashing it all day long.

Michael: Right.

Judd: But somebody is.

Michael: The funny thing about "Update" is that people have these irrational expectations. Every week, people yell at me, like, You should be fired, they never should have given you the job. But it's not like they picked me over any of the old hosts. They're gone and they're not getting this job again. I'm not Amy and Tina. You're not going to get Chevy Chase back just because you miss him.

Judd: People love to debate what works on *SNL*. In every era of the show, people love to trash it while loving it and watching it. But the audience never seems to understand that the whole show is written in a week and the fun of it is trying to see how many good ones they can uncork.

Michael: I always say that, too, when people compare the show to other sketch shows. We do a completely different thing. If we were a taped show that was condensed to a half hour, if we were able to get every perfect shot that we needed with directors, it would be the best comedy show on TV. But we can't do that. If we had the talents of Will Ferrell and Tracy Morgan and Adam Sandler and we could just focus on making a half hour of perfect comedy, it would be insane. If our star each week wasn't a person who has never done comedy before and we didn't have to write every sketch about them and their ability and skill set, it would be amazing. But that's not the way the show works—and that's what makes it so special.

Judd: Are you enjoying focusing on "Update" and not writing sketches as much anymore?

Michael: "Update" is such a specific thing. With two people, it has this strange kind of momentum—you know, you never *quite* get on a roll. In stand-up, you get on a roll. There's a flow to it. With two people, as soon as you're on a roll, the camera's on someone else. And then, when it's back to you, you've got to restart. So they're very different things. I was comfortable writing sketches. With sketches, I know what works—and if something doesn't work, I don't get suicidal over it. So at this point, sketches are more fun, but "Update" is new and I want to get better at it.

Judd: In the last year, you've had all these big experiences: writing for *SNL*, being on *The Daily Show*, then straight to "Update." That must have been a real head spinner.

Michael: It was a lot. Especially during that time when I knew I was coming back to *SNL* but I was still working at *The Daily Show*. That was awkward. It was like being a product of divorced parents, which I am, so I can say that.

Judd: How did you get out of *The Daily Show* when you just got there?

Michael: Jon was really cool about it all. He understood the opportunity and he was like, "I'm not going to hold anybody back." It was a lot like when I left *SNL* for *The Daily Show*, actually. Lorne said, "You know, I'm not going to hold you back. You'll be great at *The Daily Show*. We believe in that." So I just got lucky. Both Lorne and Jon could have easily been like, "Oh, fuck it. And fuck you for even *wanting* to go. Now you get the small office."

Judd: You didn't realize Lorne had a master plan to get you back.

Michael: I don't know that he did. I'm still not sure.

Judd: Lorne Michaels outplays everybody again.

Michael: Who knows. But that guy's smart, man.

Judd: His success rate is ridiculous.

Michael: Yeah, he knows what he's doing. What other show, what other producer, can lose Chevy Chase, John Belushi, Bill Murray, Will Ferrell, Phil Hartman, Chris Farley—who can lose all of those people and still have a relevant show? If *Cheers* lost Ted Danson and Woody Harrelson, would they be able to reload and still be relevant? *In Living Color* was one of the greatest sketch shows I've ever seen, maybe number two after *SNL*. I loved that show. I was raised on that show. It had like a five-year window. But once the Wayanses left, it was like, "Okay, well, this is over," you know what I mean? Lorne has had all these guys leave over the years, and he's been able to restock. It's amazing.

Judd: What is your relationship like with him?

Michael: I'm friendly with him in a strange way. I mean it's obviously a boss relationship—we're not getting coffee and talking about girls—but he's been super-supportive. Anytime I've had an issue I could talk to him about it and I never felt disappointed walking out of his office afterwards. He could be Darth Vader if he wanted and we'd all be okay with it and thankful to have the job. But he's not. He has helped me believe I can do this job. To get his blessing is a pretty cool feeling.

Judd: I'm considerably older than you, so I remember when *SNL* first came on. I was eight. I can't imagine that I watched the first season, but I was definitely watching it in 1976 and 1977, when I was nine and ten years old, just trying so hard to stay up. I think the whole reason I got into comedy was because of *Saturday Night Live*.

Michael: It's amazing that it's still important to people. We still have fans who are fourteen and fifteen. It's like Looney Tunes. My father grew up on Looney Tunes and I grew up on Looney Tunes. It's a thing you can share.

Judd: I would always sneak over to the show when Sandler was there. It's just fun being around it. All the musicians hanging around, the incredible collection of people. Do you enjoy that part of it?

Michael: Oh, yes. I've seen Eminem, I've seen Jay-Z, I've seen Justin. But I don't think anyone has generated as much buzz since I've been there as Prince. It was crazy. Everyone wants to be next to Prince.

Judd: Did you get any alone time with him?

Michael: Hell no.

Judd: Who have you gotten to meet who is meaningful to you? Was there anyone who blew your mind?

Michael: Steve Martin. It was at an after party. I got to talk to Steve Martin about comedy and that was just like, what the fuck. This is the biggest comedian in the world. Like, he was *the guy*. This was a stadium comic, you know. And I'm saying that to him. And he's like, "Yeah, yeah, but that was nothing. That was a long time ago." He's talking to me about comedy as if he's never done it before. He's like, "What do you do? Do you pre-pare? How do you prepare? Do you write it down first?" And I'm like, What the fuck? You're Steve Martin, man.

Judd: How many years had you been doing stand-up at this point?

Michael: Four.

Judd: Wow, your rise has been so fast.

Michael: It has been insane. If you had told me five years ago that I'd get to do all these things in the next thirty years, I would have been like, "Sign me up."

Judd: What do you think accounts for the fact that you haven't lost your mind?

Michael: Probably because I love doing this more than anything. Comedy isn't boring to me. That's where my sanity is. It's all the outside stuff that's exhausting and stressful. The onstage stuff, the crowd, the performing— that never gets old.

Judd: How closely were you following comedy as a kid?

Michael: See, I came from a funny family. You know how some families are super-athletic or whatever? In a lot of families, sports are the most important thing—who's the best football player or who's the best ball player in the family? Well, comedy was the hierarchy in my family. We'd all get together and just snap on each other and make fun of each other. The level of respect that you got in my family came from being funny. I looked up to the funny people and I wanted to hold my own against the older kids and the adults. We always watched *Raw* and *Delirious* and Damon Wayans's *One Night Stand, Hollywood Shuffle, Sucka, The Jerk, Bill Cosby Himself.* My brothers and sisters are a lot older than me, and they had these comedy tapes and I would just watch them all and recite them and perform them, but with the curses taken out. I would perform edited versions of *Delirious* and everyone would trip out because I was so young and I was doing it.

Judd: Your brothers and sisters were much older than you?

Michael: Much older. My closest brother is eight years older than me and my oldest brother is like fifteen years older than me. I'm the youngest of seven. And when you're around kids that much older than you, you have to be quiet and find something to entertain yourself. A lot of times, I would be put in front of the TV.

Judd: What was the vibe in your family in terms of career? For me, I saw comedy as a way to escape. What was going on in your family?

Michael: We came from a poor family. Everybody had regular jobs. No one did anything that was super-successful in our family. It was more like, "Don't be a bum. If you've got to be a carpet man or whatever, that's fine; we don't care what you do as long as you're not a bum." And I started comedy late. I started when I was twenty-six. As arrogant as this may sound, I knew I wasn't going to be in some cubicle and wasn't going to be a fireman. I knew I would do something creative. I was always the creative type. I worked as an artist for a while. I used to paint portraits and do graphic design and stuff. I would make a little bit of money and then lose a bunch of money, and by the time I was twenty-six, I was just really down on myself. I felt old. Twenty-six is a weird age because that's when all your friends are starting to do well—you know, they're out of college, they've gotten their careers started. And I felt like I was nowhere. I was twenty-six, but I felt like I was forty-six. That's when I decided to try comedy. And once I did, it just clicked. It was like love at first sight.

Judd: Within the year, you were working the clubs in New York, getting real gigs.

Michael: It started to roll quickly. But that's also the benefit of doing it in New York City, where you can get up five times a day if you hustle. You could go to five different open mics a night, and really get a handle on a joke. It was like I was charging a battery—every single day, just relentless. I would get certain jokes so good that they almost couldn't *not* work.

Judd: Who did you want to be, as a comedian?

Michael: Eddie Murphy made me want to be funny. But the Chris Rock and George Carlin specials, when they were saying controversial things and had points—I was like, *Man, I want to have points, too.* That was the important thing to me. That was my direction.

Judd: Now you're in a place where you can say those things and a lot of people will listen to it every week.

Michael: Nothing is more exciting than being able to say an opinion into camera and wait for a reaction. That's the ultimate goal. That's the high. You want to write something that people hear and go, "Oh fuck. How does he come up with that and he's absolutely correct? I can't believe they put that on TV."

Judd: It feels like we're in the middle of a great moment in comedy. It feels like Comedy Central and UCB [Upright Citizens Brigade] and the Internet have just turbocharged everything. And I think all this competition has made comedians better.

Michael: There's such a need for comedy now. Everything has to be funny now. A car insurance commercial might be the funniest thing you see all day. Sports announcers are funny. Everybody's funny. There's a comedy writer for every single thing. You get comedy from everywhere now, and it's breeding a society that wants to laugh. There's so much competition, but there's also so much room for more voices. It's inspiring a lot of good comedy. A lot of different comedy.

Judd: Do you love working at a place like the Comedy Cellar?

Michael: It's insane. It's like our Apollo.

Judd: Yeah, just to go in there every night and see, like, Dave Attell and then Dave Chappelle and then Chris Rock—there's just an enormous group of talented people there every night. They kill so hard. Are there particularly special moments that come to mind when you think about that place?

Michael: Yeah, my first night there. I show up and the guy at the door is like, "Yo, man, you might not be able to go on tonight because Chappelle is about to get up and we don't know when he's coming off." And I was like, "Damn." But there was another slot later on and the guy said maybe I could get on that. And I was like, "All right, cool, whatever." So you know, Chappelle's onstage. He's killing for like forty-five minutes. Uncharacteristically gets offstage after like forty or forty-five minutes; everyone assumed he was going to be up there all night. So the next comedian to get onstage is Chris Rock. He gets onstage, and does like forty minutes. And the next comedian that gets onstage is me. I'm like, Fuck you. But you know what? It was good. And you know why? Because that crowd had seen ninety minutes of the best comedians in the world. I could not ruin their night. There was nothing I could say that was ever going to wipe that smile off those faces, man.

MICHAEL O'DONOGHUE

(1983)

Growing up, I was completely obsessed with *Saturday Night Live*. Scarily obsessed. How deep did the nerd-dom go? I knew who all the writers were. (I also used to record the show with a cassette recorder, and then transcribe it by hand, and then study the transcription to try to understand how it all worked—but that's a story for another day.) I wanted to know who was responsible for making this show that meant so much to me.

There was one writer I admired above all others—he also performed on the show occasionally—named Michael O'Donoghue. He had what we used to call a sick sense of humor. He was one of those preternaturally gifted, big-brained *National Lampoon* guys, who went on to become one of the original writers of *Saturday Night Live*—and was in the first sketch ever performed on *Saturday Night Live*—and later wrote the movie *Scrooged*. When I interviewed him, he had just been fired from the show and was ready to unload. He was fucking furious, actually. It was the first time I'd heard somebody—an adult, I mean—let loose like this and insult everybody he had just worked with, and the ferocity of his rage, and the righteousness of it, definitely left an impression. Michael O'Donoghue didn't suffer fools. He didn't need to.

Judd Apatow: How would you describe your type of humor?

Michael O'Donoghue: I don't know. Everybody else calls it sick or something, but I find it healthy. I think humor should deal with the tensions that are going on in society. And our society's really different now than *The Lucy Show* or *Dick Van Dyke*, or *Mary Tyler Moore*. I try to deal with the tensions of 1983—and some of them are really dark. The psycho rings your doorbell, you know. So I reflect that in my humor. Some people say that's funny. Some think it's sick. I think it's healthy.

Judd: What would be an example of that tension?

Michael: I recently flew with Eastern Airlines, which is—as I was flying, I wrote a thing called "TransEastern Airlines." It was like flying in a cattle car with wings. It's a line like, "You'll feel like you've never left the ground because we treat you like dirt." It was entirely based on flying Eastern, where they treated you like garbage. And so I wrote a sketch about it.

Judd: What is *Mondo*?

Michael: *Mondo* is so many things. *Mondo Video* just came out in cassette form. It just sold five thousand copies, which is very good for something that's not a movie. Just coming out cold, it's doing real well.

Judd: They're going to release it as a movie in a limited—

Michael: It was careless, the movie, because it was spaced for commercials. It was really strange. And also they have not perfected that tape-to-film process, so it looks real mushy when you watch it.

Judd: What happened? You wrote it, and they okayed it, and then once it was made, they didn't want it?

Michael: That was exactly what happened, odd as it may sound. They invested a lot of money in it—three hundred thousand dollars—which I think is a lot of money. And they didn't even bother to look at it at NBC.

Judd: They didn't even screen it?

Michael: A couple of the censors looked at it, but none of the brass looked at it. A lot of television critics really liked it. It's very strange to me, the whole history of that thing.

Judd: And how did it do in the theaters when it came out?

Michael: Terrible. It looked bad. It was made for television, not for movies. When you write for late-night television, you're fighting sleep. So the way that you program is you put your best thing first, and your second-best thing second, and your third—because you're just trying to fight sleep. So the junk is at the end. That's *not* the way to make a movie. The way you make a movie is you build to a climax—it's a classic stage thing. *Mondo* was never meant to be a movie, and it didn't do very well as a movie.

Judd: How do you write a movie like that, because it's very peculiar. I mean, the skits—

Michael: Well, it was written very quickly. It was written in a couple of weeks. It was written off of a sort of video theory that it's more fun—if you can't be funny, be weird. It's just as good, maybe even better. That was the comedic theory behind it. Sometimes we would just be strange for no good reason. It keeps me amused.

Judd: What kind of reaction did you expect people to have when they watched it?

Michael: Well, some would laugh, which happens. Some would be annoyed. Ah, more were annoyed than laughed. Whatever *Saturday Night Live* was when it came out, I expected *Mondo Video* to be, five years later. You know what I mean? It would be a different kind of comedy. I got tired of working in sketch comedy. Live television is very limiting, what you can do in it.

Judd: You've had enough of TV comedy?

Michael: I've had enough. It's frustrating, live TV. Actually, there's a different way to do live television, but—

Judd: How would you like to do it?

Michael: Shoot it all with creepers.

Judd: With what?

Michael: Shoot it all with creepers—handheld cameras. Put the cameras on the stage with the actors. Can I use obscenities in this—where is this broadcast, because I'm watching my language as I talk.

Judd: We'll bleep it out.

Michael: Ah, okay. Well, then. I don't think anybody gives a flying *fuck* if they see a cameraman on a stage, okay? I don't think anybody cares. It's the liveness of it that they like. Not how technically perfect everything is.

So that frustrated me. It frustrated me when I went back to *Saturday Night Live* and they wanted to shoot it the same old way.

Judd: Do you think when they did the "new" *Saturday Night Live* they should have changed it, and tried new things instead of the same things?

Michael: Jesus, yes. All TV knows is winning combinations. Of course they should have been trying something new, something interesting. Something that made us, in the first two or three years, look like fools—like *Red Skelton* or something, you know what I mean? It's stupid.

Judd: What kind of humor don't you like?

Michael: Almost everything. Aside from the stuff I write, there's not much that appeals to me. I'll watch—I like individual performances of people like Michael Keaton, who was wonderful in *Night Shift*. I'll watch Shelley Long forever. Or somebody like Carol Kane, who's a brilliant comedic actress. I like Andy Kaufman quite a bit. Richard Pryor's great.

Judd: You don't like the normal comedy—you like a different element in it.

Michael: Well, I think Erik Estrada is the funniest man in America. I will say that. I watch *CHiPs*. I suffer for *CHiPs*. It's so stupid, those big yo-yos on motorcycles. Just kills me. You know, like most people, I like *The Jetsons*. Who doesn't? But there's not too much out there for me.

Judd: Are there any topics you think *shouldn't* be discussed in comedy? I guess that's silly to ask.

Michael: No, no, I've never found anything that's—

Judd: Even like topics like cancer?

Michael: *Especially* cancer. I've always found cancer an amusing weapon— I've always found, ah, anything that creates tension, tension and release, and cancer creates major tension.

Judd: When did you first start working in comedy?

Michael: That's hard to say. I was a serious literary writer writing for the *Evergreen Review*, doing poetry and stuff like that. And then I slid off into a comic strip called *The Adventures of Phoebe Zeit-Geist*, which I did in the late sixties, middle sixties, and then somehow I ended up at the *National Lampoon*. Then I slid into show business. It sort of shocks me to realize that I'm in the same profession as Charo and Sonny Bono. But I am—I slid into that at the *National Lampoon* radio office. Which I started in about '73, and I quit later and John Belushi took it over.

Judd: Now, what kind of comedy did you do on the radio hour?

Michael: Essentially the sort of the thing that they're doing on *Saturday Night Live*. I had very much the same cast—John and Chevy and Gilda and Bill Murray, odd people like Steve Collins, who's now been in *Tales of the Gold Monkey*. I had a great group of people, plus a lot of the writers for *Saturday Night Live*. It was very much like *Saturday Night Live*, but it was a little freer because radio's a little freer. But it's not quite as powerful. We did most of the scenes—John had some great characters, which he never created on *Saturday Night Live*—

Judd: Such as?

Michael: He did a guy called Craig Baker, the Perfect Master—the eighteen-year-old perfect master—and it was just funny. It's the concept of—instead of this guy living in India, he was just like this asshole kid who lived out in Champaign-Urbana, Illinois. Which is where John is from. And Indians would come to seek guidance from this dumb kid. It was funny. He just said, "Well, drink a lot of beer and go to Fort Lauderdale, and you need to mellow out, man."

Judd: How did this all lead into *Saturday Night Live*?

Michael: Lorne Michaels, the producer of *Saturday Night Live*, heard the show. And Chevy had let it be known that Marilyn Miller, who had been writing for *Mary Tyler Moore*, was a big *Lampoon* fan, and she recommended me to Ed Bluestone, who used to write for the *National Lampoon*. A very good writer. So Lorne had heard of me in a variety of ways. I was in the middle of starting a new humor magazine at that time, and I went in to sign a contract on this, with Stan Lee—

Judd: Then at Marvel Comics.

Michael: Yes, exactly. And the wing of that company went bankrupt and Lorne had kept offering me a television show and I didn't want to do television. Then I had no choice but to do television or magazine—I had no way to earn money, so I said, "Okay, I'll do your television show." I was sort of backed into it.

Judd: How did they decide what kind of show they wanted?

Michael: Well, they didn't—this got decided by getting a bunch of smart people in a room. The results were that show.

Judd: Now, when *Saturday Night Live* started, weren't you a prime-time player?

Michael: I was for the first show, as a matter of fact. And then, I don't know why I was eliminated from that slot—I think it was because Lorne was having some problems with Chevy. But I'm not a particularly good actor.

Judd: But you starred in the first sketch of the series?

Michael: I did. I did the first sketch. The Wolverine sketch. God, that was scary.

Judd: Why is that?

Michael: Because nobody'd ever done live television. Twenty million people are watching you. My little heart goes thump, thump, thump, thump. I thought I was going to pass out from fear.

Judd: So it was only for the first show that you were a prime-time player?

Michael: I think I was in the second show as a prime-time player, too. And then I was dumped somehow. I don't know.

Judd: Why weren't you on the show more often?

Michael: Lorne didn't like me in the show that much.

Judd: Really?

Michael: Yeah. I wish I had been on the show more. It was always a problem about writing and acting for that show at the same time. All this crap about—

Judd: Isn't there a lot of competition being on the show?

Michael: You bet.

Judd: Were you on the show straight through for the entire original run?

Michael: No, I quit after three years.

Judd: Why?

Michael: People were giving me shit. At a certain point, I didn't want to go through these comic meetings where my work was discussed. I figured I'd proven that I could write stuff. I just wanted to do what I wanted to do. I got fed up with the whole process.

Judd: Because I can see how they would question putting some of your stuff on the air.

Michael: Yeah, me, too.

Judd: I can see how somebody could question, you know, the Mike Douglas sketch. [*Michael would come out and do an impression of Mike Douglas if giant knitting needles were driven into his eyes.*]

Michael: Well, you know, they actually went for that one easy. I don't know why. I used to do it at parties with my friends. I originally did it on *National Lampoon Radio Hour.* And then I would do it to entertain the people at *Saturday Night Live,* and finally somebody said, "Let's put that on the air if it gives us laughs." That was always our standard. If it makes us laugh, it should make them laugh. And it did, in a way.

Judd: The other night, I saw—do you ever watch the repeats?

Michael: No.

Judd: Why not?

Michael: Because I don't live in the past. That just dredges—I know exactly where I was during that period. It's like asking about Beatles songs. I don't care anymore. Game over.

Judd: What kind of arguments did you get in with the censors?

Michael: Well, the censors were actually pretty nice people. They had this concept that people turning the dial would hit NBC and go, "Ah, NBC: the quality network. Oh, now my children are safe to watch this." But people have no idea what network they're watching.

Judd: What would be examples of the skits they didn't let on?

Michael: Oh, a lot of 'em. The thing I got fired over last time was this piece about NBC president Fred Silverman called "The Last Ten Days in Silverman's Bunker." It's built with Fred Silverman as Adolf Hitler and they would not let it on. It was a twenty-minute sketch starring John Belushi as Silverman. Twenty minutes. And they fired me for having written it.

Judd: They ripped Silverman up in the show, though.

Michael: But not the way I ripped him up. They *pretended* to rip him up. I ripped him up.

Judd: So this is when you left the show. This is the—

Michael: This is the last time. Grant Tinker, the president of NBC, personally axed me. That bitch.

Judd: What were the contents of that skit that were so—

Michael: It's been a long time. It, ah—you sort of had to see. Silverman always had some new wacky idea of some show that was going to bring him back on top. It was all Silverman talking to his generals. He had a show called *Look Up Her Dress*, and the camera was right under these women's dresses. Women would stand on a big Plexiglas thing, and if they missed one question, we'd look up their dress—it was all these silly giggle shows, you know, that this guy wanted. He was very clever, it was very smart.

Judd: And then you left the show—what did you do in between the time you left and when you came back?

Michael: I wrote a song for Dolly Parton called "Single Women."

Judd: Are you serious?

Michael: I am serious. Top ten. One of the top ten country songs in the country. In fact, I just wrote two more country songs. It's easy. It's just a skill I have.

Judd: I don't know if you're kidding.

Michael: I swear to God. See, I wrote a lot of music for the show. I wrote music for Madeline Kahn.

Judd: "Antler Dance"?

Michael: I wrote "The Antler Dance." Of course, the legendary "Antler Dance." I wrote "The Castration Waltz." And then I wrote "Let's Talk Dirty to the Animals" for the Gilda Radner show. And suddenly it occurred to me: *Why am I writing these novelty songs when I could be writing real songs and collecting real royalties on 'em?* So I did, and I did.

Judd: Why did you decide to come back to *Saturday Night Live* in 1981?

Michael: Money and the promise that I could do whatever I wanted. As it so happened I was totally boxed by a big towheaded dork called Dick Ebersol and his Judas accomplice, Robert Tischler. And they hired people like—ah, you know, not a box of talent between all of them. All I had was Eddie Murphy and Joe Piscopo, who's decent. Lame writers. I was totally miserable. I was nuts and finally they fired me.

Judd: So when you came back, did you know as soon as you got there that this wasn't gonna work?

Michael: Yeah, I began to get some idea. I tried. I brought in a couple people, but really—we just couldn't do anything, it was impossible, and I actually sort of engineered it so I'd get fired.

Judd: So you wrote that skit that got you fired because you wanted to get fired?

Michael: Oh, yeah, I was asking for it. "Come get me." I was just being so obnoxious. I was dressing like a maniac. I was attacking the cast. I did something so funny. There was a Christmas show, and afterwards, there was a meeting. And they came in, they thought I was gonna give them presents or something. I did. I gave them an honest evaluation of their talent. I ripped them apart.

Judd: What did you say?

Michael: I was on a roll. I was just on a tear and I went through every one of 'em. Ah, they made me angry.

Judd: Did you write anything at all that you liked?

Michael: I wrote some things—I did the TransEastern Airline ad during that period. I did, I don't know, a couple of things I like. But it was uphill all the way.

Judd: And then you left and now you're working on a screenplay?

Michael: I'm working on a screenplay with Mitch Glaser, one of the writers from *Mondo Video*, on a detective story set in Miami. I think we're about forty-five pages in.

Judd: And what kind of story is it?

Michael: It's a serious detective movie with real violence and real villains. The hero is a funny kind of guy. He's an asshole. He likes to jerk people around; that's how he gets his kicks. Somewhat like me in a way. Very much based upon me.

Judd: What's gonna be in the screenplay that the masses are going to enjoy?

Michael: Sex and violence, you know. They always go for that. This is just loaded with sex and violence. It's very funny.

Judd: And people will like it? I mean it's not just for people who like and enjoy humor, but I'm sure, you know—

Michael: I don't care about people over forty-five. They can be tossed in a shallow grave, as far as I'm concerned. I don't write to them. Let *Masterpiece Playhouse* or something write for them. I write for people younger than myself. My target group's about twenty to twenty-five—always has been.

Judd: If you could move into doing whatever you want to do in the future, what would it be?

Michael: Rule the earth. And people would have to do whatever I say, and give me their stuff—all their stuff belongs to me if I want it. It'd be great.

MIKE NICHOLS

(2012)

I met Larry Gelbart at the end of his life, and I've always regretted that I didn't get to spend more time with him. I was juggling a bunch of projects at the time, basically just being my distracted self, and when he died, I had this feeling of devastation. Because I realized I had missed it. I should have found a way to connect with him more.

So, when I was introduced to Mike Nichols, I resolved not to make the same mistake again. I was alert to the idea that every moment with him was precious. I asked questions, I listened. He was already in his eighties, but still sharp as a tack, funny as can be, but also incredibly open and willing to tell me anything I wanted to know about his journey and his work. When I would have breakfast with him, I would record our conversations because I knew he was saying so many things I would want to remember for the rest of my life.

When *This Is 40* came out, I screened it for him in New York City, and I remember him coming up to me afterward. He had tears in his eyes because he was so moved by how personal it was, which was wonderful to hear, but really what I came away thinking was: *This man is so connected emotionally, so moved by human beings and touched by our struggle.* That was his genius. He was completely plugged in to the human experience, and what was dramatic and humorous about it. I miss him.

Judd Apatow: This is so exciting. I'm such a gigantic fan of yours. Many years ago, when I first tried to write a good screenplay, I wrote a screenplay with Owen Wilson. We drove across America, trying to write it, and I remember being in a hotel, watching *The Graduate*. We took out notepads

This interview originally took place at the Museum of Modern Art in New York City with a live audience.

and outlined it because we were trying to understand how it worked and we didn't *understand*. We were trying to figure out how much information the movie gave about Benjamin, the main character. And so we just wrote down everything. Like, we don't know anything about him. All we know is he ran track and worked for the school paper and had no friends.

Mike Nichols: It's funny. I'm trying to think back to what we said to each other about Benjamin. We said very little to define him because we'd had this very strange experience, which was as we saw boy after boy come in to play him, it never seemed right. We'd seen every actor in the country in that age range, which was actually seventeen to thirty—that's how old Dustin was at the time. Thirty. He was, in fact, two years younger than Anne Bancroft. But I had seen him playing a transvestite fishwife in a play called *Journey of the Fifth Horse*, which was a sort of Russian-type play. And I said, "I like that guy. Why don't we have him in to test?" He had that strange thing, which I had experienced in the only other movie I'd ever made, *Virginia Woolf*: He was better when he was on film than when you were looking at him. Certain actors have a deal with Technicolor. In the bath overnight, they do things to them. Somehow, we couldn't get him out of our heads. The whole thing of casting—tell me, how do you feel about casting? Do you outline who you're looking for, or do you wait to see who turns you on?

Judd: That's a good question. When we did *Freaks and Geeks*, we knew we wanted real kids and we decided that they didn't even have to be actors. Wes Anderson had just made *Bottle Rocket*, which had all these strange people in it—people who were his friends from Dallas, like Kumar [Pallana], who's in all of his movies and who's, like, just a magician who owned a coffee shop. And I thought, *Wow, he's finding all these interesting guys and putting them in his movie and teaching them how to act*. And it seemed to make the work better. Once we liked someone, we tried to work with them again. It's scary meeting new people.

Mike: It's interesting that Wes, you, and Louis C.K. are all people who are deliberately going in the other direction—untheatrical, unleading people, uneverything. It's so refreshing and—in *This Is 40*, what I got excited about was that nobody has ever done a movie that was absolutely reality.

For real, actual reality, actual wife, actual daughters, actual jokes about each other and you, together. You have to have an incredibly finely tuned sense of how far you can go. You have some kind of sense of what's perfectly okay. I don't know. You either have it or you don't.

Judd: Maybe we should take a look at a clip from one of your movies, just to embarrass me.

Mike: Can we do a clip that I brought that's not from one of my movies? I'm very boring on this particular subject. This is a moment where I think we can watch an actress invent movie acting. Sound movies didn't happen until about 1930. That's how young talking movies are. And there was a stage when movies were like plays: They were photographed. And then after that, they were like plays photographed with some reality beginning to show except in the acting, because the acting was still catching up. You can see, in this clip, that they are character actors and they're very good but they, you could put them a mile away on the stage. And then here comes Garbo and you can actually see her in this clip—you can see the character thinking something, realizing something about herself. It's not *Traviata*, it's *Camille*, which is the same plot as *La Traviata*—namely, a very fancy courtesan falls in love with this young guy and they're happy and his father comes to see her and says, "Please, please give him up. You're ruining his career, he's not gonna get the post he hoped for." And she decides to do it. But the only way she can do it is to go to the man that she's most afraid of, the guy who used to own her, who she worked for full-time, which is what courtesans did. There was somebody who owned them and kept them very fancy. So she goes back to him, and—Armand is his name—he goes away unhappy. Then he comes back and there's a scene where they run into each other in the casino. And what I want you to watch for is the moment, right at the end, where she thinks, *Oh my God, look at me, I'm a cliché.* Let's look at it.

(Clip from *Camille*: Armand runs into Marguerite at the casino.)

Judd: We've come a long way, we really have.

Mike: We have. When you think that, right around this time, the whole idea of acting in a movie was being invented by Garbo and Barbara

Stanwyck and Bette Davis and a lot of people—they were doing less and less. What's interesting is that being inexpressive becomes the big deal. The most famous line in the history of movies is somebody saying something wrong. It's the line, "Here's looking at you, kid." But Bogart actually says, "He's looking at you, kid." That little inexpressive nothing became a classic thing. And the big stuff sort of went away. That's my first point and probably my last.

Judd: You started in improv. What was that transition like, from improv to acting and directing? Who taught you how to do this?

Mike: Improv taught me how to do it. Elaine and I were very lucky because our pals that we started with at this improv place had no particular idea. I mean, there were big talks about socialism and stuff, but nothing you could act. So we had to go out there and learn through horrible trial and error what you need to do to make an audience happy. And slowly, we discovered a principle. Elaine used to say, "When in doubt, seduce." Because seduction is immediately a scene. And, of course, so is conflict. If you say black, I say white, and we have a fight. There only is one other kind of scene, I discovered—there are fights, seductions, and negotiations. Most of Shakespeare turns out to be a negotiation because it's all about power and rulers and so on. When you're making it up, you learn what has to happen to keep an audience interested and excited but, most of all, laughing. And then it becomes part of you. For instance, when I started to direct my first Broadway play, which was *Barefoot*, I had them doing so much business onstage that Dick Benjamin—who replaced Redford—said, "I can't. I can't learn all the business and the lines." And that's the thing. If you keep them very busy, they're too busy to act. And then it looks like life.

Judd: The first things you did, right out of the gate, were ridiculously successful. Your comedy team, your first play, *Barefoot in the Park*, your first movie, *Who's Afraid of Virginia Woolf*? How did that happen?

Mike: Well, *Barefoot in the Park* was somebody else's idea. There was a nice producer who said, "How'd you like to"—after Elaine and I broke up, I was sort of the leftover half of a comedy team—and he said, "How'd you like to direct a play?" And I said, "Well, let's try. Let's go somewhere in summer stock and see if the play's any good. If I'm any good." I said, "I'd like to see if we can get that blond guy I saw last week—Redfield, Redford, something." And we had no time because we're going for summer stock. We had five days, so I just threw it all in and we figured it out. I felt like I'd come home because all this time I'd been thinking about it and working at it, I didn't really want to be an actor.

Judd: Why did you give up acting?

Mike: I didn't like it. I'm too good of a director to like me as an actor. I can get better people. So I did. And I just liked it more. I liked being there much more than being here. I still do.

Judd: And you did *Death of a Salesman* recently. I mean, if you started with *Virginia Woolf*, what did you learn in the middle if you—could you have done *Death of a Salesman* back then?

Mike: No, I don't think so. I think *Virginia Woolf*—I was unbelievably lucky because *Virginia Woolf*, among many, many other things, is possibly the only play that is entirely in the present. Have you noticed how plays are always somebody endlessly yammering about the past? That never happens in *Virginia Woolf*. The past is brought up but when it's brought up, it's part of a trap that's being set. Then the trap is sprung and there are terrible consequences as a result—all in the present. The present was my bag, you know. And so we just did it all in the present. It was good. Now, you: Did you start with funny?

Judd: I was a stand-up comedian. I was like you—a stand-up comedian who realized I could get better people to act. At some point, I realized my friends were way funnier than I was as a performer. So I started writing. I would write for them. And then slowly they would give me jobs, which turned into punch-ups and screenplays. But I really wanted to be Jerry Seinfeld. That was my only intention when I was younger.

Mike: What did Seinfeld mean to you?

Judd: In terms of what comedy meant to me, I liked Seinfeld, but I liked that comedians were pissed off. I liked that they said everything wasn't fair. People like George Carlin would talk about the injustices of the world. Richard Pryor and Monty Python mocked how society worked—class systems and government. I was just attracted. I must have been very hostile as a kid. I didn't know why, but I liked that people were telling everybody to fuck off. But I found that I didn't have very strong opinions when I was a stand-up comedian. I didn't have the anger to do it. So I wrote.

Mike: You saved yourself, you know. Because the one thing I understood the minute we were all comedians in this group—and I saw what happened to some people and less to others—is that it's very, very corrupting to the spirit, doing comedy. You have to be almost a saint like Jack Benny was, like Steve Martin is, to avoid being corrupted by it. There's very little work where the work and the reward are simultaneous, and comedy is that. And you can see it doing terrible things to people because it's constant, instant gratification. There are people who can resist it, like Chris Rock. People of a certain character and high intelligence know how to avoid it. Were you aware of having to build certain things in to protect yourself from that happening?

Judd: I would always get post-stand-up shame. If I was really funny, when I got home, it wasn't that I thought, *Oh, I need to do it again,* I was just so embarrassed that I had been so arrogant to feel the need to do that. Is that how you felt when you were doing the Nichols and May show? How did it feel for you?

Mike: I never told this to anybody, because it's so sort of depressing and pointless, but I had a sadist fantasy onstage. I figured each laugh was me cracking a whip. But there's this weird thing that happens to you when you're out there, dressed funny. You can wear better pants and stuff because you're not a character. You can feel like you're even sexy in everything because you're up there and the audience is doing what you want. I didn't love it but I also didn't suffer from it as Elaine did. We closed the show while we were still sold out because she couldn't take it anymore. I kept saying, "Take *what*? It's an hour and a half and all we do is talk!" But it took something out of her. She's a better actor than I am, for one thing, so she really went through stuff that I was faking. But it's also something else. It *cost* her something. It didn't cost me anything because I didn't really like it. To risk everything on a play, I mean, your feelings and ideas and secrets and everything, is, to me, much riskier than laugh, laugh, laugh. But the greatest comic writers, like Noël Coward, always had contempt for the funny stuff. They liked the prefaced boring stuff because that was so meaningful. I hate boring stuff and I like laughs, but I don't wanna do it.

Judd: Who's the funniest in person that you've collaborated with? Neil Simon?

Mike: Neil was very, very funny. I think the most difficult person to work with, because we were in such pain all the time, was Robin Williams. You just pray he'll stop because you might get in real trouble if you don't stop laughing soon. While they were lighting a scene, he would do these improvs that I can't begin to describe. Once there was an astounding one that lasted about twenty minutes—we were all begging him to stop. The next day I said, "How much of that could you do again today?" And he said, "Oh, none. It's gone." It was all unconscious.

Judd: In your directing, do you prefer doing comedy? What's the difference between doing something like *Angels in America*, which is also funny at times, and—

Mike: I think all good plays are both. You can't be only funny. And God help any play that is never funny.

Judd: I'm always happy when the idea is something serious and we find a way to get people emotional about it but still get some laughs in. We were talking about, you know, scenes where people fight, where you still can get laughs but the fight is still real and intense. Maybe we could show a clip from *This Is 40* and talk about conflict in these movies. Let's take a look at a scene.

(Clip from *This Is 40*: Debbie catches Pete playing with his iPad on the toilet.)

Mike: Your movie is so entirely about being that thing that isn't two people but something more. How you get it and how hard it is to maintain and how, since it leads to the best thing of all, which is children, how central it is to our lives. It is our lives. But your take on it, which is to concentrate on the most unsentimental parts of it, that every—even taking a dump. How much more down-to-earth can you get? But it's not only about love; it's about spirit and it's about what love really is, which is not mawkish; it's an everyday happiness that you couldn't describe to a Martian because it looks like something else. Happy people look like something else. They don't look like happy people. Have you ever noticed that? They look like involved or maybe even angry people.

Judd: Happy people look crazy. I mean, the people who *seem* happy.

Mike: Yes, there's something wrong with them, clearly. But I think that in a weird way, your trademark is: How far do we go in our ludicrousness? There's no end to it. It can go as far as you like. But the thing that happens when you have a baby and you're both in bed with a baby—for the first week, two weeks, three weeks, and then forever—is simply like nothing else in the world. You can't celebrate it in a mawkish way because then it's somebody else. To do it your way, you can't do it without laughs. You can't do it in life without laughs, either, because you're right into it. And also, I have to confess, I'm a sucker for metaphor. I go on about it too much and I keep saying metaphor is dead, nobody wants metaphor. As Nora Ephron said once: "Well, I feel terrible about the metaphor, but what can I do? It's like the whale, you know?" And then I realized it was bullshit and I was very pretentious to worry about it because it's there or it's not there and you don't have to name it or analyze it. Sometimes I get a script and I think, *How do I tell them that there's no reason to tell this story?* Here's a question that I can't answer: Why is it worth telling one story and not another? Well, the easy answer is it's, it's really secretly about all our lives. And there are plots like that, we know that. *Virginia Woolf* reminds you of the hardest parts of your own life. But to throw that all out and go and put on the screen or on the stage what actually happens without a metaphor, I think that's very exciting. That's a gearshift that we haven't had.

Judd: We've talked about the fact that life is overwhelming. There's a lot, there's too much to handle. You're trying to be a good spouse and a good parent and have your kids do well at school and you're trying to take care of your health and you're trying to deal with your extended family. And, at some point, it really brings you to the brink of losing your mind. You're trying to get along with your spouse at the same time and there always seems to be a lot of humor in this failed attempt we all make to just be able to do it all. And that was the original idea behind the movie. But I think that what happened was, as we got more specific, it became more universal. The smallest details are the details that people come up to me and say: "I've had that conversation seven times this week."

Mike: Exactly. It's everybody together saying, Oh God, that's so true. And therefore, it's not bad taste, whatever that is, and it's not a metaphor: It's life.

Judd: I didn't start out thinking that I would make personal movies. I started out writing broader comedies, but this area has interested me and I feel like, you know, you write movies to figure out why you're writing the movie. That's something I read somewhere and I thought, *Well, that does make sense.*

Mike: There's something very important here, which I think is when it's your time and when it isn't. If you make movies, your early movies are about your time. Everybody knows the story you're telling. Nobody says, "Why are you telling me this story?" Because everybody in your generation is in that place, roughly, and they recognize it. It's a direct communication. It makes perfect sense that you're making something that did not exist before. But it's also incredibly familiar because you've hit the mark. You've found a part of people that feels new. It has its own language, its own insults, its own ethos. And then, when you get to middle age, that doesn't work anymore and you've got to do other things. *The Graduate* was described endlessly as the epitome of its time. But its time didn't know that because when it was coming out, the guy who produced it made me go to campuses and show it because he felt we need to create a "market." And if I gave you the rest of the night to guess what the majority of college students said about it, you would never guess. They said, "Why isn't it about Vietnam?" Because that was the only way to get laid. To be able—to be very deeply concerned about where our country was. They wanted everything to be about that, because they hadn't yet understood that you can believe in a number of things at the same time.

Judd: Do you feel comedies don't get the respect they deserve?

Mike: That's funny you should say that. I think they get the respect they deserve. They're always more successful. People are happier with them, they live longer. What movie is enshrined like *Some Like It Hot*? No movie. To be good and funny is about as good as it gets. Who cares about Academy Awards? I mean, you used to get an Academy Award by being very sick and not dying. Maybe it could still work—who knows, try it. But I don't think any of that stuff matters. What matters is how much it connects with people.

MIRANDA JULY

(2013)

I sometimes worry that I am going through life using only a small portion of my brain. This worry is at its most intense when I spend time with people like the writer, director, and actress Miranda July, who has this way of coming at everything from a special, never-before-thought-of angle, a quality that fills me with jealousy and rage. Every thought she has is original—or at least, feels that way to me. I love her, but damn if she doesn't make me feel like I'm not seeing the world as clearly as I should.

A few years ago, she asked me to do an interview with her, and the only rule was that we were not allowed to ask each other anything related to show business. Admittedly, this is hard for me. But in the end, she brought something out of me that I don't think anyone else has. Attention all interviewers: Somewhere in here is a lesson about how to open someone up to new thoughts and ideas.

Judd Apatow: Okay, first question is: What was your scariest nightmare?

Miranda July: Like an actual asleep nightmare?

Judd: Yeah.

Miranda: Occasionally I write them down, which is probably why I remember it. I had taken this suicide pill that would kill me. Then after I took it, I strongly realized I didn't want to die—

Judd: Oh no!

This interview was originally published in Huck *magazine in May 2013.*

Miranda: But I had an antidote. I took it and was *so* relieved. Then a few minutes went by and I realized that the antidote was in my cheek and I hadn't actually swallowed it. You had to take it in a certain amount of time or it was useless so I knew, *Oh, it's too late! It was in my cheek!* And then I just felt myself fainting and was like, *I can't believe it—just this one little oversight.* And that was it. I died.

Judd: And then you woke up feeling refreshed?

Miranda: (*Laughs*) Or like, *Surely there's some way I can use that in my work.*

Judd: The one I always remember was really vivid—like it was actually happening. It's me on a plane, I'm the only one on it. It's going in and out of mountains and steep cliffs and it's clearly out of control. And I used to have nuclear war nightmares all the time as a kid. The sirens going off. I don't know why they stopped; maybe we're safer now?

Miranda: Yeah, or are we?

Judd: Actually it's worse now but for some reason I've tricked myself into thinking that's not an issue. Okay—your turn.

Miranda: What's one good thing and one difficult thing you feel like you got from your father?

Judd: Well, my dad was a big fan of comedy, and I think he thought he was funny. I can't confirm that his sense of humor *is* funny, but he carries himself as someone who's hilarious.

Miranda: Right. The idea that trying to be funny might be a "thing that one does."

Judd: His success rate is lower than he thinks. (*Laughs*) But he loved comedy and his interest in comedy sparked mine. A difficult thing I got from him was a general sense of nervousness, just not feeling comfortable in your own skin. I got that from my mom as well. They got divorced, but maybe that's why they found each other. (*Laughs*) That agitated way of thinking, *I need to stay on top of things to make it better in the future.* A lot of future thoughts. We weren't very "present" people. In my house there was a lot of "Next year will be my year!" My mom had a lot of fun energy when I was a kid. She was a really happy person, then after their divorce she became really unhappy, which threw me. During the divorce, they were more tuned in to their pain than they were to me. When your parents behave in ways that make you feel unsafe, you think, *Oh, I guess I'm in charge of myself.* And when you're fourteen, that's not a great thing. It kind of never goes away. As a producer, I'm always assuming things are going to crash and I'm trying to figure out what could go wrong before it happens. It's helpful for work. But it's a terrible way to live your life.

Miranda: I think I have some of that, too, for similar reasons. I guess that's a little bit of a director thing. I feel like it's in overdrive for me right now but it's like, *Oh, wow, this really has a purpose now that I'm a parent.* This idea of being on the lookout for calamity at all times.

Judd: (*Laughs*) As a parent, you become obsessed with anything dangerous that could happen. I remember once my mom, who's no longer with us, was babysitting my daughter and we saw her on a very busy street, and my mom was paying no attention to her whatsoever. We were like, "You're never watching our kids again." When you first have a kid and you have to make a will and you literally have to decide who gets your kids if something happens to you, that's when you realize how little you think of everyone in your world. That's a good way to get yourself to stay healthy. Put down the worst person you can think of to take care of your kids as motivation for staying alive. Okay, I have my next question. Do you have faith in humanity?

Miranda: My first instinct is to say yes and that I wouldn't be able to do what I do if I didn't. I'm counting on everyone to catch my heart, you know, to be able to understand in the deepest way that I can get it across, so in that way it's like I'm practicing that faith. But on the other hand, I was listening to the radio and it seemed that literally every day there would be a new gun violence thing. At the same time I was struggling with problematic friends and struggling with the part of myself that sometimes wants to just get rid of a friend. Like, I'm overwhelmed, I can't figure out how to deal with it, and I just think in my head, *That's it! Let's just not be* *friends and never talk to each other again!* I realized that I was feeling that same tendency about humanity. I was like, *It's too much of a mess—let's just end it now.* And then I told myself, *No, you're piling on the way you do with other things, and surely there's something that can be done—it's not all a waste.* Okay, next question for you. What are the top three things that make you feel guilty?

Judd: You've hit the mother lode! You live in a fantasyland where I can make it just three things. I am *built* for *guilt,* and if a person in my life doesn't try to guilt me to get their way, I will unconsciously train them to use guilt to manipulate me. Everything about how my family worked was based on guilt. From going to the mall with my elderly grandmother—if I had to run in and grab something, she would say, "It's okay, you can just leave me in the car." I remember as a kid my mom used to tell us who she liked best out of me and my brother and sister. We were just totally wired to please, and if we didn't please we'd feel terrible. It's a horrible thing.

Miranda: But what about right now? Top three things you feel guilty about right now.

Judd: I always feel guilty about whether or not I'm being a good enough husband and parent. I'm always guilty about not taking better care of myself. And I'm usually guilty about not being helpful enough to people in my extended family who need assistance. Because no matter what you do it's not enough. And people resent you the moment they ask for help, so it changes your relationship instantly. You have problems but then you become part of an ecosystem of their problems.

Miranda: Okay. In your experience, is it true that men are more visual and women are more mental in terms of what turns them on? I didn't make this up—this is, like, a thing. Men are more visual; just looking at a woman's body can turn them on. Whereas women, they'd rather think about sex to be turned on.

Judd: Oh, I've never thought about that before.

Miranda: Really? What do you think about? Or are you too busy being guilty?

Judd: Yeah, I'm too guilty to think about any of these issues. (*Laughs*) I'm trying to think of me. Am I visual or mental? Isn't everybody both? Well, the male figure is not pleasing. Like, the penis is weird and sloppy-looking. It's like something on the inside of your body is now on the outside and it should be on the inside. Most people don't look like David Beckham. So women need men to have a good personality because most of us don't look good.

Miranda: Even in the best of circumstances, if the man is David Beckham, Victoria is still not . . . it doesn't do anything for her. She has to pretend that she just met David for the first time, or that she's David's secretary, or . . .

Judd: Or that he's a Jewish comedy writer.

Miranda: (*Laughs*) Yeah, exactly.

Judd: She's probably bored. He has the abs. But it gets repetitive. There's only so much you can do with rock-hard abs, because there's not enough skin to work with. It's like making love to a piece of slate.

Miranda: So you don't really have anything to say about this? That's fine.

Judd: You've seen *The 40-Year-Old Virgin*, right? (*Laughs*) I'm not the guy to go to about this stuff. I'm usually just hiding in a corner, shaking. I look away when a pretty girl walks by—I feel like it's an invasion to stare at somebody. I let my eyes look up real fast and then hope that I retain some memory of it. My next question is: Who do you reach out to for guidance?

Miranda: Not too many people. I always have close women friends. There's my friend Sheila Heti, she's a writer. In fact, I sent her these questions and she just answered them all. (*Laughs*) And I have a really good therapist—which is the first time I've ever had a therapist I admire. . . .

Judd: Admire? I need her phone number. I just always think, *Oh my gosh, they look so bored. I can't believe I'm not getting better and I'm just boring them to tears.*

Miranda: Yeah, I do a certain amount of saying, "Well, this is boring," or "Here's something insignificant I want to talk about." I usually try and preface it with some sort of diminishing thing.

Judd: Do you cry during therapy?

Miranda: Not as much as I did with the old, bad therapists. I feel like I'm just a better person with this new one so I don't need to cry as much.

Judd: I don't like to cry, because then every session when I *don't* cry, he thinks, *Oh, he's not actually opening up.* Once I've showed them that's there, then it's like I'm always hiding it.

Miranda: With this therapist, the first session I ever had with her was really terrible. I was really angry with her but I forced myself to go back and tell her how she'd fucked up. It was an amazing way to start because it got to the important stuff right away and how she dealt with that was, like, really smart. I don't think in the past I would have been willing to come back. I would have quit.

Judd: I just disappear. Then I feel guilty for years that I didn't tell the doctor why I stopped coming and I assume that they're haunted by it. But they're not haunted by it.

Miranda: The therapist I left this therapist for, I've still never told her. I figure she just thinks I'm busy with the baby.

Judd: Just send a card: "Doing great! Don't need any mental health support—thank you for fixing me!"

Miranda: I really want the old therapist to know how much better this new one is.

Judd: Send them another note: "Why did you waste seven years of my life?" Okay, next question: Do you have any food issues?

Miranda: I've never had, like, "I'm going to get fat" food issues—which I have to say I credit my mom for. She just never picked up on the fact that she was supposed to worry about those things and was always like, "Let's go get a doughnut!" in a really benign way. But I love different kinds of restrictive diets. If I'm meeting a new person, and hear that they're on some kind of new restrictive diet, I want to hear all about it and possibly get on it myself. I like different forms of self-discipline. Like, I had no reason to be gluten-free, but then someone said, "Oh, you know it's not great for your breast milk." I was like, "Great! I'll go off gluten!"

Judd: We went to an allergist and it turns out our kids have no allergies to gluten. But our house is totally gluten-free. Every time we go to the supermarket my child is desperately sneaking a loaf of white bread into our cart like it's Oreos! I couldn't have more food issues. For me food is such a reward. It's all about fun. For me to think of food as fuel is extremely difficult. Food is happiness. I like being stuffed. I like being so stuffed I can't get up. Like when you're in that haze of exhaustion.

Miranda: Haze—like a drug.

Judd: How has having a child changed the way you think about your pre-child life? How has it changed you?

Miranda: I'm kind of amazed to see that the massive amount of time I spent thinking about my feelings turned out not to be vital to my existence. In fact, having less time to think and having to simply *do* is just fine. For my whole life before, I thought I needed the maximum amount of freedom, but as it turns out what I really need is to feel free for a limited amount of time and then crawl around the floor saying "I'mgonnagetcha, I'mgonnagetcha" while a very, very cute little boy squeals with glee. Before it was easy to feel alienated from most people; now I feel like I have something sizable in common with nearly every single person in the grocery store. Also, my son had a really rough start so I went through a level of trauma and fear that forever changed my relationship to catastrophe. It's more real now, so I'm more afraid of it. I suppose I'm braver, too.

Judd: I was forced to realize how self-centered I was. I found it hard to shut my brain down so I could just hang out in my kids' reality. It's easier now because my kids' realities are more like my own. We can talk about *Breaking Bad* episodes and why we think it is a bad idea to take Ecstasy. How would you like to spend your old age?

Miranda: I'd like it to be just like now—writing and surrounded by people I love—except I want there to be zero anxiety. I want to feel like I'm sitting in a Jacuzzi all the time.

Judd: I want to be like Mel Brooks. A great memory, a lot of energy, still making people laugh. I do not want to be like Jack LaLanne, pulling fifty boats as I swim across a lake. Do you have a conception of the afterlife? Are you a spiritual person?

Miranda: You know, it's funny. I just wrote that I *was* spiritual and then sat here for about ten minutes trying to put words to that feeling. Everything I came up with seemed made up or like some idea I'd had when I was fifteen. It all felt distasteful to me so I erased it. I think I'm less entranced by amorphous things at this moment.

Judd: I have some friends who had near-death experiences who felt a presence tell them to go back. It was not their time. That is all I can hold on to. When I am creative I think something more is going on, so maybe it does not end. I don't think I am going to get ninety virgins or hang out in a beautiful kingdom. My biggest fear is that I will become a ghost and be forced to hang out in some house watching a bunch of jackasses live their lives. I don't want to be a tree. I know that is supposed to be a beautiful thing, to become a tree or a beetle. I am not into that. I would like to stay me.

Miranda: What are the top three times you've been most freaked out in your life so far?

Judd: One, when I was in sixth grade my friend's brother grew pot in his room. One day my friend got his hands on a joint and we attempted to smoke it in the middle of the night at a construction site. Before we took a real puff a security guard pointed a flashlight in our direction and we ran for miles and miles and miles as if he was hot on our tail. There is no chance he took even one step in our direction. We stared out the window at my friend's house for a half hour, terrified that he would knock on the door and tell our parents. The next year I was so scared that my friends were going to become potheads that I switched social groups. My new friends eventually became the real potheads of the school, and after two years I ran back to my old friends, who never bothered to try it again. Two, when the Northridge earthquake happened it really felt like nuclear missiles were falling from the sky. The noise and the shattering of glass freaked me out. My girlfriend at the time seemed to have a bit of a mental break. Afterwards I wanted to go back to sleep. She wanted to look around so we went outside and every time we passed a cracked section of sidewalk she laughed nervously in the way bad actors pretend to be crazy people on the TV show *Quincy*. We broke up soon after when she cheated on me with a sportswriter. A year later I tried to win her back but she refused my advances because she was dating a pot dealer. Three, I got freaked out when George Bush beat Al Gore for the presidency because he was so terrible in the debates and I assumed everyone in the country saw what I saw, a man who clearly was not equipped to lead our country.

Miranda: One, aforementioned birth of baby. Two, that girlfriend you had who had a mental break during the earthquake? That might have been me. I was in bed and the next thing I know I'm on all fours growling in the corner. I was so scared I turned into a dog for a moment. Three, various flights with extreme turbulence. I grab the stewardesses, the people next to me—I pretty much do the dog/earthquake thing but without going down on all fours because the floor's gross. Last question: Can you try to give a little running narration of what it's like in your head, how the thoughts come and go? Are there fully formed words and sentences? Is it incessant and talky? Do you compose emails in your head? Or are you more in the moment than that?

Judd: My mind is a noisy place. I tend to look for problems so I can solve them before they blow up in my face. I am like a lookout for disaster. I also have a voice that tells me to calm down. I have a TM mantra and every once in a while I try to breathe and think about some piece of advice I have heard or read, usually from the book *The Power of Now* by Eckhart Tolle. Then I will think about my mantra. About one second later I am worried that I will never have a good idea again, or that I have wronged someone in my life and I try to figure out what to do. Sometimes I am really hungry. Other times I am moved by a piece of music or a deeply felt thought and I cry. Laughter has happened, too, but less often. My great love for people and my family is pushed up close to terror and my existential crisis. Occasionally I think of a great dick joke, like when Steve Carell tries to pee with an erection, and I get very proud of myself and feel like I am adding something very positive to the world. I can almost feel people forgetting their troubles and laughing, and for a moment I feel like there is a God or a higher purpose and I am truly happy. God gave me that dick joke. It all makes sense. Then I get scared again and it all starts over. You?

Miranda: Many words and fully formed sentences. Whole emails written out in my head. Lots of planning thoughts—like every single moment planning what I'm going to do in the next moment, the next hour, the next day, week, year. I have the next ten years planned, work-wise. I also think a lot about washing the dishes or vacuuming. The more boring the task, the more of my mental space I have to devote to it. I also instruct myself a lot, like: "Robot, go brush your teeth." I lay in bed and think about what I'll bring in my carry-on bag on a trip I'm going on in five months. Sometimes I instruct myself to "free fall"—exist without thinking. It feels like falling through space. I can also get super-duper focused, wormhole-style. That's the space that I go into when I'm working—about five hours a day. It goes by in a flash.

ROSEANNE BARR
(2014)

Back in the late eighties, a friend of mine—fellow comedian and *Undeclared* writer Joel Madison—told me about this guy he knew named Tom Arnold, who was moving to L.A. to write jokes for Roseanne Barr. Before we knew it, we were hearing that Tom was going to marry Roseanne, which seemed insane and impossible. It *was* insane and impossible, of course, but it happened, and Tom Arnold went on to become one of the producers of her television show as well. My secret hope was that, through my connection with Joel, I might somehow get the call to go write for *Roseanne*, one of the biggest shows on TV. As it turned out, the call I eventually got was to write jokes for Tom's act, which went well and soon led to a gig writing for Roseanne's nightclub act.

For the next several years, I spent a lot of time with Roseanne trying to craft a standup act that wasn't just about raising her family and growing up poor, but about what it was like to now be rich and mega-famous. It always felt odd to me, as a twenty-two-year-old guy without a ton of life experience, to be writing jokes for an ass-kicking middle-aged woman who happened to have multiple personalities. I used to force her to sit with me and tell me her life story, so I could try to get in her head. The depth of her experience and imagination was astonishing.

This was all happening at the absolute height of Roseanne mania, with the national anthem scandal, and the very public divorce from Tom Arnold, and the number-one show on television, year after year after year. Many people only remember the drama that surrounded her at that time, but I believe that *Roseanne* was one of the most influential shows ever on television. Because it reflected the real lives of working-class people and their daily dramas. Because it managed to be riotously funny while also exploring the deep truths about how people were living in America at the time, and still are today. It took an enormous amount of courage and madness to make that happen.

Judd Apatow: How much stand-up are you doing now?

Roseanne Barr: None.

Judd: None?

Roseanne: I'm writing jokes. I write about fifty jokes a day for nothing.

Judd: Do you get onstage at all?

Roseanne: No. I have horrible stage fright—you know, how you go through the bipolar stage fright thing? Then you go on drugs to get over the stage fright and perform but then you're not funny at all.

Judd: Were you always scared when you did stand-up, to the point where you felt like you needed to be medicated?

Roseanne: No, it was only after *The Roseanne Show* that it felt like that. I'd go on and I'd want to do edgy material and the audience would be like, "Where's Dan?" I was like, *Where's a gun so I can blow my fucking brains out all over this stage?*

Judd: Is that the worst part of success—that it defines who you are and what you do? If you succeed in one area, people think you should stay in that area.

Roseanne: They don't even know who I am. They think I'm Roseanne Conner. It's like, "You're not a writer. You're not even a comedian. You're Roseanne." And then I was like, *This is freaky because I can't get another job ever.* And I wanted to work.

Judd: It's like Archie Bunker going on tour as a stand-up.

Roseanne: I'm going to do whatever it takes and I'm not going to let them—I'm not going to let this not make me funny—so I suffered the indignities. I see other comics going through the same shit. Once you make it, it's, like, well, you're not like hungry or whatever. What the fuck am I supposed to talk about now? My maid?

Judd: I think about that, too. Did I have a different point of view when I was broke? I don't think I did. I mean, obviously a lot has happened but I don't know if my point of view about things changed.

Roseanne: Define *broke*.

Judd: Well, I shared an apartment with Adam Sandler and the rent was four hundred and twenty-five dollars a month and I was just trying to make enough money to eat and go to the Improv.

Roseanne: How old were you then?

Judd: Twenty-two, twenty-three.

Roseanne: What did you guys do to make each other laugh—or were you just depressed all the time?

Judd: It was very different because Sandler—it was clear that he was going to be a big star from the second you met him. It was fun because he had the charisma of a worldwide comedy star but he had no outlet for it, so his outlet would just be hanging out with you at Red Lobster. He had all that power and energy, and he would try to be that funny with you all day long because he had no one else to do it with.

Roseanne: Oh, shit. That's what's worth it all. That's what I miss: There are no comics to hang with and make each other laugh. I miss that a lot.

Judd: I went to the Comedy Cellar in New York recently. You go there and there's this group of people working hard, making each other laugh, hanging out all night long and—you know, when you have kids and a life, it becomes hard to say, "Honey, I'm going to go hang out at a club for a few hours. . . ."

Roseanne: That's why you need to have a screening room. That's what I used to do, but then I couldn't do it anymore because I had to homeschool my kid. So I had no life.

Judd: How did that work, homeschooling?

Roseanne: Argh.

Judd: Leslie and I always talk about that. Wouldn't it just be easier? School ruins everything. You're stuck in their schedule. The schedule doesn't make sense because the kids have to get up too early. They're too tired. They have too much homework. They have no life. Was homeschooling better?

Roseanne: It was a fucking ball. I'd be like, "We're going to Paris and we're going to go to the Louvre to study art," you know. We did awesome shit like that.

Judd: But it's a full-time job.

Roseanne: Yeah. But I had two tutors because I can't fucking read. I'm blind.

Judd: How old is your youngest?

Roseanne: He's eighteen and he graduates, please Lord, in three weeks.

Judd: And he's homeschooled?

Roseanne: No, he was. He went back to school in eighth grade because he got over the hyperactive stuff. He was so hyper, they wanted to put him on drugs.

Judd: He just pulled out of it? Some kids get over it.

Roseanne: The thing is, they've got so much focus it's like they're *not* focused. I have it, too. I'm so focused but I have my choice of a thousand things that I'm interested in—you know, too many options. I try to do too many things at once.

Judd: And then you melt down and get nothing done. It's just that your brain is trying so hard getting so much done and then you realize you're not getting anything done. I actually was diagnosed a few years ago with obsessive-compulsive thinking. That's probably from childhood trauma— from being hypervigilant. But I think it makes you a good producer and performer and writer. The thing that ruined your life makes you good at your work. And then you get rewarded at work, so you don't bother to fix it in your life.

Roseanne: That's exactly right.

Judd: So what did you do about that?

Roseanne: Things happened to me that—you know, I got pregnant with my son and I had to have a fifth baby. But let's talk about the obsessive-compulsive thing for a minute. I was told when I was a girl that every Jewish woman has to have five children to replace three-fifths of our people that were killed. That's how I was raised.

Judd: Wow.

Roseanne: In an apartment building with survivors from concentration camps. So I had trauma because I couldn't even talk.

Judd: Parents don't realize that when they teach you about the Holocaust too early, it ruins you for life.

Roseanne: It ruined me for life. I remember the exact moment well—I was like three and they had the TV on and they were of course enjoying the Eichmann trial. When they weren't talking about Eichmann, they were talking about babies on meat hooks. They used to say it in front of me. I was so horrified by the world but I looked at the TV and it showed the piles of bodies, and I was like, *I don't want to be on this fucking planet. This ain't for me. Fuck it.* And I went in the bathroom, in my grandma's house. There was this black button on the door, and I turned it. I had to stretch real hard to turn that lock. So then they were all like, "She's locked herself in the bathroom," and then it was like all this screaming. I was never—the only time they talked to me was to tell me that the Nazis used to shoot little girls right through the head in front of their parents. That's how they talked to me. Other than that, it was like, "Pick that up." They were all traumatized. Everyone was traumatized.

Judd: I didn't go to Hebrew school. My parents went the other way—everyone in the family became atheist. No one was religious. That was their way of dealing with the Holocaust.

Roseanne: God is dead, that's what they said.

Judd: But I remember I went to Hebrew school once with a friend, just visiting. And they showed the Kristallnacht documentary and it definitely messes with you. That, and a fear of Russia.

Roseanne: Yeah, no shit—the Russians. I remember having dreams of black airplanes hovering over the house, and it was Russia. Russia was coming in black airplanes and they were going to kill us all. In school, we had to practice getting under the desk for air raids and shit like that. It was drilled in — that fear, was always there.

Judd: The next holocaust, the nuclear holocaust. I used to have nightmares all the time about it. I don't know the first comedy that you were interested in, but I didn't understand how I was processing any of that. I just knew that I liked the comedy figures who told everybody to fuck off. So I loved George Carlin and the Marx Brothers. I loved that the Marx Brothers were saying that all of the rich people and the leaders were idiots. I was obsessed with them. I bought every book. I was looking for somebody to say, "Isn't the world crazy? This all makes no sense."

Roseanne: I loved the Stooges. I thought they were gods. And I still do. It was fucking godly. Because it was like, you know, one's making fun of Einstein, one's making fun of Hitler. They're making fun of the politics of the world. They were fucking deep thinkers, and their subject matter was deep, too.

Judd: It's a survival mechanism, when you're a kid, to like that stuff. When did that interest turn into being funny for you?

Roseanne: My dad was a big fan of comedy. He wanted to be a stand-up, so he made me that way. My dad loved Lenny. He also loved Lord Buckley and jazz and stuff. He was a hipster. My parents were kind of beatnicky, you know, for Salt Lake City.

Judd: Did people in Salt Lake know you were Jewish?

Roseanne: They knew. I mean we never lied about it but it's a real weird place. Like, when I was three, I fell and I got Bell's palsy in my face. My mom said the first day she called the rabbi and they said a prayer for me but nothing happened. The second day she called the Mormons and they said a prayer for me and my face was healed, so my whole life was going around as a Jew who was giving talks in Mormon churches about being healed by the Mormons. That was my life.

Judd: It's interesting that when you get older and you've raised kids and you've had your life, you look back at things that your parents did and you think, *It was just so crazy — a whole other level of crazy.* When my parents got divorced, my dad would never talk to me about how I was feeling. And that affects your whole life.

Roseanne: I think parents don't know what to say and, like, Jews—it's better to say nothing so that the kid comes and parents you.

Judd: That's exactly it.

Roseanne: I think we know—as Jewish parents, or maybe it's all parents, ethnic parents—that our kids are frigging way smarter than we are.

Judd: And they're supposed to make *us* happy. And that makes kids insane.

Roseanne: Kind of.

Judd: That's what makes you a comedian. I'm a big self-help freak and I read all those books and they're always about mirroring, that when you're with your kids, they're supposed to see themselves. They're not supposed to see your need. If they see your neediness then they just try to please you and they lose the sense of who they are because they're trying to please you. And that's what seems to create a comedian, too: How do I make other people happy?

Roseanne: Yeah, a people pleaser kind of thing. But my humor, I think, came from wanting to disarm people before they hit me. My family were hitters. And if you made them laugh, they didn't hit you. My dad wouldn't hit me if I got him with humor right between the eyes.

Judd: What age were you when he would hit you?

Roseanne: Always.

Judd: Even into like high school?

Roseanne: Oh, yeah. He'd walk over and smack me upside the head for whatever. I used to bite my nails a lot—I learned it from my dad, who bit his nails to where there was no fucking nail at all and he couldn't bend his fingers and he's like this all the time, just like anxiety, you know. And so I'd sit there biting my nails and he'd look at me and he'd go, "Stop fucking biting your fucking fingernails."

Judd: Because he loves you.

Roseanne: I'd be like, "Well, you're biting yours." And then he'd laugh. But sometimes he wouldn't. You never knew when it was coming. He'd sneak up behind you while you're biting your nail and crack you in the back of the head so hard that your knuckles would go straight up your nose and stuff. He hit me in the head constantly. He'd hit us all in the head. And hard, too.

Judd: We can't get our kids to do anything.

Roseanne: Maybe because we don't hit them.

Judd: Did you go to therapy and try to fix yourself, to learn how to not do it to your kids?

Roseanne: Yeah, but by then I had already done it.

Judd: To your first few kids?

Roseanne: Yeah. So then I'd correct it. You go to each one of them and let them curse you out and say all the shit that they want to say to you. And just go, "Oh, honey, I did it and I'm sorry." That's hard.

Judd: And how do they do after that?

Roseanne: Thank God, they are all functional and brilliant, creative people.

Judd: Well, almost no parents do that. Own up to their mistakes.

Roseanne: It's the hardest thing.

Judd: My mom could never do that. Well, right before she died, very briefly she said she was sorry for anything she might have done wrong. But for the most part—I once begged my mother to go to therapy and then sent her to my therapist. When she came back, I said, "How did it go?" And she said, "He told me that I'm right about everything."

Roseanne: That's a good one.

Judd: We have to have those conversations sometimes with our kids, where we say, you know, "We're not perfect people. We make mistakes and we have issues." And we try to explain what they are as they're happening. Like, "This is my issue and maybe that's why I did that. Sorry."

Roseanne: Well, I took all the shit off my kids because I knew they needed to say it. I was lucky enough to be able to say it to my parents, too, and do some healing.

Judd: And it somehow got you here. That's the hard thing, too, which is: If your childhood didn't happen, nothing else would have happened.

Roseanne: I don't know about that. My shrink says, "Don't say you're funny *because* of abuse; it's in *spite* of." But my whole thing is, like, I've had severe mental illness my whole life. A devastating, dissociative identity disorder—MPD, it used to be called. I had to heal from that, and that was like fifteen years of intense daily therapy. I look back and it's fucking crazy. It's nothing you can explain to people. You can't explain to people waking up in a mental institution in Dallas, Texas, with a shrink screaming in your face, "You don't have a penis!" I mean, it's like, how are you going to—

Judd: Were you high school age?

Roseanne: No, I was in my forties. It's real deep mental illness shit, man. But I got over it. Not over it, but I live with it.

Judd: Where do you think it comes from?

Roseanne: I think both of my parents and my grandparents were divided people, too. I mean, who's going to live through the Holocaust and not be fucked up? I can't blame my parents. I had a good teacher, too. I had a good rabbi. He's on the other side now, too, but he helped me put it in perspective and that was all while I was doing pretty deep therapy and I just put it all back together, all those fragments which I kind of remade the world in my mind so that it made sense. It's like, you know, this is hell.

Judd: What is hell?

Roseanne: This planet.

Judd: Can you experience reality with MPD? Do you still experience reality where you feel like different sides of your personality are handling different situations?

Roseanne: Less than in the past. I used to never sleep more than three hours a night because I always was—you know, the whole comic thing was a big thing in my head. The comic, the writer who did stand-up. That was a separate state and I'd just get into it and, fuck, I don't want to know anything else. I'd neglect my health and my life. Once it started, there was no fucking way out. It was too much. Your head's like—you have no balance at all.

Judd: Because getting successful and being a performer, it feels like safety, but it's a safety that you can't maintain because you're abandoning everything else to achieve it.

Roseanne: You can't ever be how you are. It's like, Oh you've got to do these interviews, you have to go talk to the press and stuff—which is a scary thing.

Judd: They want to set you off.

Roseanne: They do, because they're just evil.

Judd: And you *will* go off if you have things to say.

Roseanne: Yeah, and that took me a while. That's what I wanted to do. Plus I have Tourette's.

Judd: How does that show itself?

Roseanne: I have to be the one who barks out what I had conceived as the thing that must be heard. And sometimes I didn't even fucking believe it, but, you know, in my head it was the perfect state of freedom. I have to say it. Because I have all that Jew Holocaust shit, you know. I mean when I used to play Barbies with my Mormon neighbor friend, it was always, "Oh, we're going to go on a date. Ken's taking us out and we're going with Ken on a date." And I was like, "We're parachuting behind enemy lines to save the Jews." That's how I played Barbies. It was just otherly.

Judd: Were you doing stand-up before you were married?

Roseanne: No, I had three kids when I first started stand-up.

Judd: Who did you see doing stand-up who made you think, *I have to find the courage to get up and do this*?

Roseanne: When I was little, my dad and I would watch *Ed Sullivan* together. I saw all those comics on *Ed Sullivan*. I saw Myron Cohen. My grandmother loved him.

Judd: Alan King.

Roseanne: Alan King, oh my God. And Jackie Mason, Jack E. Leonard, and Leonard Barr—my dad said maybe we're related to him. And then I saw Richard Pryor and that was it.

Judd: So you're a housewife and it's floating around the back of your head somewhere that it would be great to do this?

Roseanne: I always knew since I was three. When I was little, that was one thing that I was told in a vision: I was going to have my own show when I grew up. And it's going to be funny and it's going to be like Danny Kaye, who was another one of my idols.

Judd: So you always had a vision—

Roseanne: I was always into TV. I knew I could get in the business somehow and find a place. I don't think I thought of what I could accomplish in the larger sense of it.

Judd: So in your head you knew it was going to happen and then you're having kids. At some point, you have to make the move to do it. What was the trigger?

Roseanne: I was a cocktail waitress and this guy—I got tips because I made them laugh, plus you had to have half your ass hanging out. I made them laugh so they'd give me big tips and this one guy one time, he said, "Hey, you're so funny you should go down to this comedy club downtown." And I was like *BONG, BONG, BONG, BONG.* It was literally like that. And so I'm like, "Okay, where is it?" And he's like, "It's the Comedy Works in Larimer Square in Denver." So I go down there and I watch all the comics. And I went home to write my five minutes of material—and then I just kept perfecting it. That took a fucking year.

Judd: That's incredible.

Roseanne: It was almost a year and then I went down there and did my five minutes. I look back on it now and I'm like, it was pretty ballsy that I said the things I said. They immediately banned me and said don't ever come back here.

Judd: Do you remember what was in the five minutes?

Roseanne: I made fun of male comics. I was very political.

Judd: Did you talk about being a housewife also?

Roseanne: No, it was radical, feminist politics.

Judd: Did you get any laughs?

Roseanne: The first time, I got killer laughs. And people came up, and they were nice to me. So I couldn't wait to go back the second time, and then I got way over-cocky. And I ate it like a dog's death. The indignities.

Judd: What did your husband say when you told him you were going to be a stand-up?

Roseanne: He wanted to be one, too. He helped me write. We'd sit down and we'd write jokes—my sister, too. I'd be sitting in a restaurant with her, and—when I was little my mom used to read this book *Fascinating Womanhood.* There was a character who would tell you how to get your husband to buy you a blender and shit. And it disgusted me that my mom and her friends were like that, so that's kind of why I became a feminist. But my act was called "How to Be a Domestic Goddess," and me and my sister were eating eggs one day and I was like, *Fuck*—it just came in my head, one of those things that didn't have nothing to do with me. It's like: domestic goddess. And I went, *Oh fuck, that's my door.* I just tailored it for a while and, you know, they let me on. They liked that act. Because I finally found my voice. I went to every kind of club to work it, too. I had to go to like the Episcopalian church and jazz clubs and punk clubs and biker bars. I remember performing on a punk stage with no mic in the middle of a mosh pit.

Judd: How many years of this before you moved to L.A.?

Roseanne: Five.

Judd: It is interesting, if you watch the arcs of so many comedians. At some point, they just become themselves.

Roseanne: That's exactly it.

Judd: And something amazing happens. Like everyone's looking for their angle, looking for their angle, and then they just—they become powerful.

Roseanne: You synthesize it all. You integrate it—like okay, this part of me wants to say this. This part of me is interested in that. I don't want to be ordinary. I'm willing to do the work. I'm willing to suffer the indignities of comedy. Because I want to be great. I don't want to just be good. I want to be great.

Judd: So how long was it, between moving to L.A. and getting *The Tonight Show*? It was pretty fast, right?

Roseanne: It was a dream. All these comics were coming to Denver headlining, and I'd open for them. There was a Denver "Laugh Off" thing and it was me and fifteen guys—and I won. Everyone was like, wow. That was a big accomplishment. It was an accomplishment that all the guys were rooting for me, too. That was fucking mind-blowing after all the shit I had to do. I forgot what you asked me.

Judd: How long until you got on *The Tonight Show*?

Roseanne: Oh, so everybody goes, "You need to let Mitzi see you at the Comedy Store." And so, you know, I planned it with my husband, the whole thing. I went there on a Monday night. It was like a fucking dream. Came off the stage after my first five minutes and Mitzi was like, "Go do twenty in the big room."

Judd: Immediately?

Roseanne: All the waitresses told me she had never done that before. So I went in the big room—this is all happening in one night—and I come offstage, and there's George Schlatter. And he's like, "I'm producing a show"—it was *Funny Women of Comedy* or *Funny Gals* or some shit—"and it's for NBC and I want you on it." And I'm like, "Fuck, I don't even live here, but yeah, I'll come back." So I came back in a month to rehearse for that and a guy comes up to me and he says, "I'm Jim McCawley from *The Tonight Show*, and I want to put you on Friday night."

Judd: You didn't even know he was in the crowd?

Roseanne: No. You know, with my gruff thing, I was like, "Get in line." And he's like, "No, no, I'm Jim McCawley, and I want you on."

Judd: How did your husband handle your success?

Roseanne: I was really a housewife. And then suddenly, I'm like eighteen weeks on the road without my kids and my husband—he didn't know what to do. He slept in a lot of mornings and they missed school. You know, he's a guy. I came home after like six weeks—

Judd: He was working at a post office, right?

Roseanne: No, he had quit. He quit after I started to tour. So I went and got the kids. They lived with me in a one-room apartment on Laurel Canyon Boulevard. I'd bring them to the Comedy Store and they'd just have to sit up there. It was hard.

Judd: How old were they at the time?

Roseanne: They were all under twelve.

Judd: So the two older ones kind of know what's happening?

Roseanne: Yeah, it affected them. I wasn't there to crack down on them as much. So they went wild. We all fucking went wild. You know, it's just so consuming, it's eighteen hours a day, and you turn to your husband or your sisters or family to help you but nobody can do it as well as the mom. So it's just suffering guilt every fucking minute until you've got to do drugs to handle the disappointment that you're causing your kids.

Judd: It's the aspect of show business that most people don't think about— the circus aspect of it. Whenever I see some famous person get married to another famous person, my first thought is, *How can that work?*

Roseanne: I know exactly how it works. You just talk on the phone and they're living in a world that doesn't exist like you do. I just always tried to stay in as much as I possibly could. It was really hard because, you know— you don't want to work, but you don't know when you're going to get your next job.

Judd: It could all end tomorrow.

Roseanne: And everybody's like, "You're fucking rich," but they don't get it. They don't get that you have to fucking *do* it. It's not about if you're rich or not. Because it's what you love. You have to do it because that's the only thing you know how to do.

Judd: And it keeps you sane, but it also creates all—

Roseanne: All the problems. But then it's so worth it when you're getting those laughs. It's like, *This is what I do, what I love. It's the whole fucking reason I'm alive.*

Judd: Was it possible to have balance when you were doing the TV show?

Roseanne: No.

Judd: So when you were working, you were so split off—you focused on the work so intensely that you couldn't be present in the other parts of your life?

Roseanne: Correct.

Judd: It's funny because I used to scream at everybody at the beginning of my career. I'd get really emotional. I'd project all my issues about my parents and safety onto the executives so every conversation where they gave a note was life or death and they tried to destroy me. *You don't love me. You don't get me.* And so it was really hard. It took me a very, a very long time to understand that I need to find people that understand, who like what I do, who get what I do. I need to find people who I respect so I can respect them, and they'll like being respected so they'll respect me and that's like a marriage. But early in my career, you'd get bad notes from someone who didn't appreciate what you were doing, and you would resist them. I would fight and we would always get canceled. But you had a different situation because your show was so successful that that battle of wills never ended—or was it resolved in some way?

Roseanne: Once the show was number one, it was like, "Don't ever come down here again, motherfuckers. Don't fucking come down here." I felt shut down when they'd come and stand there. I'd be like, "Nobody with a suit is allowed on this stage." They're just judging and you feel the weight of them. They're looking for a flaw. They're waiting to hurt you.

Judd: How much of that, in retrospect, was bad management or treating talent like a piece of meat or a commodity?

Roseanne: It was treating talent with contempt—and it wasn't just me. It was just the way it was then. I'm glad to see people are taking more control of their product these days, but back then it was like, whoa, they just, they didn't respect talent. They had to humiliate and belittle people who had talent.

Judd: That's how they controlled things.

Roseanne: It's a pimp mentality.

Judd: How did you take control of your show?

Roseanne: I'd be standing there during the filming, crying. I got a woman manager after every fucking guy would say the same shit: "Shut up and take it, you're getting paid." So I got, like, Diane Keaton's manager, and she was very well connected with Freddie Field and people like that, so she had power. And she was like, "Your star is in tears on this comedy. Do you even notice that *at all*?" She hooked me up with the lawyer Barry Hirsch. And I told him, "I've got to get off. I'm going to die. I've got to quit." There was one big day on set where I was sitting on the bed and the director and the producer were like, "Say the line as written." And I was like, "I'm not going to say the line as written," because Barry Hirsch had told me you can say, "I'd like a new line, please." It's a Guild thing. They were like, "You're not going to get it." But then their lawyers would tell them, "You can't force somebody to say a line." So Barry gave me the language to say, "I'd like a line change, please." And it ended up they made me do it for six hours, and then they came back with some legal shit on the loudspeaker with the cameras on. And then that shit gets back to the network and they're like, "Look what a pain in the ass she is. She needs to go." So they asked all the cast if they'd do the show without me, and John Goodman said no. If he had said yes like a lot of other fucking people in show business, I would have been off there in a heartbeat. And I was like, *Fuck that. I made it for this? All this way to have my fucking act stolen and be beaten down and disrespected?*

Judd: And then it aired and the ratings were—

Roseanne: Number one. It premiered at number three, and then it took *Cosby*. I think it was because I had done *The Tonight Show* and I had done so well there and people wanted to see it. It went to three first and then it took *Cosby* and then that was it.

Judd: Then you had the moment where you're like, "Okay, now here's how we're going to do it."

Roseanne: It was that voice that I always have with me. I said, "Either he goes . . . ," and they knew. So they go, "Well, he'll go, but he's not going until [episode] thirteen." So that was seven more or something. And I'm like, *Oh, how am I going to fucking make it through that?* And it was tough, but that voice came in and it's like, *Make a list of everybody who you're going to fire the minute that you're at fourteen.* So I did. I hung it on my door. I still have it. I said, "These people will not be here next year," and it was big so whoever walked by would see it. And they were all gone the next year, including the network president. So it was sheer will and hate and bitterness. And because it was about my kids, and I looked at it like a mom looks at it, you know. It was a fight. My husband at the time told me, "Shut up and take it. You're never going to get this chance again. Shut your fucking mouth and just do it." And I'm like, the only other person I knew then were comics and Tom Arnold, you know. And Tom was like, "Fuck them." I wanted to hear that. So I ended up getting with him and everything. I unleashed him.

Judd: How do you look back at that time—because, creatively, those first Tom years were really strong.

Roseanne: I think we had three really good years before that, too.

Judd: He came on at the end of season four?

Roseanne: The end of season three. And everyone hated him so he didn't— it was like season four that we got the comics on instead of TV writers. I always wanted that. I loved funny people over story people. It was about the jokes and I like jokes. Jokes were the only reason we were ever on that long.

Judd: How many good Tom years were there?

Roseanne: Zero good years.

Judd: Was it just batshit crazy the whole time?

Roseanne: A living hell. Unfuckingbelievable living hell. Like I didn't have enough troubles? Now I've got a drug addict running around my fucking house? You know, then I'm getting a divorce and kids are in my house. Just not fucking good at all. But at work, it was fun. Because it was like, I want this, let's try this, let's try that. It was like, Let's fucking take this down. I want gays on the air. I wanted a teenage girl who was negative like I was.

Judd: What are the parts of the show that you look back at with the most pride?

Roseanne: From the first battle, it seemed like—I felt like Wonder Woman battling back the Nazis or whatever, it was kind of like that. It was Halloween and they wouldn't let me do a show on Halloween. Because they said the Bible Belt doesn't like Halloween; they think it's witches and shit. So I'm like, "Well, then I'm a witch. And I want Halloween." I just, I couldn't stand people saying what the fuck I could do. The next thing was an unemployed husband. They didn't like that, either. They didn't like smart-mouthed Darlene. They didn't like Darlene. And you know, so Darlene was a big one for me because I'm Darlene. I was Darlene! That's who I was, you know.

Judd: Did you feel like it was an honest depiction of working-class America?

Roseanne: I liked that it was like, This shit sucks. That was real to me. And also, I wanted to show a different kind of love that wasn't that phony bullshit love. It was love through bad things. I was on a fucking mission for sure. I felt like the Messiah and Wonder Woman all rolled up into one. I felt like Robin Hood. I felt like Jesus. Plus, I had a killer cast that could make anything. I had great writers. Christ, I'll never get that again. It was like the real golden age, another golden age of television. Today they want no part of anything having to do with class on TV. No part.

Judd: Why do you think that is?

Roseanne: Because it's too true.

Judd: I think the paradox of being a comedian is you become a comedian because, on some level, you're so insecure that you need people's approval. And then you put yourself in a position where you can get an enormous amount of *dis*approval but it's worth the risk because—

Roseanne: The damn indignity.

Judd: I'm going to risk making a movie and maybe the world will tell me they hate me. Like, I want some love but I might get some hate. And there are certain people who are like totally fine with that. But there's craziness in it, too.

Roseanne: Well, I think you've got to get like that.

Judd: Is that healthy or is it also detached in some way?

Roseanne: All of it is just too hard. But when you're doing it—I remember I asked my rabbi that once. I said, "Does this shit ever stop? You know, the crazy?" And he said, "It stops when you're doing it." And I thought, *Well, Christ, isn't that right?*

SANDRA BERNHARD
(1983)

Martin Scorsese's *The King of Comedy* came out when I was fifteen, in early 1983, and it quickly became a formative movie of my childhood—and my adulthood, too, for that matter. As a kid, I was so fascinated by the stories about the making of it, especially the ones about how this young unknown woman, Sandra Bernhard, had improvised the majority of her part and, in doing so, put the great Jerry Lewis in many situations and moments that he had not been in before. That blew my mind. I interviewed Sandra not long after the movie came out, when she was on the cusp of a new, more mainstream kind of stardom. I had seen her on *Letterman*—she was a regular guest in the early eighties—and her appearances were always electric and surprising and, in terms of comedic personality, groundbreaking. There was never anyone like Sandra then, and now that I think about it, there's never been anyone like her since.

Judd Apatow: Okay, here we go. So how has your life changed since *The King of Comedy*?

Sandra Bernhard: In my career? Well, probably the most important thing that has changed is that I can get interviews for things. People are interested in finding other films for me.

Judd: Is that what you've been doing, reading scripts?

Sandra: Yeah, reading scripts and developing things of my own.

Judd: And now you're getting stand-up jobs everywhere?

Sandra: Yeah, but I'm not going to be doing comedy clubs anymore. I'm doing more musically, developing my act more as a whole package, as opposed to just comedy.

Judd: Do you get recognized on the street?

Sandra: A lot. I've always been looked at because I have one of those kinds of faces—people think they know me. But now, it's like they do. So it's kind of neat.

Judd: What do they say?

Sandra: Oh, well, most people are just incredibly supportive, and say, "God, I loved you in the film, it was a wonderful performance." You know, lots of good.

Judd: How did you get that part?

Sandra: I auditioned for it out in L.A., along with lots of other actresses. And then I met De Niro and Scorsese over a period of two months.

Judd: Were they intimidating?

Sandra: No, because I really wasn't that into their films at the time. I walked in just sort of, "Oh, hi." Real casual.

Judd: How about Jerry Lewis?

Sandra: He was more intimidating than they were.

Judd: What do you think about him? I mean he used to be such a crazy young guy, and now he's, like, an old man.

Sandra: He's a crazy old man. He's not that old, first of all. I mean, he's pretty much the same. People don't really ever change that much, you know. They slow down a little bit. But he's still totally crazy.

Judd: And did they let you improvise on this movie?

Sandra: Most of my part was improvised.

Judd: Like whole scenes?

Sandra: Yeah. A lot of what I did in the movie I improvised before I went on my auditions.

Judd: Didn't they cut a lot of stuff you did?

Sandra: No. People think that, you know. There were just different takes. I mean, I did like the same take only different improvisation. It was a matter of which improv Marty preferred.

Judd: So what do you think about your character?

Sandra: I think she's somebody that, at the time, I could relate to, and was very close to who I was emotionally. I was very needy and I wanted things to happen in my career that weren't happening. I was alienated and lonely and all those things that she felt. So she was easily understood. I mean, now that it's changed my life, I don't feel so close to that character, and I don't think I should. I don't think it would be a healthy way to relate to people.

Judd: When you saw the film, what did you think?

Sandra: I was pleased. I was especially pleased with my part.

Judd: Yeah, you got great reviews. They said you carried the film.

Sandra: To a certain degree, I guess I did. I certainly interjected a lot of excitement and energy into it. Which it needed, I think.

Judd: So what was your childhood—

Sandra: Typical and not typical. I was raised half in Michigan and half in Arizona. I was born in Michigan, in a middle-class, upper-middle-class, Jewish family. My father's a doctor, and my mother's a nurse. Three older brothers. The thing that made a difference is that I was the youngest, and the only girl. I think I got a different perspective on life than most people do, because, you know—I had to hold my own in a family of men.

Judd: You had to be tough.

Sandra: Not tough, just learn how to get attention.

Judd: Through being funny?

Sandra: Yeah, I was always funny. And pretty intense.

Judd: Popular?

Sandra: No, not really. I mean I had a lot of friends but I never thought of myself as popular because, I mean, I was always kind of thin and, you know, different. I felt more self-conscious.

Judd: So who did you idolize as a kid?

Sandra: Carol Channing. I saw her in *Hello, Dolly!* when I was eight years old.

Judd: Any other comedians?

Sandra: No, not really. I mean there were comic actors and actresses, you know. A woman had a show called *Pete and Gladys* that was on for a little while—and do you know Cara Williams? She's great. It was a great show. But it was only on for a little while.

Judd: When did you decide you were gonna be a comic? High school?

Sandra: I never made the choice to become a *comic*. I always wanted to become a singer and an actress. And I just made some friends in L.A. who thought I should be in comedy, because it's more accessible for a woman. Harder, but you get more attention. And I had a flair for comedy, but really, my first year in L.A. is when I started doing it.

Judd: And what was your first comedy stage like?

Sandra: It was pretty good. I was confident because I didn't know what to expect. I just watched other people, so I sort of imitated—

Judd: Where did you do that?

Sandra: At a place called the Ye Little Club.

Judd: How long did it take you to get confident as a performer, comfortable onstage?

Sandra: I'm still doing that. It's an endless process. I mean, you get more and more confident. Especially when I got the movie. That set me off.

Judd: How would you describe your act onstage? Because you seem very different, from—I mean, I saw you and you seem like a different person onstage.

Sandra: Well, you have to be. You have to have some sort of a persona onstage to get your point across. And you're not gonna just walk up there casual, like you're carrying on a conversation and, you know, be entertaining at the same time. That's a part of me, that character I use onstage. It's a part of who I am. But you just can't do that all the time without burning yourself out.

Judd: So how have you handled everything? Fame?

Sandra: Quite well. It hasn't radically changed—I mean, I didn't make a lot of money. If I made a lot of money, if I was rich right now, it might have changed my life a little bit more. But I'm pretty much in the same financial position. I'm okay, but—you know.

Judd: Do you think you're gonna be a superstar one day?

Sandra: Well, I think I'll be—I think I'll be pretty out there. I don't know if there's anybody that's a superstar anymore. That's sort of a thing of the past.

Judd: So what would success mean for you, then?

Sandra: Working a lot. Doing good work. Having people respect me. Being recognized by the public and having power to do what I want to do.

Judd: And if you could do anything what would it be?

Sandra: A lot of films, more money. Interesting films.

Judd: Serious films?

Sandra: Serious and comedy both.

Judd: Say Eddie Murphy gets fifteen million to do whatever he wants. You would like something like that, I guess?

Sandra: Well, I don't think I need fifteen million dollars—

Judd: Creative control over your work, then?

Sandra: Yeah, I want creative control. I'm not looking to make a billion dollars. I want to be comfortable, but I'm not starving for that kind of—

that's egotistical to me, and bullshit. And they don't do that with women, they only do that with men.

Judd: Why do you think that is?

Sandra: Because men control the business, men are in power, and men want to keep men in power.

Judd: How long did it take you to get relaxed onstage, so that you could just interact with the audience?

Sandra: I did that almost from the start. I was never really comfortable doing it, and I wasn't sure what I was gonna say, but I did it anyway. That's how I wanted to relate as a performer. I never wanted that wall up, you know. I didn't want to just tell jokes. But I wanted to relate to people so I was willing to take that risk of getting a bad reaction.

Judd: Did you ever get a bad reaction?

Sandra: Sure. A lot. I still do. Kind of a general thing in the audience. Audiences can turn real vicious sometimes. You know, collectively. Audiences are not to be trusted until you're about halfway through the show. They can turn on you. They're very—people are weird, they're like wild animals.

Judd: And that happens to you even now?

Sandra: Once in a while, there'll be a smattering of people who'll come—it's happened a couple of times at Carolines. Some people came in. And there was just—they wanted to start problems with me. They really didn't know who I was and they came anyway, so they just talked, and I said, "What the fuck are you doing here?" You know what I mean? "People are here to have a good time, I'm here to entertain them. These people know who I am, they respect my work—and if you don't know what I'm doing, and you don't like it, then get the fuck out."

Judd: And you just say that to them?

Sandra: That and a lot of other things. I'll ride their asses all night, because they don't shut up. They just keep going and I just keep going right along with them. Something interesting always comes out of it.

Judd: What would you consider your worst moment onstage?

Sandra: My worst moments are when my energy is low. When I'm really tired, and my energy is bad, then I'm vulnerable.

Judd: Do you think there's anything that a comedian *shouldn't* do?

Sandra: I don't know. I have a lot of opinions on that. I guess—I guess, you know, it depends on the person. You can't generalize.

Judd: You don't think there's anything that's off-limits? I mean, I've seen some pretty crude stuff.

Sandra: See, I have a lot of opinions on comedy. If you get me started on that, then I'll say my opinions, and I'm gonna regret it.

Judd: You're gonna say something that you're gonna regret?

Sandra: Yeah, because I don't think that there are very many people that should be doing comedy. Because I don't think most of them have a point of view or an attitude or a conviction.

Judd: Do you think comedians should make a statement, like a political or social kind of—

Sandra: I think if you're really good, you do that without trying to. You invoke emotions from an audience without being obvious about it. But the art of being a great performer is almost a dead thing. There are very few people who dedicate their lives to being a real artist and to the artistry of performing. Because there's a whole—it's not just standing up there. It's a movement and it's a tone of voice and it's a seduction and it's a school of thought. The old entertainers, they knew everything. They knew how to dance, and they knew how to sing. They *studied* it. And it's not something you just get away with being—um, you know—that's one thing I'll say about Robin Williams, even though I get tired of his comedies. He's an artist and he knows his craft. So does Richard Pryor. Richard Pryor knows movement.

Judd: I was reading somewhere that there's a Steve Allen book and it said that he didn't think that the old comedians could stand up to anybody from today. I guess he's talking about Henny Youngman and, I don't know, maybe Jackie Gleason, all of those old comedians doing stuff they did like in the Catskills in the forties. He said that they wouldn't stand up to anybody today.

Sandra: I don't know about that. I think times are different. And like I said, in those days, comedy wasn't something you just got into because it looked accessible, and easy, and you could make some fast money. I mean, those people were *raised* with that feeling. That need to entertain. I think you really have to be driven by something to be a good entertainer.

Judd: Is there anyone right now that you just like — is there anybody you look at and say, "I wish I could be that good"?

Sandra: I think people think that about me right now.

Judd: Yeah.

Sandra: I'm more interested in what I'm doing — I've been through that already. I'm beyond that. Christ, if I was still at that point, I never would have gotten the film.

Judd: So you think you have it down?

Sandra: Oh no, I don't have it down. But I'm certainly doing what I believe is true to what I think, and honest. I mean, I believe that people are talking about me. And I can't think of anybody who impresses me right now as much as I impress myself.

SARAH SILVERMAN
(2014)

I've known Sarah Silverman since she moved to California to do stand-up when she was twenty-one years old. Back then, she was the young, hilarious girl who was from the same town in New Hampshire as my friend and roommate, Adam Sandler. That always seemed so weird to me, the idea that two brilliantly funny people could come from the same small town.

I've been lucky enough to spend a lot of time with her in the intervening years, in a work capacity (we worked together at *The Larry Sanders Show*, where I was a writer and she an actor playing a writer), and in the deeply competitive world of Garry Shandling's weekly pickup basketball games (where I have tried and failed to keep her out of the paint). Not only is she way funnier than I am—I feel pretty comfortable calling her one of the most essential comedic minds of her generation—but she's also way better than me at basketball.

Judd Apatow: I was thinking recently about the first time I met you. You were so young.

Sarah Silverman: That was back when I was, like, really doing stand-up.

Judd: Did you go straight from high school into the clubs?

Sarah: Yeah. When I was seventeen, I went to summer school in Boston. I knew I wanted to be a stand-up but I'd only done it at high school assemblies and stuff. But I went up at open-mic night at Stitches when it was on Mass. Ave., and that was the first time I ever did stand-up. It was my third year of high school. I remember the comedian who was onstage when I first went in to scope it out, too. Wendy Liebman.

Judd: Wow.

Sarah: And she did two jokes. I completely remember that night. I have this sense memory of walking through the doors and the first thing I heard was her saying, "Someone thought I was Lady Di, but it turned out that they were just saying, 'Lady, die.'" And then the other one was—wow, I ruined that joke.

Judd: I was interested in comedy from a really young age, too. As a ten-year-old kid, I was watching a scary amount of Merv Griffin and Dinah Shore.

Sarah: Oh, my mother always loved Dinah Shore because she said she did her own hair. She thought that made her so down-to-earth.

Judd: What drew you to try comedy, though? Why did you like it so much?

Sarah: My dad taught me swears when I was a toddler and I saw, at a really early age, that if I shocked people, I would get approval, and it made my arms itch with glee. I got addicted to it. It became this source of power in a totally powerless life.

Judd: Did your dad get a kick out of it?

Sarah: He thought it was funny to teach his three-year-old daughter swears.

Judd: What do your parents do for a living?

Sarah: My dad is alive. I always say, "He was a retailer," and then people go, "Oh, did he die?" But no, he's just retired. His dream was to be a writer—and he wrote all these books that he self-published when he retired—but he was always a retailer. He owned a store called Crazy Sophie's Factory Outlet. And he did his own commercials. I have a bunch of them. They're amazing. He has such a thick New England accent. You can't understand a thing he's saying. He's like, "When I see the prices at the mall, I just want to vomit! Hey, I'm Crazy Donald!" He was Crazy Donald, like Crazy Eddie, only in New Hampshire.

Judd: That must have been a big deal, in a small town in New Hampshire, growing up with your dad doing commercials.

Sarah: Yeah, he was always on the radio waves talking about his sales, and jean brands that you never heard of, like Unicorn. And my mom was like Shelley Long in *Cheers*. Diction is very important to her. She says, like, *wh*en and *wh*ere. She was the opposite of my dad.

Judd: Did they stay married?

Sarah: No, they got divorced when I was like six and a half, but I was thrilled because they hated each other. I mean, I never saw a loving glance or a smile between them until long after they were divorced. Now they're close. They're like army buddies, you know. Like siblings. My mom is sickly and my stepmother checks in on her almost every day.

Judd: So your dad remarried and his wife is close with your mom?

Sarah: Yeah, they're all close. My mom remarried, too. They both found the loves of their lives, so I was able to see—unfortunately, not in my formative years—but I was eventually able to see what a loving marriage can look like.

Judd: Do you like trace your sensibility to anything specific other than your dad being amused by watching you shock people?

Sarah: I never consciously set out to talk about taboos or anything like that. That was just what the household I grew up in was like. There weren't any boundaries or a sense of, like, "Maybe let's not say that in front of the kids." It was all out there, you know, and I didn't know better. I mean, honestly, a lot of the human etiquette I learned in life I learned from, like, thank-you notes and dating Jimmy Kimmel. I have great parents and they both taught me great things, but it was just different. My formative years were boundaryless.

Judd: But was there a core of morality to it?

Sarah: Oh yeah, definitely. We had no religion at all but we were Jews in New Hampshire, and my sister—who is now a rabbi—said it best: We were like the only Jews in Bedford, New Hampshire, as well as the only Democrats, so we just kind of associated those two things together. My dad raised us to believe that paying taxes is an honor, that it goes to important things for everybody. We were never to complain about that shit, or be all about keeping your money or whatever. Now I look around and realize that was special. Money is seen as such a positive thing now, we try to get as much of it as we can and that's okay because it equals success. It's sad.

Judd: My parents didn't talk about religion, either. And then, out of the blue, my brother became an Orthodox Jew and moved to Israel. I always think it's funny how, in the same family, one person looks for answers through comedy and another through religion.

Sarah: My sister and I are so close, and so different. I don't have religion at all. Love and science are my religion. And Kermit the Frog and Mister Rogers.

Judd: That's so funny, because whenever I need to equalize myself and bawl my eyes out, I will go online and watch Jim Henson's funeral on YouTube.

Sarah: I've got to see that. I will not be able to keep it together because, honestly, I'll just fucking sing "It's Not Easy Being Green" or "Rainbow Connection" and cry.

Judd: That's what I do late at night. I just go down the Mister Rogers–Jim Henson wormhole of tears. But those two guys are a good religion. How does your sister talk about Judaism?

Sarah: It's funny because sometimes I'll get cunty with her and I'll be like, "Oh, so you believe there's a man in the sky?" I just can't get my head around it, you know. And she'll go, "Well, I like to live my life as though there is one." And I'm just like, "Oh, you're beautiful."

Judd: Why can't you get your head around it?

Sarah: I can be cynical. But I don't think of myself, at my core, as cynical. So much of it is location. Like, who is Muslim? Who is a Jew? Who is a Catholic? Who is a Christian? Who's Buddhist? Ninety-nine-point-nine percent of it is where you happen to be born. So how can one be right and another be wrong? It seems pretty clear to me that it's a coping mechanism for people who cannot handle the not knowing of things. I am okay knowing I will never be able to comprehend the world.

Judd: I wish I could convince myself to believe the way your sister believes because I'm so exhausted from not believing.

Sarah: I actually don't think that she believes in God, necessarily. I think she just loves the ritual of religion and finding meaning in every little thing. She loves living her life that way.

Judd: Do you think she believes that God is involved in people's lives?

Sarah: Yeah. But she isn't one of those "Oh, let's pray for this tumor to go away" people. You know what I mean? She just loves the ritual of finding meaning in everything. I don't know. I don't think she believes in, like, a male God or anything. She's a major feminist, a liberal hippy-dippy granola rabbi.

Judd: She doesn't believe in a God that is actively involved in people's lives, making choices?

Sarah: She doesn't believe that God is rooting for the Giants and not the Patriots. She's not fucking ridiculous.

Judd: I'm jealous of those people. I plan on tricking myself into believing in religion one of these days. I'm going to pick a religion and then hypnotize myself.

Sarah: When the rest of my family is in a crazy, neurotic tizzy, she'll be like, "It will work out." You know.

Judd: I always feel that my only connection to anything spiritual—and this might be sad—is when a joke comes to me. In that moment, I feel a different kind of connection than I do during the rest of the day.

Sarah: Because you can't make it happen. I mean, I have to sit and sit and work on my jokes. And it's just such torture for me and I think, *Why don't I love this?* Sitting down and fixing my shitty jokes should be my passion. But it's torture.

Judd: Do you put time aside to write?

Sarah: No, but when I do, it always pays off. I don't know why I'm so afraid of setting aside twenty minutes of sitting-down time. It's always fruitful, you know. But I just fight it so much.

Judd: Seinfeld said he sits and writes for two hours every single day.

Sarah: Seinfeld and Chris Rock, they're just that incredible combination of funny and not lazy, which is very rare and special and completely failure proof. I remember before I did my HBO special, Chris screamed at me—in a loving way, but still. He was like, "You need to do two hundred shows in a row and a month straight on the road before you even *think* about recording a special!" And I had literally booked two weeks on the road and then went right into the recording. It put me in a panic, but it also made me work harder and made me realize that everyone works differently, and that's okay.

Judd: Who are the comics you look up to? Who's had the greatest impact on you, would you say?

Sarah: Early on, Garry Shandling. When I first started hanging out with him, he was always so giving of what he knows and what he learned. I definitely learned to embrace the quiet moments onstage from him—relaxing and not fighting with the crowd, not raising your voice, not ever trying to win them over. I also started out with Louis [C.K.] and David Attell. I remember the very first time Louis saw me. I was just starting and I had this affectation, where I would pull the mic away from my mouth. And he was like, "You shouldn't do that. It looks weird and it's a bad habit to get into." And so I stopped, you know.

Judd: What is it like, at this point of your career, to look back on what all these people you came up with have accomplished?

Sarah: It's so exciting. You know, everyone's got their own velocity. Life goes at different speeds and there's no real time frame with comedy. Louis has been brilliant for thirty years, but it has been so exciting to see, these past five years, the world getting Louis fever. On the flip side of that, there is the waste, the ones you know that were everyone's favorite—you know, there's so many times I will find myself talking to someone, "No, no, you don't understand, he was the king, he was everyone's favorite comic," and people only see a guy as washed up, with no place to live, who can't get his shit together. It's so frustrating. You just want people to understand. Like I said about Seinfeld and Chris Rock, they're a great combination of brilliance and hard work. There are people who are brilliant and don't work hard, and there are people that are brilliant and sabotage themselves, and both are just so hard to see. Every once in a while, you forget there's nothing you can do about it, and so you scramble around, trying to get something going for them, and then you come to the realization that they'll never let it happen. You don't get what you want, you get what you think you deserve. With people like that, they're just not going to let themselves succeed.

Judd: And you end up with survivor's guilt.

Sarah: It's awful. You must know comics in their sixties who didn't parlay their act into writing or acting or producing, and so they're just fucked. Even the cruise ships don't want them anymore.

Judd: Yeah. I feel like it's a miracle when you can separate yourself from the pack enough to make a real living.

Sarah: Comedy is like alcoholism. You're surrounded by people who are getting high all day, fucking around, and just being comics—and time passes, you know.

Judd: None of us have any other skill to fall back on.

Sarah: Yeah, exactly. There are a couple of comics that—like, I have a friend who just found a whole new career as the old black man in a bunch of commercials, and it's exciting for him. Like, he can buy people drinks and stuff and it's nice. But, you know, he didn't have teeth for a while. I mean, you forget that comics, for the most part, don't pay any attention to—I mean, with women comics it tends to be different because we're not disgusting pigs, but a lot of comics don't even know to like floss and brush their teeth, you know what I mean? And their teeth, I have to tell you: There was a time where I just bought a ton of dental care products and gave them out to my guy comic friends because they didn't know any better. I mean, I don't know how they get pussy. When I drive them in my car, and they get out, I have to Febreze the whole area. It's insane. Like hygiene is just something you don't need if you're fly enough to get girls or something. But it's bad and death creeps in through the gums.

Judd: I think a lot of the reason why I've done okay was growing up with the terror of not doing okay. From an early age, I tried to teach myself how to think ahead. But I know plenty of people who are funny and don't have those types of skills.

Sarah: I'm somewhere in between. I'm so much more famous than I am financially successful. I mean, I live in a three-room apartment. I mostly make free videos on my couch. But I am fine.

Judd: Is it because, creatively, you've done what you've wanted to do?

Sarah: I've always kept my overhead low so I could do whatever I want. I think of myself as lazy with spurts of getting a lot done. I find myself rooting against things sometimes because I get excited at the thought of a clean slate. I also really like sleeping. My friends make fun of me because, you know, I love hanging out but I always hit a point in the night where I just want to get home and sleep. I have a very active dream life and I have to be there a lot.

SETH ROGEN

(2009)

When *Knocked Up* came out, Seth and I had a bit of what is known in Hollywood as "a moment." People didn't know our work that well, and the movie was this enormous, unexpected success. We felt, for a second, like we were fully in the zeitgeist, the flavor of the month. At the height of it, we were interviewed by the critic David Denby at The New Yorker Festival—which is a series of words I never thought I would type. It was a real collision of worlds, because the festival, at least to us, felt very literary, and here we were, onstage, talking about an emotionally thoughtful but dirty, dirty movie.

People talk a lot about me being a mentor to Seth, or having discovered Seth when he was a kid, but here's the truth: Seth's sense of humor has influenced everything I have done. I feel very maternal toward Seth—so when he makes a movie like *This Is the End* and it includes a scene where Jonah Hill is being fucked by the devil, I'm as proud as a parent whose kid graduated from Harvard and became a brain surgeon.

David Denby: One of my distinguished predecessors, Pauline Kael, used to put down movies by saying that they were "deep on the surface"— meaning that there was nothing underneath. *The 40-Year-Old Virgin* was shallow on the surface with endless depths underneath. It was certainly foul-mouthed, but it was also about, oh God, shyness and bluster and illusion and delusion and many, many other fascinating things. If anything, it was a song of innocence, which ended with this amazing hilltop hymn to love, which was very dangerous to have shot. But you pulled it off. It was earned. Now, those of you who had seen *Freaks and Geeks* on television from 1999 to 2000 already knew something about this comic sensibility. I'm just catching up to some of that. The great thing about these two guys is that, even though Seth is disgustingly young, he's been working with Judd for almost nine years. Now, if you print out Judd's credits on IMDb, you get three single-spaced pages of stuff. So I'm just going to run through the highlights quickly: The pride of Syosset, Long Island. Mother worked in a comedy club in Southampton. Interviewed established comics when he was in high school on the high school radio station, which had ten watts of power. Attended USC for two years, dropped out. Roomed with Adam Sandler for a while and knew other young comics as well as Garry Shandling. Wrote for a lot of them. Did stand-up and gave it up. Wrote *The Cable Guy* in '96. Paul Feig created *Freaks and Geeks* in '99 and Judd wrote a fair amount of it and directed three episodes. It was canceled after eighteen episodes—

Judd Apatow: After thirteen. We shot eighteen.

David: You shot eighteen and only thirteen aired?

Judd: Thirteen aired and then they dumped it.

David: And then *Undeclared* was two years later?

Judd: Yes.

David: And was also canceled. Do you ever wake up at night and have revenge fantasies?

Judd: Well, the same guy who canceled *Undeclared* also canceled *The Ben Stiller Show*. And uh, I don't want to start out with a randy joke, but, uh—

David: Oh yes, yes you do.

Judd: As I realized that we were about to be canceled, that day *Time* magazine put out a list of the ten best shows on TV and they had *Undeclared* on there. I knew we were about to get canceled so I framed it and put a Post-it on it and sent it to him, and the Post-it said, "I don't understand how you can fuck me in the ass when your penis is still in me from last time."

David: I'm sure that you will—

Judd: This is *The New Yorker,* you know. You don't hear John Updike say that.

David: Mr. [William] Shawn, the very squeamish editor of *The New Yorker* for thirty years, has probably turned over in his grave so many times in the last fifteen years, he's burrowed to Hackensack. But that document, I'm sure, will be deposited at Harvard University in the Apatow Papers. Among your most recent feats was that you held off Stephen Colbert during a pretty rough outing in the summer, and managed to get the words *Jew* and *penis* onto national television—although not always in conjunction with each other. You have described the penis in a movie as the last frontier. Is that the Jewish penis you were referring to and—

Judd: I guess the first frontier is the Jewish penis and then the last frontier is the uncircumcised penis.

Seth Rogen: I won't touch that.

David: We're not going to go there. Okay, Seth was born and raised in Vancouver and started performing stand-up comedy in a lesbian bar when he was thirteen. Is that correct?

Seth: It is.

David: Now, was this before or after your bar mitzvah—and what in the world was your material?

Seth: It was after my bar mitzvah and it was just about my life, about my grandparents and my bar mitzvah and high school and trying to meet girls and stuff like that.

David: I don't want to get too personal here, but were you prematurely testosteroned? When did you get that bottom octave?

Seth: The bass? I don't know, I always had a raspy voice from years of physical mistreatment to myself.

David: So you were in Vancouver and Apatow shows up with a casting call for *Freaks and Geeks*? I'd love to hear that first encounter from both sides.

Seth: I had been doing stand-up for a while and it became clear I was going to fail out of high school, so I thought I should try to get some money. I had gotten an agent and I said, you know, maybe I should start to audition for things because stand-up comics don't make a lot of money from just doing stand-up comedy. So she said okay, and *Freaks and Geeks* was the first or second audition I got sent out on. Judd was in there and Paul Feig was in there, who I actually recognized from the movie *Ski Patrol*, which I was a big fan of. The whole time I didn't actually pay that much attention to Judd because I was like, *The fucking guy from* Ski Patrol *is here!* That was shocking to me. No one warned me. I thought they warned you when something like that happens. But I got in there and read the scene and I remember they laughed really hard. I remember walking out thinking, *If I don't get that role I don't know what they're looking for, because they really seemed to laugh—unless it's bullshit and they do that with everybody.*

Judd: They do that for everybody.

Seth: Yeah, they do.

Judd: I saw Seth on a videotape at home. They sent me like thirty or forty people from Vancouver and we wrote a generic *Freaks* scene to see who had an interesting personality. The scene was about a kid explaining that he was going to grow pot underground and if the cops came, he would explode the entrance to the tunnel and then they would just see that he had grown corn aboveground and he would say that he was a corn farmer. That was the premise of it and, uh—

Seth: I related to it.

David: Seth, you were writing from a very early age with Evan Goldberg, and I think that I read that the first version of *Superbad* was commenced when you were fifteen. You were writing about guys who were seventeen when you were fifteen?

Seth: Actually, I think we were a little younger—around thirteen or fourteen—but no, it was about guys our age. The characters just slowly got older as we got older until we graduated and then we couldn't take the characters with us beyond that point.

David: So you just kept writing it and rewriting it over a period of years.

Seth: Yeah, for around twelve years. If they made it when we were twelve—I mean, it would be pathetic.

Judd: But the penis sequence was in draft one.

Seth: It really was. What's sad is that a fair amount of the jokes in the movie were in the draft we wrote when we were twelve years old. It's sad reading it because I have not gotten any funnier in the last fifteen years of my life.

David: Judd, you said somewhere when you were doing stand-up comedy that you found it hard to develop a persona for yourself as a stand-up comic, and that struck me as interesting because I never heard anyone say that. Explain what you meant.

Judd: Well, I did stand-up when I was seventeen years old, and you really don't have any life experience to draw on and so I wasn't mad about anything. I was just kind of like a really bad Bill Maher. I would go on the road and open up for Jim Carrey, and I would watch him and think, *Wow, he's a lot better than I am. He seems to have gifts that I don't have.* And so I gave up.

David: You wrote for a lot of people and—

Judd: It was easier to write for other people. I could sit in my house when I was twenty years old and write jokes for Roseanne Barr about stretch marks, which is very weird, but I could write it. I remember I had one joke—and I really don't understand how I wrote this at twenty because I didn't even know what a stretch mark was—which was, the only way to get rid of stretch marks is you have to put on another ten pounds just to bang it out. I wrote for Roseanne for a year and I'd go to her house and hang with her and Tom and write jokes, but I really wasn't thinking about my own personality.

David: When Seth and his partner, Evan Goldberg, were working with you in Los Angeles, I read somewhere that you sent them writing exercises like: Come up with ten comic ideas in the next three days. Were there other writers you were schooling this way? You sound like a fencing master or Karate Kid or something.

Seth: I didn't even finish high school.

Judd: Oh Jesus. And you know, I saw from day one that this was one of the funniest guys I've ever encountered. He was capable of anything. I thought that when he was sixteen years old, watching him act on the show, watching how his mind worked. And so Evan would come out sometimes in the summer and they would do rewrites of *Superbad* and it would get rejected and they'd do more rewrites and table reads and more rejections, and then I just started to find ways for them to make money so they wouldn't have to go back to Canada.

David: Let's get into *Freaks and Geeks*, and we can get the first clip going. It doesn't go zing, zing, zing like a sitcom. It's actually very slow—it plays very slowly and meditatively. It's melancholy, some of it, about all sorts of painful things as well as funny stuff. Was that a very radical thing to do? Is that why NBC lost faith in it?

Judd: Paul Feig hated all the high school shows that were on TV at the time, which were all filled with very handsome, pretty people. He thought there should be a show about slightly less pretty people. He just thought there should be a show about his goofy group of friends, and that was his inspiration to talk about his childhood in Michigan and—you know, that's how it all began. He had this idea of a show that moved a little slower. His theory was it would be like what storytelling was before everything got sped up by MTV editing. I was heavily influenced by *Welcome to the Dollhouse*—that's a movie that I thought about a lot when we were working on the show. And *Fast Times at Ridgemont High*, which Paul Feig claims he never saw.

Seth: That's bullshit.

David: I've been looking at it recently and some of them really go deep. There's the episode where Jason Segel plays the guy who is not terribly bright, just wants to more than anything else be a drummer, and he plays with his friends and goes to an actual audition for a real band and totally bombs.

Judd: It's the end of the episode.

David: That's getting kids where they live.

Judd: It was a pretty dark episode. "Here's your dream. You suck at it. End of episode." And we wondered why we were canceled.

Seth: I know. People don't want that?

David: And there's a kind of neo–Howard Stern episode—

Judd: We were trying to come up with a story line for Seth to have a girlfriend. And it was near the end of the run and we clearly knew that we were going to get canceled, so we were being a little bolder with our ideas. As kind of a fuck-you to the network, like, If you're going to cancel us then we're going to do the episodes that we want to do and we'll just go down swinging—or as Michael O'Donoghue said when he was at *SNL*, go down like a burning Viking ship. The episode is about Seth's girlfriend telling him that she was born with ambiguous genitals and that the doctor had to choose what sex she would be. And so it's basically Seth's reaction to that and the question of, will he break up with her or will he be able to handle it? We tried to handle it sensitively. We did it right.

David: Do you remember shooting that scene?

Seth: I do. Me and Jason and James really got along well on the show and we had a good dynamic and it was never our instinct to rush through things, I would say. I mean, we would make a fucking meal out of it if we can. I'd say one line all day if I could, but it was always really easy and it never seemed like a *laborious* process. It never seemed like it would take a long time to get somewhere. Everyone was collaborative. It always seemed clear how to do it, I think.

Judd: I remember watching that scene and thinking, *Seth's a movie star*. I mean, it just was clear. Like this is the kind of guy I want to watch in a movie. In fact, if you look at *Knocked Up*, a lot of it is the same kind of comedic idea of something happening that's unexpected and having to figure out if you're man enough to handle it correctly.

David: When are girls going to figure out that the jocks become used car salesmen and the nerds become, you know, Judd Apatow and Bill Gates? Why aren't they on to that by now?

Judd: You know, that's—uh, maybe they are. Any high schoolers here getting laid? Any nerds getting a lot?

Seth: Have you seen Kelsey Grammer's wife?

Judd: David Spade.

Seth: David Spade. Bill Maher, even. Come on.

David: *The 40-Year-Old Virgin* started as a skit, right, that Steve Carell did about a middle-aged guy who had never had sex?

Judd: Steve was really funny when we were shooting *Anchorman*—crazy funny, like we were all watching him every day going, What is going *on* with this guy? He's just playing so over his head every day.

Seth: Oh, it was crazy.

Judd: And so I said, "Hey, if you ever have any idea of something you can star in, let's do it." And he came up to me and said, "You know, I did this sketch at Second City that I played around with and never finished. It was about a guy playing poker with his friends and they were all telling really dirty sex stories and slowly you realize that he's a virgin and his stories make no sense." And then he said—and you know his example was, "You know how like when you're with a woman and you feel her breasts and it feels like bags of sand, and you know how like when you put your hand in a woman's panties and there's the baby powder?" I just clicked in and thought, *That's the greatest idea I've ever heard.* I was afraid to direct a movie and had not really pursued it because I didn't feel, I don't know, I just didn't feel like I would do a good job. But then I heard that idea and I said, "Unfortunately, I understand what that is." It's not like I was a virgin until I was forty but I certainly had very long spans in between sex. You know, I'd go a decade here and there. I understood the issue.

David: Did the two of you then sit down and co-write it, and work together in a room somewhere?

Judd: He would come to the office and we would just bang it out. Very quickly, we realized that it should be real and that the character should be quiet. Steve and I talked about it as almost a Buster Keaton–type character. That he would be quiet and then he could get mad but he wouldn't be a wallflower. He would be a really normal person. And that came from going on the Internet and finding all these blogs from middle-aged virgins — they all seemed a little scared, like it just got by them.

David: But his whole personality is shaped around this thing — his consumer choices, his temperament, everything. Because he just can't get past that one thing. So it's one of the most incredible pictures about neurosis —

Judd: It's something that I kind of understood. That's what a lot of *Freaks and Geeks* was, too: terror of intimacy, the fear that people will think that you're a freak. They'll discover the thing that you're afraid might be true. Seth was in my office when we got green-lit for *40-Year-Old Virgin* and got very aggressive about being in it.

Seth: I saw my moment. Judd was very happy. He was on the phone. He was like, "We're *making* it?" And I was like, "Put me in it." I tried to ride the celebration wave. He'll say yes to anything right now.

Judd: Well, in my head I'd always wanted Seth to be in it. I tried to get Seth to be the lead of *Undeclared* and Fox network said no.

Seth: They literally laughed.

Judd: And so I was just so afraid that, like, what if I want Seth to be the lead and they say no? I was just hoping I could get it approved without telling him and then he got aggressive in the meantime. But Seth was a giant inspiration on that movie. We couldn't get *Superbad* made, and as a result, his theory of people want a really dirty movie, we put onto *The 40-Year-Old Virgin*. Seth was aggressive with Steve about being dirty.

Seth: Steve had his reservations, I would say, about it. He actually had me write up a version of the script that was rated PG-13 at one point and I did it just so he could see how lame it was. I think he was underestimating his own sweetness and how much that would come across. I always thought he's so likable and so nice that you could have the most despicable language and activity in the world surrounding him but he's like the, the anchor of niceness, so you can get away with any of that stuff.

Judd: We did a table read with all the actors and I was so nervous that the script wouldn't be good enough to amuse Catherine Keener—

Seth: Yeah.

Judd: We worked really hard on Catherine Keener's part because she's scary. You know, you don't want Catherine Keener mad at you. She literally had just finished a Daniel Day-Lewis movie and a Sean Penn movie and then she's, like, with us idiots, you know? I don't want her to notice that this was a career mistake for her. So then we did a table read and Catherine and Steve murdered and Seth and Romany [Malco] and Paul just ate it.

Seth: Ate shit.

Judd: Yeah, and then we went into rehearsal and played around and we started telling sex stories and talking about our relationships, and Paul was very funny, getting mad about women who broke his heart and playing the guy who couldn't get over it. And Romany had the craziest sex stories. He was like, "I lost my virginity when I was eight." And we were like, "What?" And he says that in front of Sharon Waxman from *The New York Times*. And I'm like, you know, "Let's not print the 'Romany lost his virginity when he was eight' story, okay?" Of course, it was in *The New York Times*. I said, "Isn't that like a molestation?" He said, "No, I was into it."

David: How did *Knocked Up* originate?

Judd: I had a lot of ideas about pregnancy because every time my wife and I went through childbirth, terrible things would happen with the doctors and the nurses—people being mean and not showing up or me cursing someone out, or them cursing me out. And so I thought, *I've got to write about this because it's so awful that I must get something from it.* I liked the idea of a rushed pregnancy or something that sped it up, because even when you plan it, it's so terrifying the entire time. Anyway, Seth was talking to me at the time and he was pitching some science fiction movie ideas and I was trying to explain to him that "I don't think anyone would make a hundred-million-dollar Seth Rogen movie at this point. But you *could* do something simple because you're funny in *40-Year-Old Virgin* when you're just sitting there on the phone. You don't need ghosts and goblins and fairies." I said, "You could just get a girl pregnant and that would be enough for a whole movie because you with the gynecologist—" And I went, *Wait a second, this might be worth writing.* That's how it began.

David: I know you had an early version of the script and you called in actors and you did a table reading. Explain how that works.

Judd: Yes, well, I wrote the first draft when I was producing *Talladega Nights*. It was just going well, so I would just go in my trailer and work on the movie. And then I came back and we very quickly did a table read with some people who weren't ultimately in the movie, just to see where we were. From that point on, you know, basically everyone is involved in the process. I'm asking everyone's help on ideas and I'm trying to make each role as specific to their personality as possible. Seth is very uncomfortable around my kids so I thought, *Well, that's funny.* Seth's not one of those people that you're like, "You know what, I've got to run out for twenty minutes, will you hang out with the kids?"

David: It's unusual. There are legendary directors like Bergman and Ford who have worked with stock companies, but this must be fairly unusual in studio Hollywood today, to be able to draw on this many people. I mean, some of them were working. Some of them were not working. You were able to call them in and get them to read for you just like that? It's an amazing advantage, isn't it?

Judd: The stock company is mainly Seth.

Seth: Yeah, and my idiot friends.

Judd: I love all the people from *Freaks and Geeks* and thought it was a missed opportunity to show what they can do, but the thing that really makes a lot of these movies possible is that when we do the auditions, Seth reads with every actor trying to get a part in the movie. So by the time the movie is shot, he has read with like two hundred people. Through that process, we figure out who his character is and we try to problem-solve all the issues of the movie. So we'll hold auditions for parts even though we kind of know who we want for the part, just to hear it with that person— and that almost becomes the rehearsal of the movie.

David: And the guys in the movie were your friends.

Seth: Yeah, those are my actual friends. I lived with almost all of those people at one point or another in conditions similar to that of the movie. It's funny because they kept coming to me during the rehearsal process and saying, like, you know, "I don't *get* my character." And I kept saying, "It's you, Jonah." And he was like, "Am I *for* the pregnancy? Or am I against it?" I'm like, "It doesn't matter. It's just you, man. Be for it one take, and against it in another take. It really doesn't matter. It'll just be you." It's surreal for me to watch those scenes because they all use their real names and it's amazing how our actual group dynamic worked its way into the movie.

David: I don't have to tell you that there were some women who were upset because the Katherine Heigl character goes through with the pregnancy and there isn't more, at least, discussion in the film about abortion—

Judd: We knew this would be an issue. To me, the interesting part of the movie is the people deciding not to have an abortion and, you know, from my perspective I think that there's certainly people that the second that they get pregnant, no matter what the circumstances are, there's a part of them that says, *I'm not doing that.* And there's people who *would* do that. This is just a story about somebody that would not do that, and I knew people would say, "Why don't they talk about abortion more?" Which is a hilarious comedy area. When people say that I'm like, "You're clearly not a funny person."

David: Your wife, Leslie Mann, gets angry in this movie.

Judd: And at home.

Seth: Yeah, exactly. I wasn't going to say anything.

David: Elaborate on the connection between the home arguments and the movie arguments.

Judd: In a lot of ways, the movie is two phases of my and Leslie's relationship. What I wanted to do—and was really happy that she had the courage to do—was to explore us at our worst. And yes, Leslie *did* kick me out of the car on the way to the gynecologist's office. She got mad about something, I don't remember what, and was like, "Get out of the car. Get out of the car." And I'm like, "Oh come on." "Get out of the car." And then I'm out of the car and I'm thinking, *Am I supposed to go to the appointment now? Or do I go home? And if I go home, will she be mad that I didn't get to the appointment? How do I get through this hormonal madness?* There's something that my wife said to me once: Just because you don't yell doesn't mean you're not mean. That's actually the interesting lesson that I took from my marriage, which is when you're married to an actress, they're very emotional and they're expressive, and as a weird nerd writer who likes hanging out in his room watching *The Merv Griffin Show*, I'd be kind of quiet, and so I thought that I was always right in fights just because I didn't get upset. I was in a superior position because she was getting upset. And then actually that realization was kind of a big moment in our marriage. She convinced me that I'm the dick.

SPIKE JONZE

(2014)

One of the most rewarding parts of putting this book together was that it was really an excuse to continue my artistic education. I don't know if you would call Spike Jonze a comedian, at least not in the classic sense, but it is definitely not a stretch to say that certain moments in his films — in *Her*, for example, or *Being John Malkovich* — are as funny and moving as anything I can think of.

Spike is a true individual, one of the few people whose work I watch and then think, *Should I just quit the business?* I was thrilled to have the opportunity to sit down with him for a few hours in my office and ask him all the questions that I hoped might jog something loose in my brain and push my work in a more original direction. I may never get to puppets and orchids, but surely there's a less smart equivalent I can find and make my own.

Spike Jonze: It's interesting how you've become, like, this mentor to so many comedians. I mean, at one point, you were just a young kid, but somewhere along the line, you made the transition to being this mentor who enables all these other creative people to be creative, as well as doing your own stuff.

Judd Apatow: Well, when I was a kid I spent all this time interviewing comedians and they would, in turn, sort of mentor me. Later, I opened on the road for Jim Carrey, and then Garry Shandling hired me on *The Larry Sanders Show*, which was really just another mentoring —

Spike: How old were you when you were on that show?

Judd: Twenty-six.

Spike: That was a great show.

Judd: I learned everything from watching Garry. We had a similar sense of humor, so he liked having me around. It put him in a good mood. Some guys pitch jokes and when they're really off, it throws you.

Spike: It kind of takes energy from the room. It's like, Okay, now we have to dig out.

Judd: Exactly. Because some people, they pitch jokes, they're in the ballpark and they make you laugh and think of something else. Other people pitch jokes and the room dies. I was mostly in the ballpark and I think it helped Garry get to what he had to think about. But I wasn't thinking about mentoring anyone when we started working on *Freaks and Geeks*.

Spike: Was that your first solo show?

Judd: Well, I created *The Ben Stiller Show* with Ben in 1992.

Spike: You were really young then.

Judd: I was twenty-four and I didn't know what I was doing. I just watched Ben to figure out what *he* was doing. But when we did *Freaks and Geeks*, there were so many kids around and all of my guilt kicked in because none of them were going to college—they had this job but I knew the show was going to get canceled and then I somehow spoiled them because they were all super-weird. Hilarious and brilliant, but super-weird. I didn't think they would necessarily get work again.

Spike: Like who?

Judd: Like everybody. Even Rogen, who was sixteen years old. Riotously funny, but a strange guy. And as we watched we thought, *We're going to chuck this guy in the show a lot.* And then one day we were watching him in the dailies, we said: *He's a movie star. Is this possible?* Back then, we used to talk about him as a John Candy type. But I did worry: *What's going to happen to all these people?* Rogen wasn't going to finish school. Jason Segel wasn't going to go to college. Sam Levine didn't go to college. I mean—

Spike: It's crazy that all of those guys were on that show.

Judd: Yeah. And so, for me, the idea of mentoring came from a place of: *I'm going to ruin their lives. Maybe I have already. And what can I do to help them?* It came from an insecure place. But I'm fascinated by groups of people that come together in a moment in your life, when you're just figuring out how to do it—and then what happens to all of us. Like Tamra Davis, who directed *Billy Madison.* That's when I met her. And I was fascinated to hear that she was instrumental in your early days, too.

Spike: Totally. There are so many people I met through her and opportunities I got through her. She recommended me for videos and let me tag along with her as she did a Sonic Youth video. She gave me a crash course in making music videos by letting me do that. And the way I met her was so roundabout in the first place. I did a skate video with my friend Mark Gonzales. It was called *Video Days* and I was like twenty-one and Mark gave it to—he went to a Sonic Youth show and gave it to Kim Gordon and Thurston Moore in a parking lot outside of their show.

Judd: Just handed it to her cold?

Spike: It wasn't planned. It was just—he had it in his car and he was driving by. He's like, "Oh, yeah, there she goes," and he stops. "Hey, guys."

Judd: And it changes your life.

Spike: It changes my life. And then Kim called me up and left a message at my house. It's like, "Hey, this is Kim Gordon from Sonic Youth and we want you to come shoot a video with us," and I'm like, *What?*

Judd: That is crazy. Let me ask you a question, because I actually don't know much about the earliest part of your life. You grew up in Maryland? Were you a part of the skateboarding thing in Maryland?

Spike: Yeah.

Judd: Did you do videos there as a kid, or just when you came out here?

Spike: I did, but not skate videos. In high school, we made these little videos on camcorders but they were always edited in camera.

Judd: I remember doing that, too.

Spike: You'd press the button and it would take two seconds for the thing to start recording and then it would always be like somebody waiting and then they'd start moving.

Judd: Who were you hanging out with back then? The nerds? Indie kids?

Spike: There was one video class in our school, and it lasted for one semester, until they realized they didn't have a teacher to teach it. So most of us would just go down to this basement room where there were these 1950s cameras and a switcher and we kind of fooled around with it. Mostly, the kids just used it as study hall. But then one kid brought in a camcorder from home and we started making videos. I don't know what kind of kids they were. My world was outside of school. I went to school as little as possible. I went to the BMX shop instead and went on tours in the summer.

Judd: You were racing BMX?

Spike: Freestyle, not racing. I was skating, too.

Judd: And that eventually took you out to L.A.?

Spike: I started going out there when I was fifteen or sixteen. I was going on these summer tours with this bike team called Haro. Even before that, I met these guys named Andy Jenkins and Mark Lewman at a magazine called *Freestylin'*. *Freestylin'* was like—even without me really thinking about what authentic meant, it was authentic. It was written by guys that ride bikes for guys that ride bikes and it's in the language of that world and it didn't try to explain anything to anyone outside of it. You just *knew*. When I was thirteen or fourteen, I got to know them a little bit because of this BMX shop that I worked at called Rockville BMX—it was sort of the epicenter of the East Coast BMX scene. So when I went to California when I was like sixteen, I met them in person. And then I started writing for their magazine in high school.

Judd: So you went back to Maryland, and you'd write for them from Maryland?

Spike: Yeah.

Judd: And *then* you came out to L.A. for good?

Spike: Yeah. In my senior year, they asked if I wanted to be an assistant editor after I graduated.

Judd: And what did you think was going to happen? What were you trying to do?

Spike: I was worried. I was worried that adulthood sounded scary. I thought I was going to go work at this BMX magazine for a year before I went to college because I thought you were supposed to go to college and you had to go to college.

Judd: It was a gap year.

Spike: It was a gap year.

Judd: You've had a long gap year.

Spike: Yeah, I still haven't gone back. But I just thought I had to go to college or I was going to be a fuckup and a failure. My parents went to college and it just, it was scary—that question of what am I going to do for the rest of my life, and how am I going to support myself?

Judd: What were you going to study if you went to college?

Spike: I didn't know. I did apply in my senior year, before I got that job offer. I applied to all these film and TV schools, communication schools.

Judd: I went to USC film school.

Spike: I applied there. I applied to all of them.

Judd: I had terrible grades but I wrote an essay that was all about how much money I was going to give them when I was successful. I went into great detail.

Spike: That's way more sophisticated than I could have ever been at that age. I wouldn't have had the confidence to put my point of view and personality into it.

Judd: I had an English teacher in eleventh grade who asked us to write our autobiography. I didn't want to write it because my parents were going through a difficult divorce. So I just made one up about how I was undercover at school and I was sleeping with all the teachers. I just wrote this very aggressive, funny essay and she pulled me aside and said, "You're funny. You could be like Woody Allen." I always wished someone would say something like that to me.

Spike: You mean you wished that before? I had no idea who Woody Allen was in high school. Like, I was so beyond—

Judd: You weren't watching movies then?

Spike: I was a late bloomer in a lot of ways.

Judd: But so I tried to get into film school because I couldn't think of a major that matched up with wanting to be a stand-up comedian. What made you want to go to film school?

Spike: I definitely knew I liked film. I mean, I liked photography. I didn't understand how film worked, but I would certainly be hypnotized. I liked *Star Wars* and *Empire Strikes Back*, movies that made me fall into a world. I spent a lot of time playing in my room and making up worlds.

Judd: Did you read?

Spike: Not a lot, but yeah. I think that I might have had some reading problems. I'm still a super-slow reader. If somebody wants me to read their script, it's like dread—I know it'll take me a good six hours to read it. But, you know, I wish—I think it's rare to find a teacher like you had. I had a photography teacher in high school who was cool and encouraging, Mr. Stallings. But for the most part I would write something that I thought was funny, a short story or something, and the teachers would say, "Bad handwriting, bad grammar, no paragraphs." They would rip it apart and give me a bad grade.

Judd: No acknowledgment of the soul of it?

Spike: No acknowledgment of the humor or imagination or whatever. In elementary school, they thought I had learning disabilities and they wanted me to get tested, you know, at the room down the hall. There was a special classroom for kids with learning disabilities.

Judd: Do you think your reading problems made you more visual?

Spike: Maybe. I mean, it does seem like directors often come to directing through either photography or writing and I was definitely more, you know, I liked writing. But as soon as I got to the magazine in California, I started focusing on photography because it was more exciting to me.

Judd: What were you getting paid?

Spike: Fifteen grand a year, and then I got a raise to eighteen grand a year.

Judd: That's not bad.

Spike: That was amazing, actually. For back then, a kid right out of school? And I loved what I was doing. After a year I thought I was going to stay out here for another year and then go to school *next* year. And it was halfway through that second year that it dawned on me: Most of the kids getting out of college would love to have the job I had. And I started to realize how much I was learning and that this was kind of—

Judd: This was your college.

Spike: This was my college. And I was around all these other really creative writers and photographers and interesting people. I would just watch them, watch how their minds worked, ask them all a million questions, and be inspired by them.

Judd: I had such a similar trajectory, because I came out to college and I knew I couldn't afford it. There was this ticking clock. I only went for a year and a half but I knew from day one that my parents wouldn't be able to afford it. I knew it could end any day. I got a job at school making burritos and I was making a little money trying to do stand-up comedy at night, but it dawned on me that no one in my family was obsessed with figuring out how we were going to pay for it. My whole family was happy when I dropped out. But when I was in high school I wrote for *Laugh Factory* magazine. And through the magazine I interviewed David Brenner and Henny Youngman and that was my first connection to comedians. Then I was an intern at Comic Relief. When I was in college, they did their first benefit, and I worked it for free. Afterwards, they said, "Do you want to stay on?" They paid me like two hundred dollars a week and then after two–three years I got it up to four hundred dollars a week. I was writing jokes for comics on the side and before I knew it I'm like, *Oh my God, I'm making like eight hundred dollars a week*—half from Comic Relief and half just writing jokes. And it was the same thing. I was around people that I could watch.

Spike: From the time I was thirteen, I was so into the BMX and skate world—that was like the comedy world to me—but I kept thinking, *That's not a job.* You know, *I've got to go to college and get a* real *job.* But it was the thing that I loved. Getting to work on the thing that you're always thinking about anyways is like the biggest—that's the goal.

Judd: What did your parents think of you going deep into the BMX world?

Spike: My mom was very encouraging, I think, because she saw how excited I was about it.

Judd: She recognized that sense of fun.

Spike: Yeah, I think so. I think she trusted me. Looking back, I had a point of view about what things meant to me and she saw that. Like if you're told that something should be taken seriously, you should try and figure out why before you take it seriously. I always wanted to know why before I believed something.

Judd: The thing I was thinking when you were talking was when we were young, there was no Internet. When I was interested in a subject—like, oh, *I wonder what happened to Lenny Bruce*—I would have to go to the library and get out the microfiche. Today, kids are so savvy. All that information is just sitting there. You can look up Martin Scorsese and watch hundreds of interviews with him. But we were really in the fucking woods. If you wanted to know something, it was hard to find out. Like, I didn't even see a picture of USC before I went there. I didn't visit. There were no photos. Where would you get a photo of it? You'd have to write a letter: "Can you send me a brochure of USC?" My parents didn't even know what I did at school. I filled out all my applications. Like today, if you have a kid, you're there constantly. You're so deep in their lives. But my parents didn't know what the hell I was doing, most of the time. Was that what your experience was like?

Spike: Yeah, but my mom was really encouraging in wanting me to work at this BMX shop in Rockville or to go on tour, or letting me move out to California. She was super-supportive of it. But, yeah, I'd be gone for three months on summer tour and she wouldn't know where I was.

Judd: I would never think to do that in a million years. My daughter's sixteen. The idea of shipping her out . . . But I did the same thing. I would just jump on the train and go to Poughkeepsie to interview Weird Al Yankovic. I didn't know where I was. I used to go to the city by myself all the time when I was fifteen.

Spike: My dad lived in New York so I would go back and forth. I went to school a little bit in New York and, yeah, by the time I was ten, I was wandering around the city by myself all the time.

Judd: That's when the city was dangerous.

Spike: We got mugged in Central Park. I'd get chased on my BMX bike. But also, going back to the idea of—one of the things I got from working in the bike shop and just being a part of skateboarding in general is that everything—and I would have never known this intellectually at the time—but in skateboarding, the city is a playground. The city is for you to reinvent. You're looking at it in a different way than everybody else is. You're looking at handrails in a different way. The things that people might sit on to have lunch, the ledges, you're looking at what you can do, tricks you can do or lines you can do and everything is to be invented.

Judd: Is skateboard culture progressive? Because it seems like there are so many artists that come out of it. Like, I love Mike Mills. There's so many others, too—Templeton and all of the *Beautiful Losers* artists. Is that part of what they're taking from that culture?

Spike: There's no one way to do skateboarding. It is athletic but it is also really creative. It's a very individual, individual-minded thing. And especially in the eighties or early nineties, when it wasn't that popular. It wasn't on TV. It didn't have the X Games. We didn't have skate parks. You had to go out of your way to be a part of it.

Judd: No tennis player or baseball player has ever directed a good movie. I mean, it is interesting when you think about how many filmmakers and artists come out of skateboard culture and zero come out of football, baseball, tennis, soccer. It's not part of any other sport.

Spike: I think it's—there's a number of things. One is that you're not told how to skate. In other sports, somebody's telling you: "This is the way to do things." There's a discipline to it. In skateboarding, you create your own discipline. You're in a bank parking lot with your friends at night and you keep throwing yourself down a set of stairs trying to land a trick. Your friends are skating, too, and you are all supporting each other, but you keep slamming and getting up because you want that feeling of mastering it and rolling away. There's no coach. Also, and this is in other sports, too, when you're trying to land a trick, the methodology of getting that—it's like this sort of OCD thing, where you're getting closer and closer every time you flick the board. The way you're sort of visualizing your body doing it. I remember being about seventeen or eighteen and there was this kid Matt Hoffman, who is this amazing BMXer. We are great friends and used to travel together and shoot photos a lot. He's probably one of the most notable BMX guys. He invented so much. He was the first guy to ever think of building a mega-ramp and almost killed himself learning to ride it. He told me about the idea of visualizing a trick and he never read it anywhere, he just discovered it. He realized that he had to start picturing in his head what he was going to do because he was inventing stuff that no one had ever done. Once you see somebody else do it, you can do it. But if no one's ever done it before, you don't know it can be done. You have to do it in your head and *imagine* it can be done.

Judd: That's like thinking you can do a video with a man running on fire that's shot in twelve seconds and then slow it down and that's a video. That's visualizing something that hasn't been done before.

Spike: We never asked permission.

Judd: Studios today are in a weird position because they want to do the thing that will make the most money but they also know that they need innovation and they have to have something new and exciting for the audience to get them into the theaters.

Spike: And they have a fiscal responsibility to the people giving *them* the money to make movies. I don't want to rail against the studios here, because I'm so fortunate and I have friends that work at the studios and I get to work with them and they are real friends and collaborators. But I see what their jobs are and understand the situation they're in. When I did *Where the Wild Things Are*, I had so much trouble getting that movie through when I was editing it because it was so not—you know, I think they were expecting a "family film."

Judd: They thought you were going to do *The Grinch.*

Spike: Yeah, maybe.

Judd: And when did they find out that they weren't getting *The Grinch*?

Spike: About ten months after we shot, I showed them a rough cut, and that's when they were like, *Oh shit. We have to put this in front of an audience right away.* I could tell there were things that they were worried about. If somebody's going to give me money to make a movie, I'm going to be very collaborative with them and listen to their concerns, but it's also my job to protect the idea of the film because, without that, we're all lost.

Judd: When you were making it, did you think, like, *Oh, if I do this correctly it will connect in some deep way and reach a certain amount of people*, or did you think, *I have this idea and I'm lucky enough to be able to do it, so let's go?*

Spike: I want the studio to make their money back and I want to be able to make movies in the future. And when I'm making a movie, I want to be responsible and listen to the concerns of the people who gave me the money. But at a certain point, I have to put that all out of my mind because it's not the responsibility of that movie. That movie's responsibility is to be true to itself. If I don't get to make another movie, I'll make something else. I'll make a movie for a million dollars. I'll go write a short story. I'll go write a book. I believe that. I mean, if I'm put to the test, I hope it's true. I hope it's not just a romantic idea.

Judd: That approach frees you up to be as creative as possible because you're not completely reliant on Hollywood or the studio system to keep you working.

Spike: With *Where the Wild Things Are,* there was a point where I was told, during the editing process, that they were worried about what the movie was and the problem was also it was financed by multiple companies, so—

Judd: They all wanted their say?

Spike: They were all nervous about—

Judd: Isn't that the worst, when you can sense that jobs are on the line? I've made movies and then the next year people have been fired and it's not necessarily *because* of your movie, but you're definitely a part of what brought down the administration. When we did *The Cable Guy,* Sony had had a few bad movies in a row and then, suddenly, everybody was gone.

Spike: I feel like even if they're going to lose their jobs they can't possibly care about the movie as much as I do. And they can't possibly go to the lengths that I'll go to protect it. With every film, I'm so grateful that they made my movie and I will extend myself to keep the conversation open and hear their thoughts. But with *Wild Things,* there was a point where it started to feel abusive. There was a point where I said to somebody at the studio that I was working with, whom I'm actually close friends with now, I was like, "If I came to you and talked to you about your child the way you're talking to me about my movie right now, you wouldn't listen to me. If I came to you and said, 'Man, your kid is fucked up. He's a problem child and he is freaking me and everyone out. I think you should put him on medication. You know, he's really a fucked-up kid,' you're never going to listen to me because I'm judging your kid and I clearly don't like or get your kid. But if you came to me and said, 'Your kid is really special. I see how special he is. I sat and talked to him the other day and what he was talking about was amazing. But there's a school that might be better for him than the school that he's in right now and I'll go visit it with you if you want . . . ,' that's a different thing. I'll listen to you."

Judd: It takes a long time to find the people who get what you do. The first half of my career, I was always at war with people. We would fight and scream and curse and cry and I was a terror because people didn't understand what I was trying to do. They were so mad at me, like I was letting them down. Because *Freaks and Geeks* didn't have more viewers or *The Ben Stiller Show* wasn't beating *60 Minutes*. But *The Ben Stiller Show* was up against *60 Minutes* at seven-thirty on a Sunday! It was an edgy sketch show but they, you know, you get into these battles because either they feel you're unimportant or they feel like you're not doing what they want you to do. And then finally you find someone that gets your joke and so you make *Superbad* and then you say, "Hey, I've got another one. Do you want to do *Pineapple Express*?" and they say, "Yeah." And suddenly you're in this great rhythm with a studio because they get your tone. They got the joke. With comedy, as soon as you succeed, you have some credibility and then they trust you more. It must be much more extreme with you because you're doing things that are always very new to the studio. You have a track record of succeeding doing something that's completely original, but yet it must also scare them because you are reinventing the wheel every time out.

Spike: We've been lucky for sure. *Wild Things* was the only one that I've ever gotten in those kinds of fights with because the budget was so much higher. I was on a different playing field because what I wanted to do required a lot more money. And so when you're taking that much money from somebody, there's going to be a danger.

Judd: They do the math: Okay, it cost us a hundred, it needs to gross three hundred.

Spike: And it's a weird movie. Some people find it very sad and strange or dark and that doesn't feel like a "family film."

Judd: It's a remarkable movie, but it's so daring. When I watch it, I think, *This feels like it was made in another land.*

Spike: There are people who like it and people who don't like it. I don't even know how to judge that kind of thing. I just know it's true to what I set out to make, and it feels dangerous in the way I promised Maurice Sendak it would feel. When I first started talking to him about the movie, it always scared me because I loved the book and I didn't want to fuck it up and I didn't know what I could possibly add to it. And then I finally had the idea of what I'd add to it, which is: Who *are* the wild things? And, you know, who are they to *Max*—they are emotional volatility and emotional wildness in his life—in him and the people he is close to. If I could make a movie that captured what it felt like to be a person at nine years old trying to understand a confusing and sometimes scary world—that was my goal. I remember talking to Maurice about it and saying, "Maurice, I'm a little nervous about what I want to do because this is what it is to me but I know this book is a lot of things to a lot of other people." And he said, "I don't care." He said, "Just promise me that you're not going to pander to children, that you're going to make something dangerous and personal and true to you. If you do that, then you've done the same thing I did when I wrote the book when I was your age. The book was mine and now this movie has to be yours." With his blessing . . . and not only blessing but his artistic integrity challenging me and pushing me and inspiring me, I felt like as long as I'm true to the assignments that he gave me, I will have done right by him.

Judd: With a movie like *Where the Wild Things Are*, you get incredible praise and vicious attacks. How do you keep your center when you have both?

Spike: The thing I'm realizing is that I just don't start to make another movie until I feel clean again from the last one.

Judd: That can mean years in between.

Spike: I took a while after *Where the Wild Things Are* before I was ready to start again—it was almost a year after we released it before I sat down to write. I had all the notes for it. I had two years of notes for what became *Her*. But I let myself take time before I sat down to write, until I felt *excited* to write—excited in that feeling of curiosity and wanting to get into this for myself.

Judd: Because you do get a kind of post-traumatic stress from making these movies.

Spike: It maybe seems obnoxious to say that, but it's true.

Judd: I think it's because you're so vulnerable. You put so much of your heart into it and some people are deeply moved and touched, and other people could give a fuck. Twitter is a funny expression of that. You can get so much praise and then just someone's just like, "This was forty minutes too long." You know.

Spike: It's like, "Meh." (*Laughs*) I love that, that you can work on something for three years and somebody will give you just three letters: M-E-H. It makes me think of two things. One of which is, I feel like my job really isn't to know how many people are going to like something. My job is to know what a movie's *about* to me, and to know that I need to make it. It's somebody else's job to say, "Okay, that budget makes sense or doesn't make sense." Once they gamble on it, that's their gamble and I'm gonna be their partner in it, but we have to support each other. That's how I feel with Megan Ellison. I feel like we are partners. And then the other thing made me think about what you were talking about before, the anxiety of not being able to get another movie made. I don't want to come off as flippant about that. Because it is an anxiety I had, of course. But it's my job to not let that anxiety affect the creative decisions. That's not fair to the movie.

Judd: So you decided to make a movie about a guy who wants to fuck a computer. Am I going to get to work again? (*Laughs*) Seriously, though. What do you take from the success of *Her*? You know, what I notice from a lot of people is that . . . I feel like, as creative people, we're all on this journey to get comfortable with who we are, to understand who we are, to find a way for our art to express that. And as the years go by, you can see the journey that people take to be themselves and find themselves, whether it's Garry Shandling as a comedian who then does *The Garry Shandling Show*, which then turns into *The Larry Sanders Show*. Or Louis C.K. being a comedy writer who works for Conan and does stand-up until he suddenly reveals himself and does *Louie*.

Spike: I love the story of Louis C.K. I love the story of him finding his voice when he's thirty-five and, like, and a lot of it having to do with his kids, having kids, and—

Judd: Just realizing that's interesting. See, I never thought I was interesting. I stopped doing stand-up because I thought, *Jim Carrey's* interesting.

I could write jokes for him. I could work on a movie with him. But my feelings? Not interesting.

Spike: And when did that change?

Judd: My Maurice Sendak moment happened with Warren Zevon. I wrote a movie with Owen Wilson in the late nineties and I went to meet with Warren Zevon about scoring it. I was talking about handing it in to the studio and being anxious about getting their notes. And he looked at me like I was crazy for even getting notes, or wanting notes, or caring about what the notes would say. He's like, "What do you care what they say? That's not what this is about." And then I just clicked in, like: *Oh, that's what it is.* And then even as something as silly as *The 40-Year-Old Virgin* perfectly captured my neurosis, how insecure I felt and how much like a freak I felt. You're just hiding in your cubby, afraid to interact with the world. And as soon as I let go, everything went better. The second I made that adjustment, my career took off. But it took me forever to believe, to get my self-esteem out of the gutter enough to think that my story, my thoughts, were interesting. And I felt that when I watched *Her*, which is such a personal expression of a worldview and how you feel about other people and relationships. And then the world rewards you because you went all the way. And it leads to success and an Oscar. Do you look at it that way? Like, *Wow, I finally did it all alone, I fully committed?*

Spike: It's so complicated. There's so many thoughts and feelings I have about all that. One of which is maybe slightly defensive. Which is: I feel like *Her* is not a radical departure. Maybe it was, I don't know. But to me, it was just the next step like any next step that came before—following what I had to do. But I have to say, I don't think I could've written *Her* in my twenties. I don't think I could've written screenplays like that in my twenties because I didn't understand everything you're talking about, in terms of exploring yourself through writing. I couldn't even have written the story you wrote to get into college about all the teachers having sex with you. I don't think I knew how to go that raw. I knew how to explore things I was curious about. My daydreams, my fantasies—as I said, I'm a late bloomer. When I think about certain writers, like the Coen Brothers or Paul Thomas Anderson, they came out writing those things so *young*. That's incredible to me. But I also want to say that most everything I've done feels personal to me. Even the two movies that I did with Charlie [Kaufman] or the music videos—a music video that would start with a song that Björk would send me, and I would try to make it my thing. It's all an extension. They are all personal to me, because that's who I was and what I was interested in and trying to explore at that time. Maybe that's a little defensive. But it's a bit of a defensive answer because, you know, I just finished doing a lot of interviews about the movie and that point was made a lot: This is the first thing that wholly came from me. Which is, you know, true in some ways. But *Wild Things* feels like it came from the same place, to me.

Judd: There's something about being alone in the woods.

Spike: Yeah, so now that I've been defensive, I'll answer your question. I think *Wild Things* was the beginning of that. And after *Wild Things* I went and made a few short films that was like, I wanted to sort of exercise that muscle of having an idea that came purely from my own imagination and my confusion and my excitement and wasn't inspired by something else, that was inspired purely by my gut and heart. I was excited by that. I'm excited by giving myself permission to write what's in my daydreams.

Judd: What do you think people took from *Her*? Like what do people talk to you about when they say they've connected with the movie?

Spike: Um, what . . . I'm not sure. . . . I think to answer that question honestly makes me anxious because I'm still recovering from six months of talking about that movie. Maybe I'm a bit fried right now since it's still fresh. It took a lot out of me. But to be clear, I'm so grateful for the response it got, the reception it got. And grateful that I get to make movies and that anyone is interested in talking to me about it in the first place. But it's also complicated just because of how *much* I've had to talk about the movie and—

Judd: The experience of making movies is—if you do work that's personal, you're putting yourself out there in a way that people don't understand. They really don't. I made a movie with my family and it was made up, but it did cut to the core of everything we're debating and worried about and thinking about. And it takes years to recover.

Spike: Yeah. I feel ridiculous to complain about it but I'm just giving myself time to recuperate. Making a movie takes so much out of you, but it also gives you so much. When I lock picture—it's like a relationship ending, and there's something bittersweet about it, too. It's a love relationship in one way, in terms of negotiating what you need from it, and what it needs from you. It's also a parent relationship, in that you can't need too much from it. You have to give to it unconditionally and you have to allow it to be who it is—not to put your needs on it. And then you let it go—it graduates high school and you send it off into the world; you've done everything you can do. When I finished *Her*, I thought, *Okay, I've done everything I can do to give this as much love as I could give it and now it's gonna go off and be what it's gonna be. If it gets loved I'll be proud and if it gets hated it'll hurt, but I also know that what I have done with my friends and collaborators will never change.* That is what the movie is to me, that's my relationship with my movie . . . the experience and life I lived with it.

Judd: It's deeply sad that it ends. If I think about anything I've done— when we made *Freaks and Geeks* and it ended, I thought: *How do I keep these people around? How do I keep these ideas around?* I never recovered in a lot of ways. I miss making *Funny People*. I miss going to see Sandler every day and talking about it. It's devastating. I mean, I come from a divorced family. It's devastating that each experience comes to this . . . instant violent conclusion, and then you're alone again in your room. So many of those ideas went into *Her*. I'm such a—I'm fascinated by relationships, self-help, the struggle we all have, and I thought—in the last thirty-five minutes of that movie, you brought so many ideas together in such an elegant way, that are really hard to capture. The idea of loving your ex, even though it doesn't work. And getting to that place where you feel like you understand why it melted down, and it can't work but . . . It's like an impossible thing to express. I don't think I've ever seen people talk about it in that way. About letting go and what it means.

Spike: I don't know what to say.

Judd: Am I in the ballpark of what you were exploring?

Spike: For sure, for sure. You know, relationships are so infinitely complicated. And I think that intimacy is equally so. . . . I was trying to write about all of that, trying to write about it in as complicated a way as I knew how at this time in my life. As you said earlier, every day we're in a different mood and see things differently. And our emotions are so completely convincing to us, so I tried to write about all the confusion of that . . . but also the way we believe things so truly—the way, there's the moment, you know, where Joaquin is talking about how he is never going to feel anything new again. And he believes it so convincingly and then, the next day, he's believing something totally new. And feeling that with complete conviction that that is true, too. Luckily, we have these irrational emotions, emotions that make life large and—it's just not like this series of rational decisions and logic. It's the magic of it and the poetry of life. I don't know. You saying that definitely moves me. When you're talking about the idea of loving your ex, and being able to hold on to that amidst all the other feelings of being heartbroken or sad or missing something that's gone—something dies when a relationship ends. It is a death because that thing that was the two of you together was alive and now it won't be and the only two people who really knew that thing that was alive are the two of you. No one else knows.

Judd: I think about my girlfriend from high school and all of our dreams at the time and I almost . . . You know, a lot of times I'm tempted to reach out to her but I don't because it's almost, it's so *present*. It doesn't feel old. It feels brand-new. I'm always afraid to see exes in front of my wife because I feel like she'll know in my face that I'm as devastated today as I was the day that girl broke up with me. Do you think it sometimes takes making a movie—do you feel like you evolve in your personal issues as a result of making a movie like *Her*?

Spike: Yes, every movie, I'm working stuff out.

Judd: Joaquin Phoenix is so amazing in *Her*. It's just so tight on him, and he does so many amazing, funny things. And it's so intimate.

Spike: So many times I felt, *I just don't want to cut away from this performance. I just want to sit here on this take and be close and feel him.*

Judd: In the writers' room on *Larry Sanders*, we would always have this debate: Would you rather work with someone who is easy and not as good or someone who is a pain in the ass who is a genius? There were writers in that room that would say, "I'll take the easy guy, life's too short." I was always like, "Nah, you've got to go with the genius."

Spike: Or you are really lucky if they're a genius and easy to direct, like Meryl Streep or Rooney Mara. They are easy and amazing and they work in a different way. I don't even understand it. Somehow they are both emotionally in tune, totally real in the smallest moments and completely directable and able to make the smallest or biggest adjustment from take to take.

Judd: It's not pure pain. But some of those pure pain people are remark-able.

Spike: Like Gandolfini. He was so raw. It was so exciting to work with him, but it was intense, too. Scary even, because he would get so upset at him-self if he did something that felt false. But what he gave me and that char-acter and the movie was a piece of himself. He breathed his life into the film with all his heart and pain and sensitivity. I loved that man.

Judd: Do you ever think, like, you're like the guy in the BMX shop, for so many people? That they look at you as somebody who doesn't follow the rules and lives in this fully creative world and does things differently, and promotes "newness"?

Spike: I'd be flattered if I was.

Judd: Was Maurice Sendak like that as well?

Spike: For me, for sure. He's a real artist. And to be able to have the kind of friendship and collaboration I had with him was like—you know, a gift for life. He's somebody who's unafraid to be honest in all its messiness. The same thing with Charlie Kaufman. Being friends with Charlie and being able to work with Charlie is hugely inspiring.

Judd: It's like you continue to find that person. When you think of Maurice Sendak, is there a thought or philosophy that immediately comes to mind?

Spike: I met him when I was twenty-six and we worked on a movie that didn't end up happening. And at that point, I really don't think I understood what being an artist meant. He would talk about it often and I would nod. And over the years, we stayed in touch, we stayed close, but it wasn't until the third time he offered me the book that I had the idea I was talking about earlier. I was like thirty-three, and that's when we started working together. And we became close. I just think he was an artist till the day he died. I think now I know what that means in terms of living honestly and creating honestly. Actually, Maurice and Charlie remind me of each other. They're very similar people in terms of their willingness to throw down against anything they think is bullshit. They are not careerists; they are making what they are making because they have to. Out of all the people that have influenced me, those guys are two of the biggest.

Judd: What about something like *Jackass*? How do those guys, and that experience, fit into what you're talking about?

Spike: Similarly. I mean, funnily enough, the two guys—so it's me and Johnny Knoxville and Jeff Tremaine that created the show and later the movie, and we are really close, too. I met Knoxville in my early twenties out here in L.A. when we were both figuring out what we were doing. And Jeff I've known since I was twelve. Jeff introduced me to the Ramones, took me to my first hard-core shows in D.C. He was two years older than me. And when he was sixteen, he had a car and we'd build ramps together and skate.

Judd: He sounds like the coolest guy in the world.

Spike: He was cool. Oh, Jeff was cool.

Judd: You're twelve and have a cool fourteen-year-old who showed you all of that stuff. That's a big deal.

Spike: And then I helped Jeff get his first jobs out here. One of them was at the skate magazine where I was working, *Big Brother*.

Judd: Is that where they did the first Johnny Knoxville getting shot?

Spike: Yeah, it was all through the *Big Brother* videos. I introduced Knoxville to Jeff. At the time he was doing extra work.

Judd: A professional extra?

Spike: And he also landed a Taco Bell commercial. And he was like, "I got a Taco Bell commercial!" We were all in our mid-twenties and I introduced Jeff to Knoxville and they started doing stuff for the *Big Brother* videos. And a few years later, it was Jeff who had the idea to take that and make a TV show out of it. It just came out of what we were already doing. It was natural, what made us laugh in skate videos. We thought if we can get twenty minutes on national TV and do whatever we want, we were getting away with murder. We thought it would last eight episodes. And we got an eight-episode order from MTV! That was all we thought we would do. We had no idea anyone would care; we were really just doing it because we thought it was funny. And then as soon as it came out, it just blew up. Knoxville was on the cover of *Rolling Stone* two months later and we got to make another fourteen episodes. We did the show for a year, twenty-two shows total, and then we canceled the show ourselves, which was unheard of.

Judd: For your own safety?

Spike: No, we did what we wanted to do. We also felt like MTV wasn't really promoting it that much because they were so nervous about it. They were really into it because it was so successful but they were also nervous about it and getting shit for it. And it just felt right to end it. We ended it on a high.

Judd: What was the criticism? That it was bad for our culture?

Spike: I mean, yeah. It was the downfall of Western civilization.

Judd: It wasn't just that it was something that kids have done forever.

Spike: Certain age groups would view it as nihilistic. So anyways, we ended up canceling it. But they didn't want us to cancel it, obviously. So we said, "What if we do a movie as our last episode?" The movie was so fun and we had such a blast doing it.

Judd: What a great fraternity of people that is. The camaraderie of it.

Spike: We've been through life together. We've done so much together now. I've known Jeff for over thirty years. That's crazy. I've known Knoxville for twenty years, and a lot of the guys—we've been through it together. And we have a lot of it on tape, too.

Judd: It may be the funniest thing ever. I remember watching a little bit of it with my daughter—and she was too young to watch it. I was surprised at how dirty it is. But I couldn't resist showing it to her. I don't know if she was nine or ten at the time, but I'd fast-forward past anything bad. The next thing I know, someone's balls are on the screen and she's laughing as hard as I've ever seen her laugh in my life. I mean it just brings such joy to people. When you watch it, you think: *I never laugh this hard. Like, nothing can get me to this place of total hysteria where you fall to pieces laughing.* That's a real gift to the world, and it cannot be underestimated.

Spike: We just stumbled on it. I don't think we had any idea.

Judd: It makes you feel like you're fifteen again. The friendship and craziness and that tension before they do crazy things—it's that nervous energy that really brings you back to middle school. In the best possible way.

Spike: That's what it's like when we're out there, feeling it. We are laughing. We are laughing more than anybody else. We just think it's the funniest thing in the world. You can't force that kind of chemistry, and we're very protective of that. We only do it if it feels right. It was fun to do the last one, *Bad Grandpa*.

Judd: I watched that with my eleven-year-old. I was like, *My daughter can handle seeing balls.* When you're watching *Bad Grandpa* there's a moment where the big, long ball comes out and, as a parent, you think, *Okay. It's probably going to go away in a second, so I'm not going to cover her eyes.* And then you think, *Wait, what's wrong with testicles? Is there anything wrong with seeing a testicle when you're a kid?* And then you just say, *Fuck it, she's laughing too hard.* This was one of the great father-daughter moments, watching this ridiculous movie. I mean, God, we laughed so hard. I took pictures of her laughing, it felt so momentous.

Spike: That's so sweet.

Judd: That's how life works in our house.

STEPHEN COLBERT
(2014)

Sometimes I would watch *The Colbert Report* and I'd be literally stunned at how funny it was. The writing and performing on that show were at a level never before seen on television.

Stephen Colbert is so funny, and such a nimble and versatile comedian, but he also seems to be a spiritual man who has found a measure of true happiness. That's something I don't understand at all, so I was thrilled to get the chance to ask him how this happy-funny combination is possible, with the small hope that he would say something that would change my life forever. I think he did say it at one point, and I intend to have it printed on a plaque that I can put on my refrigerator. I can't remember what it was, though, because I was too pissed off to hear it.

Judd Apatow: It's hard to believe you're in the final few weeks of your show. Is it tough to focus on making this last run great when you have this giant new thing looming?

Stephen Colbert: It is. When you do a hundred and sixty shows a year, it's really hard to produce that much material. As I used to say, "All I want to do is eighty hours of comedy this year that I wouldn't mind my friends seeing."

Judd: (*Laughs*) Yeah.

Stephen: This year I'm just working on an eighty-hour comedy project. That's it. Listen, before I knew how horrible it would be, the strike in 2007 sounded like a great idea.

Judd: Are you burned out?

Stephen: I'm not, really. I'm not burned out—people may be reading this book centuries from now, so I'll have to remind them that I play a character on my show, and he's modeled on punditry, and I no longer respect my model. That's my problem. Regardless of whether I was moving on to something else after this show, I don't know if I could have done it much longer, because you have to be invested in your model. And I really am not. I can't watch that stuff anymore. That's what burns me out, not the grind. I *like* the grind. I like showing up every day with people that I respect, and doing the show with them. I always say that by the time I go out onstage, we've already done the show for each other, all day long. It's my responsibility, and privilege, to then translate that to an audience. You know? I'm the bottom of the funnel.

Judd: Yeah.

Stephen: And that's part of the skill, to be able to coalesce and synthesize everything into a single mouth. So, I don't mind that. That doesn't burn me out. But now that I only have ten shows left, everything is harder. It's harder to only have ten left, because the way you prepare for a hundred and sixty shows is to build this enormous machine that is constantly firing information or jokes or script ideas that you're collecting as you go along: That one will work, that one will work, that one will work, throw that one away. And then you sweep them into a pile and say, "What does that mean? What are those about?" And then you go, "Oh, *that's* what that one's about. Put this one together with that, and then that's what you want to say." But now, we only have ten shows left. We can't just fire things randomly out of the cannon. Not that it was ever random. What I mean is, our level of output is no longer useful.

Judd: And sometimes the speed of things and the sense of it never ending is what keeps you from feeling nervous.

Stephen: Exactly. And when you have a certain number of shows left, you get afraid that, right at the end of the race, you're going to drop the baby.

Judd: It seems like people in this position respond differently. Like, when Conan O'Brien was getting canceled at *The Tonight Show*, he started turning out his best shows.

Stephen: He seemed very free.

Judd: The rage fired him up.

Stephen: Yeah.

Judd: It's like you're in a David Chase situation right now. You're ending *The Sopranos.*

Stephen: (*Laughs*) I wish.

Judd: Looking back, what was the main input for the show: the comedy or the politics?

Stephen: I once had a teacher who would say, "Write what you know, and write what you are interested in." I also had an improv teacher who said the first thing you are emotional about onstage is what the scene is about. So, regardless of what it is, you have to follow that rabbit hole. That's where you'll make your discoveries. I am an actor who became a comedian, and I wanted to do something with the skill set that I established; someone who was an actor who became an improviser, and through improvisation, learned dramatic structure and applied that to comedic scenes and sketch comedy—and then, for some weird reason, got hired by *The Daily Show.* It was kind of a mistake, and I went, Oh, but I also really care about the news. I enjoy it. I have eclectic interests, so maybe I could apply this little tool set that I've built up over the years to a lot of different subjects that might be covered in the news, and I also look like—wait, I look like a white guy.

Judd: (*Laughs*)

Stephen: I look like the Man. I look like a very hegemonic figure. So, I said, *Okay, I am an anchor.* I look like an anchor, anyway, and so I did that for Jon for years. Acting was a tool toward doing comedy. I was a straight actor for years, actually, until I realized how much more I loved being in comedy, writing comedy, and being with comedians. The joy I felt with other comedians, that was the healthiest thing. I thought, *Oh my God, look how much we're laughing and how agonizing it was for that to have gone that poorly. The healthy choice is to do this for the rest of my life.*

Judd: I've realized that later in life, too. For a long time, I thought getting into comedy was an unhealthy choice. Only recently did I begin to think it's a healthy choice.

Stephen: Yeah, exactly. To me, it was. It's almost like committing myself to flossing and exercise. I don't really want to do anything other than comedy, and so did we talk about things that mattered to me? Did we occasionally invest our scripts with a satirical meaning that was overt? Yes. But, it's always comedy first. Because that's what I love. That's what keeps me going and alive.

Judd: When did that kick in for you, comedy as a point of view, as a way of dealing with life?

Stephen: I don't know if there was necessarily a moment. I remember when I was younger—I knew a guy, a great improviser, and I'm not going to name his name because of the advice he's about to give in this little story. He said, "You have to see the world differently than the audience does." Like, you have to put yourself in a state where you see the world differently than the audience does, because then you will surprise them with your choices. Comedy is all about surprising the audience with your choices. It might be something that is familiar to them, but they're surprised you're willing to say it. He said, "If you have to do heroin, do heroin. I would recommend you do heroin."

Judd: Okay. (*Laughs*)

Stephen: But also, when I was a kid, we had a tragedy in my family. My father and two of my brothers, Peter and Paul, the two closest in age to me, died in a plane crash. I was ten years old, and my mother, who had always been a very religious person—not overtly related to their death—would say to me—if anything was wrong with my life, if anything was going wrong—she would say, "Look at this in the light of eternity. What is this in the light of eternity?" In other words, don't worry about this little thing.

Judd: Yeah.

Stephen: And that light of eternity is another way of looking at everything. See it in the light of eternity. Don't see this as your momentary worry. So, that helped me not worry, and because my father and brothers had died, what could worry you more than that? From that point on, I never worked in school again. I maybe did my homework six times from age ten to eighteen.

Judd: Wow.

Stephen: I barely graduated. I just read a lot of books, so I incidentally learned enough to bullshit by. There was no threat that anyone could hold over me. Nothing seemed important. So that made me think differently about almost everything that normally happened to a child. What are you going to threaten me with? What could a teacher possibly threaten me with?

Judd: Your mom sounds wonderful.

Stephen: She was a lovely lady.

Judd: It's a great piece of wisdom, and her strength must have been ridiculous to be able to communicate that to you in a way that it landed. Because some kids—their parents would look at the big picture and then go take drugs and disappear.

Stephen: Well, I did take drugs.

Judd: (*Laughs*)

Stephen: But my mom was not bitter. She did not become a bitter person. She had an excuse to be, and she did not. She stayed grateful for life. And her example kept me from—I was a broken kid, don't get me wrong, but I did not compound that by feeling guilty about not doing work, which is actually beside the point. The real point is it forced me to look at the world differently because, suddenly, the value system of checks and balances against the young mind did not mean anything to me anymore.

Judd: I can sense that spirit in your work. I noticed it when you performed for George Bush at the White House Correspondents' Dinner in 2006, that level of confidence and not caring. I don't think many people have that. I watched Leno do it once and he looked exhausted and nervous, and he had a rough set. Actually, what made me laugh the most is that he had to sit next to the first lady for like two hours before he had to do his set, and it was fun to watch them run out of things to talk about.

Stephen: I sat next to Helen Thomas. And she said, "So, are you going to do *all* of your jokes?"

Judd: (*Laughs*)

Stephen: And she goes, "How did you like the party beforehand?" Because there's this big party beforehand, with the president, a few cabinet members, heads of news organizations, and maybe the Super Bowl quarterback, you know.

Judd: Yeah.

Stephen: And my mom, who loved the president, was there, with my brothers and sister. And Helen Thomas says, "Did you like the party?" I say, "I liked that party, yeah. It was nice. My mom had a good time." And she said, "Now, after that party, are you going to do all of your jokes? Because that's a smart party. There's a lot of people—I've sat next to a lot of comedians who are cowed by that party."

Judd: Oh, wow.

Stephen: Because you're there, you're being chummy with the guy you're going to be making fun of. So I say, "Oh, yeah, I know what that means, but I think I can do it because *I'm* not doing it, my character is, and my character loves the guy." That actually helped a lot.

Judd: I've always thought there should be a documentary about that performance.

Stephen: Well, there's a lot to talk about.

Judd: Looking back on it, after 9/11, everyone was afraid to say the president didn't know what he was doing or was making terrible mistakes. And that felt like the first time that someone said, "Oh, by the way, this guy might not know what the fuck he's doing at all."

Stephen: I wouldn't say I was the first person to do it, because Jon certainly was doing it on his show.

Judd: But not to his face.

Stephen: Well, you don't get an opportunity to do that very often.

Judd: Yeah.

Stephen: You know, there's a woman I get my coffee from every morning. She is not a native to our country, she wasn't born here. And she said to me the week of that dinner, she said, "Stephen, you look so tired, why do you look so tired?" I go, "Well, Anna, I been working late after the show. I'm writing a script to get ready for the Correspondents' Dinner. I'm going to perform for the president." She said, "You perform in front of the president?" I said, "Yeah, I'll be like five feet from him." She goes, "But you're a satirist. You're a critic. You're going to do your jokes right next to him?" And I said, "Yeah." She took my face in her hands and said, "This is a good country."

Judd: Did you have a sense of the importance of the moment *in* the moment?

Stephen: Oh, no. Hell no. I knew what it was. I was thrilled to do it, because I knew I'd never be—I knew I'd never get this shot again. I just wanted to get to the next joke and the next joke and the next joke.

Judd: Yeah.

Stephen: I did ten minutes on the president and I did ten minutes on the press, too, which people forget. The last ten minutes were on the people in the room. And it was—there was something you were talking about earlier that made me think of the story about the party beforehand. Oh, I know what it was: It was feeling nervous sitting next to the first lady before you go in.

Judd: Right.

Stephen: After Helen Thomas asked me if I was going to do all my jokes, she looks down the table and the president is sitting there with his cards, about to go up and do his bit. And she goes, "He's going over his cards, too."

Judd: (*Laughs*)

Stephen: I said, "Oh, Helen, I can't look at him right now." And she goes, "Why not?" And I said, "Because he can't be a person. He has to be his ideas." He has to be his policies. I feel for another performer, but he has to be the object—he has to represent his policies and the actions of the administrations for these jokes to come out of my mouth. I can't make a joke about a guy worried about his bit at a banquet.

Judd: When you did the routine, were you registering the reaction from him or the first lady?

Stephen: No, no. I know I've said this to some people before, but C-SPAN is not an entertainment company, and they don't mic the room. So, what you didn't know, if you watched at home, was that a lot of material was landing.

Judd: Yeah.

Stephen: It just wasn't landing for the people on the dais, or the people in the front row, who were all from the news organizations who need to not piss off the people on the dais. But, you know, as a comedian, if a thousand people are laughing, that sounds like a lot of people. That sounds like bacon frying. It's a big crowd. There were three thousand people in that room, so if a thousand of them laughed, it still felt like a great response.

Judd: Yeah.

Stephen: So, I did not feel like I was grinding my way through the indifference of a hostile audience. I didn't think I was throwing Molotov cocktails. And that wasn't my intention, either. I was there to do jokes, just like I did them on the show. I didn't do anything different there than I did on the show.

Judd: What's fun is that now you'll probably end up talking to the president about it at some point, because it's inevitable he will be a guest on your new show.

Stephen: I don't know about that. Nothing's inevitable. I would like it, though. I wrote him a letter afterwards saying I hope he enjoyed it, it was an honor. Maybe he burned it.

Judd: What is your sense of how Republicans and Democrats feel about your show?

Stephen: I mean, it has been hard to get Republican politicians to come on the show. But I saw this study once many years ago, from Ohio State University, the graduate program there. They did a study of self-identified conservatives and self-identified liberals, and they got a group that self-identified in those categories, and that also both sides identified as fans of the show, and they had them watch the same video, then they said, "What do you think his actual political position is here?" Democrats believed that I was a liberal or liberals believed I was a liberal pretending to be a conservative, and conservatives who enjoyed the show tended to think that I was a conservative pretending to be a liberal pretending to be a conservative.

Judd: (*Laughs*)

Stephen: And I don't really want to correct either side, because there are times I agree with my character. And I really don't want the audience to know when I do. I love that, man. That's the triple gainer. I purposefully jumped over the line a lot at the beginning of the show so people would be confused.

Judd: Is it strange for you, as a comedy person and an improviser, to be tossed into the center of public political life, and to be surrounded by the players—

Stephen: That was the point of it. The whole point of it was to do that. Jon Stewart used to say when we were over there, "We're the kids in the back of the class shooting spitballs, you know?"

Judd: Yeah.

Stephen: And I wanted to be the spitball. I remember when I ran for president for the first time in South Carolina, people—people who have known me for years and really understand me—would call me up and say, "Listen, you got to help me out here. I am trying to deal with people who are freaking out about this. Is this real or is this a joke?"

Judd: (*Laughs*)

Stephen: And that's the first time I realized what I really liked about this. If it wasn't real, it wouldn't be a joke. Or it wouldn't be a joke I'd want to do.

Judd: Yes.

Stephen: I wanted to do it to see what it was really like, because when I really ran, I really had to deal with federal election law. I really had lawyers up my ass. I really had to find out, like, Wait, I can actually be sponsored by Doritos? Okay, my candidacy can be sponsored by Doritos, but I can't actually talk about Doritos when I talk about my candidacy? Or I can eat Doritos that I bought myself, but I can't eat Doritos that Doritos gave me? Or, like, when I actually formed a super PAC, or sponsored the Olympics, or testified before Congress, or held a rally with Jon on the

Mall, or . . . We always say here that we can make jokes about anything. Where do we point the gun?

Judd: Yeah.

Stephen: The hard part is deciding what's worth shooting.

Judd: How much money did you raise?

Stephen: Over a million dollars. Significantly over.

Judd: Why do you think people gave you money?

Stephen: They wanted to play the game. We established this lovely relationship with our audience where—early on, we called them the Colbert Nation, okay? "I've got to watch where I point this thing, okay? You people are powerful, I'm your leader. We're going to change things. We're going to make the world a better place." I said that on the first night, and I started calling them the Nation. Well, what we didn't realize is our audience was accepting our initiation that they were a character in the show. And that super PAC was the ultimate game they played with us. We went and held rallies. We raised money. We ran commercials. We got in trouble. We said, "You give us the gun and we'll go fuck shit up. We'll start shooting it in ways that are both legal and unethical."

Judd: (*Laughs*)

Stephen: And our audience enjoyed being in a little gang. That's a fun thing. We all had a place. There was an intimacy that I would never want to lose again. I know that's possible now, and I never want to lose it.

Judd: Were you thinking about winding down the show before the offer to do the talk show came in?

Stephen: Yes. As I said earlier, I was sick of the model. And I realized: *If I want a change, I've got to leave.*

Judd: What are your thoughts about switching to something that is just transparently your personality—and about, on some level, sincerity?

Stephen: We shall see, Judd Apatow. We shall see.

Judd: Were you a fanatical Letterman fan?

Stephen: Yeah, yeah. I mean, I am the ur-audience. His show started in '82, the year I started college. Dave was it. Johnny was great, I loved Johnny. I'm the youngest of eleven children, and my elder sisters would wake me up to watch Carson with them because they didn't want to watch it alone. I would be like a toddler watching Carson with them, but Dave — Dave was like us. Dave was stupid. And I loved it. His disrespect was to his own form.

Judd: I was completely obsessed with Letterman, too. When I was in college, I — this is a terrible story. I haven't told it in a long time, but I sent a letter to every single staff member at *Letterman* asking for an internship, and someone called me, and I flew to New York, on my own dime, for the interview. When I got there, the woman told me there was no job, it had already been filled. I flew home and wrote her the meanest letter, using words that could end my career right now.

Stephen: Oh my God. You know, I was offered a *Letterman* internship.

Judd: And you didn't take it?

Stephen: My girlfriend my senior year of college — she was coming out to New York and I came with her. She was interviewing for an internship at *Letterman*. I don't know how she got it. I didn't know internships existed. I didn't know anything like that, didn't know that was an option. I went with her to the interview. It was at 30 Rock, and she went in and she was having her interview and somebody opened the door next to that room and said, "Are you the next guy?" I said, "No, I'm just here with my friend who is in there talking." He goes, "Well, do you want to come talk?" So I went in and we had a nice conversation, and then they called me and said, "You got the internship," and she didn't get it.

Judd: Did the breakup soon follow?

Stephen: We did not last the summer. But I turned the job down, because I was like, "What? You don't pay? How can I go to New York and not — what? What do you mean I move to New York and you don't pay me? What do I do, live in a trash barrel?"

Judd: See, I would have lived in the trash barrel.

Stephen: It would have been fun, but again, it wasn't on my radar.

Judd: And when did you—just so I understand the trajectory a little bit, you were attempting serious theater at this point?

Stephen: Yeah, I was studying at Northwestern University's theater program, and you know, I was doing Stanislavski and Meisner and I was sharing my pain with everyone around me—it was therapy as much as it was anything. I met a guy there who said, "Hey, have you ever seen comedy improv?" I said no. He said, "Well, I'm going down to see these guys in Chicago do something called *The Harold*. Do you want to go see it?" I said sure. So I went down to a place that doesn't exist anymore called CrossCurrents, which was beneath the Belmont L in Chicago, right near Ann Sather's. Best Swedish cinnamon rolls in the city.

Judd: Yeah.

Stephen: And I went and saw people improvise one-act plays based on a single word, and I was immediately hooked. I went, "I don't know what that is, but I have to do it. I have to get onstage and perform extemporaneously with other people." I loved the ensemble feel of it. I continued to do straight theater, kind of avant-garde black box kind of theater, but I was getting paid to do comedy. And then realized I really like it actually. I really love these people. I met Amy Sedaris and Paul Dinello at Second City. They changed my life. If I hadn't met Paul and Amy, I don't think I would have gone into comedy. They became my family.

Judd: But before that, you didn't think, *I'm a comedy person in high school*? That wasn't—

Stephen: I didn't know what it meant to do comedy in high school. I didn't even perform until I was a senior.

Judd: Wow.

Stephen: On anything. I was just a kid in the back of the room, you know?

Judd: Let me just switch topics here. The one time I was a guest on your show, which I enjoyed a great deal—

Stephen: I'm glad to hear that. You came on pretty early, when we hadn't had many entertainment figures on. I wasn't sure how to adjust. I'm glad you had a good time, because I was very nervous to have you on.

Judd: The background of it is very strange, which is, I was in the car on the way to the show, and my mom, who has since passed away, called me right as I'm pulling up to the studio, to tell me that her chemotherapy didn't work. It felt like I had just been told that she was going to die.

Stephen: Oh God.

Judd: Then I had to get out of the car and do *The Colbert Report* with you, and I was just white as a ghost—

Stephen: I'm so sorry.

Judd: It was an out-of-body experience.

Stephen: I have performed after someone I love died. Like finding out moments before and having to walk onstage. It's possible.

Judd: Oh, it is. I actually felt I did much better as a result of it because it freed me up to not be nervous and roll with it. It was actually a great thing to do, and you were so nice and came into the dressing room beforehand and said, "Okay, I'm about to be really awful to you. Enjoy yourself!" It's one of my strangest showbiz moments.

Stephen: I can imagine.

Judd: I need to look back and look at it.

Stephen: Twice I have performed having just found out that someone I loved passed away, and I had to go on immediately, and I can't watch— I haven't watched either one of them and it's been many years. I just can't bring myself to watch whoever that guy was that got through it.

Judd: And in the middle of all this—

Stephen: I just know that nobody knew. I also said to everybody, "It's important that no one knows this happened. I don't want to be a brave person, I just got to do my job."

Judd: That's why I didn't tell you.

Stephen: I'm glad you didn't. I probably would have burst into tears and threw my arms around you.

STEVE ALLEN

(1983)

Steve Allen was the first interview I ever did. We met at the St. Regis hotel, in New York City. I had no idea what I was doing. He was someone I had seen on numerous talk shows, and I had a sense that he was somehow integral to the history of television and, more specifically, late-night comedy. He didn't have to be kind to me, a pimply kid with a tape recorder, but he was. He sat there for an hour, in his suit and tie, answering all my questions in great detail and with total respect. I remember thinking, *Oh, so this is how you're supposed to behave in the world.* He was a man of manners and generosity.

I was too young to know much about his show, beyond some clips I'd seen on TV, but I was aware that many of the things I loved about *Late Night with David Letterman* and *The Tonight Show* had been invented by, or influenced by, Steve Allen decades before. And this sweet old man was actually this subversive creator, the one guy who would have Lenny Bruce and Jack Kerouac on all the time. Who's cooler than that?

Judd Apatow: So what is the point of rereleasing these old comedy albums?

Steve Allen: None of your business, Judd. I can't go around telling every Jack, Tom, and Harry what I'm up to. It's for me to know and you to find out. Ha, ha, ha. The point of rereleasing these records, Judd, is to make a bundle. I used to be in the laundry business and I miss all that bundle making. No, I'll tell you why: It's a public service. We did the albums originally—well, I did the calls on the air, back in '62, '63, '64—and the

This interview appears by permission of Meadowlane Enterprises, Inc.

albums were big hits at that point. *Funny Fone-Calls* and *More Funny Fone Calls*. And I have been annoyed to the point of tears ever since by whippersnappers like you coming up to me and saying, "Where can I get a copy of those albums?" I say remarkable things such as, "Ever try a record store?" And for the first year or two that worked. Because they *were* in record stores. But all albums go out of print eventually, so they were not available. And the Polygram people finally realized that since there was this untapped market, and if they got a market tapper, they could go around and rap a few knuckles.

Judd: Do you have a lot of other albums?

Steve: I haven't done many comedy albums over the years. There was, besides *Funny Fone-Calls* and *More Funny Fone Calls*, there was one called *Man on the Street*, which consisted of tapes from another comedy show I was doing—a weekly prime-time sketch comedy series, in which I interviewed three supposed men on the street. They were, in fact, Louie Nye, Don Knotts, and Tom Poston. That was a funny album. And I've done a few individual comedy recordings, forty-fives and seventy-eights in the old days. We've recently been taking inventory of old tapes and films, videotapes and so forth that I have, and discovered there's a lot of pure gold there.

Judd: One thing I noticed about the albums was, when I listened to them—I have to say that I went home one night and listened to both of them straight through and I was up till four in the morning because I was wide awake from laughing—

Steve: (*Laughs*)

Judd: I was up, hysterical. And the thing that I noticed was that the laughter in the background—I never hear laughter like that on TV, ever.

Steve: Yeah. That's a very important thing you put your finger on. It has nothing to do with me, because on some of the calls I hardly make any contribution at all. Jerry Lewis was ninety-eight percent of the funniness there. But you're absolutely right. There was something about television comedy in those days. The laughter was fresh and genuine and real and warm. Those shows were never sweetened. That started with *Laugh-In*.

Laugh-In was all done with, you know, Scotch tape. They had to do seventeen minutes of this and two minutes of that and tape it all together. And for the most part, there was no audience, and therefore most of the laughter you heard was canned. That was unfortunate. It may have been the only way, technically, they could do that kind of a show, so as not to keep an audience there for fourteen hours. But it was unfortunate. Because, as you say, you don't hear laughter like that very much now. There was nothing forced about it, and nobody even had to bother to warm the audience up. Some nights, we had to cool them down. They laughed so much, they covered up jokes.

Judd: The thing I noticed was that everything you did, *you* originated. And now everything that they do has been done already.

Steve: Yeah, that's it. First of all, it was new to the audience. They hadn't seen it fifty-seven times. Whereas now—in a talk show or a comedy talk show setting, it's really quite difficult to do anything totally unlike stuff that's been done before. It's not that I'm so much more creative than any of the other guys. It's just that I had the good fortune to do it first. But at the moment, I can't think of any feature of those shows which was not originated on one of our early shows.

Judd: Right now, most shows on TV are formulized. Johnny Carson comes on, does his monologue, does a skit or his little thing, and interviews three people. There's nothing like what you were doing. Do you think they could reproduce what you did today?

Steve: I don't think most people could, no. I don't say that in any conceited sense. It's just that I prefer to work loose. In the case of Johnny, it's hard to criticize him personally on this, because he's been there for twenty years. Why should he bother to be inventive now? It'd be as pointless as Bob Hope suddenly doing inventive things. It could hurt them, you know. But it would drive me nuts to do the same thing every night. I'm not saying I'm better or worse than they are, it's just that I don't work that way. For my own peace of mind, I had to do new stuff every night, and I learned very early in my career, even before I was working in television, that the biggest laughs in show business, for me, came the same way the biggest laughs in reality do: out of whatever the reality of a given exchange of a social situation is. One example that pops into my mind was back—oh, when was it? Forty-eight, let's say. In addition to a regular late-night comedy and talk show I was doing in L.A., I was doing some evening network things for the CBS Radio Network. And right in the middle of a live show one evening, there was an ungodly noise, an annoying noise, just behind some closed doors at the back of the stage. And I knew it could be heard all around the country. I mean, what was this *(loud whisper voice)* "chuck-a-chuck-a-chuck-a-chuhhh . . ."? We had to stop everything and—you know, we were on the air live so we couldn't say, "Stop tape." So I just did what I think was the sensible thing. I didn't do it because it was funny, I did it because it was sensible. I said, "Ladies and gentlemen, um, obviously those of you at home can hear this annoying distraction in the background here. I don't know what it is and—" I said, "Do any of you know?" And nobody on the stage knew, so I said, "Well, let's find out." So I took the mike with the long wire on it. And we had somebody open the doors, and there was an old man, an old Italian gentleman—or with an Italian accent, I should say—who was using a cement mixer, a small portable cement mixer outside those doors. To this day, he does not know he was on the air for ten minutes. I went in and whistled and screamed at him to, you know, turn it off. So he finally got the point, and turned it off. And then I asked him, I said, "What are you doing here?" And he said, "I lay the cement, you know." And we talked and had a lot of laughs and he—I don't know if he could hear the people laughing in the other room or not, I don't remember anything I said to him. But it was just funny, live on the air, with maybe nineteen million people listening all over America. That's not one of the great moments in the history of comedy, but the point is it's an example of looseness. I think everybody ought to do that.

Judd: One of the things you originated was talking with the audience at the beginning of your show, which they do on other shows now. How did that come about?

Steve: I didn't originate taking a hand mic into the audience. There were noncomic fellows who did that before me. Notably Tom Breneman and a fellow named Don McNeill. They were very popular on the radio in the mid-1940s chiefly. They were sort of genial masters of ceremonies. And sometimes Art Linkletter would go into the audience with some specific gimmick in mind. Like, let's see who has the most outlandish thing in her purse. "All right, madam, will you stand up and open your purse? Oh, look here, it's a dead mouse," or whatever, you know. Except that's a funny joke. They wouldn't say that. They would just talk about whatever was really in the purse, and "Thank you, here's fifty dollars" and sit down. So they had done that before. But I was the first comedian to do it.

Judd: And you had regular audience members that were there all the time.

Steve: I don't know how that came about. I guess it was just that they were lonely people who had nothing much else in their lives and they could go to this party every night and have a few laughs and be given some recognition. I used to love to talk to the regulars, as they were called, on the old *Tonight Show*. The classic instance of this, which people over fifty still remember, was a woman named Mrs. Sterling. She was what we would call a bag lady. She usually had a couple of big paper bags with her, and she dressed quite poorly. She usually wore a man's khaki army overcoat and tennis shoes. And she was in our audience every night. And I don't think I ever saw her laugh at anything. It was all very serious for her. But you know, she would be given attention. Her motivation, chiefly, was greed. Because at the end of the interviews we used to give away prizes, toasters or a pair of silk stockings or salami or something. At the time one of my sponsors was Polaroid cameras. She never could get the name straight. I would interview her; the interviews were very much the same. She didn't seem to hear my questions very well. But she knew that if she could get to talk to me at all, she was good for a toaster or a fan or a deep-fry pot or something. She must've had a room full of all these things. Probably sold them out on the street after the show. So she would resort to flattery. I'd say, "Good evening, Mrs. Sterling." She'd say, "Mr. Allen, you're wonderful." I'd say, "Well, the degree of my wonderfulness is irrelevant, but how have you been?" And she'd say, "Oh, we love ya. Everybody loves you, you're great, Mr. Allen. Give me one of them Palmeroid cameras." She always called them Palmeroids. And she never knew why the audience was hysterical. I never even had to do jokes. I just turned around and it was funny. So, she was like a known quantity. I knew that I would get laughs if I talked to her, so I talked to her practically every time I went into the audience.

Judd: Didn't you turn one of your audience members into a movie reviewer?

Steve: His name was John Fisher. He was—I guess now we would call him a hyperkinetic personality. He talked sort of uncontrollably fast and effusively. He was an upstate farmer type. And I asked him one question when I first met him one night. It was something like, "Hello, sir, what's your name?" And most people say, you know, "Charlie Feldman," and just hang there. Which is really more sensible, because I only ask that, I didn't ask for their serial number, you know. And he gave me about a nine-minute answer. He just couldn't stop his mouth. "I'm John Fisher, and I live up in Solo, New York, and I have a potato farm up there and I just come to talk, because I seen the movies, the one with Clark Gable and Myrna Loy." And he sort of reviewed the whole movie for us. Obviously that's hysterically funny and I have nothing to do with it. He's the one that's getting the screams, did not know why he was getting laughs. So when he finally shut up, I said, "Well, John, that was a very interesting movie review, would you like to come back and join us from time to time?" He said, "Yeah, sure," and gave me another six-minute answer. So we signed him up and we would get tickets to the new movies and he would go see them and come in and give us these dumb reviews of them. You know—it's funny. And he never knew why it was funny.

Judd: And you used to do remotes from the street in the beginning of the show?

Steve: I've always loved the idea of getting cameras right out into the street. Sometimes I was out there with them, but more often I was not. More often I was just onstage looking at a television screen. So I could see what the cameras were seeing, and just saying, I hoped, funny things about them. And there again, people would say, "Boy, you were funny." It was nice of them to say that but what often was funny was the situation. My contribution may have accounted for only, you know, fourteen percent of the funniness. Some years back, when Dick Cavett was doing his talk show on ABC, he took a week's vacation and asked me to fill in for him, so I did. And we did the camera on the street every night and had tremendous luck. First of all, you see different things on the streets of New York than you do in Hollywood. And you have the advantage in New York that you're generally right on some street. Whereas at NBC Burbank, if you open the back door, you just see part of the parking lot. In this case Dick was—I guess up at Forty-eighth Street. Anyway, one evening, we punched up the camera, just at random. And just in time to see one of those city trucks that hauls away illegally parked cars. It was a mystery thing and the whole audience went, Whoa boy, who's going to get hauled away? So I was doing a play-by-play and the truck stopped right in front of the theater and the guy jumps out and, you know, does the thing with the hook and the chain, and suddenly from the balcony you see a guy say, "Oh no"—it was his car that they were hooking the bumper up. I said, "Is that your car, sir?" And he said, "Yeah." And I said, "Well, come on, run down!" And the band played chase music, and we had a shot of this poor guy running down from the top level of the balcony. And he runs out into the street, now he's on camera and it's like a silent movie and he's pleading, you know. And the guy says, "No, it's just my job." He flicked his cigar all over him, and took his car away. Well, that was sad for him, but hysteria for the audience.

Judd: One thing I read was that they dressed you up as Superman in the street. And people just looked at you like you were just anybody and you just flew away and they didn't even say anything.

Steve: That was when we were doing the talk show in the early sixties from Hollywood. We were opposite a crazy hangout for Hollywood eccentrics, an open-all-night place called the Hollywood Ranch Market. And we did our show late, so it was kind of a pretty zany neighborhood—perfect for our purposes. And I had done a number of Superman sketches over the years. Because anybody with glasses, dark hair, an old fedora, and a gray suit looks like Clark Kent. I never looked that much like Superman, but I did a great Clark Kent. However, as soon as I put on the Superman suit, it never seemed to fit trimly, it always looked like baggy underwear. So right away it was funny before I did anything. So I had the Superman suit and the Clark Kent attire over it. One night I ran out and the cameras were there and they had a phone booth set up across the street—you know, so I could change clothes like Superman. I ran in and I tried to change like I did in my dressing room, where I had plenty of room, but you don't have much room in a phone booth. If you're not Superman, it's tough. I need a lot of elbow room. So I couldn't get my pants off. I looked like a jerk. A man trying to take his pants off in a phone booth. At this point a guy walks by carrying a bag of groceries, coming out of a grocery store. So I say, "Hey, Mack, you got a minute?" He says, "What?" I say, "Can you give me a hand here?" He puts his bag down. He says, "What's the problem?" I say, "I can't get my pants down." So I sit down on the little seat in the thing and I stick my legs out and this guy pulls my pants off for me. And then I stand up and I throw the hat off and now I'm dressed like Superman. I say, "Thanks a lot." He says, "Don't mention it," and he walks away. Now, if that happened in Cleveland, the guy'd say, "Hey, what are you, some kind of a nut?" But in Hollywood and New York, they don't even notice. Because they see craziness around them all the time.

Judd: They used to make you do those weird things all the time. I remember I saw one sketch where you were made into a human tea bag.

Steve: Yeah, they had a big—I don't know where it came from—but they had this big plastic tank. See-through plastic. It was about maybe seven feet deep and six feet wide and four feet the other way. They filled it with warm water and then they attached about a hundred tea bags to my body, and so I made tea for the whole neighborhood. They would never let me know—by "they" I mean the production staff—exactly what was planned. Sometimes just at the last minute, you know, I'd have to find out because I would see what I was getting into. But whenever they could keep it from me, they would. Because they had discovered that I was much funnier if I did not know for sure what was going on. I would often have a hint that it would be messy. They would come to the dressing room and say, "Underdress." So I would wear a pair of swimming trunks or a tight kind of a jockey short thing or something underneath. And sometimes they would say, "Wear one of your Hong Kong suits." They meant, we don't want one of your nice suits to get cream pie on it or dog food or mustard or whatever they were gonna hit me with. But beyond that, I did not know what the heck was up.

Judd: What do you consider the highlights of the show? Comedic highlights?

Steve: My weekly check was hysterical.

Judd: (*Laughs*)

Steve: I don't know. It was funny every night, actually. Just recently, I was listening to one particular show, because we're putting together the comedy albums. And it's remarkable how many of them hold up, if you can just hear them. Often, we're just describing what's going on. Once we had a woman—a nurse—come in from the blood bank and just take my blood. The point of it was to show how simple it is and that all of us should give blood. That's not an inherently comic notion—certainly there's nothing funny about giving blood. But when you do it in front of three or four hundred people, it somehow *becomes* funny, especially if you're a comedian.

Judd: What was it like having Lenny Bruce appear on the show?

Steve: Lenny was a brilliantly inventive and original comedian, as the world now does not have to be told. There was never any fear in my mind that he would say or do anything in poor taste, although at the time he was saying things that would've been construed as poor taste in a club. But he was very intelligent and we were friends, and he would've never done anything of that sort on the air. And in fact, he did not.

Judd: The last time he was on, didn't they have to cut something out, something he was talking about?

Steve: I don't know. Sometimes there would be discussions about production details, which did not come to my personal attention because I was usually busy enough the day of the show. What Lenny did do at the time—and nobody censored it because nobody knew what it meant—is a little routine about glue sniffing. This was probably the first time sniffing of glue was mentioned on a nationwide basis in the comic context. In fact, the nation as such knew nothing about that at the time. That there were just a few weird kids sniffing airplane glue. But anyway, Lenny did about four lines on that and nobody cut them out, because it would be like today somebody wrote a thing about spaghetti sniffing. You know nobody would cut that because they think, *What's the harm in sniffing spaghetti?*

Judd: What kind of man was he?

Steve: He was neurotic and self-destructive, but absolutely brilliant in his comedy. A true original. He was the first guy—first comedian, I should say—to speak the language of musicians. Which is now common. Even squares now say "hip" and "cool" and "I dig" and "you know, baby" and all that stuff. But in the thirties and forties only jazz musicians used that language. And Lenny was the first of the comedians to do so in his performing. He had sort of a musician's sense of humor. It was very hip and courageous. He would discuss politics or religion or sex or social attitudes. And he was a true pioneer.

Judd: How do you choose the subjects for your books, *Funny People*?

Steve: Very much at random. It's all a matter of personal judgment. For the most part I write about people I personally think are funny. And that solves one problem, because the world does not need Steve Allen explaining why Joe Dokes is terrible when he does comedy. Therefore, when I write about somebody, it's because I like their work and it's very easy to make the appropriate compliments. There was one exception to that, but I did it only after the performer had died. He was a great performer, a great song-and-dance man. A very important figure on Broadway and in films, an old comedian of the 1920s and '30s named Eddie Cantor. In my opinion Eddie was a cute, likable, lively, vivacious personality. But I never thought he was terribly funny. So I took about twenty-seven pages to say that. But again, since he was already dead, I couldn't hurt his feelings.

Judd: You did the same with John Belushi. That wasn't very complimentary.

Steve: On the contrary. If you'll reread it you'll find it was highly complimentary. But it gave both the bright and dark sides of it.

Judd: You said other performers were a lot more talented.

Steve: I considered Aykroyd funnier, I considered Bill Murray funnier. I considered Chevy Chase funnier. But there are a lot of compliments for John in the chapter. But I could not avoid discussing John Belushi, simply because Belushi himself sort of forced that on the public consciousness. It was not anything particular in my own reaction to him. I'd already discovered that, although I could laugh at what was funny in his work. I liked a lot of what he did in the *Blues Brothers* movie, for example. In this, I was very much alone in the over-fifty generation. Now, it is generally true that people over fifty don't laugh that much at comedians, let's say, under forty. Whether they should or not is a separate question. I'm simply reporting the fact that they do not. I, on the other hand, do. Some of the funniest people in the world are young guys in their twenties and women in their twenties. I don't care how old a person is. If he's funny, that's all there is to it as far as I'm concerned.

STEVE MARTIN
(2014)

I don't think anybody has made me laugh longer or louder than Steve
Martin. When I was young, I loved him without even understanding the
premise of his act. I didn't realize that he was poking fun at the self-
importance of showbiz personalities, or the clichés of comedy. There was
this whole meta thing going on that was completely over my head. As a
ten-year-old kid, I just thought he was insanely weird and funny, and I
didn't know why, and I didn't want to know why, because it didn't matter
to me.

I can remember my dad bringing home Steve's *Let's Get Small* album,
and then us listening to it for fourteen hours straight as we drove from
Long Island to South Carolina on vacation. Okay, maybe we didn't listen
to it the entire time; I do remember hearing a lot of the Little River Band
on the radio, too. But I remember laughing, as my parents laughed right
along with me, and thinking, *I am beginning to understand a little more
about how the world really works.*

As I entered middle school, my obsession with Steve Martin only deep-
ened. I had a grandmother who lived in California, and when we would
go visit her, I would beg her to drive by Steve Martin's house. (Yes, I'd
found out where he lived.) It was this solid white house with no windows.
I imagined it as this bunker filled with light. I begged her to drive by not
because I thought I would see him—although I badly wished that would
happen—but because I just couldn't believe there was a structure that
actually contained him. It seemed impossible to believe he existed and
was somebody you could talk to.

Then one day in the summer of 1980, as we drove by his house, I saw
him standing there in his driveway. I can't quite remember what he was

doing; maybe he was washing his car, maybe he was raking leaves. All I know is I yelled for my grandmother to stop the car. My brother and I got out. I ran up to Steve and said, "Hey, can I get an autograph?" And he said, "No, I'm sorry, I don't sign autographs at my house." "Well," I responded, "then can you sign it in the street?" (Which, looking back, was not a bad joke for a thirteen-year-old.) No, he said, sorry, he didn't sign autographs at his house, because if he did, then everybody would walk up to his front door and ask for things and that wouldn't be good. I did not understand this logic at the time. (I understand it today, however: If you knock on my door, even if you are from a charity, I will call local security.) I wasn't done yet, though. I started begging him, "Please, please, I'm from out of town, I won't tell anyone where you live, I'll never bother you again. . . ." But he wouldn't break. He smiled—and kept to his policy.

So I ran straight home and went to my room and wrote him a long, crazy letter, the spirit of which was: I have bought everything you've ever made, and you wouldn't live in that house if it weren't for people like me. And then I demanded an apology.

I went back to his house a few days later and slipped the letter into his mailbox. (Notice that I didn't mail it, for that extra stalker touch. Yes, Steve: I know where you live.) I'm pretty sure it was several pages long.

About six months later, long after I stopped thinking about how I was wronged, I received a package in the mail, which contained two copies of Cruel Shoes, his seminal collection of essays and short stories. In one of the copies, he wrote: "This is for your friend. Steve Martin." That friend, of course, was my brother, who did not appreciate Steve Martin on nearly the same level as I did, and has since turned into an Orthodox Jew and lives in Israel. I still have his book. The other one said, "To Judd: I'm sorry I didn't realize I was speaking to the Judd Apatow. Your friend, Steve Martin."

This story always gets a laugh, but to me, it's more meaningful than that: This moment with Steve made me think I must have made him laugh, or he wouldn't have gone through the trouble of sending me that book. And if I could make Steve Martin laugh, maybe I was funny enough to go into this comedy business I'd always dreamed about, after all.

Decades later, I met Steve Martin—formally, in a non-stalkish way—for the first time at a work-related meeting, to discuss a project he was kicking around. At the meeting, I was urged to tell that story, and so I did. When it was over, someone said to Steve, "Is that how you remember it?" And Steve responded, "Actually, I believe I was the one who knocked on Judd's door."

Judd Apatow: It takes a lot to get up onstage and perform. What drove you to try it?

Steve Martin: I didn't even know what stand-up was in the beginning. I started off in magic so I liked the idea of performing onstage and stand-up—I kind of defaulted into it because, at some point, I realized the magic thing was a dead end and stand-up had a future. So I started to pare away the magic tricks. I fell into stand-up because it seemed like there was opportunity in it. It was the path of least resistance.

Judd: What about before that? When you were a teenager, did you just want to get out of the house and be in front of people? For me, my parents got divorced. And so, as a teenager, I thought, *These people are crazy. Whatever advice they're giving me, I shouldn't listen to.* It made me ambitious. But it's a big leap to get out of the house, isn't it?

Steve: I definitely wanted to get out of the house and I wanted to have a job. I don't know why, but the idea of working at Disneyland—that was, you know, fantastic.

Judd: You lived near there, as a kid, right?

Steve: I lived two miles from there and I would ride my bike there. Two miles seemed like such a long way to a kid of ten.

Judd: You did it at ten? Wow, times have changed. Most people today won't let their kids leave the driveway until they're seventeen years old.

Steve: Yeah.

Judd: My parents never knew where I was. My whole childhood, they would have no idea how to find me, from after school until seven at night.

Steve: I had the same thing.

Judd: What did your parents do?

Steve: My dad was a Realtor, and my mom stayed home. She was fascinated with show business.

Judd: So you had one parent who was fascinated by show business, and the other who—

Steve: Oh, my dad wanted to be in show business, too.

Judd: What did he want to do?

Steve: He wanted to be an actor, but he gave it up for the family. He had to. He couldn't earn money.

Judd: Did he actually attempt it?

Steve: Yeah. I have a photo somewhere of him in a play. He was very young. I also have a photo of him—a publicity photo—that I'm in with him. I was like four or five. I didn't understand it as a kid. In the photo, the police are taking him away and I am the forlorn child.

Judd: My dad quietly wished that he had pursued a career in comedy, but he never said that to me. He only told me decades later. But there were always a lot of comedy albums around the house. I would put on one of your albums when we were driving somewhere—like, we would drive to South Carolina on vacation—and he didn't mind if I kept playing it for five hours straight. He would laugh his ass off. But he never told me he was *interested* in it. Did your dad resent your success at all?

Steve: I think there was an element of that. There was almost a condemnation of the type of material, the type of act it was, yeah.

Judd: Because it was the sixties and everything was changing?

Steve: Yeah, everything was changing out from under him.

Judd: Did he like any of the comedians that you were making fun of?

Steve: I don't think he perceived what I did as parody. I think he just—you know, he was critical. The first time I did *Saturday Night Live*, he thought that was a bad move, you know.

Judd: That's terrible show business advice. My dad, when my parents got divorced—and I'm just saying this because I think it's so funny how men acted, pre-therapy and pre–the days of people talking about their feelings. When my parents got divorced, I lived with my dad. My mom moved out. And one day, he left out a book on the coffee table called *Growing Up Divorced*. He just left it there. He never asked me to read it. He never checked to see if I did read it. He just hoped I would find it. That was his child-rearing approach.

Steve: I had the same. My dad said to me once—and this was after I'd grown up: "I didn't teach you about sex because you learn about that on the school yard."

Judd: Oh, that's funny. But what I found fascinating in *Born Standing Up* is when you wrote that you made a conscious choice at some point to spend time with your parents, and then you did it every week for fifteen years.

Steve: Yeah.

Judd: I was struck by that kind of commitment to healing or connecting. It's difficult to do that.

Steve: Well, part of it is selfish. I didn't want my parents to die and then have all this guilt, you know.

Judd: Their guilt or your guilt?

Steve: My guilt. You know, they raised me. And now I'm raising them. That's what it is when they get older. You can't just strand somebody.

Judd: When you were starting out in the early seventies, did you feel like you were a part of the comedy scene?

Steve: There wasn't really a comedy scene.

Judd: What about when you were doing *Saturday Night Live*? Did you feel like you were part of it then, or did you still feel like you were visiting?

Steve: I was always on the road, so I didn't have that opportunity to feel like a part of *SNL*, but I really liked the people. I liked Danny Aykroyd. I had a few moments with Belushi, who was very sweet. He had just done *Neighbors* and was excited about acting. He was calm and well-spoken, very intelligent about what he wanted to do—and then he was dead a few months later, you know. I had this moment with him. I remember one night, this was after an *SNL* show, and we were in this caravan of cars. At one point he got out—this was on Seventy-second Street—and just started directing traffic. It was one of those crazy moments. And I just had the feeling he didn't really want to direct traffic, but he felt that he had to for his persona. That he was doing something to fulfill others' expectations of him rather than it was coming from his heart. I felt he was a little caught in a vise. And then when I saw him many years later in California, he was expressing this other side of himself. He seemed sober. I felt he had overcome that need to be the party guy.

Judd: And then the other side won.

Steve: You can do that for a while, and then—

Judd: It seems like everyone has a kind of transitional moment in life. Adam Sandler and I tried to put it in *Funny People*, actually. There was this line we cut, where he said something like, "I'm not a young guy anymore. I've got to switch to my Walter Matthau period." But for you, it feels like you've made an effortless transition across eras, from stand-up to—

Steve: Did you ever do stand-up?

Judd: I did it from the time I was seventeen until I was twenty-three or twenty-four.

Steve: That's a long time.

Judd: But then I stopped because I was getting a lot of writing offers and not a lot of performing offers. I just thought, *Oh, the universe is telling me not to perform live.* But lately, I've been going out and performing again. Last summer, I went out and started performing a few times a week. And I just felt like, this is why I got into the business in the first place, for the fun part. I felt like I had lost sight of the fun part of working in comedy because, as a director, I spend all my time in small rooms with sweaty editors and everything's so stressful. The whole time you're thinking, *Oh God, I hope it works.* I don't get that much fun out of it. I just feel like I escape humiliation.

Steve: That's the way I feel, too. I found it really hard to make a funny movie. Plus, in movies, the strikeout ratio is so against you.

Judd: But your ratio, when you write, is like one hundred percent. You haven't written that many movies in the last ten years or so, but do you like the writing part of it?

Steve: It's excruciating.

Judd: Did you stop because it was exhausting, or because you had a bad experience?

Steve: It's just so frightening. The pain of it. And that first screening is so awful.

Judd: We just had a great screening of a movie, and the numbers were fantastic. And then someone at the studio called and sounded disappointed. That haunts you.

Steve: Yeah.

Judd: It's like, *Oh my God, am I wrong?*

Steve: It's like what Brian Grazer said to me once. He was giving me advice as an actor or as a deal maker or whatever. And he said, "Always be just a little bit disappointed."

Judd: Albert Brooks told me the reason he doesn't make more movies is not about the difficulty of writing the movie or making the movie, it's about the release. He said, It's so painful. The press, the response—

Steve: It's hard.

Judd: But isn't that also why it's so fun, that uncertainty and pain? Is that what you feel when you're out making music now, touring with your band?

Steve: It has been a joy to get those chops back. Get a new joke. Get a new thing, you know.

Judd: How many years ago did you start performing live?

Steve: Five years ago.

Judd: Was that terrifying?

Steve: It was. But doing those shows made me sharper on the talk shows, gave me more material. And it made me sharper in my stand-up career because the last ten years have been nothing but award shows—giving them and receiving them.

Judd: But that's a lot of appearances. And don't you find that there's a moment when you go, *How much can we all honor each other?*

Steve: Absolutely.

Judd: On the other hand, Martin Short's speech about you at the Oscars for lifetime achievement was incredible.

Steve: He was great.

Judd: Was that as special a night as it seemed?

Steve: It was a big deal for me, yeah. First, I never thought I would get an Oscar. Although, you know, Nora Ephron said once, I don't care who you are, when you sit down to type the first page of your screenplay, in your head you're also writing your Oscar acceptance speech. And when you're an actor and you're giving your performance you're also thinking, *You know, I think I can win an Oscar. I'm going to win an Oscar for this.* And comedy gets the short end of the stick at the Oscars because nobody understands it. So I was honored to be acknowledged for a body of work, I really was.

Judd: All those movies exist and they're on all the time.

Steve: Yeah. And, you know, I saved all the scripts. That's the only thing I saved. I never got them autographed or anything but I had them bound in leather. Sometimes I look at them, look at the titles, and think, *It's all shit.*

Judd: All of them?

Steve: All of them. But then sometimes I think, *Well, that was pretty good, and that was pretty good, and that was good,* and so I can get like eight out of forty that are pretty good. All it takes is eight to make a good career. Because no one has twenty.

Judd: It's like baseball.

Steve: It's hard to hit a lot of good movies. Very hard. I didn't know that at the beginning. I thought every movie I did was going to be good. To me, there's like three levels of knowing if a movie is good. One is when it comes out. Is it a hit? Then after five years. Where is it? Is it gone? Then again after ten–fifteen years if it's still around. Are people still watching it? Does it have an afterlife? Like, *Three Amigos!* was a flop.

Judd: But then it becomes the most beloved—

Steve: Well, I don't know if it's beloved. They tell me it is, but I don't know.

Judd: When I was working for *The Larry Sanders Show*, Warren Beatty was on an episode and I had lunch with him. And he told me, "You don't know for ten years if a movie is truly good, so don't even think about it. At some point, you gradually realize, *Oh, people are still amused by this.*"

Steve: Absolutely true. I find that the joke you put in that really shouldn't have been in the movie because it was a personal favorite or something is the joke that stands out ten years later.

Judd: Let's talk about *The Jerk*. It made a hundred and eighty million dollars in 1980. That's like the equivalent of making six hundred million today dollars or something. Did it feel that big when it came out?

Steve: I didn't have any way of comparing. It was my first movie. Everything I'd done had been a hit, so I just assumed that it'd be a hit, too. You know.

Judd: It's one of those movies that completely holds up.

Steve: It's held up for a long time, yeah.

Judd: Would it be painful to sit and watch it now?

Steve: Yeah. It would.

Judd: What is the high point of your career, then? What film or moment do you instantly go to in your mind?

Steve: You mean, in terms of movies that I've done? I can think of scenes that feel really funny to me, but I don't resee a lot of my movies. I actually avoid it. Unless it's by accident. In terms of movies, they are usually the ones done by somebody else—*Planes, Trains and Automobiles; Father of the Bride; Parenthood.*

Judd: You should watch *Planes, Trains and Automobiles* again.

Steve: I know that film pretty well. John Hughes was a special kind of genius.

Judd: It is a masterwork, and I refer to it when I'm working with people because I think that movie has a lot to teach people who are trying to do comedy. That scene where you and John Candy have a fight in the hotel room is as perfect as, you know, Albert Brooks and Holly Hunter's fight in *Broadcast News*.

Steve: Why do you think that was? Because it turns around or because I realize that I hurt him?

Judd: You go off on him so hard because you're so frustrated and you've lost your sense of his humanity and then he stands up for himself and just says, "Well, I like me." It goes from riotously funny to almost mean-spirited to truly sad. It can make you cry in an eighth of a second. It's just your chemistry with him. How vulnerable he instantly becomes, and how you react to that, how it stops you in your tracks. Like, *Oh my God, what have I done? How am I behaving?* I don't know if I've seen another movie with a sequence that works like that. Two actors in total sync.

Steve: We really got along, John and I. There's a scene in that movie that makes me laugh—we're in a car going the wrong way, and then we pull over. John and I are just sitting on a suitcase talking, but we're also scared, and we look at the car and it spontaneously bursts into flames. Poof. John Hughes was the master of those comic timing moments. That guy really knew something.

Judd: Did you become close with him?

Steve: It was funny. I did for a while, but then he just sort of stopped. He was a strange guy.

Judd: There comes a moment when your kids start asking to see your movies. For a while, my daughter would give me a hard time because she wasn't allowed to see my movies because they're all R-rated. It's hard to delay kids to fifteen, sixteen years old, especially when they have the movie on every gadget in the house. But I finally opened up the door. It was this big deal. I was like, "Okay, you can watch them now"—and then she had no interest in watching them. So now, anytime she watches a movie that's not one of mine it's an insult to me. "Why are you watching *Schindler's List*? You haven't seen *Funny People*! When are you going to watch it?" She's like, "I don't know, Dad."

Steve: I loved *Funny People*, by the way.

Judd: Thank you. It was fun writing about comedians. Adam Sandler and I thought a lot about Rodney Dangerfield when we were making that movie. Rodney was someone who just seemed unhappy with the ride.

Steve: I met him once in Vegas, in the seventies. And immediately, when we sat down, it was like, "So-and-so stole that joke from me." I remember thinking, *Well, that was fast.* I liked him, though. He was great. You know who used to love Rodney? David Brenner.

Judd: Brenner is so funny. I used to watch him on *The Mike Douglas Show* all the time.

Steve: He actually helped my career quite a bit.

Judd: How so?

Steve: It was '73 or '74, and I went to see him somewhere in Washington, D.C. He was really hot at the time, hosting *The Tonight Show*, with a beautiful girlfriend. I remember after the show, they came out and they were both wearing full-length mink coats. Anyway, I wrote to him. I was living in Santa Fe at the time. I said, "I can't make any money. I can get paid maybe three hundred dollars for a gig, but it costs me two hundred dollars to get there." And he writes back and says, "Here's what I do. I tell the club owner, 'I'll take the door, and you can have the bar, and I'll have a guy stand at the door with a clicker.'" I couldn't, you know, with my WASPy thing, I couldn't ever say that, but I did ask the club owner to give me the door. That's when I decided I would only be a headliner—and it changed my career. The opening act doesn't get any traction and a headliner does.

Judd: How did you arrive at the ideas in your act, early on? I mean, you were taking apart what it means to be a comedian. It was not observational comedy. The act itself was fascinating.

Steve: I was lucky to have come up in that era because today, every area is covered and there's so many good people. If I was starting now, I'd be lost.

Judd: But no one's doing the type of comedy you were doing. There are really smart comedians, but there's not a lot of conceptual comedy out there.

Steve: I think it's a dead end, you know.

Judd: Because it runs out of gas?

Steve: Yeah.

Judd: You can't keep doing it?

Steve: I mean, I'm still around, but I couldn't have kept doing *that* act, I don't think.

Judd: You've developed a different comic persona now, which feels distantly related to that. When you host the Oscars, I can sense that you've redefined your persona.

Steve: Yeah, I have. I didn't want to do the same old thing and I didn't want to look like I was doing the same old thing. That extreme physical thing has totally gone out of it. And I love playing the egotistical asshole.

Judd: I'm always fascinated by people's comic journey—when they get bored and say, That's enough. There are people like you, who seem to find new things to keep them interested, and there are people who say, I'm just going to hang out at the house. It's a real challenge because success never satisfies whatever you thought it was going to do for you. You think, *Oh, I thought success would heal me and it doesn't.* So you have to look for new reasons to keep making things.

Steve: I read a book in college called *Psychoanalysis and the Arts.* And it compared Picasso and Chagall. Picasso was a guy who just kept changing his whole life and Chagall essentially painted the same things, over and over. And it talked about there being two types of creative people and I think that applies.

Judd: When you got bored of doing stand-up, was there a part of you that thought, *Okay, this next thing will bring me happiness*?

Steve: No. I was just beaten down.

Judd: And you feel the joy again, now that you're out touring and making music?

Steve: I really enjoy doing the shows, but the wear and tear—I have a daughter at home. It gets a little painful.

Judd: When did you start playing the banjo?

Steve: I've been playing it for over fifty years now.

Judd: The second I hear that instrument, it makes me feel that happy Disney feeling. I read something where you talked about how fun it was to be creative with something that's completely nonverbal.

Steve: I think playing the banjo has extended my brain life by another ten years.

Judd: Because it just connects everything?

Steve: Yeah, just thinking in another way.

Judd: Do you feel like this is a common trait, among the people that you've chosen as intimate friends? This creative searching? Is this how your friends also deal with this ride?

Steve: Yes.

Judd: Everyone around you seems to have a sense of humor about it, but they're also working really hard.

Steve: Everybody I know—I'm talking about Tom Hanks, Mike Nichols—

Judd: Lorne.

Steve: Lorne, yeah. Marty. All of us, we know how lucky we are. Everybody says, Oh, God, we have such a nice life, you know. We're lucky to have had this happen to us.

Judd: Yeah.

Steve: Everybody is grateful.

ACKNOWLEDGMENTS

I'd like to thank Andy Ward, Michael Lewen, Dave Eggers, Andrew Wylie, Kaela Myers, and Amy Reed for their invaluable work putting this collection together.

I'd also like to thank my representatives: Jimmy Miller (since Comic Relief '87), David Kramer, Matt Labov, Bryan Wolf, and Sam Fischer.

Thank you to these special people who believed in me early in my career, before there was any reason to: Jack DeMasi, Josh Rosenthal, East Side and East End comedy clubs, Governor's Comedy Club, Chuckles Comedy Club, Budd Friedman and the Improv, Jamie Masada and the Laugh Factory, Joe Drew, Sammy Shore, Bob Zmuda, Chris Albrecht, Rick Messina, James L. Brooks, Al Jean and Mike Reiss, Garry Shandling, Roseanne Barr, Tom Arnold, HBO, Ben Stiller, Jim Carrey, Adam Sandler, Steve Brill, Kevin Rooney, Allen Covert, Jack Giarraputo, Paul Feig, Adam McKay, Will Ferrell, Jake Kasdan, and Steve Carell.